World Economic Situation and Prospects 2019

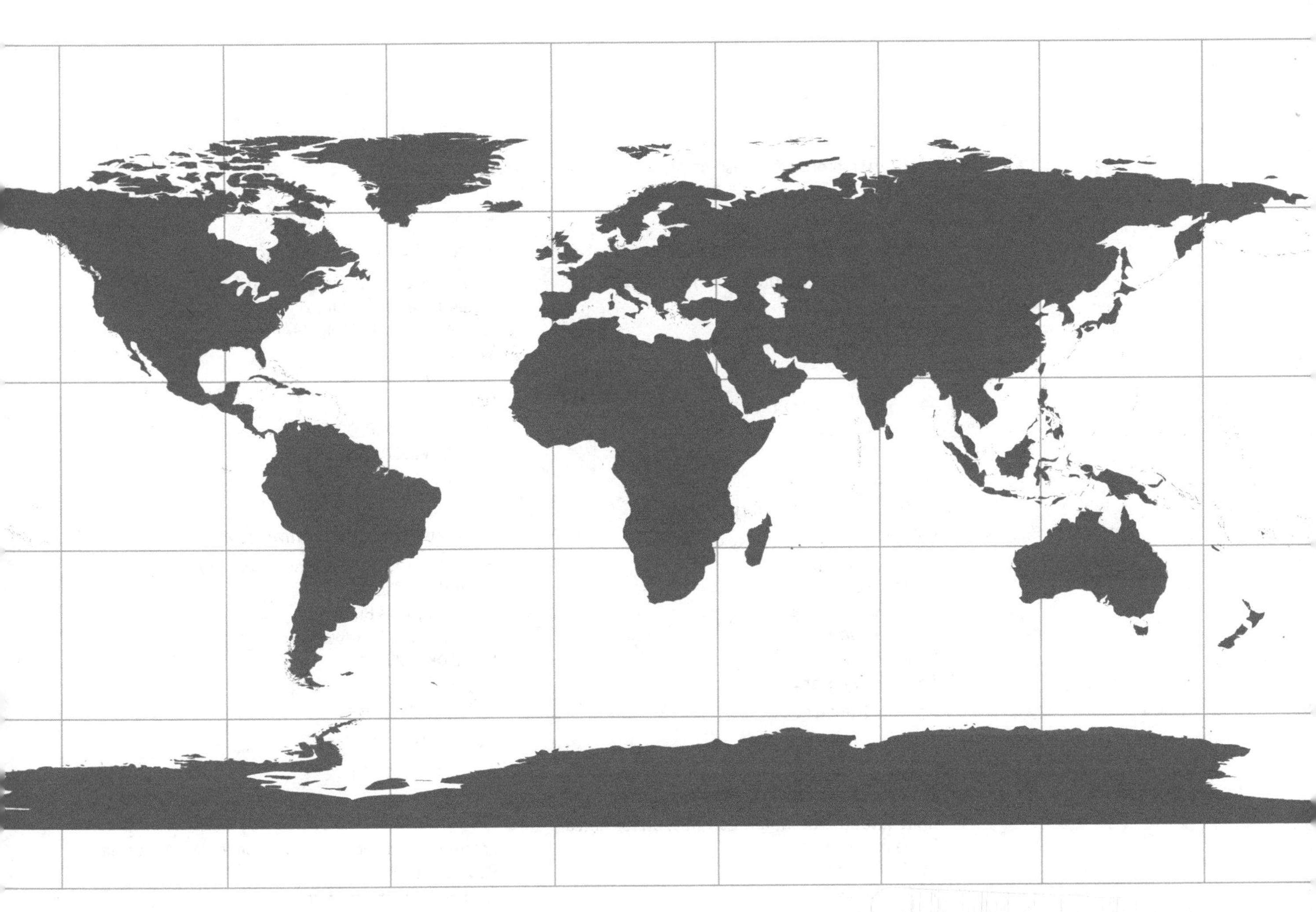

United Nations
New York, 2019

The report is a joint product of the United Nations Department of Economic and Social Affairs (UN/DESA), the United Nations Conference on Trade and Development (UNCTAD) and the five United Nations regional commissions (Economic Commission for Africa (ECA), Economic Commission for Europe (ECE), Economic Commission for Latin America and the Caribbean (ECLAC), Economic and Social Commission for Asia and the Pacific (ESCAP) and Economic and Social Commission for Western Asia (ESCWA)). The United Nations World Tourism Organization (UNWTO) also contributed to the report.

For further information, visit https://www.un.org/development/desa/dpad/ or contact:

DESA

Mr. Liu Zhenmin, *Under-Secretary-General*

Department of Economic and Social Affairs
Room S-2922
United Nations
New York, NY 10017
USA

☎ +1-212-9635958
✉ undesa@un.org

UNCTAD

Dr. Mukhisa Kituyi, *Secretary-General*

United Nations Conference on Trade and Development
Room E-9042
Palais de Nations, 8–14
1211 Geneva 10
Switzerland

☎ +41-22-9175806
✉ sgo@unctad.org

ECA

Ms. Vera Songwe, *Executive Secretary*

United Nations Economic Commission for Africa
Menelik II Avenue
P.O. Box 3001
Addis Ababa
Ethiopia

☎ +251-11-5511231
✉ ecainfo@uneca.org

ECE

Ms. Olga Algayerova, *Executive Secretary*

United Nations Economic Commission for Europe
Palais des Nations
CH-1211 Geneva 10
Switzerland

☎ +41-22-9174444
✉ unece_info@un.org

ECLAC

Ms. Alicia Bárcena, *Executive Secretary*

Economic Commission for Latin America and the Caribbean
Av. Dag Hammarskjöld 3477
Vitacura
Santiago, Chile
Chile

☎ +56-2-22102000
✉ secepal@cepal.org

ESCAP

Dr. Shamshad Akhtar, *Executive Secretary*

Economic and Social Commission for Asia and the Pacific
United Nations Building
Rajadamnern Nok Avenue
Bangkok 10200
Thailand

☎ +66-2-2881234
✉ escap-scas@un.org

ESCWA

Mr. Mounir Tabet, *Acting Executive Secretary*

Economic and Social Commission for Western Asia
P.O. Box 11-8575
Riad el-Solh Square, Beirut
Lebanon

☎ +961-1-981301
@ https://www.unescwa.org/contact

ISBN: 978-92-1-109180-9
eISBN: 978-92-1-047611-9
Print ISSN: 1995-2074
Online ISSN: 2411-8370
United Nations publication
Sales No. E.19.II.C.1

Acknowledgements

The *World Economic Situation and Prospects 2019* is a joint product of the United Nations Department of Economic and Social Affairs (UN/DESA), the United Nations Conference on Trade and Development (UNCTAD) and the five United Nations regional commissions (Economic Commission for Africa (ECA), Economic Commission for Europe (ECE), Economic Commission for Latin America and the Caribbean (ECLAC), Economic and Social Commission for Asia and the Pacific (ESCAP) and Economic and Social Commission for Western Asia (ESCWA)).

The United Nations World Tourism Organization (UNWTO), and staff from the International Labour Organization (ILO) also contributed to the report. The report has benefited from inputs received from the national centres of Project LINK and from the deliberations in the Project LINK meeting held in Santiago, Chile on 5–7 September 2018. The forecasts presented in the report draw on the World Economic Forecasting Model (WEFM) of UN/DESA.

Under the general guidance of Liu Zhenmin, Under-Secretary-General for Economic and Social Affairs, and Elliott Harris, United Nations Chief Economist and Assistant-Secretary-General for Economic Development, and the management of Pingfan Hong, Director of the Economic Analysis and Policy Division (EAPD), this publication was coordinated by Dawn Holland, Chief of the Global Economic Monitoring Branch of EAPD.

The contributions of Helena Afonso, Grigor Agabekian, Peter Chowla, Ian Cox, Daniel Gay, Andrea Grozdanic, Matthias Kempf, Leah C. Kennedy, Poh Lynn Ng, Ingo Pitterle, Michał Podolski, Gabe Scelta, Nancy Settecasi, Yifan Si, Shari Spiegel, Sheilah Trotta, Sebastian Vergara, Mathieu Verougstraete, Thet Wynn, Yasuhisa Yamamoto and Stephanie Gast Zepeda from **UN/DESA**; Bruno Antunes, Regina Asariotis, Rodrigo Cárcamo, Stefan Csordas, Taisuke Ito, Nicolas Maystre, Viktoria Mohos-Naray, Janvier D. Nkurunziza, Bonapas Onguglo, Julia Seiermann, Mesut Saygili, Claudia Trentini, and Liping Zhang from **UNCTAD**; Hopestone Chavula, Adam Elhiraika, Khaled Hussein, Allan Mukungu, Sidzanbnoma Nadia Denise Ouedraogo, and Duncan Ouma from **ECA**; José Palacín from **ECE**; Claudia De Camino, Pablo Carvallo, Michael Hanni, Esteban Pérez-Caldentey, Ramón Pineda, Daniel Titelman, Cecilia Vera, and Jurgen Weller from **ECLAC**; Goksu Aslan, Shuvojit Banerjee, Zhenqian Huang, Achara Jantarasaengaram, Zheng Jian, Daniel Jeong-Dae Lee, Hamza Ali Malik, Sanjesh Naidu, Kiatkanid Pongpanich, Ma. Fideles Sadicon, Sweta C. Saxena, and Vatcharin Sirimaneetham from **ESCAP**; Seung-Jin Baek, Moctar Mohamed El Hacene, Mohamed Hedi Bchir and Ahmed Moummi from **ESCWA**; Sandra Carvao, Michel Julian and Javier Ruescas from **UNWTO**; Florence Bonnet and Juan Chacaltana from **ILO** are duly acknowledged.

The report was edited by Mary Lee Kortes.

Explanatory notes

The following symbols have been used in the tables throughout the report:

..	**Two dots** indicate that data are not available or are not separately reported.
–	**A dash** indicates that the amount is nil or negligible.
-	**A hyphen** indicates that the item is not applicable.
–	**A minus sign** indicates deficit or decrease, except as indicated.
.	**A full stop** is used to indicate decimals.
/	**A slash** between years indicates a crop year or financial year, for example, 2018/19.
–	**Use of a hyphen between years**, for example, 2018–2019, signifies the full period involved, including the beginning and end years.

Reference to "dollars" ($) indicates United States dollars, unless otherwise stated.

Reference to "billions" indicates one thousand million.

Reference to "tons" indicates metric tons, unless otherwise stated.

Annual rates of growth or change, unless otherwise stated, refer to annual compound rates.

Details and percentages in tables do not necessarily add to totals, because of rounding.

Project LINK is an international collaborative research group for econometric modelling, coordinated jointly by the Economic Analysis and Policy Division of UN/DESA and the University of Toronto.

For **country classifications**, see Statistical annex.

Data presented in this publication incorporate information available as at **30 November 2018.**

The following abbreviations have been used:

ASEAN	Association of South East Asian Nations
BEPS	base erosion and profit shifting
BIS	Bank for International Settlements
BoJ	Bank of Japan
CEMAC	Central African Economic and Monetary Community
CFA	Communauté financière africaine
CIS	Commonwealth of Independent States
CO_2	carbon dioxide
DAC	Development Assistance Committee
DSM	dispute settlement mechanism
ECA	United Nations Economic Commission for Africa
ECB	European Central Bank
ECE	United Nations Economic Commission for Europe
ECLAC	United Nations Economic Commission for Latin America and the Caribbean
ECOSOC	United Nations Economic and Social Council
ESCAP	United Nations Economic and Social Commission for Asia and the Pacific
ESCWA	United Nations Economic and Social Commission for Western Asia
EU	European Union
FDI	foreign direct investment
Fed	United States Federal Reserve
G20	Group of Twenty
GCC	The Cooperation Council for the Arab States of the Gulf
GDP	gross domestic product
GHG	greenhouse gas
GNI	gross national income
GVCs	global value chains
HLPF	United Nations High-level Political Forum on Sustainable Development
IEA	International Energy Agency
IFF	illicit financial flows
ILO	International Labour Organization
IMF	International Monetary Fund
IPCC	Intergovernmental Panel on Climate Change
LDCs	least developed countries
MNE	multinational enterprises
MTS	multilateral trading system
NAFTA	North American Free Trade Agreement
ODA	official development assistance
OECD	Organisation for Economic Co-operation and Development
OPEC	Organization of the Petroleum Exporting Countries
PPP	purchasing power parity
R&D	research and development
SDGs	Sustainable Development Goals
SDT	special and differential treatment
SIDS	small island developing States
UNCTAD	United Nations Conference on Trade and Development
UN/DESA	Department of Economic and Social Affairs of the United Nations Secretariat
UNWTO	United Nations World Tourism Organization
VAT	value-added tax
WAEMU	West African Economic and Monetary Union
WESP	World Economic Situation and Prospects
WTO	World Trade Organization

Sustainable Development Goals

Goal 1. End poverty in all its forms everywhere

Goal 2. End hunger, achieve food security and improved nutrition and promote sustainable agriculture

Goal 3. Ensure healthy lives and promote well-being for all at all ages

Goal 4. Ensure inclusive and equitable quality education and promote lifelong learning opportunities for all

Goal 5. Achieve gender equality and empower all women and girls

Goal 6. Ensure availability and sustainable management of water and sanitation for all

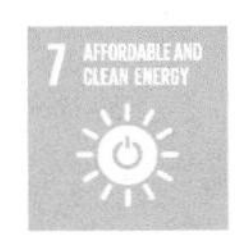

Goal 7. Ensure access to affordable, reliable, sustainable and modern energy for all

Goal 8. Promote sustained, inclusive and sustainable economic growth, full and productive employment and decent work for all

Goal 9. Build resilient infrastructure, promote inclusive and sustainable industrialization and foster innovation

Goal 10. Reduce inequality within and among countries

Goal 11. Make cities and human settlements inclusive, safe, resilient and sustainable

Goal 12. Ensure sustainable consumption and production patterns

Goal 13. Take urgent action to combat climate change and its impacts

Goal 14. Conserve and sustainably use the oceans, seas and marine resources for sustainable development

Goal 15. Protect, restore and promote sustainable use of terrestrial ecosystems, sustainably manage forests, combat desertification, and halt and reverse land degradation and halt biodiversity loss

Goal 16. Promote peaceful and inclusive societies for sustainable development, provide access to justice for all and build effective, accountable and inclusive institutions at all levels

Goal 17. Strengthen the means of implementation and revitalize the Global Partnership for Sustainable Development

Table of contents

Acknowledgements ... iii
Explanatory notes ... iv
Sustainable Development Goals ... v
Foreword ... xv
Executive summary ... xvii

Chapter I
Global economic outlook ... 1

Prospects for the world economy in 2019–2020 ... 1
Robust global growth masks an increase in risks and vulnerabilities ... 1
Investment is contributing more to growth ... 9
Employment is rising, but job quality is low ... 13
Economic conditions remain challenging for many commodity exporters ... 18
International trade ... 20
Global trade growth moderates, amid heightened trade tensions ... 20
Impact of tariff hikes is heterogeneous across sectors and firms ... 23
International financial flows ... 30
Financial market volatility has increased ... 30
Official development assistance declined in 2017 ... 36
Risks to the outlook ... 37
Escalating trade policy disputes ... 37
Abrupt tightening of global financial conditions ... 40
Appendix
Baseline forecast assumptions ... 47
Commodity prices ... 47
Monetary policy ... 49
Fiscal policy ... 52
Exchange rates ... 55

Chapter II
Macroeconomic prospects and the implementation of the 2030 Agenda for Sustainable Development ... 57

Strengthening international cooperation and multilateralism ... 58
International trade policy ... 58
Revenue mobilization for sustainable development ... 64
Macroeconomic conditions and climate change ... 69
Overcoming domestic structural challenges ... 78
Excessive commodity dependence ... 78
Poverty and inequality ... 87

Page

Chapter III

Regional developments and outlook 97

Developed economies 97

United States: GDP growth to moderate as impact of fiscal stimulus wanes amid rising capacity constraints 97

Canada: housing market has cooled, but household debt may pose a risk as interest rates rise 99

Japan: economy at capacity despite a slower expansion..................... 100

Australia and New Zealand: robust economic growth continues despite emerging uncertainties 101

Europe: robust growth ahead, but risks to the outlook are shifting 102

Economies in transition 109

The Commonwealth of Independent States and Georgia: commodity price increases and remittances sustained growth 109

South-Eastern Europe: positive economic trends set to continue 114

Developing economies 117

Africa: improving short-term outlook but with significant medium-term vulnerabilities.................................... 117

East Asia: growth outlook remains robust, but downside risks are high 133

South Asia: economic outlooks diverge as short- and medium-term challenges remain... 143

Western Asia: gradual recovery as oil markets improve 149

Latin America and the Caribbean: growth is projected to gradually pick up, but major downside risks remain 157

Page

Boxes

I.1 Graduation from the United Nations least developed country category 8
I.2 Informal employment around the world: recent data and policies......... 14
I.3 Impacts of large-scale electric vehicle deployment on battery metals markets.. 19
I.4 International tourism 22
I.5 Technological capabilities and export dynamics in developing countries ... 25
I.6 Trade in services as a driver of development in times of tension: inclusiveness, resilience and diversification 28
II.1 Strengthening multilateralism and international cooperation to achieve SDG target 17.11 60
II.2 Climate change adaptation for coastal infrastructure in Caribbean small island developing States 75
II.3 Nigeria: from economic boom to prolonged slump.................... 82
II.4 Case studies of successful natural resource management: Botswana and Costa Rica.. 86
II.5 Finance, growth and inequality 93
III.1 Emerging labour shortages in Eastern Europe....................... 106
III.2 New fiscal rules in energy-exporting countries of the Commonwealth of Independent States.. 112
III.3 African Continental Free Trade Area: opportunities and challenges for achieving sustainable development................................ 124
III.4 China's economic transition and its potential impacts on Asia and the Pacific... 137
III.5 Exploring exchange-rate misalignment in Arab countries.............. 153
III.6 The determinants of investment and their relative importance 159

Figures

I.1 Growth of world gross product, 2012–2020 2
I.2 Contributions to change in world gross product growth, 2017–2018 3
I.3 GDP per capita growth, 2018 6
I.4 Average annual GDP per capita growth by region 7
I.5 Contribution to GDP growth by expenditure component, 2018 9
I.6 Annual growth of private investment, decomposed by asset type (constant prices) 10
I.7 Annual growth of gross fixed capital formation in selected developing economies... 11
I.8 Inflation in 2017 and 2018 12
I.2.1 Extent and composition of informal employment, 2016 14
I.2.2 Level of GDP per capita and informal employment share............... 15
I.9 Real household disposable income, developed economies.............. 17
I.10 Major commodity prices.. 17
I.3.1 Battery metals prices and EV sales 19

Page

I.11 Contribution to global merchandise export volume growth by region, 2011–2018 21
I.12 Contribution to global merchandise import volume growth by region, 2011–2018 21
I.13 Steel prices in the United States and world, January 2017–October 2018 . . . 24
I.5.1 Economic complexity and R&D investments, 2015 25
I.5.2 Technological capabilities and GDP per capita, 2015 26
I.14 Growth of world trade and world gross product, 1992–2020 27
I.6.1 Services and goods exports (value), 2005–2017 28
I.6.2 Exports value growth by deciles of export value, 2005–2017 29
I.15 Stock market performance in the United States and the emerging economies 30
I.16 Chicago Fed National Financial Conditions Index 31
I.17 CBOE equity volatility index (VIX) 31
I.18 Current account vs fiscal balance in selected emerging economies 32
I.19 US dollar exchange rates and foreign reserves of selected emerging economies, January–October 2018 33
I.20 Non-resident portfolio inflows to the emerging economies 35
I.21 Net official development assistance, by main expenditure component 37
I.22 United States: tariffs introduced and proposed, 2018 38
I.23 Price-earnings ratio of S&P 500 index vs long-term interest rates 41
I.24 Breakdown of non-financial sector debt of developed and emerging economies 42
I.25 Dollar-denominated credit to non-bank borrowers in selected emerging economies 43
I.26 Government interest payments as a share of general government revenue, 2018 44
I.A.1 Selected commodity prices, January 2011– September 2018 47
I.A.2 Price of Brent crude: recent trends and assumptions 49
I.A.3 Key central bank policy rates: recent trends and assumptions 49
I.A.4 Total assets of major central banks, January 2007–December 2020 50
I.A.5 Monetary policy stances 51
I.A.6 Fiscal policy stances 53
I.A.7 Major currency exchange rates: recent trends and assumptions 55
II.1 Total number of active trade disputes, 1996–2018 59
II.1.1 LDC share of world merchandise exports, population and the SDG target, 2011–2020 60
II.2 Median tax revenue by country groupings, 2000, 2010 and 2015 65
II.3 Schematic representation of components and channels of illicit financial flows 69
II.4 Global anthropogenic GHG emissions, 2015 71
II.5 GDP and emissions growth
A. GDP and GHG emissions growth, 1991–2016 71
B. Decomposition analysis of global CO_2 emissions, 1990–2017 71
II.6 Number of registered weather-related loss events worldwide, 1981–2017 . . . 73

Page

II.2.1 Projected flooding of George F.L. Charles International Airport and Port Castries, Saint Lucia 75
II.7 GDP per capita growth 1980–2016 vs 2017–2018 79
II.8 Countries by type of commodity dependence and country grouping 80
II.9 Commodity price volatility between 2000–2017 81
II.3.1 Nigeria's macroeconomic indicators 83
II.10 Government revenue as a share of GDP in selected commodity-dependent countries, average 2010–2016 84
II.4.1 Real GDP per capita trends in Botswana and selected regions 86
II.11 Extreme poverty headcount ratios, scenarios for 2030 88
II.12 Distributions of per capita consumption growth and inequality change across countries 89
II.13 Income share held by the lowest 40 per cent of the population in income distribution, 2000–2004 vs 2012–2016 91
II.5.1 Relationship between financial development and economic growth 93
II.5.2 Share of pre-tax national income in the United States and the world 95
III.1 Job openings in the United States by sector, relative to unemployment, 2001–2018 98
III.2 Total credit to households, selected developed economies 100
III.3 Diffusion indices on employment and production capacity in Japan, 2000–2018 101
III.4 Sectoral share of gross value added in Australia, 2000–2018 102
III.5 Public debt in the European Union, 2017 104
III.1.1 Unemployment rate, selected countries in Eastern Europe 106
III.1.2 Beveridge curves
A. Czech Republic, 2008–2018 107
B. Finland, 2012–2018 107
III.6 Exchange rate vs the US dollar in the Russian Federation and Kazakhstan, January–October 2018 110
III.2.1 Oil price and exchange rate in the Russian Federation, 2014–2018 112
III.7 GDP growth and inflation in Africa, 2010–2020 118
III.8 Income distribution by population quintiles, Africa 118
III.9 GDP growth rates by African subregions, 2016–2020 119
III.10 GDP growth in North Africa, 2018–2020 120
III.11 Changes in income distribution, by income group, selected East African countries 122
III.12 Labour market structure of selected East African countries, by sector 122
III.13 Changes in savings and investment as ratios of GDP, 2000 and 2018. 123
III.14 GDP per capita growth in selected Southern African countries, 2015–2020. 126
III.15 Changes in income distribution, by income group, in selected Southern African countries. 127
III.16 Labour market in selected Southern African countries, by sector 127
III.17 GDP growth in West Africa, Nigeria and WAEMU, 2014–2020. 128
III.18 Gross official reserves, Central African Economic and Monetary Community, end of period, 2011–2020 130
III.19 GDP growth and inflation in East Asia, 2006–2020 133

III.20 Share of selected East Asian countries' total exports sent to China, 2017 . . . 134
III.4.1 Computable General Equilibrium (CGE) model simulation: the impact of China's economic transition on its development in 2030 137
III.4.2 CGE model simulation: the impact of China's holistic structural reforms on the Asia-Pacific region in 2030 138
III.21 International reserves of selected East Asian economies, months of import coverage 140
III.22 GDP growth in South Asia, 2018–2020 143
III.23 South Asia: total reserves over external debt, 2015–2017 144
III.24 Economic Complexity Index, selected countries and regions, 2016. 146
III.25 GDP growth prospects of GCC countries. 149
III.5.1 Modelling results on exchange-rate misalignment in Arab countries 154
III.26 Annual GDP growth and consumer price inflation in Latin America and the Caribbean, 2010–2020 157
III.27 Fiscal balances and government debt in Latin America and the Caribbean, 2017. 163
III.28 Selected Latin American exchange rates against the US dollar 163

Tables

I.1 Growth of world output and gross domestic product, 2016–2020 4
I.2 Growth of world output and gross domestic product per capita, 2016–2020. 5
I.A.1 Key commodity prices 48
II.1 Per capita tax revenue by region, 2015. 66
III.5.1 Exchange-rate arrangements in Arab countries 153
III.6.1 Latin America (selected countries): results of the estimation of the relative importance of investment determinants, 1995–2017 160

Statistical annex

Country classifications

Country classifications 167

Data sources, country classifications and aggregation methodology 167

A. Developed economies 169
B. Economies in transition 169
C. Developing economies by region 170
D. Fuel-exporting countries 171
E. Economies by per capita GNI in June 2018 172
F. Least developed countries (as of March 2018) 173
G. Heavily indebted poor countries (as of October 2017) 173
H. Small island developing States 174
I. Landlocked developing countries 174
J. International Organization for Standardization of Country Codes 175

Annex tables 177

A.1 Developed economies: rates of growth of real GDP, 2010–2020 179
A.2 Economies in transition: rates of growth of real GDP, 2010–2020 180
A.3 Developing economies: rates of growth of real GDP, 2010–2020 181
A.4 Developed economies: consumer price inflation, 2010–2020 185
A.5 Economies in transition: consumer price inflation, 2010–2020 186
A.6 Developing economies: consumer price inflation, 2010–2020 187
A.7 Developed economies: unemployment rates, 2010–2020 191
A.8 Economies in transition and developing economies: unemployment rates, 2010–2018 192
A.9 Selected economies: real effective exchange rates, broad measurement, 2009–2018 194
A.10 Indices of prices of primary commodities, 2009–2018 196
A.11 World oil supply and demand, 2010–2019 197
A.12 World trade: changes in value and volume of exports and imports, by major country group, 2010–2020 198
A.13 Balance of payments on current accounts, by country or country group, summary table, 2009–2017 200
A.14 Balance of payments on current accounts, by country or country group, 2009–2017 201
A.15 Net ODA from major sources, by type, 1996–2017 204
A.16 Total net ODA flows from OECD/DAC countries, by type, 2008–2017 205
A.17 Commitments and net flows of financial resources, by selected multilateral institutions, 2008–2017 206

Bibliography 207

Foreword

The *World Economic Situation and Prospects 2019* offers timely warnings about a range of macroeconomic challenges facing policymakers as they aim to deliver on the 2030 Agenda for Sustainable Development.

Last year's report noted that after a long period of stagnation, the world economy was strengthening, creating opportunities to reorient policy towards the longer-term pursuit of sustainable development. The intervening year has been punctuated by escalating global trade disputes and episodes of financial stress and volatility, amid an undercurrent of geopolitical tensions.

While global economic indicators remain largely favourable, they do not tell the whole story. The *World Economic Situation and Prospects 2019* underscores that behind these numbers, one can discern a build-up in short-term risks that are threatening global growth prospects. More fundamentally, the report raises concerns over the sustainability of global economic growth in the face of rising financial, social and environmental challenges. Global levels of public and private debt continue to rise. Economic growth is often failing to reach the people who need it most. The essential transition towards environmentally sustainable production and consumption is not happening fast enough, and the impacts of climate change are growing more widespread and severe.

One overarching message is clear: while it is important to address the short-term challenges of today, policymakers must remain steadfast in advancing a long-term development strategy to meet the economic, social and environmental goals of tomorrow. Decisive policy action relies on multilateral, cooperative approaches in key areas such as pursuing climate action, mobilizing sustainable finance and redressing inequality.

I commend the efforts of the United Nations Department of Economic and Social Affairs, the United Nations Conference on Trade and Development, the five United Nations regional commissions and other contributors on the production of this joint report. I recommend its analysis to a wide global audience as we strive to implement the 2030 Agenda, achieve a fair globalization and build a peaceful, prosperous future in which no one is left behind.

António Guterres
Secretary-General of the United Nations

Executive summary

Prospects for global macroeconomic development

Urgent and concrete policy action is needed to reduce risks to the global economy and secure the foundations for stable and sustainable economic growth. A dynamic and inclusive global economy is central to delivering the ambitious targets of the 2030 Agenda for Sustainable Development. Policymakers must work to contain short-term risks from financial vulnerabilities and escalating trade disputes, while advancing a longer-term development strategy towards economic, social and environmental goals. Decisive policy actions rely on a multilateral, cooperative and long-term approach to global policymaking in key areas, including combatting climate change, sustainable finance, sustainable production and consumption, and redressing inequality. This also requires progress towards a more inclusive, flexible and responsive multilateral system.

On the surface, global economic growth appears firm, masking underlying risks and imbalances

Economic growth accelerated in more than half the world's economies in both 2017 and 2018. Developed economies expanded at a steady pace of 2.2 per cent in both years, and growth rates in many countries have risen close to their potential, while unemployment rates in several developed economies have dropped to historical lows. Among the developing economies, the regions of East and South Asia remain on a relatively strong growth trajectory, expanding by 5.8 per cent and 5.6 per cent, respectively in 2018. Many commodity-exporting countries, notably fuel exporters, are continuing a gradual recovery, although they remain exposed to volatile prices. The impact of the sharp drop in commodity markets in 2014/15 also continues to weigh on fiscal and external balances and has left a legacy of higher levels of debt.

Global economic growth remained steady at 3.1 per cent in 2018, as a fiscally induced acceleration in the United States of America offset slower growth in some other large economies. Economic activity at the global level is expected to expand at a solid pace of 3 per cent in 2019, but there are increasing signs that growth may have peaked. The growth in global industrial production and merchandise trade volumes has been tapering since the beginning of 2018, especially in trade-intensive capital and intermediate goods sectors. Leading indicators point to some softening in economic momentum in many countries in 2019, amid escalating trade disputes, risks of financial stress and volatility, and an undercurrent of geopolitical tensions. At the same time, several developed economies are facing capacity constraints, which may weigh on growth in the short term.

Beneath the headline figures, economic growth is uneven and is often failing to reach the regions that need it most

These headline figures conceal fragilities and setbacks in many developing economies and the uneven pace of economic progress across the world. While economic prospects at the global level have improved over the past two years, several large developing countries have seen per capita income decline. Further declines or weak per capita income growth are anticipated in 2019 in Central, Southern and West Africa, Western Asia, and Latin America and the Caribbean—homes to nearly a quarter of the global population living in extreme poverty.

Even where per capita growth is strong, it is often driven by core industrial regions, leaving peripheral and rural areas behind. While unemployment rates are at historical lows in several developed economies, many individuals, notably those with low incomes, have seen little or no growth in disposable income for the last decade. More than half of the world population has no access to social protection, perpetuating high levels of subsistence activities. These imbalances push the targets of eradicating poverty and creating decent jobs for all further from reach. Inadequate income growth also poses risks to many of the other Sustainable Development Goals, as countries strive to alleviate infrastructure bottlenecks, improve health, upgrade human capital and broaden opportunities.

Resource-rich countries often struggle to tap into their development potential

Many of the developing economies that are falling behind depend heavily on commodities, both in terms of export revenue and financing fiscal expenditure. The combination of high volatility of export and fiscal revenues often translates into large swings in economic activity, and lower rates of growth over the longer term. These effects are exacerbated in countries with weak governance and poor institutional quality, where the lack of diversification may act as a barrier to socioeconomic development. Among the commodity-dependent growth laggards, many have also been mired in long-standing armed conflicts or have faced civil unrest and instability in recent decades.

Uncertainties, risks and implementation of the 2030 Agenda for Sustainable Development

Increasing downside risks and vulnerabilities threaten the short-term sustainability of economic growth

The steady pace of global economic growth masks the build-up of several short-term risks with the potential to severely disrupt economic activity and inflict significant damage on longer-term development prospects. This would make many of the targets of the 2030 Agenda for Sustainable Development much harder to accomplish. Countries with significant vulnerabilities, such as large macroeconomic imbalances and high levels of external debt, are particularly susceptible to such disruptions. As policy space has narrowed considerably across the world, any external shock could have severe and long-lasting implications for global growth and socioeconomic conditions.

Escalating trade policy disputes pose short-term threats…

Over the course of 2018, there was a significant rise in trade tensions among the world's largest economies, with a steep rise in the number of disputes raised under the dispute settlement mechanism of the World Trade Organization. Moves by the United States to increase import tariffs have sparked retaliations and counter-retaliations. Global trade growth has lost momentum, although stimulus measures and direct subsidies have so far offset much of the direct negative impacts on China and in the United States.

A prolonged episode of heightened tensions and spiral of additional tariffs among the world's largest economies poses considerable risk to the global trade outlook. The impact on the world economy could be significant: a slowdown in investment, higher consumer prices and a decline in business confidence. This would create severe disruptions to global value chains, particularly for exporters in East Asian economies that are deeply embedded into the supply chains of trade between China and the United States. Slower growth in China and/or the United States could also reduce demand for commodities, affecting commodity-exporters from Africa and Latin America. There is a risk that the trade disputes could aggravate financial fragilities, especially in some emerging economies. Rising import prices, coupled with tighter financial conditions and high debt-servicing costs, could squeeze profits and cause debt distress in certain industries.

…with longer-term repercussions

A protracted period of subdued trade growth would also weigh on productivity growth in the medium term, and hence on longer-term growth prospects. Trade supports productivity growth via economies of scale, access to inputs, and the acquisition of knowledge and technology from international contacts. Trade in services also contributes to inclusiveness, resilience, and diversification. These trade channels are strongly intertwined with investment decisions, productivity gains, economic growth and ultimately sustainable development.

An abrupt tightening of global financial conditions could spark localized financial turmoil…

Rising policy uncertainties and deepening country-specific vulnerabilities generated bouts of heightened financial market volatility in 2018. Investor sentiments were affected by escalating trade tensions, high levels of debt, elevated geopolitical risks, oil market developments, and shifting expectations over the monetary policy path of the United States. Against this backdrop, global financial conditions experienced some tightening during the year. In the current uncertain environment, any unexpected developments or sudden shift in sentiment could trigger sharp market corrections and a disorderly reallocation of capital. A rapid rise in interest rates and a significant strengthening of the dollar could exacerbate domestic fragilities and financial difficulties in some countries, leading to higher risk of debt distress.

…with potential for more widespread contagion

Investors may become particularly wary of countries with significant domestic vulnerabilities, such as high current account and fiscal deficits, large external financing needs, a lack of transparency in their debt obligations, or limited policy buffers. Financial stress can also spread between countries through banking channels and other financial market linkages. In addition, there is evidence of recent financial market contagion through discrete shifts in investor confidence, irrespective of underlying fundamentals, placing emerging markets more broadly at risk.

Monetary policy adjustments or policy missteps in major economies could trigger heightened financial stress

Considerable uncertainty surrounds the monetary policy adjustment path in the developed economies, particularly the United States. Against a backdrop of a highly pro-cyclical fiscal expansion and an increase in import tariffs, a strong rise in inflationary pressures could prompt the United States Federal Reserve to raise interest rates at a much faster pace than currently expected, triggering a sharp tightening of global liquidity conditions.

The possible failure of policymakers in Europe to finalize legal and regulatory arrangements in advance of the intended withdrawal of the United Kingdom of Great Britain and Ireland from the European Union in March 2019 poses risks to financial stability, given the prominence of European banks in driving global cross-border financial flows.

Recent policy easing in China, while likely to support short-term growth, could exacerbate financial imbalances. This may raise the risk of a disorderly deleveraging process in the future, with large repercussions on real economic activity, and regional and global spillovers.

Climate risks also threaten economic prospects, especially for small island developing States

Climate risks are intensifying, as the world experiences an increasing number of extreme weather events. Over the last six years, more than half of extreme weather events have been attributed to climate change. Climate shocks impact developed and developing countries alike, putting large communities at risk of displacement and causing severe damage to vital infrastructure. Nevertheless, the human cost of disasters falls overwhelmingly on low-income and lower-middle-income countries. Many small island developing States (SIDS) in the Caribbean and Indian and Pacific Oceans are particularly exposed to climate risks, through flooding, rising aridity, coastal erosion and depletion of freshwater. Climate-related damage to critical transport infrastructure, such as ports and airports, may have broader implications for international trade and for the sustainable development prospects of the most vulnerable nations. Risks from marine inundation of coastal infrastructure will increase substantially when global warming reaches 1.5°C, which may be reached as early as in the 2030s.

Underlying vulnerabilities of a longer-term nature endanger the sustainability of global economic growth along financial, social and environmental dimensions

Global public and private debt levels have continued to rise. In several countries, high debt service obligations already constitute a heavy burden on government finances. More broadly, the rise in debt in developing economies has generally not been matched by an equivalent expansion of productive assets. This raises concerns about the longer-term sustainability of debt, as well as concerns about productive capacity over the medium term, given large infrastructure gaps, degradation of existing capital and their related impact on productivity.

Eradicating poverty by 2030 will require both double-digit growth in Africa and steep reductions in income inequality

Along social dimensions, economic growth is often failing to reach those that need it most. Weak per capita income growth in regions where poverty levels and inequality remain high acts as a severe impediment to social development. Despite substantial progress over the last two decades, more than 700 million people remain below the extreme poverty line, of which more than half are in Africa. Achieving the target of eradicating poverty by 2030 will require dramatic shifts in countries where poverty rates remain high, both in terms of sharp accelerations in economic growth and steep reductions in income inequality. In Africa, economic growth needs to rise to double-digit levels to reach poverty reduction targets, well beyond growth rates recorded over the last 50 years.

A fundamental shift in the way the world powers economic growth is imperative

To avoid substantial changes to current human and natural systems, global CO_2 emissions must start to decline well before 2030. While some progress has been made in reducing the greenhouse gas intensity of production, the transition towards environmentally sustainable production and consumption is not happening fast enough, allowing the level of carbon emissions to rise and accelerating climate change. A fundamental and more rapid shift in the way the world powers economic growth is urgently needed if we are to avert further serious damage to our ecosystems and livelihoods. Such a fundamental transformation requires policy action on many fronts, the acceleration of technological innovation, and significant behavioural changes.

Policy challenges and the way forward

The multilateral approach to global policy making is facing significant challenges

There has been a growing perception that the benefits of increasing economic integration have not been equitably shared between or within countries. The benefits from trade and financial liberalization are now increasingly viewed as exacerbating income and wealth inequality within countries, limiting policy space and even, in some cases, undermining national sovereignty. Institutions and agreements at the heart of the multilateral system have been facing increased pressure. These pressures have materialized in the areas of international trade, international development finance, and tackling climate change.

The threats to multilateralism come at a time when international cooperation and governance are more important than ever. Many of the challenges laid out in the 2030 Agenda for Sustainable Development are global by nature and require collective and cooperative action.

There is need to work towards a more inclusive, flexible and responsive multilateral system

In today's closely integrated world economy, internationally agreed rules and institutions are vital for ensuring well-functioning markets, resolving disagreements and guaranteeing stability. Strengthening multilateralism is, therefore, central to advancing sustainable development across the globe. To be effective, multilateral systems must respond to legitimate concerns and criticisms. The architecture of the multilateral trading system needs to be better aligned with the 2030 Agenda for Sustainable Development, creating an inclusive, transparent and development-friendly framework for international trade. Progress in international tax cooperation must enable all countries to receive their fair share of taxes from international companies, which is especially important for the poorest countries. To halt global warming, greater international cooperation on green technology, including affordable technology transfer, is needed to support transition towards sustainable production in many developing countries, especially the least developed countries (LDCs).

International tax cooperation must complement effective national tax policies

The international community must continue to work for a fair, sustainable and modern international tax system, supported by pro-growth tax policies. Efforts should be universal in approach and scope, and should fully take into account the different needs and capacities of all countries. In the digitalized era, a multilateral approach to taxation is essential. Nevertheless, this must leave space for countries to adopt effective tax policies that enhance domestic public finance for sustainable development. Effective and well-managed mobilization, budgeting and use of domestic public resources are critical to providing essential public goods and services, strengthening infrastructure, reducing inequality and supporting macroeconomic stability.

Delivering environmentally sustainable growth requires fundamental shifts in policy and consumption

Economic decision-making must fully integrate the negative climate risks associated with emissions, thereby reducing the demand for carbon-intensive services and fossil fuel-based technology. This can be achieved through tools such as carbon pricing measures, energy efficiency regulations such as minimum performance standards and building codes, and reduction of socially inefficient fossil fuel subsidy regimes. Governments can also promote policies to stimulate new energy-saving technologies, such as research and development subsidies. In countries that remain highly reliant on fossil fuel production, economic diversification is vital.

Managing natural resource wealth requires far-sighted policy strategies

Natural resource wealth can create vast development opportunities for an economy when matched with effective management and far-sighted policy strategies. Returns from the commodity sector can provide vital revenue to support broader access to education and health care, investment in critical infrastructure, provision of crucial social protection services and to promote economic diversification. Diversification will strengthen resilience, and in many cases is also an environmental necessity. Achieving this requires a comprehensive approach to commodity management embedded within a broad sustainable development strategy. Key elements include strengthening institutions, increasing transparency, developing countercyclical policies, and targeted investment in human capital.

Education, employment policies and rural infrastructure are central to reducing inequality

High levels of inequality are a major barrier to achieving the 2030 Agenda for Sustainable Development. Broadening access to education and improving its quality are crucial to redressing this obstacle. Employment policies, such as raising minimum wages and expanding social protection, have also been shown to raise the living standards of the lowest income earners. Prioritizing rural infrastructure development, through public investment in transport, agriculture and energy, can also support poverty alleviation and narrow the rural-urban divide.

Chapter I
Global economic outlook

Prospects for the world economy in 2019–2020

Robust global growth masks an increase in risks and vulnerabilities

Strong headline figures mask shortcomings in the foundations and quality of global economic growth

On the surface, global economic growth appears robust. The world economy is projected to expand at a steady pace of 3 per cent in 2019 and 2020. Growth rates in many developed economies have risen near to what is widely considered their potential, while unemployment rates have fallen towards historical lows. Among the developing economies, the East and South Asia regions remain on a strong growth trajectory, while many commodity-exporting countries are continuing a gradual recovery. However, a closer look below this surface reveals significant shortcomings in the foundations and quality of global economic growth.

Short-term risks are rising, with the potential to severely disrupt economic activity and inflict significant damage on longer-term development prospects. These include escalating trade disputes, financial stress and volatility, and an undercurrent of geopolitical tensions. Amid the significant build-up in global public and private debt, policy space has narrowed considerably across the world, and any negative shock could have severe and long-lasting implications for global growth. Waning support for multilateralism also raises questions around the capacity for collaborative policy action in the event of a widespread global shock.

Short-term risks compound underlying structural vulnerabilities

These short-term risks compound underlying structural vulnerabilities of a longer-term nature. Economic growth is often failing to reach where it is needed most. Per capita incomes are stagnant or declining in several regions, including some with high rates of poverty. With persistently high levels of inequality, the goal of poverty eradication by 2030 is moving increasingly out of reach. In addition, the critical transition towards environmentally sustainable patterns of production and consumption is not happening fast enough. While some progress has been made in reducing the greenhouse gas intensity of production, this progress remains insufficient to reduce aggregate emission levels, given the increased volume of production. The level of carbon emissions continues to rise, accelerating climate change.

Urgent and concrete policy action is needed to change the trajectory of the global economy towards a sustainable path and implement the actions and policy changes needed to deliver the ambitious goals of the 2030 Agenda for Sustainable Development. This includes sound macroeconomic and macroprudential policies, structural and redistributive reforms, and industrial policies, adapted as appropriate to country-specific circumstances. At the international level, progress relies on a cooperative and long-term strategy for global policy in key areas such as climate change, sustainable consumption and responsible finance, supported by declines in income and gender inequality. A withdrawal from multilateralism will pose further setbacks for those already being left behind.

The rest of this chapter focuses on the short-term outlook for the global economy, world trade and international financial flows, and key risks to that outlook. Chapter II considers the implications of this macroeconomic backdrop for the implementation of the 2030 Agenda for Sustainable Development. Policy challenges are discussed, emphasizing the need for multilateral solutions in the areas of international trade, international finance, and climate change. The chapter also discusses important domestic structural challenges, including overcoming excessive commodity dependence and persistently high levels of poverty and inequality. Chapter III looks in more detail at economic prospects in individual regions and country groups.

At the global level, economic growth remains steady, but may have reached a peak

In 2018, global economic growth remained steady at 3.1 per cent when calculated at market exchange rates, or 3.7 per cent when adjusted for purchasing power parities (figure I.1).[1] A fiscally induced acceleration in the United States of America offset slower growth in some other large economies, including Argentina, Canada, China, Japan, Islamic Republic of Iran, Turkey and the European Union (EU) (figure I.2). Despite these slowdowns, economic growth accelerated in more than half of the world's economies in both 2017 and 2018.

There are growing signs that global growth may have reached a peak. Estimates of global industrial production and merchandise trade growth have been tapering since the beginning of 2018, especially in trade-intensive capital and intermediate goods sectors, signalling weaker investment prospects. The annualized expansion of global industrial production slowed to 3.0 per cent in the first 9 months of 2018, compared to 3.5 per cent

Figure I.1
Growth of world gross product, 2012–2020

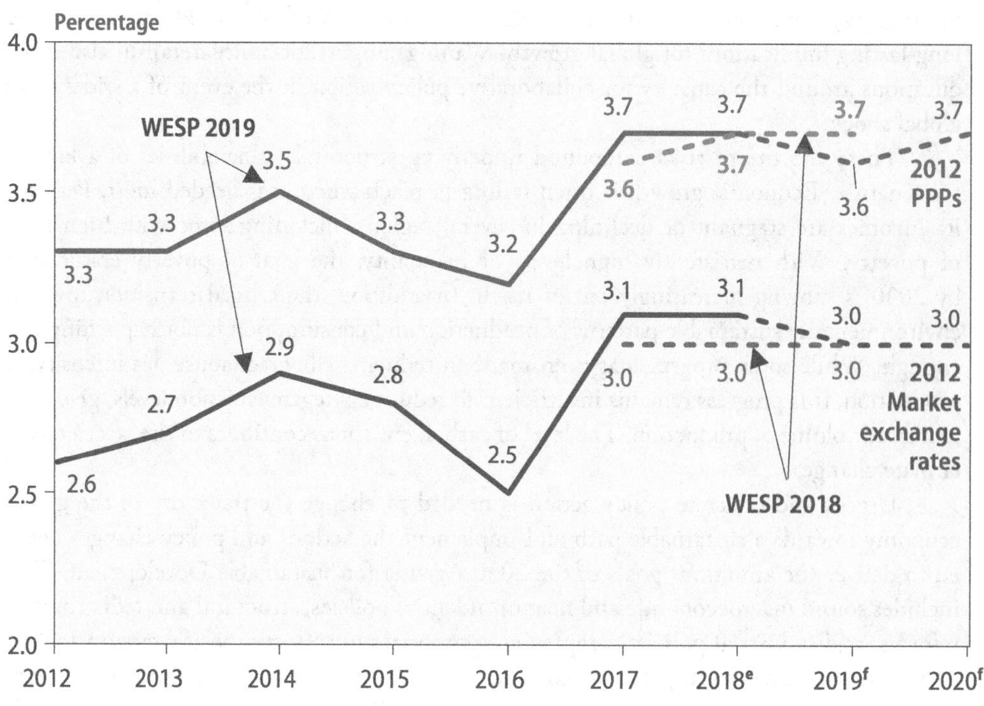

Source: UN/DESA.
Note: e = estimates, f = forecast.

1 Purchasing power parities (PPPs) adjust for differences in the costs of living across countries. Developing countries get a higher weight in PPP-based aggregations. Since developing countries have been growing significantly faster than developed countries, the level of global growth is higher when using PPP exchange rates.

Figure I.2
Contributions to change in world gross product growth, 2017–2018

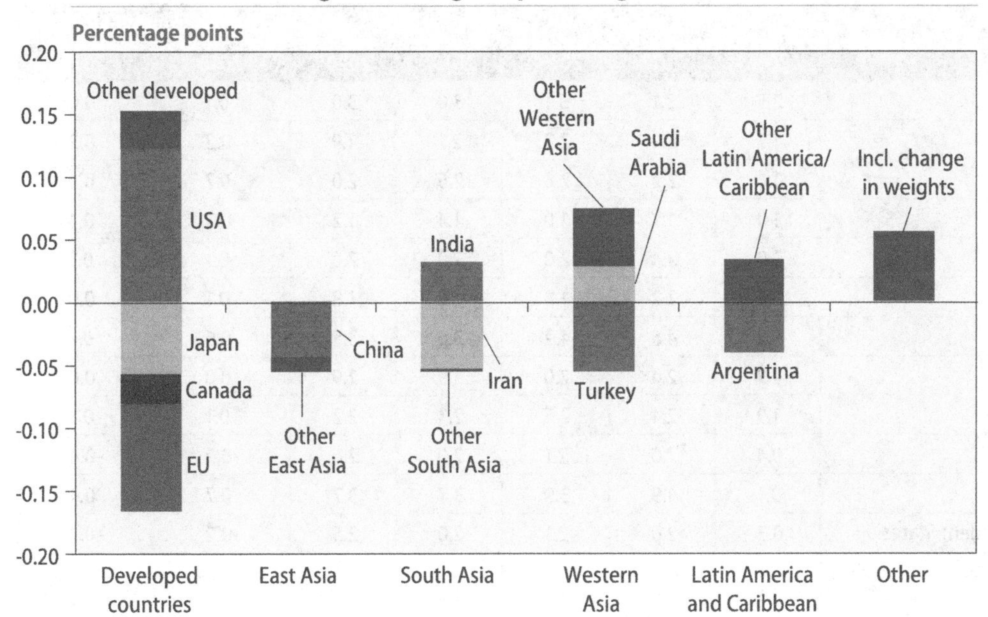

Source: UN/DESA.

growth in 2017. World merchandise trade growth averaged 3.7 per cent in the 9 months to September, compared to 4.7 per cent growth in 2017.[2] At the same time, several developed economies are facing capacity constraints, which may constrain growth in the short term.

Leading indicators point to some softening in economic momentum in many countries in 2019. The Organization for Economic Cooperation and Development (OECD) Composite Leading Indicator for the 36 members of the OECD plus 6 large non-member countries (Brazil, China, India, Indonesia, the Russian Federation and South Africa) has drifted down since the end of 2017. According to Moody's Analytics Survey of Business Confidence, expectations about business conditions and investment intentions over the next six months have weakened. Both the ifo World Economic Survey and Ipsos Global Consumer Confidence Index indicate a moderation of economic activity in the coming months. These expectations are closely associated with heightened uncertainty, both in terms of financial market volatility and global economic policy uncertainty.

Slower growth in China and the United States will be largely offset by mild recovery in large commodity exporters

At the global level, growth is expected to moderate slightly to 3 per cent in both 2019 and 2020 (table I.1).[3] Slower growth in China and the United States will be largely offset by continued recovery in some developing regions and economies in transition that have been hardest hit by the commodity price collapse of 2014/15. Among developed economies, US growth is projected to decelerate notably as the impulse from fiscal stimulus wanes and the effects of higher interest rates are increasingly being felt. While steady growth is projected for the EU, the risks are tilted to the downside, including a potential fallout from Brexit. Among developing and transition economies, the gradual moderation of growth in China is likely to continue, with policy support partly offsetting the negative impact of trade tensions. Several large commodity-exporting countries, such as Brazil, Nigeria and the Russian

2 Data comes from the CPB Netherlands Bureau for Economic Policy Analysis.

3 Country-level forecasts underlying this summary table are reported in the Statistical annex. Unless otherwise specified, regional aggregations are based on 2012 market exchange rates. Key assumptions underpinning the forecasts are reported in the Appendix to chapter I.

Table I.1
Growth of world output and gross domestic product, 2016–2020

						Change from WESP 2018	
Annual percentage change	2016	2017	2018[a]	2019[b]	2020[b]	2018	2019
World	2.5	3.1	3.1	3.0	3.0	0.1	0.0
Developed economies	1.7	2.2	2.2	2.1	1.9	0.2	0.2
United States of America	1.6	2.2	2.8	2.5	2.0	0.7	0.4
Japan	1.0	1.7	1.0	1.4	1.2	-0.2	0.4
European Union	2.0	2.4	2.0	2.0	2.0	-0.1	0.1
EU-15	1.9	2.2	1.8	1.8	1.8	-0.1	0.0
EU-13	3.2	4.6	4.2	3.6	3.5	0.6	0.1
Euro area	1.9	2.4	2.0	1.9	1.9	0.0	0.0
Other developed countries	1.9	2.4	2.5	2.3	2.2	0.1	0.1
Economies in transition	0.4	2.0	2.1	2.0	2.6	-0.2	-0.4
South-Eastern Europe	3.1	1.9	3.9	3.7	3.7	0.7	0.4
Commonwealth of Independent States and Georgia	0.3	2.0	2.1	2.0	2.5	-0.2	-0.4
Russian Federation	-0.1	1.5	1.5	1.4	2.1	-0.4	-0.5
Developing economies	3.9	4.5	4.4	4.3	4.6	-0.2	-0.4
Africa	1.6	3.4	3.2	3.4	3.7	-0.3	-0.3
North Africa	2.9	5.3	3.7	3.4	3.5	-0.4	-0.7
East Africa	5.5	6.1	6.2	6.4	6.5	0.4	0.2
Central Africa	-0.5	-0.2	2.2	2.5	3.8	0.1	0.0
West Africa	0.2	2.4	3.2	3.4	3.8	-0.1	0.0
Southern Africa	0.3	1.5	1.2	2.1	2.6	-1.1	-0.4
East and South Asia	6.1	6.1	5.8	5.5	5.6	0.0	-0.4
East Asia	5.7	6.1	5.8	5.6	5.5	0.1	0.0
China	6.7	6.9	6.6	6.3	6.2	0.1	0.0
South Asia	8.0	6.1	5.6	5.4	5.9	-0.9	-1.6
India[c]	7.1	6.7	7.4	7.6	7.4	0.2	0.2
Western Asia	3.1	2.5	3.0	2.4	3.4	0.7	-0.3
Latin America and the Caribbean	-1.3	1.0	1.0	1.7	2.3	-1.0	-0.8
South America	-2.9	0.5	0.4	1.4	2.3	-1.4	-1.0
Brazil	-3.5	1.0	1.4	2.1	2.5	-0.6	-0.4
Mexico and Central America	3.1	2.4	2.4	2.5	2.3	-0.2	-0.1
Caribbean	-0.7	-0.4	1.9	2.0	2.0	0.1	0.0
Least developed countries	3.6	4.6	5.0	5.0	5.7	-0.4	-0.5
Memorandum items							
World trade[d]	2.5	5.3	3.8	3.7	3.9	0.3	0.1
World output growth with PPP weights[e]	3.2	3.7	3.7	3.6	3.7	0.0	-0.1

Source: UN/DESA.
a Estimated.
b Forecast, based in part on Project LINK.
c Fiscal year basis.
d Includes goods and services.
e Based on 2012 benchmark.

Table I.2
Growth of world output and gross domestic product per capita, 2016–2020

Annual percentage change	2016	2017	2018[a]	2019[b]	2020[b]
World	1.3	2.0	2.0	1.9	2.0
Developed economies	1.3	1.9	1.9	1.8	1.6
United States of America	0.9	1.5	2.1	1.8	1.3
Japan	1.1	1.9	1.2	1.6	1.5
European Union	1.8	2.3	1.9	1.8	1.8
EU-15	1.6	2.0	1.6	1.6	1.6
EU-13	3.4	4.9	4.4	3.9	3.8
Euro area	1.8	2.2	1.8	1.8	1.7
Other developed countries	0.8	1.3	1.4	1.2	1.2
Economies in transition	0.1	1.7	1.9	1.8	2.4
South-Eastern Europe	3.3	2.1	4.0	3.8	3.8
Commonwealth of Independent States and Georgia	-0.1	1.7	1.8	1.7	2.3
Russian Federation	-0.2	1.5	1.5	1.4	2.2
Developing economies	2.6	3.2	3.1	3.1	3.4
Africa[c]	-0.9	0.5	0.6	0.9	1.2
North Africa[c]	1.3	2.5	1.7	1.7	1.8
East Africa	2.5	3.1	3.3	3.4	3.6
Central Africa	-3.1	-2.8	-0.4	-0.1	1.1
West Africa	-2.5	-0.3	0.5	0.7	1.1
Southern Africa	-2.0	-0.8	-1.1	-0.2	0.3
East and South Asia	5.1	5.1	4.8	4.6	4.7
East Asia	5.0	5.4	5.2	5.0	4.9
China	6.2	6.4	6.2	5.9	5.9
South Asia	6.6	4.8	4.4	4.1	4.7
India[d]	6.7	5.1	6.2	6.5	6.4
Western Asia	1.1	0.6	1.1	0.6	1.7
Latin America and the Caribbean	-2.3	0.0	0.0	0.8	1.4
South America	-3.8	-0.4	-0.5	0.5	1.4
Brazil	-4.2	0.2	0.6	1.4	1.8
Mexico and Central America	1.8	1.1	1.2	1.3	1.2
Caribbean	-1.2	-0.9	1.4	1.5	1.5
Least developed countries	1.2	2.2	2.6	2.6	3.3

Source: UN/DESA.
a Estimated.
b Forecast, based in part on Project LINK.
c Figures for Africa and North Africa exclude Libya.
d Calendar year basis.

Federation, are projected to see a moderate pickup in growth in 2019–2020, albeit from a low base. The prospects for commodity exporters remain clouded by several factors. The price collapse in 2014/15 has left a legacy of higher levels of debt and depleted fiscal buffers, severely constraining policy space. While prices have partly recovered, they remain highly volatile and subject to wide fluctuations, as exemplified by the sharp decline in oil prices in the fourth quarter of 2018.

Global growth is not reaching areas where it is needed most

The robust headline global growth figures conceal an uneven pace of economic progress across the world. While economic prospects at the global level have improved since 2016, several large developing countries have seen per capita income decline in 2018 (figure I.3). Despite a modest improvement, per capita incomes will stagnate or grow only marginally in Central, Southern and West Africa, Western Asia, and Latin America and the Caribbean in 2019 (figure I.4 and table I.2). These regions combined are home to nearly 20 per cent of the global population, and nearly one quarter of those living in extreme poverty. Furthermore, among developing countries where per capita growth is strong, economic activity is often driven by core industrial and urban regions, leaving peripheral and rural areas behind—thereby contributing to increasing internal inequalities.[4] This pushes the targets of eradicating poverty and creating decent jobs for all, with an adequate level of

Figure I.3
GDP per capita growth, 2018[a,b]

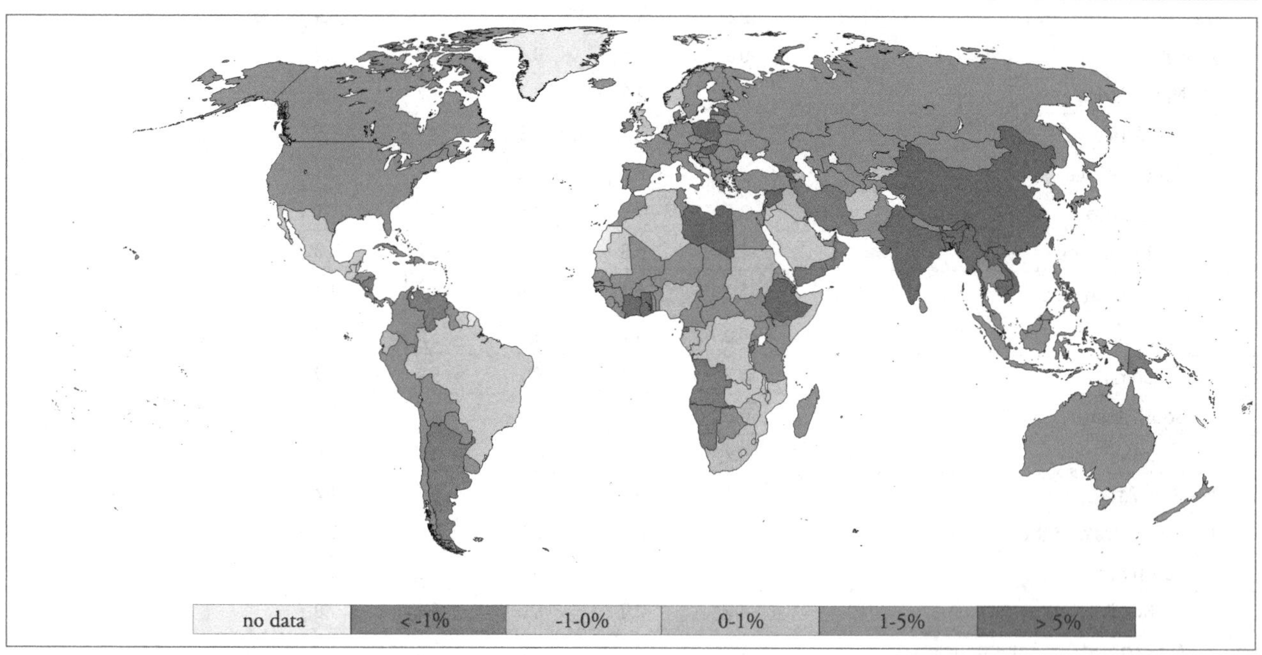

Source: UN/DESA.

a Disclaimer: The designations employed and the presentation of material on this map do not imply the expression of any opinion whatsoever on the part of the Secretariat of the United Nations concerning the legal status of any country, territory, city or area or of its authorities, or concerning the delimitation of its frontiers or boundaries. Dotted line represents approximately the Line of Control in Jammu and Kashmir agreed upon by India and Pakistan. The final status of Jammu and Kashmir has not yet been agreed upon by the parties. Final boundary between the Republic of Sudan and the Republic of South Sudan has not yet been determined. A dispute exists between the Governments of Argentina and the United Kingdom of Great Britain and Northern Ireland concerning sovereignty over the Falkland Islands (Malvinas).

b The map represents countries and/or territories or parts thereof for which data is available and/or analysed in *World Economic Situation and Prospects 2019*. The shaded areas therefore do not necessarily overlap entirely with the delimitation of their frontiers or boundaries.

4 See, for example, Rodríguez-Pose and Hardy (2015).

Figure I.4
Average annual GDP per capita growth by region

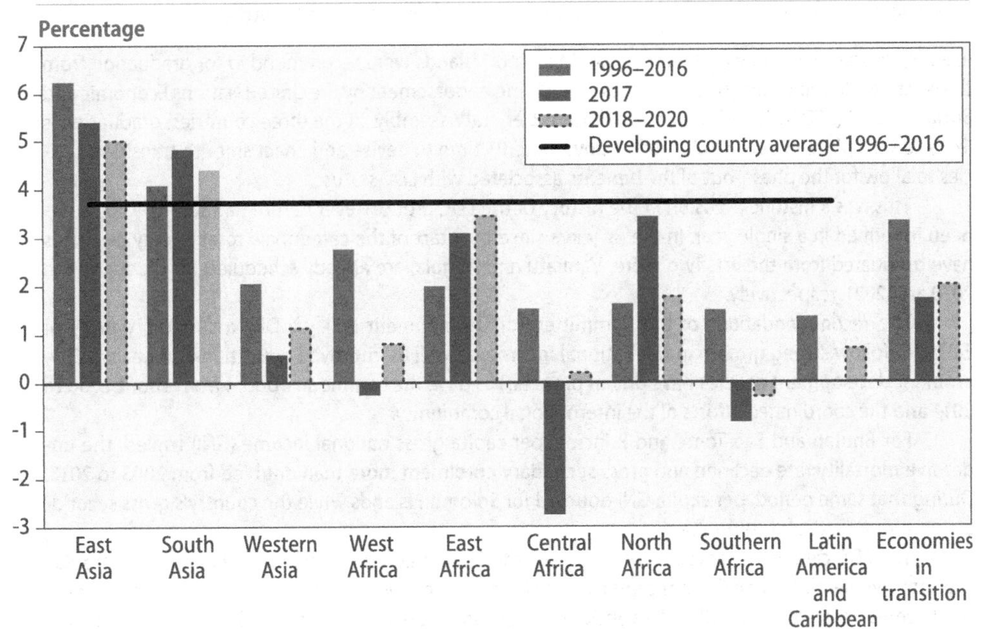

Source: UN/DESA.

social protection, even further from reach. Inadequate income growth, coupled with high levels of inequality, also pose risks to many of the other Sustainable Development Goals (SDGs), as countries strive to alleviate infrastructure bottlenecks, strengthen the business environment, upgrade human capital and broaden opportunities.

Poverty eradication requires double-digit growth and steep reductions in income inequality

GDP growth in the least developed countries (LDCs) is estimated to average 5.0 per cent in 2018 or 2.6 per cent in per capita terms, continuing a steady acceleration since 2015. Three countries—Bhutan, Sao Tome and Principe, and Solomon Islands—were recommended for graduation from the LDC category in 2018 (box I.1). Although most countries have participated in the upturn, which is partly driven by some recovery of commodity prices, almost one third of the LDCs have grown by less in 2018 than in 2017. Some large LDCs are expanding at an average annual rate of 7 per cent or more, including Bangladesh, Bhutan, Burkina Faso, Cambodia, Ethiopia, Lao People's Democratic Republic, Myanmar and Senegal. By contrast, growth in many small island developing States (SIDS) and conflict-affected countries remains well below what is called for in target 8.1 of SDG 8 (promote sustained, inclusive and sustainable economic growth, full and productive employment and decent work for all). In the majority of LDCs, per capita GDP growth is significantly below levels needed to eradicate extreme poverty. Longer-term growth projections point to nearly 30 per cent of the population in LDCs remaining in extreme poverty by 2030. Changing this outcome would require both double-digit economic growth and a significant reduction in income inequality (see discussion in chap. II). This, in turn, will require a significant rise in well-targeted investment, including rural infrastructure development; well-managed public resources and targeted social protection programmes; and supportive education and employment policies.

Box I.1

Graduation from the United Nations least developed country category

In 2018, Bhutan, Sao Tome and Principe, and Solomon Islands were recommended for graduation from the least developed country (LDC) category, following endorsement by the United Nations Economic and Social Council (ECOSOC) and the United Nations General Assembly. In the three countries, graduation is likely to take place in 2023–2024, giving Governments time to devise and enact smooth transition policies to allow for the phase-out of the benefits associated with LDC status.

This was a historic occasion in the history of the LDC group. Never before had so many countries been identified in a single year. In the 47 years since the start of the category, a total of only five LDCs have graduated from the list. Two more, Vanuatu and Angola, are already scheduled for graduation in 2020 and 2021, respectively.

The recommendations of the Committee for Development Policy (CDP), a subsidiary body of ECOSOC, follow strong growth in the national income, as well as improved education and health. Government development policies have driven progress, as have the commodity boom from about 2000 to 2014 and the coordinated efforts of the international community.

For Bhutan and Sao Tome and Principe, per capita gross national income (GNI) tripled, the under-five mortality rate declined and gross secondary enrolment more than doubled from 2003 to 2018. During that same period, per capita GNI doubled for Solomon Islands while the country's gross secondary enrolment rate almost doubled.

The LDC category is assessed using three criteria: human assets (health and education targets), economic vulnerability and GNI per capita. Countries must meet two of the three criteria at two consecutive triennial reviews of the CDP to be considered for graduation. The CDP sends its recommendations to ECOSOC for endorsement, which then refers its decision to the General Assembly.

Bhutan, Sao Tome and Príncipe and Solomon Islands each continue to meet the GNI per capita and human assets criteria but not the economic vulnerability criterion.

The CDP found that while Nepal and Timor-Leste also met the criteria for graduation, they were not recommended for graduation at this time owing to economic and political challenges. These countries may again be considered for graduation at the next triennial review of the CDP in 2021 if they still meet the criteria. ECOSOC deferred a decision on Kiribati and Tuvalu, which also meet the criteria, to 2021.

Bangladesh, Lao People's Democratic Republic and Myanmar met the graduation criteria for the first time in 2018, but would need to do so again for a second time at the next triennial review in 2021 to be considered for graduation.

Graduating LDCs stand to lose several benefits delivered exclusively to members of the category—including trade preferences, certain forms of technical and financial support, dedicated climate financing, and other measures such as travel assistance and smaller contributions to the United Nations budget.

Multilateral trade preferences for LDCs, such as duty-free quota-free market access under the European Union's (EU) Everything But Arms (EBA) initiative, are particularly important. Bangladesh, for instance, the biggest LDC and the world's second-largest garment exporter, sends half of its garment exports to the EU and enjoys a tariff preference margin of 9.6 per cent on many of its exports to that market.

The country is unusual in that it has no bilateral trade agreements (although it is a member of regional agreements Bay of Bengal Initiative for Multi-Sectoral, Technical and Economic Cooperation (BIMSTEC) and South Asian Free Trade Area (SAFTA)). As Bangladesh becomes unable to rely on multilateral preferences, following its probable loss of EBA in 2027, it may consider negotiating free trade agreements (FTAs) or bilateral agreements with a number of major trading partners, such as China. Talks with Sri Lanka have already begun. An FTA with Europe could be an alternative to EBA and the Generalized System of Preferences Plus (GSP+).

For Bangladesh, therefore, the next few years will be crucial, given that any bilateral agreements or FTAs negotiated now are likely to set a precedent for future agreements. The power-based nature of bilateral negotiations, however, makes this a much more challenging environment than the multilateralism that has governed trade up to this point.

An associated trend is the increasing "Africanization" of the LDC group. The next 10 likely graduations, except Angola, are in the Asia-Pacific region. Lao People's Democratic Republic and Myanmar

(*continued*)

are on track to graduate by the mid-2020s and Cambodia by about 2027. By the end of the decade the LDC group will probably comprise about 30 African countries, plus Afghanistan, Haiti and Yemen. This has implications for the preference schemes of trading partners such as the EU, which has separate Economic Partnership Arrangements with African, Pacific and Caribbean countries. If partner countries and regions, and their companies, wish to keep benefiting from trade preferences with low-wage manufacturing countries, they will have to develop new trade regimes for former LDCs in Asia.

The graduating countries are, in a sense, victims of their own success, and new measures need to be put in place to help them after graduation. Whether or not they maintain current market access arrangements is, to some extent, a test of global attitudes towards multilateralism.

Box I.1 (*continued*)

Author: Daniel Gay (UN/DESA/EAPD).

Figure I.5
Contribution to GDP growth by expenditure component, 2018

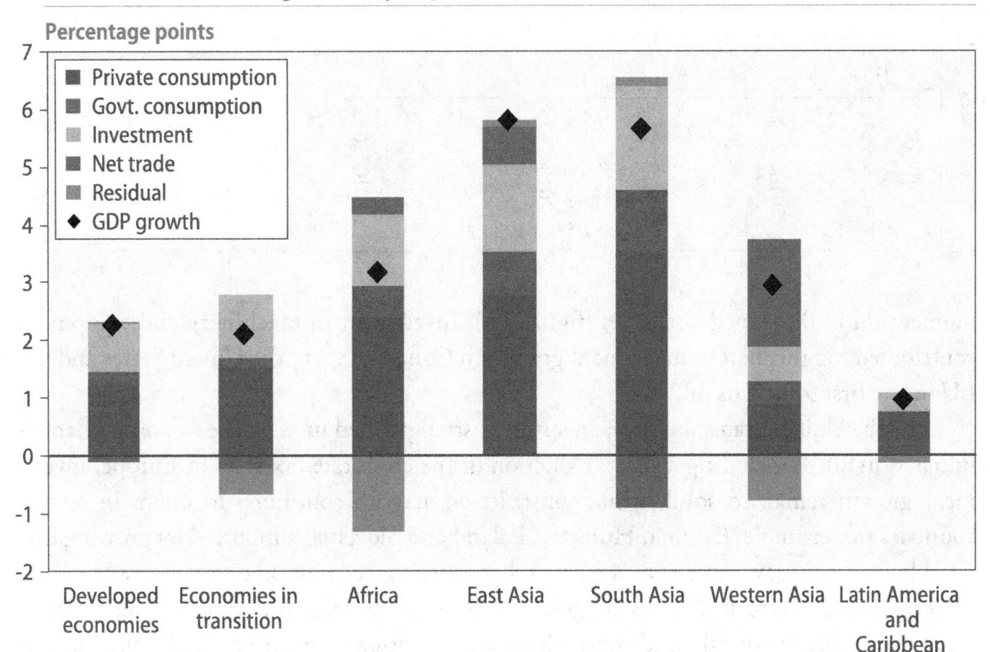

Source: UN/DESA estimates.

Investment is contributing more to growth

Private consumption remains the main contributor to growth in most regions

A decomposition of economic growth by expenditure reveals some differences in the drivers of GDP growth across regions in 2018 (figure I.5). Private consumption remains the largest contributor to growth in many regions, most notably in Africa, Latin America and the Caribbean, and South Asia. In Western Asia, net trade contributed significantly to growth as higher average oil prices boosted oil-related export revenues in the Cooperation Council for the Arab States of the Gulf (GCC) countries, while Turkey experienced a sharp contraction of imports. Meanwhile, East Asia's broad-based growth during the year was underpinned by robust domestic demand conditions and positive net trade. In both the East and South Asia regions, investment growth has been driven by the implementation of large infrastructure projects in several economies.

Investment playing a more important role in driving growth

While private consumption continues to be a key driver of overall GDP growth for most regions, investment activity has strengthened in many developed and developing economies over the past two years. In particular, private non-residential investment gained

Figure I.6
Annual growth of private investment, decomposed by asset type (constant prices)

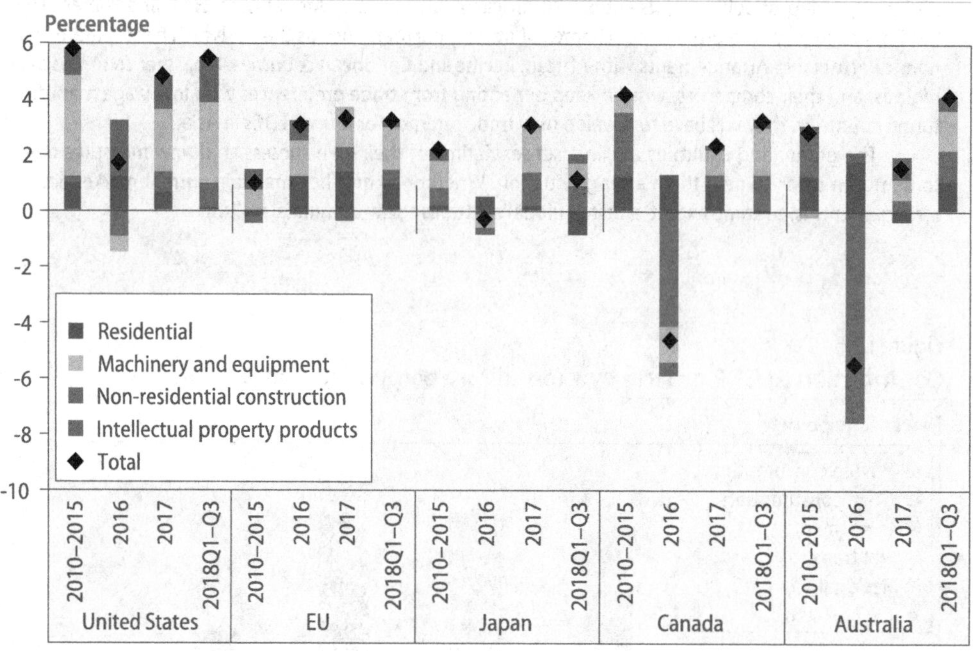

Sources: United States Bureau of Economic Analysis, Eurostat, Statistics Canada, Cabinet Office of Japan, Australia Bureau of Statistics.

Note: Figures for the EU and Japan include public sector investment.

momentum in developed countries (figure I.6). Investment in machinery and equipment contributed roughly half of investment growth in Canada, Japan, the United States and the EU in the first 9 months of 2018.

In the United States, business investment strengthened in response to policy changes initiated in 2018, including a sharp reduction in the corporate tax rate. In Europe, investment growth remained solid, while construction activity continued to boom in several countries (for example, Estonia, Hungary, Poland and Slovenia) supported by growing disposable incomes, government measures and continuing accommodative monetary policy. Nevertheless, forward indicators suggest that investment growth may moderate in 2019, amid tightening financial conditions, rising trade tensions, and protracted policy uncertainties.

Investment ratios in developed economies remain low by historical standards

This upturn across developed economies comes after a prolonged period of subdued investment in the aftermath of the global financial crisis. Despite the recent improvement, the average investment-to-GDP ratio remains lower than in the pre-crisis period. Changes in investment ratios may reflect a wide range of factors, including shifts in production structure, price adjustments of capital goods relative to consumer goods, broad changes in savings behaviour, or even the impact of technological changes that are difficult to measure in statistical terms, such as the contribution of the digital economy. A decline in the investment ratio in itself may not necessarily give rise to concern. Concerns are warranted, however, if debt continues to increase unabated, while a smaller share of current income is invested into productive assets that will provide a future flow of income to pay down those debts. Since the 2008/09 crisis, corporate non-financial debt has risen notably in developed economies as interest rates remained ultra low. The International Monetary Fund (IMF) recently highlighted that a significant part of the new loans—particularly in the segment of highly indebted speculative-grade companies—has been used to "fund mergers and acquisitions and leveraged buyouts (LBOs), pay dividends, and buy back shares from investors—in other words, for financial risk-taking rather than plain-vanilla productive investment" (Adrian, Natalucci and Piontek, 2018). This trend is evident in both Europe and the United States, and could pose a risk going forward.

Many developing economies experienced a pick-up in investment growth in 2018

Many of the major developing economies also experienced a pick-up in investment growth in 2018 (figure I.7). Following a protracted downturn, private investment saw some recovery in Brazil, supported in part by accommodative monetary policy. Investment activity in several other commodity exporters, including Chile, Colombia, and Peru, also improved during the year. In Mexico, capital spending benefited from reduced uncertainty as the new trade agreement with the United States and Canada was finalized. In India, the acceleration in investment growth was mainly driven by public infrastructure spending. In China, fixed asset investment remained solid but moderated at a gradual pace, amid efforts to reduce excess capacity in several industrial sectors.

Looking ahead, investment prospects in several large commodity-dependent economies will depend highly on developments in global commodity markets. The high oil price volatility, amid shifting policy stances, has brought about renewed concerns over the growth outlook of these economies. In the Russian Federation, the tightening of economic sanctions is expected to weigh on investment activity in the near term, compounding high business borrowing rates. For several developing economies, elevated corporate debt may constrain the pace of investment growth going forward. In many African economies, investment levels appear insufficient to achieve a more sustained and inclusive growth. More broadly, as in developed economies, the rise in debt in developing economies has generally not been matched by an equivalent expansion of productive assets, but has often been used to finance short-term consumption or has been channelled towards share buy-backs or real estate and financial assets. This raises concerns about the longer-term sustainability

Figure I.7
Annual growth of gross fixed capital formation in selected developing economies

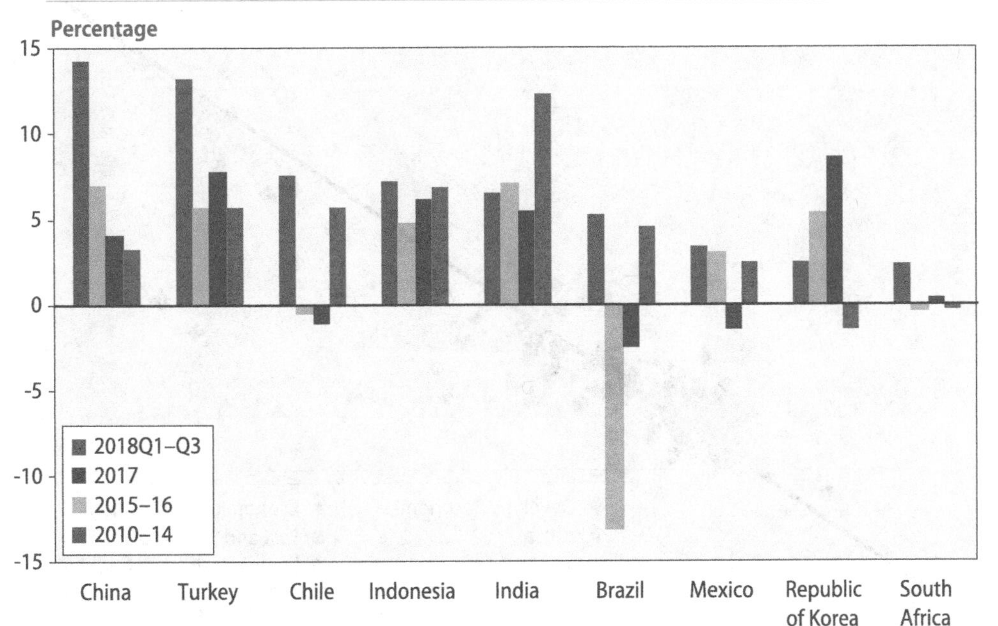

Source: CEIC.

Note: Data for Mexico and Turkey up till 1H 2018. Figures for China are estimated using fixed asset investment data, deflated by the CPI index.

of debt, as well as concerns about productive capacity over the medium term, given large existing infrastructure gaps, degradation of capital and the implications for productivity. Against this backdrop, macroprudential policies, in coordination with monetary, fiscal and foreign-exchange policies, are needed to promote financial stability and contain the build-up of financial vulnerabilities.

An expansion of infrastructure investment is crucial to the success of the SDGs. To meet the challenge of delivering universal electricity, clean water, health care, education and well-diversified economies—and to facilitate the exchange of goods and services between countries—total annual financing needs, according to recent estimates, range between $4.6 trillion and $7.9 trillion at the global level. Many states must double current levels of infrastructure investment to meet these needs (UNCTAD, 2018a). Securing the finance for infrastructure investment is only one facet of a well-designed national sustainable development plan. Making the most valuable use of limited resources requires long-term strategic planning, expertise in procurement and contract negotiation, a transparent business environment and the labour force skills needed to deliver the projects. Policymakers need to develop clearly designed development strategies that actively foster the positive feedback loops between infrastructure, productivity and growth (ibid.).

Inflationary pressures remain contained

Global inflation remains moderate, but is on an upward trend in the majority of countries (figure I.8). Rising oil prices contributed to additional inflationary pressures in oil-importing countries over the course of most of 2018, while currency depreciation against the US dollar put upward pressure on imported prices in many countries. By contrast, some of the commodity-exporting countries in Africa and the Commonwealth of Independent

Figure I.8
Inflation in 2017 and 2018

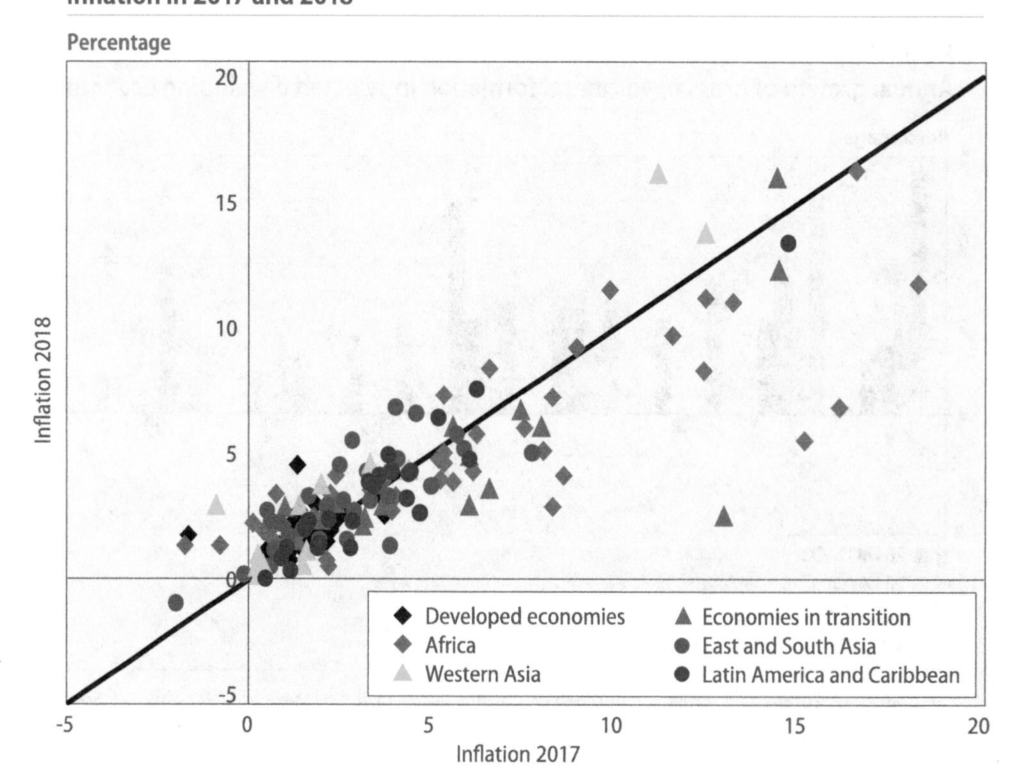

Source: UN/DESA.

Note: Countries with inflation above 20 per cent are excluded from the figure for clarity (Angola, Argentina, Egypt, Islamic Republic of Iran, Libya, South Sudan, Sudan and Venezuela).

States (CIS) that experienced sharp currency depreciations in response to the commodity price shocks of 2014/15 have seen inflation recede in 2018, as the exchange-rate shock has been absorbed into the price level. Ongoing trade disputes can be expected to put some upward pressure on inflation in 2019, as the impact of tariffs passes through value chains to consumer prices. In developed economies, rising capacity constraints have put some upward pressure on inflation, and headline inflation generally exceeds central bank targets in Europe and North America.

Employment is rising, but job quality is low

Tight labour markets and capacity pressures are evident in some developed economies

The upturn in the world economy has been associated with a slight rise in global employment, although some caution should be used in interpreting headline figures, which give an incomplete picture of the quality of jobs discussed further below. According to International Labour Organization (ILO) estimates, the global unemployment rate stood at 5.5 per cent in 2017. Developed economies have seen notable gains in recent years, with the average unemployment rate declining from a post-financial crisis high of 8.7 per cent in 2010 to 5.4 per cent in 2018. In several large economies, including Germany, Japan and the United States, unemployment rates are currently at their lowest level in decades (see table A.7 in the Statistical annex for country-level detail and projections). In all three countries, firms have reported a lack of qualified workers as a factor restraining production levels. In the United States, capacity limits in internal delivery transport by rail and trucking have pushed up prices of freight transportation sharply, while firms in Japan cite an extremely high utilization of production equipment.

Unemployment is rising in some large developing countries

At the global level, falling unemployment in developed economies has been largely offset by rising unemployment in several large upper-middle-income countries, such as Argentina, Brazil and South Africa, which have been deeply impacted by political and economic crises, inequalities, and continuous socioeconomic imbalances (see table A.8 in the Statistical annex). Worldwide, an estimated 190 million people are currently unemployed. While the global unemployment rate has remained largely stable in recent decades, the total number of unemployed people has increased by approximately 40 per cent since the early 1990s. This means that there is a consistently growing population that is not able to fully participate and benefit from the advances in the global economy.

Job quality remains low in many parts of the world

Reducing unemployment remains a crucial development challenge for policymakers. But equally as important as reaching targets for job creation is strengthening the quality of employment. The 2030 Agenda for Sustainable Development strives to create decent work for all, which requires not just an increase in employment opportunities, but also reductions in informal employment and in labour market inequality (particularly in terms of the gender pay gap), and the provision of safe and secure working environments.

Of those employed in 2017, 300 million workers were nonetheless living in extreme poverty. Progress towards reducing the numbers of the working poor remains slow. Many of the working poor hold informal jobs or are in other vulnerable forms of employment. In developing countries, three out of four workers are in vulnerable forms of employment, which entails lower levels of job stability and limited access to social protection. Over 60 per cent of all workers worldwide are in informal employment (box I.2). Moreover, more than half of the world population has no access to social protection. This tends to perpetuate high levels of subsistence activities, which generally provide very low levels of income.

Box I.2
Informal employment around the world: recent data and policies

Today, two billion workers, or 61.2 per cent of all workers worldwide, are in informal employment (ILO, 2018). The informal economy involves all economic activities by workers and economic units that are, either in law or in practice, not covered or insufficiently covered by formal arrangements (ILO, 2015). It is primarily characterized by its high heterogeneity. Informal employment is the reality of more than 85 per cent of own-account workers and one out of two employers. Their economic units are not legally recognized; they face non-compliance with fiscal obligations as well as serious difficulties in engaging in commercial contracts and gaining access to financial resources, markets or property. It is also the reality of 40 per cent of employees whose employment relationship is, in law or in practice, not subject to national labour legislation, income taxation, social protection, or entitlement to certain employment benefits. Informality is, finally, the reality of all contributing family members, who are considered as having informal jobs by definition.

Informality has multiple adverse consequences for individuals, firms and societies. Individuals who work informally are exposed to pervasive decent work deficits and limited access to social protection. Enterprises that operate informally are a source of unfair competition for those enterprises that comply with fiscal and labour laws. In addition, they face high barriers in terms of access to capital, financial resources, public infrastructures and markets, with negative implications for productivity and business sustainability. Finally, for Government and societies, informality means reduced government rev-

Figure I.2.1
Extent and composition of informal employment, 2016

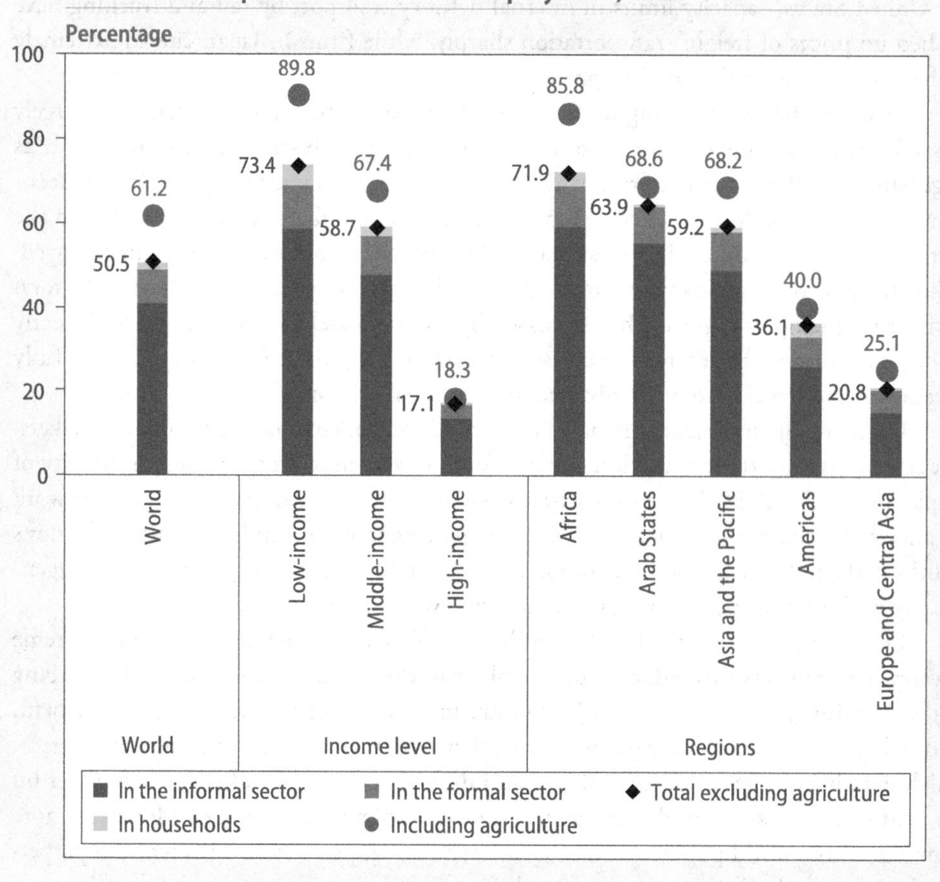

Source: ILO calculations, based on national labour force survey or similar household survey data.

Note: Data represents harmonized definition of informal employment. Global estimates are based on 119 countries representing 90 per cent of total employment.

(continued)

Box I.2 (*continued*)

enues. This, in turn, limits the scope of government action and weakens the rule of law, undermining social cohesion and inclusive development.

The level and forms of informality vary depending on the level of economic development. The share of informal employment ranges from 18.3 per cent in high-income countries to 67.4 per cent in middle-income countries and as high as 89.8 per cent in low-income countries (figure I.2.1). Nevertheless, countries with similar levels of GDP per capita show very different levels of informal employment (figure I.2.2). The dispersion reflects cross-country differences, such as the composition of GDP, the institutional setting and also characteristics of workers that may act as barriers to formal employment. Indeed, the poor face higher rates of informal employment, and poverty rates are at least two times higher among workers in informal employment compared to workers in formal employment. The majority of workers with no education (93.8 per cent) are in informal employment compared to 23.8 per cent of workers with a tertiary level of education. More than half of all workers in informal employment have, at best, a primary level of education. Further, more than three quarters of the youth and older workers are in informal employment compared to 57 per cent among those aged 25–64 years old. Finally, the share of informal employment is almost twice as high in rural areas compared to urban areas. This results partially from the higher exposure of agriculture to informal employment compared to industry and services. Rural areas are also impacted by the institutional and economic environment (limited access to public infrastructure and services; differences in the quality of services; local governance), personal and employment characteristics of the rural population (higher incidence of poverty; lower levels of education; over-representation of small economic units), or traditions and rural actors' perception of laws, regulations and social norms.

Firm size is also linked to the prevalence of informality. It is estimated that enterprises of less than 10 workers account for 75 per cent of total informal employment. However, despite the greater ability of large enterprises to cover the cost of formalization, a significant share of wage employment is informal in medium and large enterprises, including in formal enterprises (Bonnet, forthcoming).

Figure I.2.2
Level of GDP per capita and informal employment share

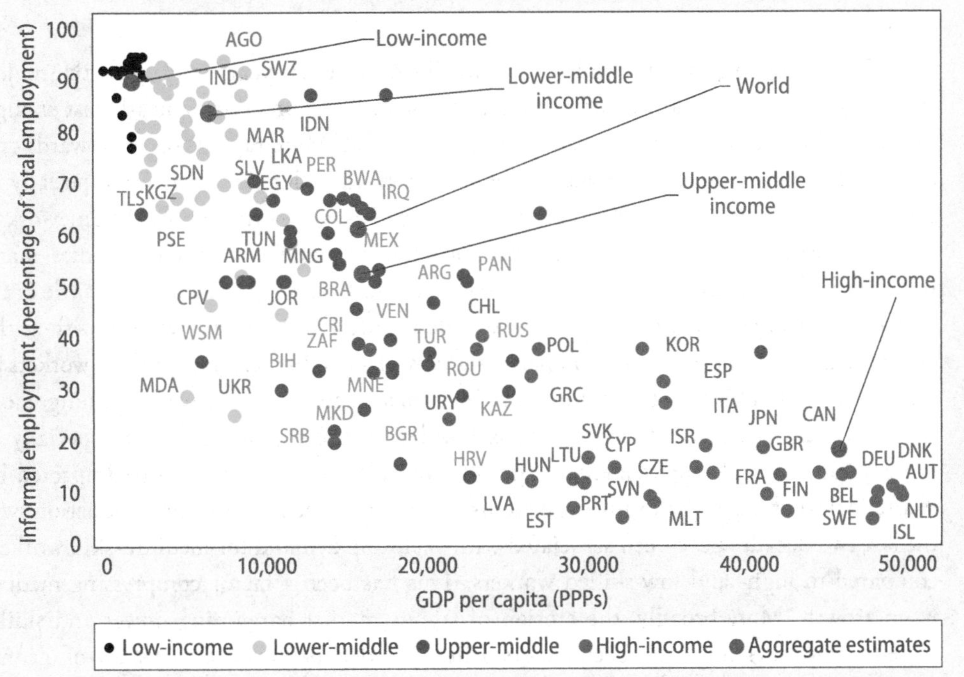

Sources: ILO and World Bank's World Development Indicators.

Note: Only selected country labels are included for visibility.

(*continued*)

Box I.2 (*continued*)

Formalization policies

Recommendation 204 (R204) of the International Labour Organization (ILO) suggests that reducing informal employment must be tackled along three policy channels:

- Formal employment generation (via growth, structural change, etc.);
- Policies for the transition from the informal to the formal economy (tax incentives, social security schemes for specific population groups, etc.);
- Policies to impede the informalization of formal jobs (firm and labour enforcement systems for example).

It is important to take into account that transition to formality will require time and cannot rely on one-time policy interventions. This view is well supported by the example of Latin America in 2005–2015. It is estimated that over this period, the region generated 51 million jobs, and 39 million were formal jobs (Salazar and Chacaltana, 2018). This brought the share of non-agricultural informal employment as a whole down from 52 per cent in 2005 to 47 per cent in 2015. The ILO Regional Programme for the Promotion of Formalization in Latin America and the Caribbean (FORLAC)[a] argues that countries in the region embarked on four pathways to formality: productive development, regulation simplification/ improvement, incentives (tax, social protection), and enforcement. In his study, Infante (2018) underscores the relative importance of different drivers of the transition to formality: it is estimated that economic factors, such as growth and structural transformation, that boosted formal employment generation, account for 60 per cent of the reduction in informality in the region, while institutional policies account for the remaining 40 per cent.

Other recent studies on the impact of institutional policies tend to find that specific policies have positive but small effects that are short lived (Salazar and Chacaltana, 2018; Jessen and Kluve, 2018). A key to understanding these results is that impact evaluation studies tend to focus on single interventions in a particular time frame—the time frame usually being soon after the intervention has started. However, the Latin America experience shows that the most impressive results have occurred in those cases where multiple interventions accumulated progressively over time, and where the political will towards formalization was sustained for more than a decade. Informality will persist for a long period, unless an integrated and consistent approach is implemented, as ILO R204 recommends.

a Available from https://www.ilo.org/americas/temas/econom%C3%ADa-informal/lang--es/index.htm.

Authors: Florence Bonnet and Juan Chacaltana (ILO).

Even where income inequality has come down in recent years, wage growth and job creation for those at the lower end of the income scale is not proceeding nearly fast enough to lift the threat of poverty from those being left behind. More rapid progress towards creating decent jobs requires both active labour market and education policies, especially to support youth, women and vulnerable groups, as well as well-managed fiscal frameworks.

At the country level, returns from growth are failing to reach many individuals most in need

While unemployment rates are at historical lows in many developed economies, many individuals, notably those in the bottom 10 per cent of income scales, have seen little or no growth in disposable income for the last decade (figure I.9). Low real wage growth at the bottom end of the wage distribution partly reflects a lack of bargaining power of workers in low-skilled jobs. This may result, for example, from a decline in collective bargaining, more stringent social security conditions, or a lack of labour protection legislation, especially in the case of informal employment. Wages in particular sectors may also be impacted by technological change. For example, structural changes to technology and production over the last two decades have been associated with declining demand for medium-skill workers compared to high- and low-skilled workers. This has been a factor compressing median wage growth. More broadly, the erosion of labour market bargaining power and skills-biased technical change have been factors behind the decline in the labour share of income over the last several decades.

Figure I.9
Real household disposable income, developed economies

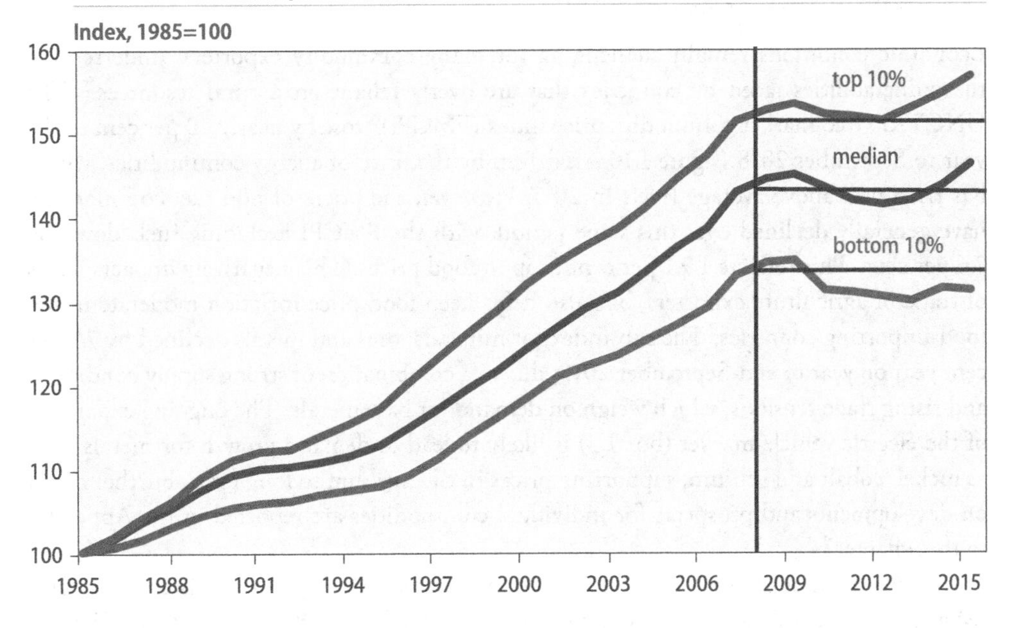

Source: UN/DESA, based on OECD Income Distribution and Poverty Database.

Note: Simple average of 17 countries: Australia, Canada, Czech Republic, Denmark, Finland, France, Germany, Greece, Italy, Japan, Luxembourg, Netherlands, New Zealand, Norway, Sweden, United Kingdom, United States.

Figure I.10
Major commodity prices

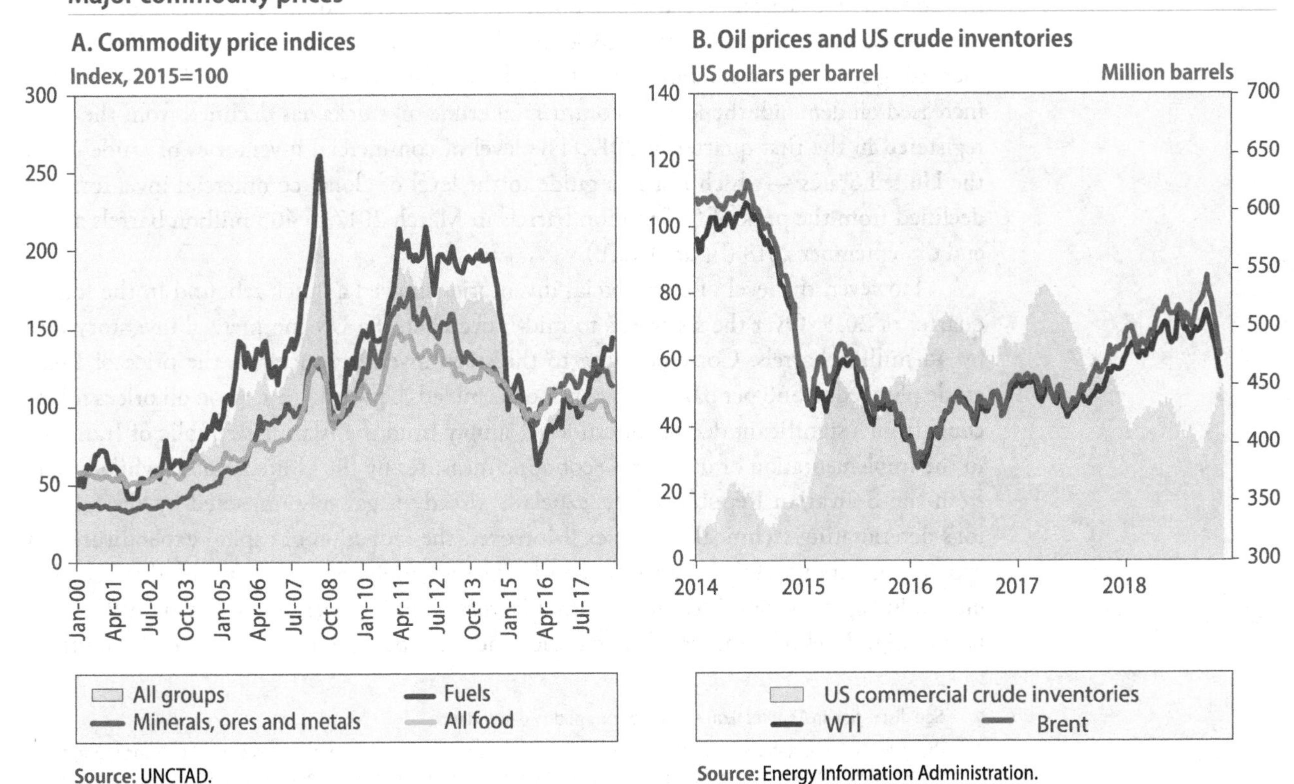

Source: UNCTAD.

Source: Energy Information Administration.

Economic conditions remain challenging for many commodity exporters

Economic conditions remain challenging for many commodity exporters, underscoring the vulnerabilities faced by countries that are overly reliant on natural resources.[5] The UNCTAD free-market commodity price index (FMCPI)[6] rose by nearly 20 per cent in the year to September 2018 (figure I.10.A), driven by the price of energy commodities, which has risen well above average levels in 2017. However, the prices of non-fuel commodities have generally declined over this same period, with the FMCPI excluding fuels down by 7.6 per cent. This reflects a 9.1 per cent drop in food prices. This negatively impacts terms of trade of agriculture exporters, but also helps keep food price inflation moderate in net food-importing countries. The sub-index for minerals, ores and metals declined by 7.9 per cent year on year to end-September 2018, due to a combination of strong supply conditions and rising trade tensions, which weigh on demand for base metals. The ongoing expansion of the electric vehicle market (box I.3) is likely to lead to demand growth for metals such as nickel, cobalt and lithium, supporting prices in the medium to long term. Further detail on developments and prospects for individual commodities are reported in the Appendix to this chapter.

Oil prices remain volatile

Over the first three quarters of 2018, oil prices rose steadily, and the Brent spot price recovered to reach $80 per barrel at the end of September 2018 (figure I.10.B). The rise largely reflected a rebalancing of excess supply. Since 2017, the Organization of the Petroleum Exporting Countries (OPEC), the Russian Federation and some other oil producers have operated under an agreed crude oil production cap, entailing a reduction of 1.8 million barrels per day relative to 2016 levels. The supply cuts have partially offset rapidly increasing crude oil production in the United States. As the expanding world economy has increased oil demand, the level of commercial crude oil stocks has declined from the peak registered in the first quarter of 2017. The level of commercial inventories of crude oil in the United States[7]—which is also a guide to the level of global commercial inventories—declined from the peak of 535 million barrels in March 2017 to 403 million barrels at the end of September 2018 (figure I.10.B).

However, the level of commercial inventories showed a quick rebound in the fourth quarter of 2018. Over the six weeks to mid-November, the US commercial inventory rose by 44 million barrels. Corresponding to the steep inventory increase, the price of Brent crude plunged to $60 per barrel. The outlook is mixed. Upward pressure on oil prices might come from a significant decline of crude oil supply from the Islamic Republic of Iran, due to the implementation of unilateral economic measures by the United States, while supply from the Bolivarian Republic of Venezuela is already negatively impacted by the oil sector's deteriorating technical capacities. Moreover, the reduction of capital expenditures on exploration activities for the last few years limits the supply capacity, particularly in smaller oil-producing countries. Meanwhile, other factors point to lower prices, based on the stubbornly high level of commercial inventories and an expectation that the rate of growth of

5 See discussion in Chapter II on excessive commodity dependence.

6 The UNCTADStat database on commodity prices and indices underwent substantial revisions in 2018, including the introduction of a new commodity price index, which includes energy commodities and has 2015 as the base year. The old commodity price index was discontinued as of December 2017.

7 See U.S. Energy Information Administration, available from https://www.eia.gov/dnav/pet/hist/LeafHandler.ashx?n=PET&s=WCESTUS1&f=W.

Box I.3

Impacts of large-scale electric vehicle deployment on battery metals markets

The market for electric vehicles (EV) is expanding at a rapid rate, driven by regulation and a trend towards the reduction of carbon emissions from the transport sector combined with falling costs of EVs relative to vehicles with internal combustion engines. EV sales have increased almost tenfold in the past five years, from 118 thousand vehicles in 2012 to 1.15 million in 2017. Current estimates put EV sales at 11 million in 2025 and 30 million in 2030 (Bloomberg New Energy Finance, 2018).

EVs are powered by lithium-ion batteries, which contain cobalt, lithium and nickel as key components. The massive increase in demand for these battery metals over the coming years poses challenges but also creates opportunities for commodity-dependent developing countries where a large share of these battery metals is mined.

The battery industry is the dominant end-use of cobalt and currently absorbs about half of global production. Since cobalt is almost exclusively mined as a by-product of copper and nickel and given the commodity's low elasticity of supply, price signals do not necessarily trigger a supply response. Furthermore, cobalt mining is highly concentrated in the Democratic Republic of the Congo, which accounted for 58 per cent of global cobalt mine production in 2017 and has the world's largest reserves (U.S. Geological Survey, 2018). These supply-side features, in combination with growing demand from the battery industry, have caused tension in the cobalt market and a dramatic price increase in 2017 (figure I.3.1). While producers are working on formulations that reduce the cobalt content in lithium-ion batteries, the rapid expansion of the EV market is going to drive demand growth and likely create upward pressure on prices, at least over the short to medium term.

Figure I.3.1

Battery metals prices and EV sales

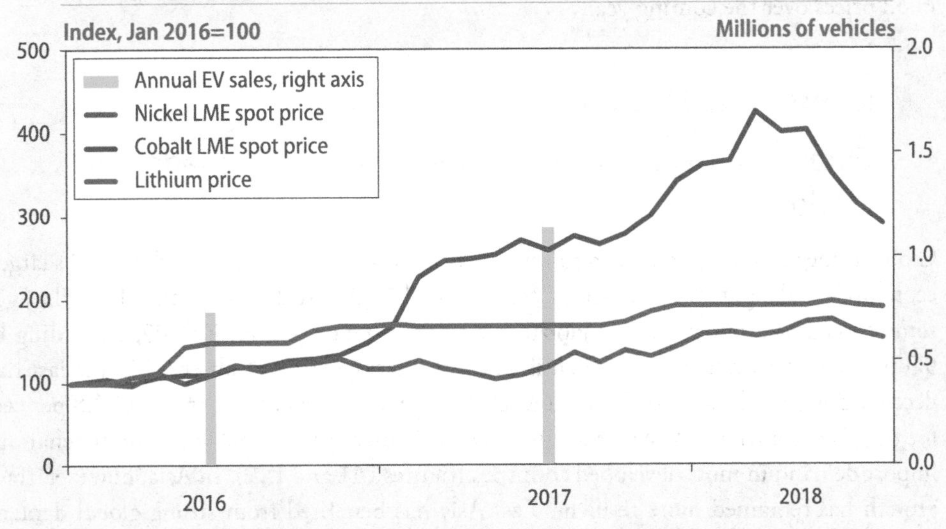

Sources: Quandl, World Bank, Thomson Reuters, International Energy Agency.

Batteries are also the largest end user for lithium, absorbing 46 per cent of lithium used (ibid.). Australia, Chile and Argentina jointly accounted for 89 per cent of global mine production in 2017 (ibid.).[a] Since lithium is not a homogenous commodity that is sold on a major exchange, but rather comes in different compounds that are traded between a small number of suppliers and buyers, price data is not readily available. However, existing data suggest that lithium prices have increased significantly in 2016 and 2017. Unlike cobalt, lithium is mined as a primary metal so that price signals have a more immediate effect on supply. Consequently, suppliers have announced the expansion of existing mine production as well as new operations, including in the Argentina-Bolivia-Chile "lithium triangle," which has attenuated

a Figure excludes mine production in United States.

(continued)

Box I.3 (*continued*)

the price increase in 2018. Going forward, the surging lithium demand from the EV sector can be expected to lead to an expansion of production rather than supply tensions or steep price increases.

While nickel is an essential component of lithium-ion batteries, the battery industry currently represents only 3 per cent of global nickel consumption.[b] However, only class-I nickel, about half of the global production, is suitable for battery production. Hence, at current EV market growth rates, the battery industry could become the dominant end user for class-I nickel within a decade. An additional driver of incremental nickel demand is the anticipated change in battery chemistries towards a higher share of nickel. Given the high capital intensity and long lead times of new nickel mines and increasingly depleted nickel sulphide deposits, the emerging growth in nickel demand is likely to put upward pressure on prices.[c]

The EV revolution is just gathering steam and projected growth rates are enormous. For developing countries that own many of the reserves of battery metals, this increases the urgency to strengthen environmental, social and ethical standards of mining operations and to ensure local value retention in order to support the sustainable development of mining communities. Recent developments in this context include the classification of cobalt as a strategic metal by the Government of the Democratic Republic of the Congo, which allowed it to increase royalties fivefold from 2 per cent to 10 per cent. Other developing countries with significant reserves of battery metals—such as Cuba, Madagascar, the Philippines and Zambia for cobalt, Brazil, Indonesia and the Philippines for nickel and Argentina, Bolivia, China and Chile for lithium—will need to find ways to align potential ramifications of the rapidly emerging global EV market with their national sustainable development efforts.

b Authors' estimates.

c See UNCTAD and FAO (2017) for a case study on the Indonesian nickel ore export ban.

Authors: Authors: Stefan Csordas and Janvier D. Nkurunziza (UNCTAD/DITC/ Special Unit on Commodities)

crude oil demand will moderate. These opposing forces are expected to create large swings in oil prices over the coming year.

International trade

Global trade growth moderates, amid heightened trade tensions

Global trade growth is moderating alongside rising trade tensions among the world's largest economies and tightening monetary conditions that are escalating financial fragilities in some emerging economies. The global trade performance peaked in 2017, expanding by 5.3 per cent in volume terms, which is above the average growth observed in the last half decade. But growth tapered throughout 2018, with an estimated expansion of 3.8 per cent for the year as a whole. The slowdown was mainly driven by a weaker rise in merchandise import demand in most developed countries (figures I.11 and I.12). In Asia, however, trade growth has remained more resilient. East Asia has benefited from strong global demand for electronics, boosting intraregional trade, given the region's deep integration into the industry's global production networks. Meanwhile, global trade in services continued to expand more rapidly than merchandise trade, up by more than 10 per cent in value terms in the first half of 2018. International tourism revenues contribute 30 per cent of global services trade, and tourist arrivals increased by 6.0 per cent in the first half of 2018 (box I.4). Tourism is also closely correlated with market sentiment, suggesting that as of mid-2018 the build-up of economic risks had not materially impacted global sentiment.

So far, trade disputes have affected trade flows only moderately...

In 2018, there was an escalation in trade tensions and a sequence of rising tariffs among the largest world economies, most prominently between China and the United States (see the discussion on escalating trade policy disputes below). While these tensions

Figure I.11
Contribution to global merchandise export volume growth by region, 2011–2018

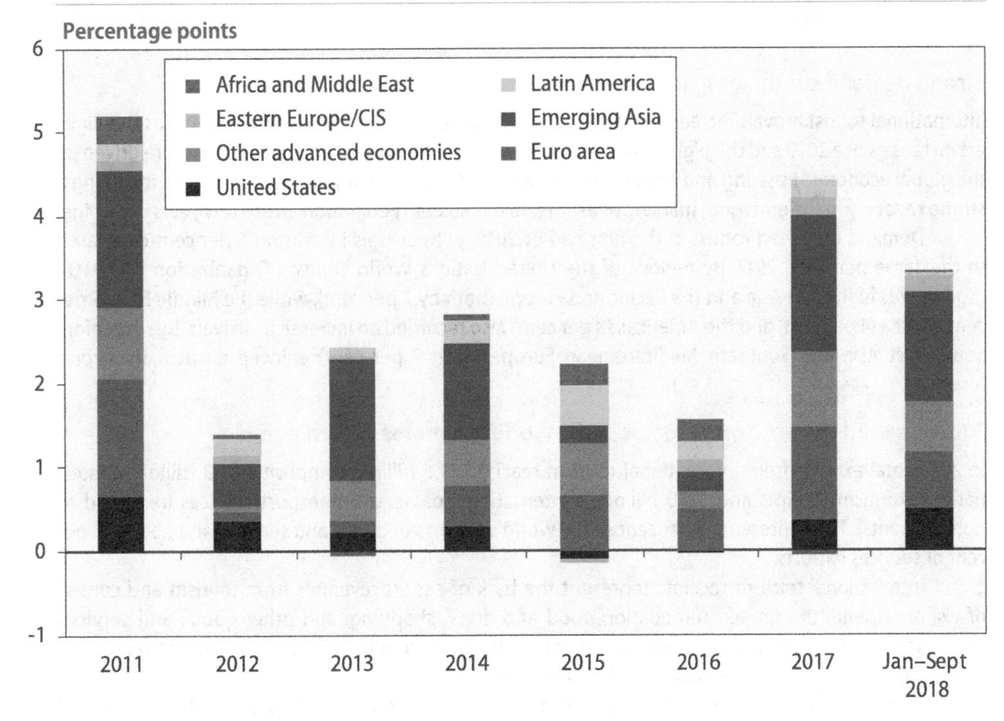

Source: UN/DESA, based on data from CPB Netherlands Bureau for Economic Policy Analysis.

Note: Regional groupings are not strictly comparable to those in the *WESP*, but are illustrative of regional tendencies.

Figure I.12
Contribution to global merchandise import volume growth by region, 2011–2018

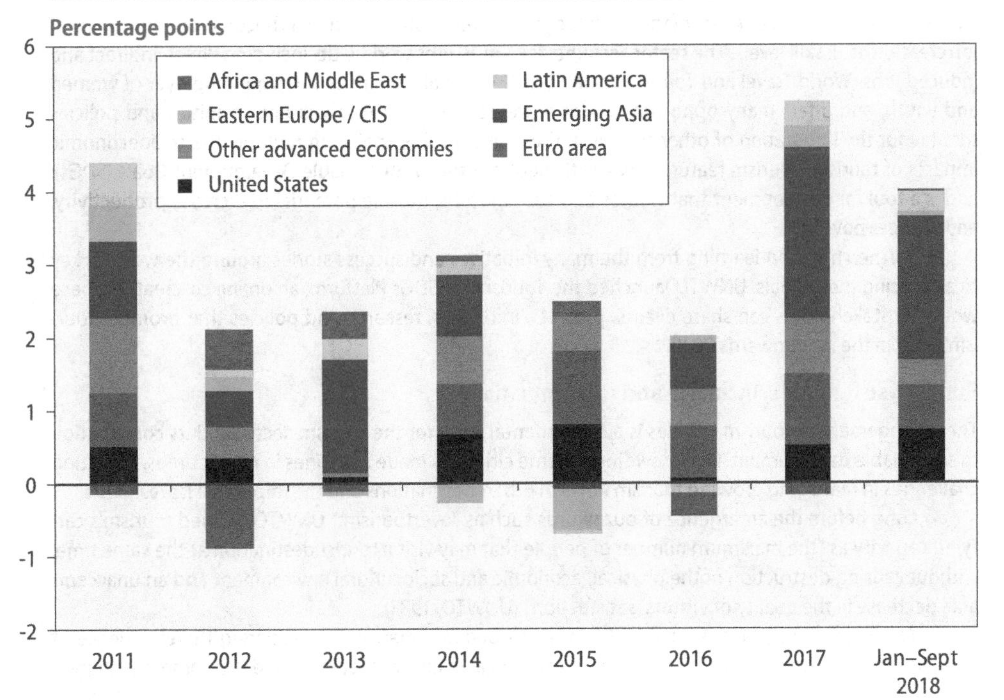

Source: UN/DESA, based on data from CPB Netherlands Bureau for Economic Policy Analysis.

Note: Regional groupings are not strictly comparable to those in the *WESP*, but are illustrative of regional tendencies.

Box I.4
International tourism

Strong demand continues in international travel

International tourist arrivals increased 7 per cent in 2017 to reach 1.3 million worldwide. It was the highest increase since 2010 and the eighth consecutive year of above-average growth. Results were driven by the global economic upswing and solid outbound demand from virtually all source markets, including a strong recovery in the emerging markets of Brazil and the Russian Federation after a few years of decline.

Demand remained robust in the first half of 2018, with arrivals increasing 6 per cent compared to the same period in 2017. By regions of the United Nations World Tourism Organization (UNWTO), growth was highest in Asia and the Pacific and Europe (both by 7 per cent), while the Middle East (5 per cent), Africa (4 per cent) and the Americas (3 per cent) also recorded an increase in arrivals. By subregion, South-East Asia and Southern Mediterranean Europe (both 9 per cent) enjoyed particularly strong results.[a]

Tourism: third largest export sector in the world generates $1.6 trillion

In 2017, total exports from international tourism reached $1.6 trillion, comprising $1.3 trillion in international tourism receipts and $240 billion in international passenger transport services (rendered to non-residents). This represents 7 per cent of the world's exports of goods and services and about 30 per cent of services exports.

International tourism receipts represent the bulk of export revenues from tourism and consist of visitor expenditure on accommodation, food and drink, shopping, and other goods and services purchased in destinations. Global receipts increased by $95 billion in 2017, or 5 per cent in real terms (accounting for exchange-rate fluctuations and inflation).

Tourism is a crucial source of foreign revenues for both emerging and advanced economies and an essential component of national export strategies. It is the third largest global export category after chemicals and fuels, ahead of automotive products and food. In many developing countries, tourism is the top export category.

Tourism: creating jobs and opportunities on the road to 2030

Tourism accounts for 10 per cent of the world's gross domestic product and has become a major source of job creation at all skill levels. The sector accounts for 1 in 10 jobs worldwide, including direct, indirect and induced jobs (World Travel and Tourism Council, 2018). Globally, tourism is a major employer of women and youth, and offers many opportunities for entrepreneurs. Decent work opportunities and policies that favour the integration of other sectors in the tourism value chain can multiply the socioeconomic impacts of tourism. Tourism features heavily throughout the 17 Sustainable Development Goals (SDGs), and is a tool for development that creates and sustains jobs, has the potential to increase productivity, and reduces poverty.

Partnerships and learning from the many initiatives and success stories around the world is key to advancing these goals. UNWTO launched the Tourism for SDGs Platform, an online co-creation space where all stakeholders can share events, projects, initiatives, research and policies that promote tourism's role in the road towards 2030.[b]

Building sustainable, inclusive and resilient cities

The management of tourism in cities is a fundamental issue for the tourism sector and its contribution to sustainable development. Overcrowding in some cities has made headlines in recent times, reflecting challenges in managing growing tourism flows in urban destinations and the impact on its residents.

Long before the emergence of buzzwords such as "overtourism," UNWTO defined tourism's carrying capacity as "the maximum number of people that may visit a tourist destination at the same time, without causing destruction of the physical, economic and sociocultural environment and an unacceptable decrease in the quality of visitors' satisfaction" (UNWTO, 1983).

Tourism will only be sustainable if it is developed and managed considering the experience of both visitors and local communities. It is therefore critical to ensure that tourism development is aligned

a For the latest tourism data and trends, please refer to the UNWTO World Tourism Barometer, available from mkt.unwto.org/barometer, or the UNWTO Tourism Highlights, available from mkt.unwto.org/highlights.

b More information about the Tourism for SDGs Platform is available from http://tourism4sdgs.org/.

(continued)

Box I.4 (*continued*)

with the United Nations New Urban Agenda and the SDGs, namely Goal 11 (make cities and human settlements inclusive, safe, resilient and sustainable).

The UNWTO (2018) report, *Overtourism? Understanding and Managing Urban Tourism Growth Beyond Perceptions*, examines how to manage tourism in urban destinations to the benefit of visitors and residents alike by proposing 11 strategies and 68 measures to better understand and manage visitor growth. These include measures to stimulate community engagement, reduce seasonality, promote less-visited parts of the city, improve infrastructure and develop plans that take into account the destination's capacity.

Examples of successful initiatives to manage urban tourism include Berlin, which has promoted the organization of conferences and seminars in community buildings and schools, preferably those linked to the conference subject. This provides conference organizers with innovative locations, allows for direct financial benefits in a neighbourhood, and stimulates a different form of exchange between residents and visitors. Turismo de Portugal, in collaboration with NOVA School of Business and Economics and NOS (Telecom Company) designed a pilot project to study the various pressures created by tourism in Lisbon and Porto. The project aims to measure and monitor tourism by using telecom traffic (CDR data), social media usage, Airbnb data and arrivals at airports. A second phase of the project will design policy recommendations and concrete actions to be taken by relevant tourism authorities to address the key challenges. Most of these strategies are naturally applicable to other types of tourism destinations, considering they are based on key principles of sustainable tourism such as community engagement, partnerships and coordination of all players, as well as the definition and management of carrying capacity at destinations.

Authors: Sandra Carvão, Michel Julian and Javier Ruescas (UNWTO).

have materially impacted some specific sectors, stimulus measures and direct subsidies have so far offset much of the direct negative impacts on China and the United States, and disruption to trade flows at the global level remains moderate. The magnitude of trade flows subject to new tariffs is still limited, even following the decision of the United States to impose tariffs on an additional $200 billion worth of Chinese goods beginning in mid-September 2018. Although China and the United States are the two biggest traders in the world, bilateral trade between the two countries represents just 3–4 per cent of global merchandise trade, as the bulk of global trade is concentrated in intraregional flows in East Asia, Europe and North America.

...but the economic impacts may build

Temporary trade barriers act as a supply shock that reduces output and raises inflation. While often introduced to "protect" the domestic economy, trade barriers are generally not effective tools to provide macroeconomic stimulus or to promote rebalancing of external accounts (Barattieri et al., 2018). Directly impacted sectors have already witnessed rising input prices and delayed investment decisions, and these impacts can be expected to spread, especially through production networks. A rise in trade barriers can have large, non-linear effects on trade volumes, and these impacts tend to increase with deeper vertical specialization along the value chain (Goldberg and Pavnick, 2016).

Impact of tariff hikes is heterogeneous across sectors and firms

Recent tariff hikes and counter measures, if prolonged, are expected to increasingly reduce and divert trade, disrupt cross-border operation of global value chains (GVCs), and entail costs for consumers, producers and workers in China, the United States and elsewhere. The firm-level impacts depend critically on their position in the production networks of the impacted sectors. For example, industries in the United States that use steel as a major production input, such as construction and transport equipment, have faced higher production costs since US steel tariffs were announced in early 2018. The after-tax price of steel in the

United States has risen by nearly 30 per cent relative to world export prices since the beginning of 2018 (figure I.13). While the direct impact of steel tariffs may preserve or create jobs within the steel industry, the indirect effects in the much larger steel consuming industries will squeeze corporate profits and potentially reduce employment and wages (Afonso and Holland, 2018).

The agricultural sector in the United States is also under stress given the retaliatory tariffs implemented by China on products such as soybeans and corn. Meanwhile, US automobile producers with operations in China are facing higher costs from new tariffs implemented by both countries (AmCham China, 2018). The export exposure of Chinese firms to the United States is also a major factor in spreading economic and financial effects in the corporate sector in China—for example, in the machinery and electronic sectors (Huang et al., 2018).

The high import content of Chinese exports suggests that developing countries integrated into these supply chains will also be impacted. For those products where China or the United States have market power, for example, cascading effects could be felt through downward pressure in international prices, with adverse implications for suppliers in other developing countries. In addition, if business performance and confidence deteriorate from the ongoing trade disputes, then changes on investment plans might become more widespread, including not only lower capital expenditures but also production and employment reallocations across countries. Some Chinese manufacturers might consider shifting their production to other countries that are not affected by tariffs, such as Mexico or Viet Nam.

Countries' sensitivity to trade shocks depends on their trade openness, exchange-rate regimes and diversification across markets and products

At the country level, vulnerabilities to the negative fallout from global trade disputes differ substantially. Trade openness and the composition of trade flows, together with exchange-rate regimes, are crucial determinants of the degree of exposure to trade shocks and of how they are absorbed in different economies. Macroeconomic policy space also plays an important role in counteracting, or deepening, potential negative effects. For instance, China is considering the implementation of a tax cut to boost consumption, while at the same time implementing several policy measures to inject liquidity into commercial

Figure I.13
Steel prices in the United States and world, January 2017–October 2018

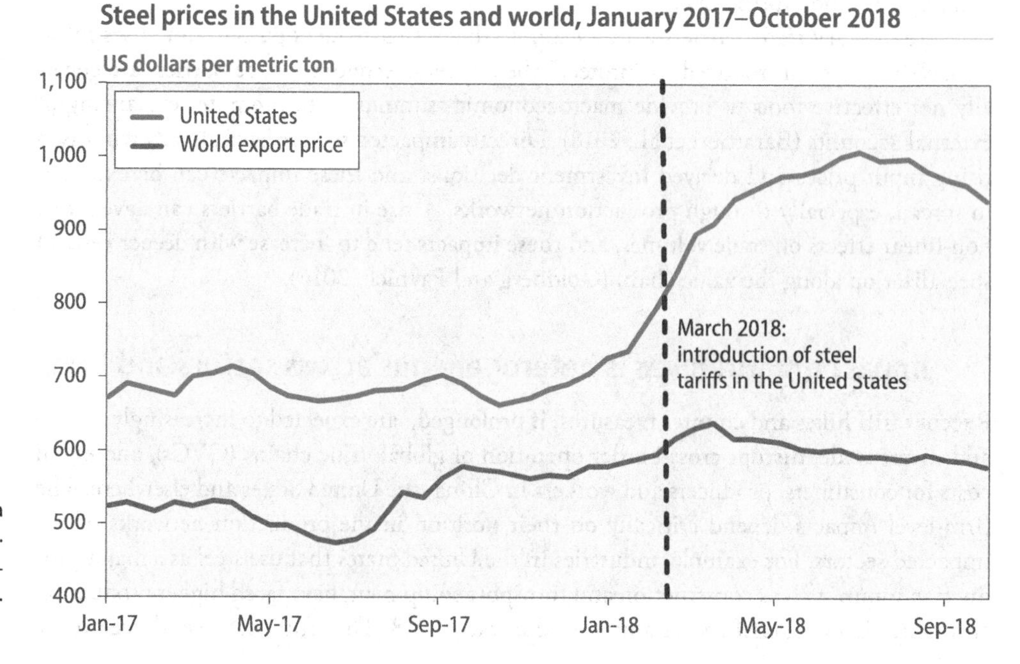

Source: UN/DESA, based on data from SteelBenchmarker™ Data.

Note: Prices correspond to hot-rolled band (HRB) steel prices.

banks, offsetting much of the direct impact of ongoing trade disputes on the domestic economy. In addition, targetted subsidies and support can temporarily offset the direct impact of tariffs on specific industries. For example, the United States is implementing an emergency bailout plan worth $12 billion to support corn and soybean farmers.

At a more disaggregated level, exporters' product and market diversification helps them to navigate adverse trade shocks. This provides exporters with some flexibility to confront higher trade costs. More generally, technological capabilities shape how countries integrate into foreign markets. For example, even comparing only developing countries, those economies with higher technological capabilities have more exporters, and their exporting firms are larger, more diversified and charge higher prices for their products, suggesting a higher product quality (box I.5) (Vergara, 2018).

Global trade growth is projected to remain below 4 per cent in 2019–2020

Manufacturing output surveys in the euro area and some economies in the Association of Southeast Asian Nations (ASEAN) point towards a further slowdown in trade activity in the near term. Given the current prospects for the world economy and the height-

Box I.5

Technological capabilities and export dynamics in developing countries

An engine of export growth, economic growth and development, technological capabilities have long played a central role in economic literature. Early contributions on development theory emphasized that technological progress was a critical factor in upgrading production structures and shaping the patterns of international specialization. Also, while Schumpeterian ideas emphasized the importance of research and development (R&D) investment and innovation in shaping market dynamics, modern growth theories highlighted the role of human capital, R&D and, more broadly, knowledge as major drivers of growth. Despite these long-standing contributions, many open questions remain regarding how technological capabilities shape export dynamics at the microeconomic level, especially in developing countries.

Figure I.5.1

Economic complexity and R&D investments, 2015

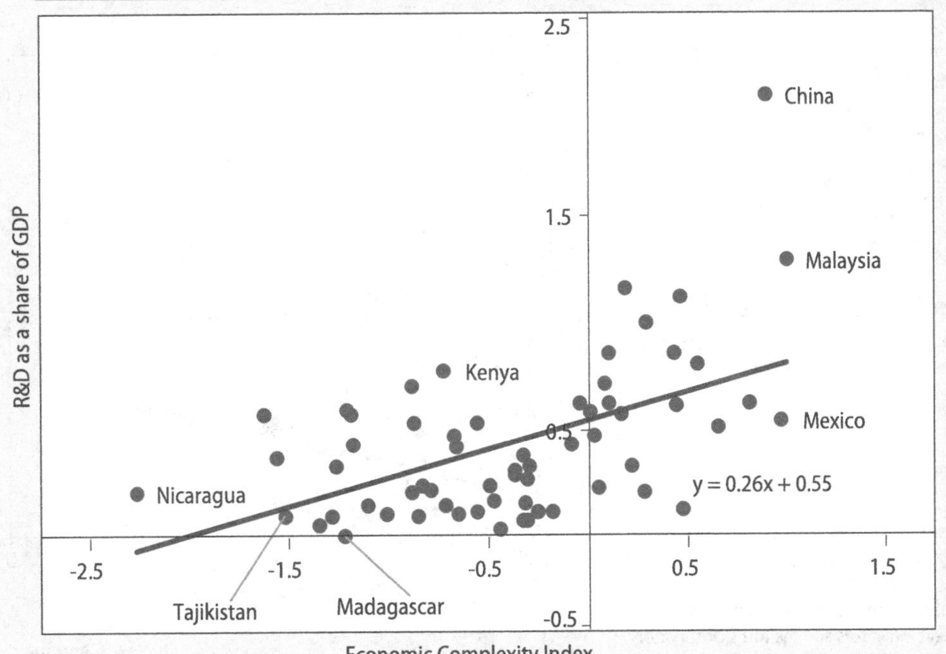

Source: Author's own elaboration, based on data from World Bank's World Development Indicators and the MIT's Observatory of Economic Complexity https://atlas.media.mit.edu/en/.

(continued)

Box I.5 (*continued*)

There are several different measures that capture aspects of an economy's technological capabilities. In recent years, one measure that has gained prominence is the Economic Complexity Index (ECI).[a] The ECI measures the multiplicity of productive knowledge in an economy by combining information on the diversity of a country's exports (based on the number of its export products) and the ubiquity of its products (based on the number of countries that export the same products). Another traditional variable to measure capabilities is R&D investment, which reflects the level of effort that countries spend to foster knowledge creation and absorption. In fact, a firm's R&D activities not only encourage product and process innovation, but also enhance its absorptive capacity to assimilate external knowledge.

Figure I.5.1 displays the levels of ECI and R&D investment for selected developing countries. As expected, there is a positive correlation, but the dispersion of observations also underscores that ECI and R&D investment reflects distinctive aspects of technical capabilities. For example, Mexico displays a relatively high ECI as its export structure is diversified, with a relatively large share of medium-high and high technology products because of the significant presence of transnational firms. However, technological efforts in the Mexican economy are limited, with relatively low levels of R&D investment—only 0.55 per cent of GDP—illustrating the weaknesses of its national innovation system. By contrast, Kenya exhibits a relatively low level of ECI, as its export structure is highly concentrated in a few vegetable products and textiles. Nevertheless, Kenya has strengthened its efforts to visibly increase R&D investment in recent years—to about 0.8 per cent of GDP, a relatively high figure for a developing country. This should have some effect on the diversification and technology upgrading of its exports in the medium term. Meanwhile, figure I.5.2 displays the plots for ECI and R&D against the level of development, using GDP per capita as a proxy. As expected, both variables are positively correlated with the level of development, but the relationship differs significantly across countries. For example, some heavily commodity-dependent countries in Western Asia and Latin America exhibit relatively low levels of capabilities and high GDP per capita compared to other developing countries.

In analyzing the role of technological capabilities on a country's export dynamics, Vergara (2018) used a range of export indicators from the World Bank's Exporter Dynamics Database.[b] This database compiles export information from national sources exporter-level customs data for 40 developing countries between 2002 and 2012. It comprises statistical information at the sectoral level (two digits of the HS 2002 Classification) for the number of exporters (total and per product), average value of exports

a See https://atlas.media.mit.edu/en/rankings/country/eci/.

b For details about the database, see http://www.worldbank.org/en/research/brief/exporter-dynamics-database.

Figure I.5.2
Technological capabilities and GDP per capita, 2015

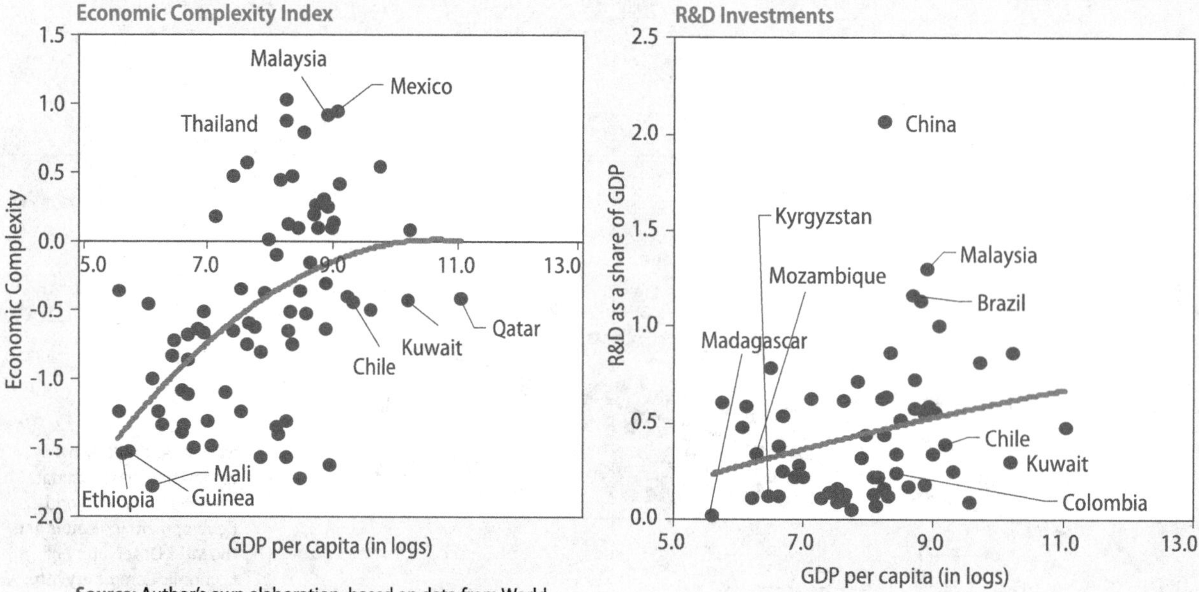

Source: Author's own elaboration, based on data from World Bank's World Development Indicators and the MIT's Observatory of Economic Complexity https://atlas.media.mit.edu/en/.

(continued)

Box I.5 (*continued*)

per exporter and per new exporter, average unit prices per exporter, average number of products per exporter, and the average number of destinations per exporter. In particular, the analysis tackles the following questions: Do countries with more technological capabilities have more and larger exporters? Do exporters from countries with more capabilities receive higher unit prices for their products? Are exporters from countries with more capabilities more diversified by product and destination? In doing so, the empirical approach controls for other country dimensions that are relevant for export dynamics, such as the size of the economy, level of development, trade openness, size of manufacturing sector, and commodity dependency.

The empirical analysis provides several interesting outcomes.[c] First, the results show that, within sectors, countries with higher technological capabilities have more exporters (total and per product) and the exporters are larger and charge higher prices for their products, suggesting a higher quality of their products. Second, the results confirm a positive and strong relationship between technological capabilities and diversification: within sectors, exporters in countries with more capabilities tend to export a higher number of products and to more destination markets. Moreover, technological capabilities seem to play a crucial role in promoting market diversification in high technology exporters.

Thus, even comparing exporters' behaviour only among the developing countries, stronger technological capabilities are significantly related to the "extensive" and "intensive" margin of exports, diversification across products and destinations, and product quality—all of which are relevant aspects of developing countries' insertion in global trade markets. Importantly, these features should make countries with stronger technological capabilities more resilient to trade shocks, while also helping their medium-term growth and development prospects. These findings reinforce the importance of economic diversification, a policy environment that supports innovation and technological progress, and investment in workforce skills to accelerated development prospects.

c For full details of the empirical approach—definition of variables, econometric specification, estimation methodologies and robustness checks—see Vergara (2018).

Author: Sebastian Vergara (UN/DESA/EAPD).

ened trade disputes, global trade growth is expected to remain below 4 per cent per year in 2019–2020, well below the average trade growth observed in previous decades (figure I.14). This trend also reflects the diminishing effects of structural factors that boosted trade in previous decades, such as the rapid expansion of GVCs and the information and communications technology revolution. Global trade in services is expected to continue to show greater resilience than merchandise trade. Service sectors offer significant opportunities for

Figure I.14
Growth of world trade and world gross product, 1992–2020

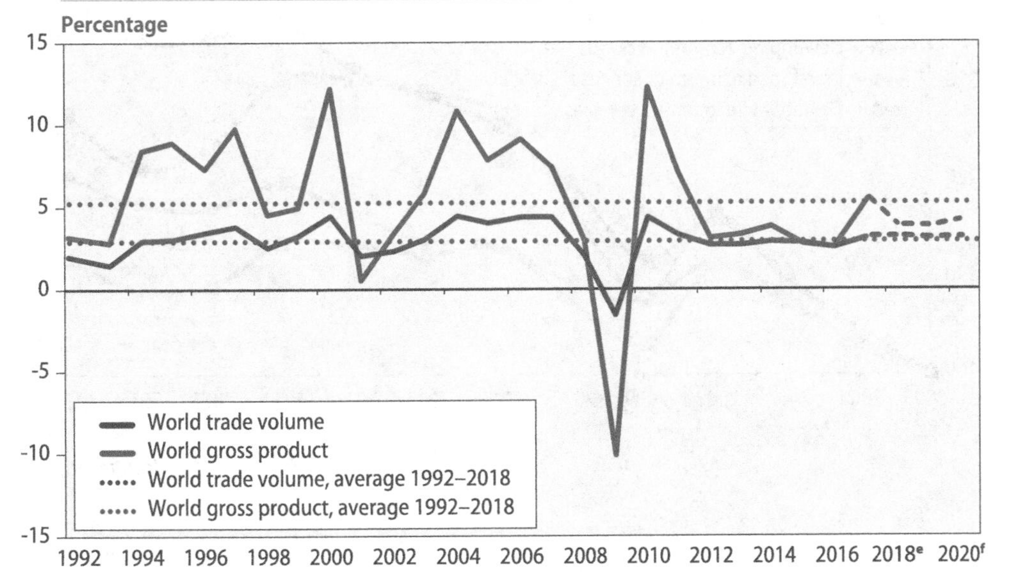

Source: UN/DESA.
Note: e = estimates, f = forecast.

Box I.6

Trade in services as a driver of development in times of tension: inclusiveness, resilience and diversification

Following the trend of recent years, trade in services has continued to expand at a relatively fast pace—about 7 per cent in 2017. This trend seems to hold in 2018 with year-over-year growth of 15.0 and 9.6 per cent in the first two quarters, respectively. In developing countries, relatively fast growth of services exports has allowed their share in global services exports to rise from 23 to 30 per cent between 2005 and 2017. In this period, developing Asia registered the fastest growth in trade in services, about 9 per cent per year on average. Africa showed the weakest performance, but nevertheless recorded an average annual expansion of 5 per cent. Least developed countries (LDCs) also saw significant growth in services exports but have started from a low base and still account for less than 1 per cent of global services exports. Still, services account for 19 per cent of total exports in LDCs, underscoring the importance of the contribution of services for the achievement of target 17.11 of the Sustainable Development Goals (SDGs), which calls for a significant increase in exports from developing countries and LDCs (see box II.1).

Despite this expansion, restrictions to services trade in the world economy remain noteworthy. They are particularly acute in trade in services through the temporary movement of people, where restrictions related to quotas, labour market tests, durations of stay (IMF, World Bank and WTO, 2017), visa and work permit rules, and the recognition of qualifications and licences persist. Trade policy needs to pay attention to addressing the restrictions to services trade, as the costs are high and restrictions are declining more sluggishly than for goods.

Services trade is not a direct target of recent tariff hikes. However, in times of trade tensions, tightening visa requirements and other measures restricting foreign visitors may also affect service categories such as education and tourism. Tension-related tariff hikes will also disrupt global value chains (GVCs), impacting their services components. Nonetheless, in the current international trade environment, the heightened trade tensions with a focus on tariffs may increase the relevance of services in pro-development trade strategies.

Data on services exports also point to the important role of services in contributing to inclusiveness, resilience and diversification. In addition to growing more in developing countries than in developed countries, services exports are also more dynamic than goods exports in both country groups (figure I.6.1). Thus, services' contribution to total exports has increased, from 24 to 28 per cent in devel-

Figure I.6.1

Services and goods exports (value), 2005–2017

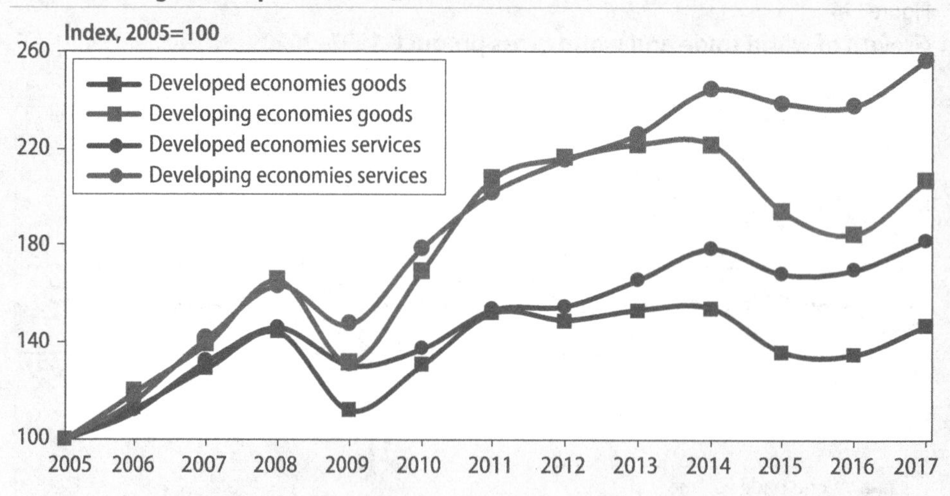

Source: UNCTAD secretariat calculations, based on UNCTADstat.

(continued)

Box I.6 (*continued*)

oped economies and from 14 to 17 per cent in developing economies since 2005. Services exports have also been more resilient, as shown by the much lower declines in services trade compared to goods trade, both during the global financial crisis and during the trade downturn in 2015 and 2016.

The inclusive potential of services is also revealed by figure I.6.2, which illustrates the annual growth rate in exports between 2005 and 2017 in small and large exporters. The figure groups countries according to the value of their global exports, with the first decile representing small exporters—that is, the 10 per cent of countries that account for the smallest global export revenue. The tenth decile represents the top 10 per cent of global exporters. In goods, exports have declined in countries with the smaller export revenue, increasing their distance from other countries. In services, although exports have grown less in countries with smaller export revenue, growth has nonetheless been positive since 2005. Moreover, services exports grew more in countries with medium export revenue (deciles 5 and 6), pointing to some reduction of the gap with large services exporters.

Figure I.6.2
Exports value growth by deciles of export revenue, 2005–2017

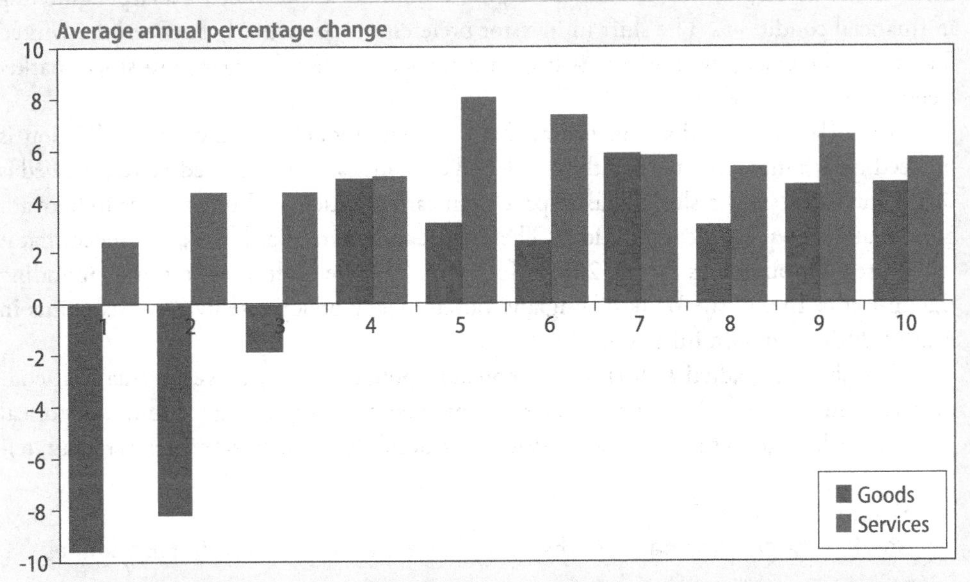

Source: UNCTAD secretariat calculations, based on UNCTADstat.

Importantly, trade in services plays a vital role in promoting horizontal and vertical diversification in most economic sectors. This role is reflected in the substantial value added component of services in goods exports, in intermediate inputs and in services bundled with goods, for example distribution services provided by manufacturing companies. While direct exports of services in 2011 accounted for 25 and 14 per cent of total exports in developed and developing economies, respectively, services represented much higher shares of 44 and 32 per cent of the value added in total exports in developed and developing economies, respectively. In addition, while directly exported value added has increased in recent years, close to two thirds of the growth of services value added in exports is due to an increase in services embodied in exports of other sectors (UNCTAD, 2017a). The export of this services' value added within products in all economic sectors, referred to as the mode 5 of services trade, is the reflection of the "servicification" in international trade. Global gross domestic product gains from the multilateral liberalization of mode 5 of services trade could reach €300 billion by 2025 and global trade could increase by over €500 billion (Antimiani and Cernat, 2017).

Author: Bruno Antunes (UNCTAD/DITC).

both developed and developing countries in the medium term, even more so in the current context of heightened barriers for trade in goods (box I.6).

International financial flows

Financial market volatility has increased

Financial market volatility rose in 2018, particularly in the emerging economies

Rising policy uncertainties in the global economy and deepening country-specific vulnerabilities generated bouts of heightened financial market volatility in 2018, particularly in the emerging economies. Alongside the escalation in trade tensions, investor sentiments were also affected by high levels of debt, elevated geopolitical risks, oil market developments, and shifting expectations over the monetary policy path of the United States. Against this backdrop, global financial conditions experienced some tightening during the year, albeit at an uneven pace across regions and countries. Notably, while liquidity remained high in most of the developed world, many emerging economies experienced a sharp tightening in financial conditions. The shift in investor preferences, particularly between the United States and the emerging markets, is in part evidenced by the divergence in stock market trends in 2018 (figure I.15).

Despite periodic spikes in volatility, financial conditions in the developed countries remain generally benign

As inflation rises closer to central bank targets, monetary policy normalization is proceeding at a measured pace in the developed economies. In the United States, the Fed is lifting interest rates at a slightly faster pace than earlier anticipated in response to buoyant growth and labour market conditions. The European Central Bank has announced that it will cease asset purchases by end-2018. Meanwhile, despite high uncertainty surrounding the impact of Brexit, the Bank of England raised its key policy rate by 25 basis points in August 2018 to contain inflation.[8]

Despite the gradual tightening of monetary policy stances, however, financial conditions in most of the developed countries remained generally benign. From a historical perspective, long-term sovereign bond yields are still subdued, corporate spreads remain rel-

Figure I.15
Stock market performance in the United States and the emerging economies

Sources: Financial Times and CEIC.

8 Additional information on monetary and fiscal policy assumptions underpinning the forecast is reported in the Appendix to this chapter.

atively low, and equity market valuations are still high. Notably, in the United States, financial conditions remained loose during the first three quarters of 2018 (figure I.16). While long-term Treasury yields have recently risen considerably, they remain well below pre-crisis averages. However, the Chicago Board Options Exchange Volatility Index (CBOE VIX), which measures expected equity market volatility in the United States, saw sharp spikes, particularly in the early months of the year and in October (figure I.17). Notwithstanding periodic bouts of volatility, equity markets in the United States recorded new highs in 2018, reinforcing concerns over excessive valuations and an underpricing of risk.

Figure I.16
Chicago Fed National Financial Conditions Index

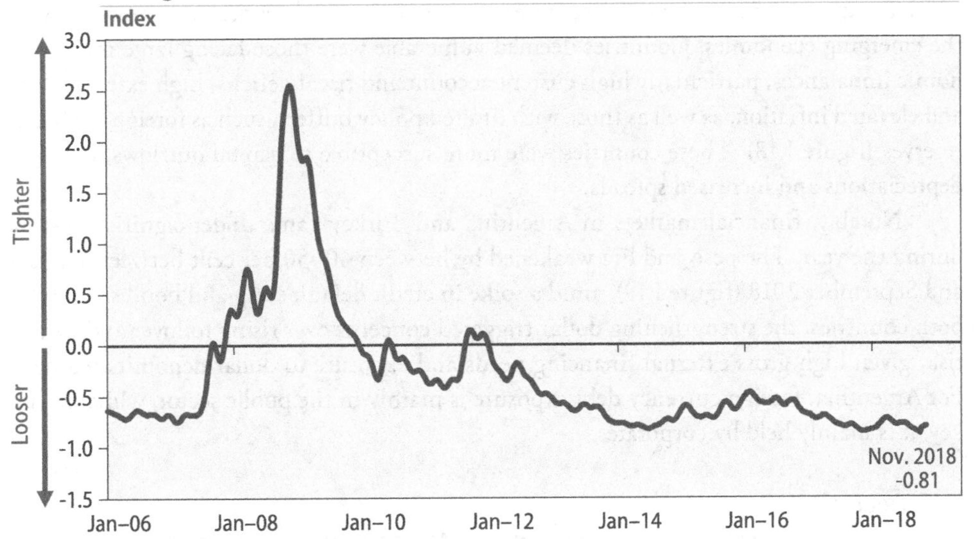

Source: Federal Reserve Bank of Chicago.
Note: Positive values of the NFCI indicate financial conditions that are tighter than average, while negative values indicate financial conditions are looser than average.

Figure I.17
CBOE equity volatility index (VIX)

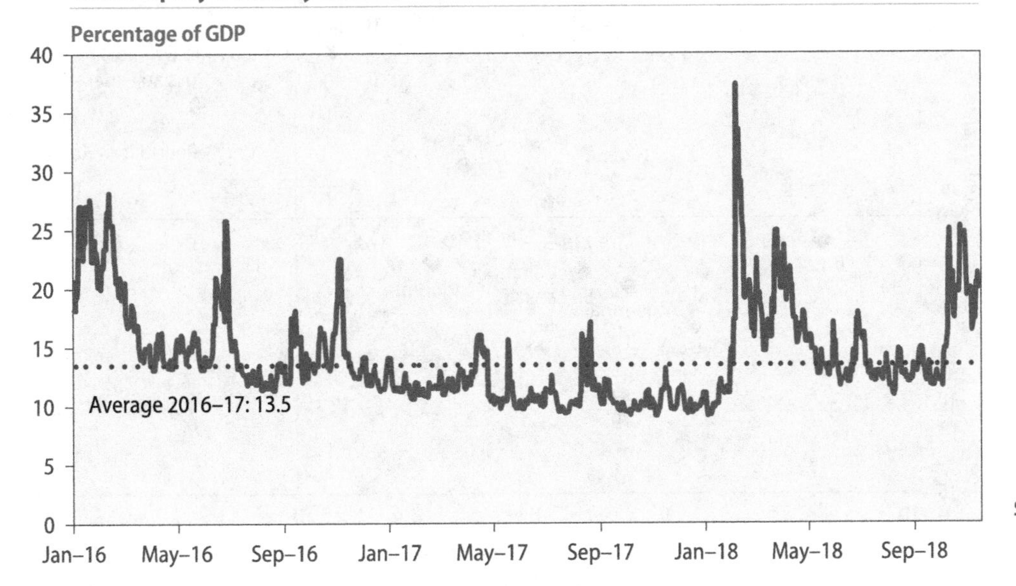

Source: CBOE Global Markets.

Emerging economies experienced a sharper increase in financial market pressures, due to both external and domestic factors

In contrast, the emerging economies experienced a sharp increase in financial market pressures, which intensified in the second half of 2018. The reduced demand for emerging market assets was driven by a confluence of both external and domestic factors. On the external front, the escalation in trade disputes, heightened oil price volatility, and rising interest rates in the United States, were the main factors driving the increase in risk aversion. This was reflected in a broad-based strengthening of the dollar—signalling increased demand for "safe" assets—and a decline in short-term capital flows into the emerging economies.

External factors expose domestic vulnerabilities

For several emerging economies, financial markets were subjected to stronger pressures as the impact of external headwinds was compounded by the presence of significant domestic vulnerabilities. As the global environment became more challenging, investors began to increasingly scrutinize the strength of fundamentals in each country. This resulted in a marked differentiation in the performance of financial market indicators between the emerging economies. Countries deemed vulnerable were those facing large macroeconomic imbalances, particularly high current account and fiscal deficits, high external debt, and elevated inflation, as well as those with limited policy buffers, such as foreign-exchange reserves (figure I.18). These countries were more susceptible to capital outflows, currency depreciations and increased spreads.

Financial markets in Argentina and Turkey came under significant stress

Notably, financial markets in Argentina and Turkey came under significant stress during the year. The peso and lira weakened by between 40–50 per cent between January and September 2018 (figure I.19), amid a spike in credit default swap and bond spreads. In both countries, the strengthening dollar triggered concerns over rising rollover and default risk, given high gross external financing needs and exposure to dollar-denominated debt. For Argentina, foreign currency debt exposure is mainly in the public sector, while in Turkey, it is mainly held by corporates.

Figure I.18
Current account vs fiscal balance in selected emerging economies

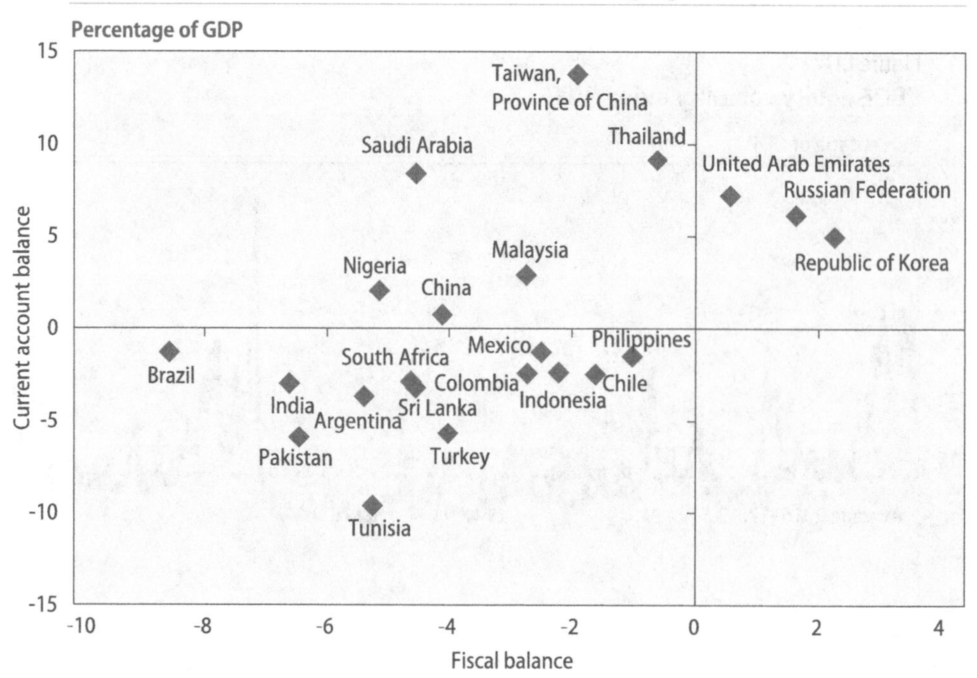

Source: IMF World Economic Outlook October 2018 database.

Figure I.19
US dollar exchange rates and foreign reserves of selected emerging economies, January–October 2018

Percentage change

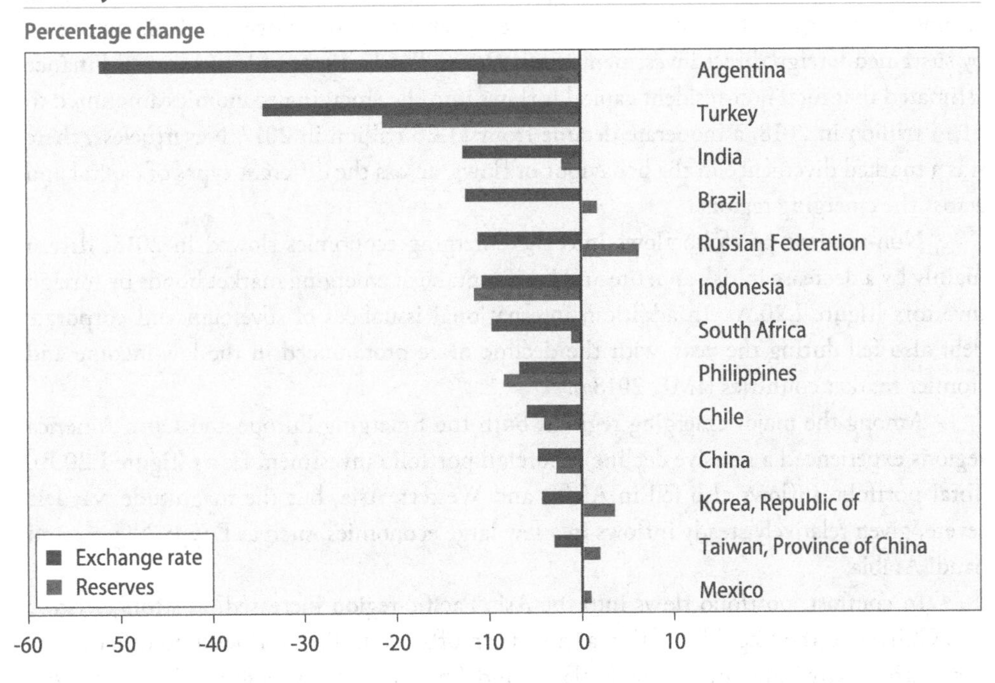

Source: CEIC.
Note: Reserves data for Argentina, India, and Turkey are for end-September 2018.

The loss in investor confidence in Argentina and Turkey was also exacerbated by country-specific weaknesses. In Argentina, large fiscal and current account deficits, combined with the Government's inability to rein in inflation, led to growing pessimism over the economy's prospects. Emergency measures, such as raising the key policy rate to 60 per cent and agreeing on a large Stand-by Arrangement with the IMF, have temporarily calmed the markets. However, with the economy entering recession amid severe fiscal austerity measures, the outlook is highly uncertain. Meanwhile, in Turkey, strong growth over the past few years has been accompanied by large current account deficits and a rapid increase in private sector indebtedness, fuelling concerns of overheating in the economy. Furthermore, elevated policy uncertainty impacted by unilateral trade measures as well as rising geopolitical tensions also contributed to a deterioration in investor's sentiments.

Financial market conditions also deteriorated in several large emerging economies, as investor sentiments weakened

Several large emerging economies, including Brazil, India, Indonesia, and the Russian Federation, also experienced considerable declines in equity markets and depreciation of domestic currencies. In Brazil and South Africa, the deterioration in investor perception reflected a weaker growth outlook and persistent macroeconomic imbalances, exacerbated by high political uncertainty, while in the Russian Federation, financial markets were affected by the imposition of new sanctions. The sharp reversal of foreign portfolio flows from these countries drove overall portfolio investment trends in their respective regions during the year.

An increase in financial market turbulence prompted several central banks to raise interest rates

In response to the increase in financial market turbulence, many central banks in the emerging and developing economies tightened monetary policy or reduced their degree of monetary accommodation in 2018. As risks to financial stability increased, central banks in several large economies, including Argentina, India, Indonesia and Mexico, raised interest rates to stem outflows and support domestic currencies. This in turn contributed to even tighter domestic financing conditions, weighing on the short-term growth outlook.

Notwithstanding the increase in global financial market volatility, the emerging economies on aggregate continued to receive sizeable capital inflows in 2018, supported by sustained foreign direct investment (FDI) flows. The Institute of International Finance estimated that total non-resident capital inflows into the emerging economies amounted to $1.14 trillion in 2018, a moderate decline from $1.26 trillion in 2017. Nevertheless, there was a marked divergence in the behaviour of flows, across the different types of capital and across the emerging regions.

Portfolio inflows slowed, reflecting a decline in investors' risk appetite

Non-resident portfolio flows into the emerging economies slowed in 2018, driven mainly by a decrease in risk appetite and lower uptake of emerging market bonds by foreign investors (figure I.20.A). In addition, international issuances of sovereign and corporate debt also fell during the year, with the decline more pronounced in the low-income and frontier market countries (IMF, 2018a).

Among the major emerging regions, both the Emerging Europe and Latin America regions experienced a massive decline in foreign portfolio investment flows (figure I.20.B). Total portfolio inflows also fell in Africa and Western Asia, but the magnitude was less severe, given relatively steady inflows in a few large economies, such as Egypt, Nigeria and Saudi Arabia.

In contrast, portfolio flows into the Asia Pacific region increased, as stronger flows into China and the Republic of Korea more than offset a decline in flows into other countries, particularly India, Indonesia, Malaysia and Thailand. Despite a noticeable weakening in the Chinese stock market and a depreciation of the domestic currency, China experienced a rapid increase in foreign portfolio inflows in 2018. This was largely attributed to the decision of Morgan Stanley Capital International (MSCI) to include Chinese stocks in its benchmark index as well as the Chinese Government's announcement of measures to further liberalize domestic bond markets (Institute of International Finance, 2018).

Growth in cross-border bank lending to the developing economies continued to lose momentum

Bank for International Settlements (BIS) data showed a slowdown in overall international banking activity in the second quarter of 2018, but with some variation in trends across regions. Compared to the same period last year, cross-border claims on the United States slowed considerably, but continued to grow at a rapid pace for Japan. At the same time, cross-border claims on the euro area continued to contract on an annual basis, weighed down mainly by a decline in credit to non-bank financial institutions (Bank for International Settlements, 2018).

For the emerging market and developing economies, growth in cross-border bank lending has been slowing since the end of 2017. In the second quarter of 2018, several large emerging countries, including Brazil, India, and Mexico, experienced a contraction in cross-border credit compared to the previous quarter (ibid.). While this may reduce risks associated with rising foreign currency debt, it may also constrain available finance for investment.

In recent years, banks have continued to strengthen their balance sheets, as reflected by higher capital and liquidity buffers. Nevertheless, several fragilities remain in the global banking system, which could weigh on international banking flows. Notably, banks in several countries have a large share of borrowers with stretched debt-service ratios, which could in turn lead to an increase in non-performing loans in the event of an income shock or steep rise in interest rates (IMF, 2018a). Meanwhile, tighter global liquidity conditions and the

Figure I.20
Non-resident portfolio inflows to the emerging economies

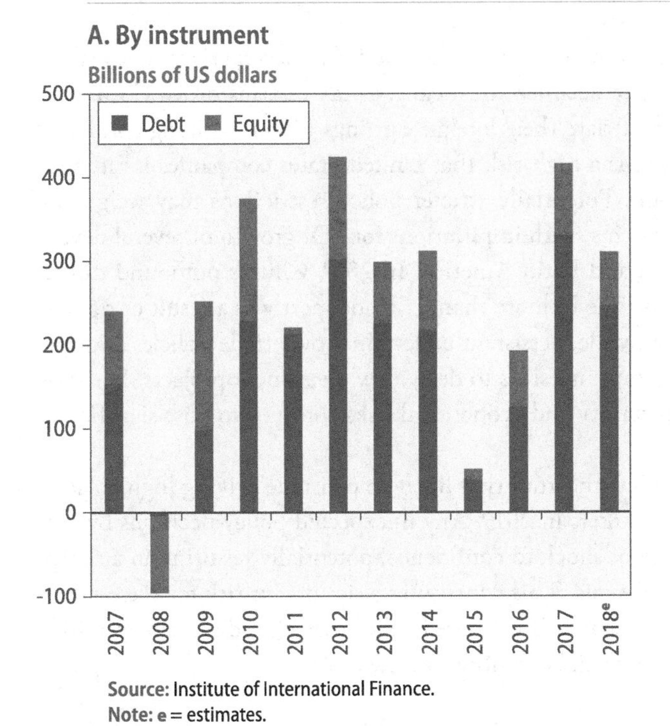

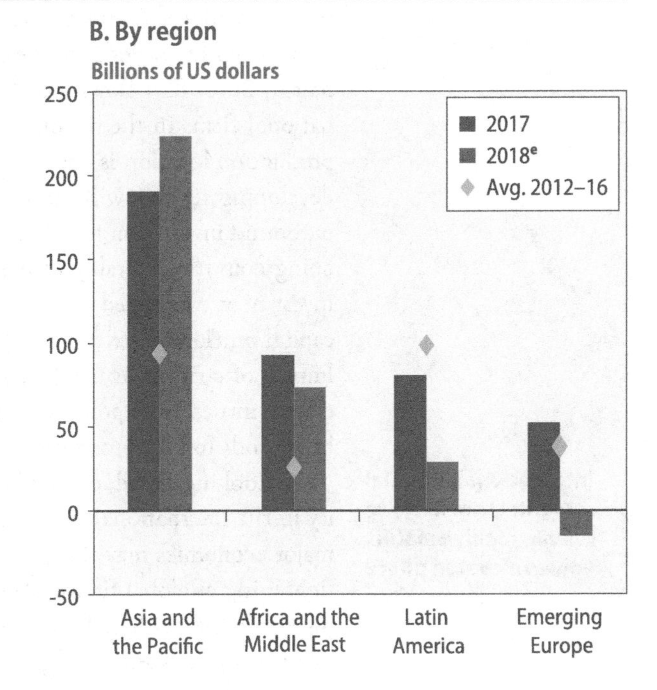

Source: Institute of International Finance.
Note: e = estimates.

projected moderation in global trade are also factors that are likely to constrain growth in cross-border banking activity.

FDI flows remain relatively stable across the developing regions

Despite higher external uncertainty, FDI flows have remained relatively stable across the developing regions. In its recent report, the United Nations Conference on Trade and Development (UNCTAD) estimated that total FDI inflows to the developing economies stood at $310 billion in the first half of 2018, a modest 4 per cent lower than the first half of 2017. Developing Asia remained the largest host region, with China emerging as the largest global recipient of FDI during this period (UNCTAD, 2018b). For the developing Asia economies, FDI prospects are supported by relatively robust and stable growth prospects. Furthermore, several countries in the region, including Cambodia, China, and Viet Nam, have recently outlined a range of policy initiatives to attract more foreign investment and to improve the business environment.

In the Latin America region, FDI inflows to the commodity exporters, including Chile, Colombia and Peru, were buoyed by the moderate recovery in global oil and metal prices. In Brazil, however, high political uncertainty weighed on investor confidence. From a medium-term perspective, FDI into the region is gradually shifting away from natural resources, and increasingly into the manufacturing and services industries, particularly renewable energy and telecommunications (ECLAC, 2018a).

In Africa, the partial recovery in global commodity prices has yet to translate into a recovery in FDI flows in the large commodity-dependent economies, including Algeria, Angola and Nigeria. For the region as a whole, weakness in FDI inflows seen in 2017 extended into the first half of 2018. Looking ahead, the implementation of the African Continental Free Trade Area agreement may increase attractiveness of the region for FDI in the outlook period (UNCTAD, 2018c). The high concentration of Africa's FDI in natural resources, however, is a cause for concern, particularly given limited productivity gains and positive spillovers to the broader economy.

The FDI outlook for the developing economies is clouded by several risks. In the first half of 2018, FDI flows into Europe declined drastically, as tax reforms drove US multinational firms in the region to repatriate their foreign earnings (ibid.). Although shifting production location is costly, there is a high risk that United States companies located in developing regions will follow suit. Potentially stricter policy restrictions may weigh on outbound investment by Chinese firms, with implications for FDI growth of several developing countries, notably in Africa and Latin America. In 2017, China's outbound direct investment contracted for the first time in more than a decade, partly as a result of tighter capital outflows restrictions. Meanwhile, persistent uncertainty over trade policies and the impact of tariff measures may prompt investors to delay new investment projects. For several countries, high political uncertainty and geopolitical risks continue to pose significant headwinds to FDI prospects.

International financial markets are likely to remain highly volatile, given elevated policy uncertainty

Looking ahead, elevated policy uncertainty is likely to continue driving high volatility in the international financial markets in 2019. Any unexpected policy decisions by the major economies may trigger a major shock to confidence, potentially resulting in a sharp tightening of global financial conditions. This constitutes a significant risk for the emerging economies with high indebtedness as well as limited policy space (see discussion on risks of an abrupt tightening of global financial conditions below).

Official development assistance declined in 2017

ODA flows declined marginally in 2017, but assistance to LDCs rose

Net official development assistance (ODA) flows from members of the OECD Development Assistance Committee (DAC) amounted to $146.6 billion in 2017, representing a marginal decline of 0.6 per cent in real terms compared to 2016 (figure I.21). These flows constituted 0.31 per cent of DAC combined gross national income, which remains well below the United Nations target of 0.7 per cent. The decline in aggregate ODA flows in 2017 was mainly due to lower spending on in-donor refugee costs. Excluding these expenditures, ODA grew at a modest pace of 1.1 per cent in real terms compared to the previous year.

In 2017, bilateral aid to the LDCs increased by 4 per cent in real terms, in part reversing the weakness in flows to these countries that has been observed in the past few years. ODA flows account for more than two thirds of external finance for the LDCs, and donor countries are pushing for ODA to be better utilized towards generating private investment and domestic tax revenue (OECD, 2018). Bilateral aid flows to sub-Saharan Africa also saw a turnaround in 2017, expanding by 3 per cent, in contrast to a cumulative contraction of 13 per cent seen between 2011 and 2016. In addition, the total volume of development finance globally is increasingly being supported by providers of aid beyond the DAC members, including countries such as Turkey, the United Arab Emirates, and South-South cooperation providers (ibid.).

Nevertheless, several recent developments could be a cause for concern. While most ODA remains in the form of grants, the volume of loans to developing countries has been on the rise, growing by 13 per cent in real terms in 2017 (ibid.). While this expands available finance, it also increases the risk of currency mismatches for loans in foreign currency (United Nations, 2018a). Meanwhile, although urgently needed, the increase in the share of ODA

Figure I.21
Net official development assistance, by main expenditure component

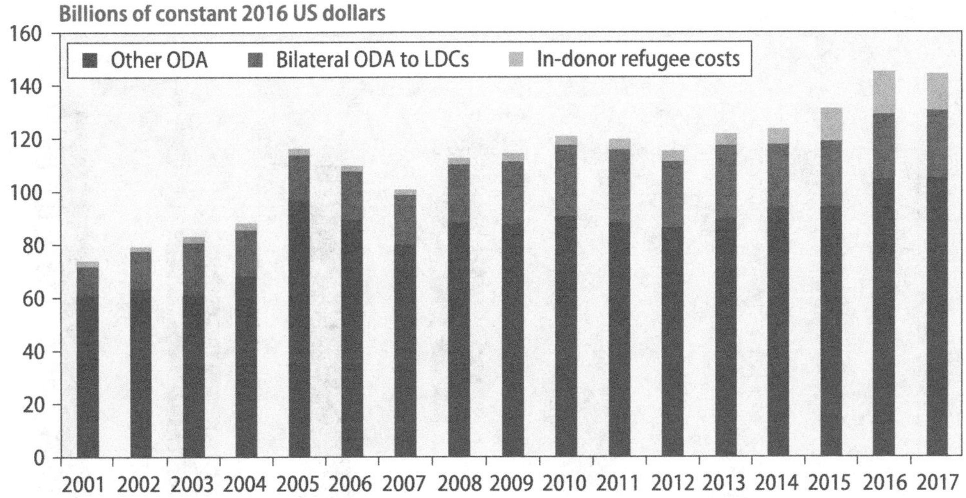

Billions of constant 2016 US dollars
160
140
120
100
80
60
40
20
0
Other ODA
Bilateral ODA to LDCs
In-donor refugee costs
2001
2002
2003
2004
2005
2006
2007
2008
2009
2010
2011
2012
2013
2014
2015
2016
2017

Source: OECD (2018), DAC statistics.

flows channelled towards humanitarian aid may have an impact on the resources available for long-term development projects, including to address critical infrastructure gaps.

Risks to the outlook

The steady pace of global economic growth masks the build-up of several short-term risks with the potential to severely disrupt economic activity and inflict significant damage on longer-term development prospects. Countries with significant vulnerabilities, such as large macroeconomic imbalances, limited policy buffers and high levels of external debt, are particularly susceptible to such disruptions. A prolonged escalation of trade tensions and an abrupt tightening of global financial conditions pose the main economic risks and are discussed further below. Geopolitical tensions in several regions also present potential threats to the global economic outlook. Meanwhile, climate risks to economic prospects are also intensifying. Over the past decades, the world has observed an increasing number of extreme weather events, of which more than half in the last six years have been attributed to climate change. The human cost of disasters falls overwhelmingly on low- and lower-middle-income countries, putting large communities at risk of displacement and causing severe damage to vital infrastructure. Many SIDS in the Caribbean, Indian and Pacific Oceans are particularly exposed to climate risks.

Escalating trade policy disputes

Rising trade disputes pose a significant risk to economic prospects

A prolonged escalation of trade disputes among the world largest economies poses a significant risk to the global trade outlook, with potentially large consequences for the short- and medium-term prospects for the world economy. While this section discusses the trade risks for the global economy in the short term, the uncertainties that this trend imposes on the evolution of the international trading system are discussed in chapter II.

Figure I.22
United States: tariffs introduced and proposed, 2018

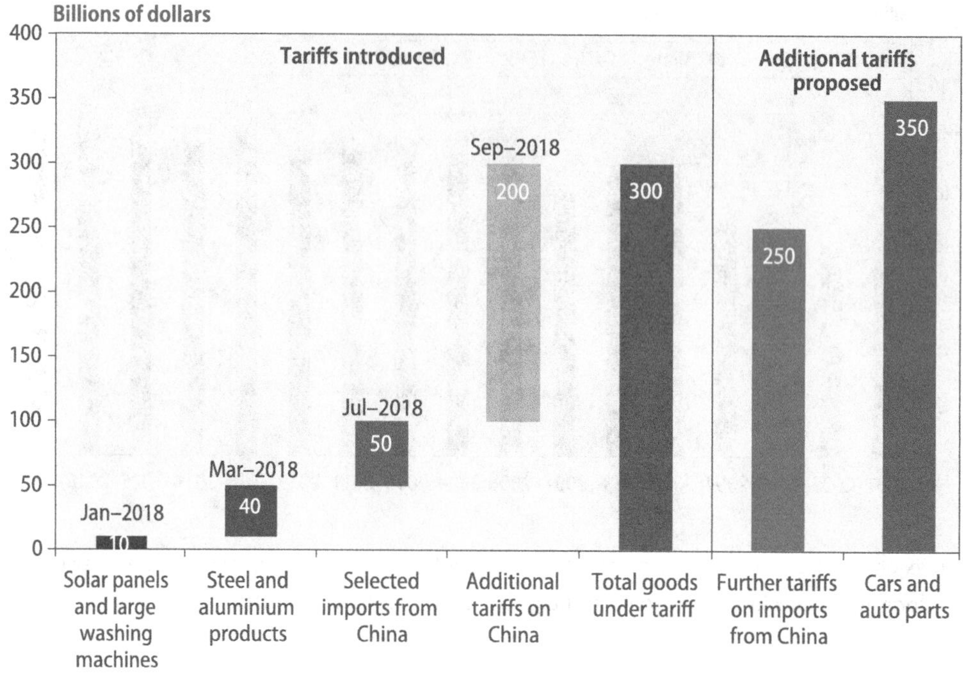

Source: UN/DESA.

Rising tariffs have been met by retaliations and counter-retaliations

New tariffs were imposed on solar panels and large washing machines in January 2018, as safeguard measures, affecting imports worth $10 billion. In March of 2018, the United States introduced a global tariff of 25 per cent and 10 per cent, respectively, on steel and aluminium products, covering an estimated $40 billion imports (figure I.22). The tariff measures were matched with retaliatory tariff increases on United States exports by several countries—including by Canada and China as well as the EU, who have all raised disputes at the WTO to contest the compatibility of the unilateral measures with WTO rules. By mid-2018, the United States introduced new additional tariffs of 25 per cent on more than 1300 products imported from China, worth $50 billion, to counter what the United States considers “unfair” policies and practices in China regarding technology transfer, intellectual property and innovation. Tariff measures are being complemented with tightening restrictions on foreign investment and visa regimes. China brought the case to the WTO Dispute Settlement Mechanism and reciprocated by introducing equivalent levels of tariffs on some 100 products covering $45 billion worth of imports from the United States, including soybeans, its major bilateral import item.

While some bilateral trade disputes were negotiated throughout 2018…

Some of the bilateral trade disputes among large economies were negotiated throughout 2018. For example, in July the United States and the EU agreed to negotiate a reduction in tariffs and other trade barriers, defusing for the moment the risk that the introduction of steel and aluminium tariffs could potentially escalate to automobiles. Nonetheless, the United States is continuing to examine the possibility of a global tariff on cars and automotive parts of 25 per cent, justifying such a move on national security grounds under Section 232 of the Trade Expansion Act of 1962. If introduced, the tariffs could affect an estimated $350 billion of automotive imports (cars, truck and parts) from major trading partners.

In October 2018, the new United States-Mexico-Canada Agreement (USMCA) was announced, which will replace the North American Free Trade Agreement (NAFTA). The automotive sector was a focus of NAFTA renegotiations, as well as renegotiations of the South Korea-United States Free Trade Agreement (KORUS-FTA). USMCA raises the local value added requirement of automobiles for tariff-free access from 62.5 per cent to 75.0 per cent and requires that a certain proportion of the final assembly be done by workers earning a wage of at least $16 per hour. Under KORUS-FTA, the Republic of Korea has accepted a quota on its auto exports to the United States. These measures have been introduced in an effort to support the automobile sector in the United States.

...the trade disputes between China and the United States gained further momentum

By contrast, the dispute between China and the United States continued to gain momentum throughout 2018. In September, the United States imposed a new tariff of 10 per cent on an additional $200 billion worth of Chinese imports as a counter-retaliation against tariffs imposed by China. Together with the initial tariffs, the new tariffs are set to cover about half of the United States bilateral imports from China, which totalled about $500 billion in 2017. To counter the counter-retaliation, China imposed tariffs on an additional $60 billion worth of US products. While threats of a further increase in tariffs on US imports from China loom in 2019, an agreement reached between China and the United States at the Group of Twenty meeting in Buenos Aires in early December has temporarily de-escalated tensions. According to the official declaration from the United States, the deal postponed a further increase of import tariffs and specified a 90-day window to negotiate a more comprehensive agreement over technology transfer, intellectual property rights, non-tariff barriers and cyber theft, among others.

A full-blown trade war between China and the United States would have severe economic effects...

There remain significant risks that the global trade tensions may persist for an extended period. The impact of a spiral of additional tariffs and retaliations could be significant, causing a slowdown in investment, higher consumer prices and a decline in business confidence. While the magnitudes of such impacts are difficult to project and depend on the extent and depth of the trade disputes (Bollen and Rojas-Romagosa, 2018), higher trade barriers can be expected to have negative consequences for domestic and global growth, with limited impacts on addressing external imbalances.

... with significant disruptions to GVCs

In addition, this would imply much wider disruption to GVCs, particularly exporters in East Asian economies that heavily rely on Chinese exports to the United States. Economies that seem to be more exposed to the trade dispute between China and the United States include Hong Kong SAR, Malaysia, Republic of Korea, Singapore and Taiwan Province of China, and especially in sectors such as electrical and optical equipment and transport equipment (Saxena, 2018). In addition, slower growth in China and the United States could also reduce the demand for commodities, affecting commodity exporters from Africa and Latin America.

Higher trade costs, coupled with elevated levels of debt, could become a significant risk in the corporate sector

Importantly, there is a risk that the trade disputes could become intertwined with the financial fragilities and elevated levels of debt in the corporate sector, especially in some emerging economies. For example, exporters facing rising trade costs can be further affected by tighter financial conditions and higher debt-servicing costs. As a result, the deterioration in the earning and profit outlooks could cause significant corporate distress in certain industries, such as automobiles, machinery and electronics.

This channel could be especially relevant if economic and financial distress affects large global firms, which dominate many industries and participate in the world economy along multiple margins with interconnected trade, investments and innovation decisions across countries. Recent research emphasizes the role of these firms in spreading trade shocks and other shocks across countries, as a rise in individual tariffs can lead to a broad reorganization of the complete global value chain (Bernard et al., 2018). In addition, higher trade costs due to higher tariffs can also generate changes in firm productivity, magnifying the potential impacts on trade flows as firms respond by adjusting export and import products and markets.

From a medium-term perspective, subdued trade will act as a drag on productivity growth

A protracted period of subdued trade growth also imposes a constraint on productivity growth in the medium term, and hence longer-term growth prospects. Trade supports productivity growth via economies of scale, access to inputs, and the acquisition of knowledge of new production techniques and product designs from international contacts. These channels are strongly intertwined with investment decisions, as firms take decisions regarding entering or expanding operations in foreign markets, together with investment, technology adoption, product mix and innovation decisions. Thus, revitalizing trade growth and promoting developing countries participation in GVCs, especially from regions that so far have limited participation such as South Asia and Africa, could become a powerful engine to encourage productivity gains, economic growth and sustainable development.

Abrupt tightening of global financial conditions

Overstretched asset valuations remain a concern in global financial markets

Despite some recent corrections, overstretched asset valuations and high-risk behaviour remain concerns in global financial markets. The protracted period of abundant global liquidity and low interest rates fuelled an increase in investor risk appetite and an intensified search for yield, resulting in the build-up of financial imbalances across both the developed and developing economies.

Notably, the global stock of high yield bonds and leveraged loans has doubled in size since the global financial crisis (Goel, 2018), driven by low borrowing costs, high risk appetite, and looser lending standards. Instead of being channelled towards productive investment, a large share of the capital raised through leveraged financing has been used to fund share buy-backs and mergers and acquisitions. This has contributed to elevated valuations across several financial asset classes, most evidently in the United States. Despite high economic policy uncertainty, cyclically adjusted price-earnings ratios of listed companies in the United States remain well above long-term averages (figure I.23). In addition, corporate bond spreads, particularly those of high-yield bonds, appear very low after accounting for expected default rates (IMF, 2018a), suggesting a certain degree of underpricing of risk.

In the current highly uncertain environment, particularly with shifting global financial conditions and rising trade tensions between China and the United States, investor behaviour remains highly sensitive to major data releases and policy announcements. Any unexpected developments could induce a sudden reversal of the risk-taking cycle, triggering sharp market corrections and a disorderly deleveraging process.

The Fed's monetary policy normalization process could trigger a sharp tightening of global liquidity conditions

High uncertainty surrounding the monetary policy adjustment process in the developed economies, particularly the United States, is a potential trigger of a sharp tightening of global liquidity conditions. While inflation so far remains contained, there is a risk that the highly procyclical fiscal expansion and increase in import tariffs could spark a strong rise in inflationary pressures, prompting the Fed to raise interest rates at a pace much faster than expected. The rise in interest rates would reduce equity valuations and impact other financial assets, which could reverberate through the global financial system. This is likely to generate adverse spillover effects on the rest of the world, particularly the emerging economies.

Figure I.23
Price-earnings ratio of S&P 500 index vs long-term interest rates

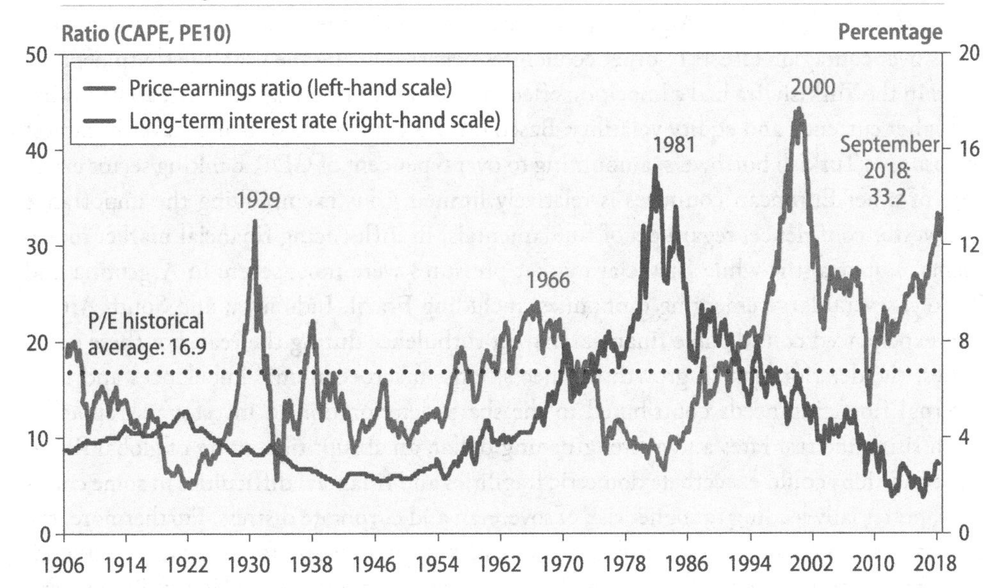

Source: Online data Robert Shiller, available from www.econ.yale.edu/~shiller/data.htm.

Note: CAPE, PE10 refers to the cyclically adjusted price-earnings ratio applied to the S&P 500 Index. It uses 10 years of real earnings to smooth income fluctuations arising from business cycles. Long-term interest rates refer to 10-year US Treasury rates.

There are several transmission channels through which monetary policy changes made by the Fed can significantly affect the emerging economies. First, a US monetary policy shock can generate large global spillovers through changes in cross-border bank lending to the private sector (Buch et al., 2018). Second, higher interest rates in the United States affect emerging bond markets through an increase in term premiums, and this transmission channel appears to have become more prominent in the post-crisis period (Albagli et al., 2018). Furthermore, as rising US interest rates exert upward pressure on the dollar, countries with a high exposure to dollar-denominated debt face greater refinancing and currency mismatch risks. Koepke (2016) found that the emerging economies face a substantially higher probability of a banking, currency or sovereign debt crisis when the Fed is tightening monetary policy.

Brexit poses considerable risks to financial stability

The possible failure of policymakers to finalize post-Brexit legal and regulatory arrangements in a timely manner poses additional risks to financial stability, given the massive cross-border financial linkages between the United Kingdom of Great Britain and Northern Ireland and the EU. For instance, the Bank of England recently reported that firms based in the EU hold derivatives contracts with a notional value of £69 trillion at United Kingdom clearing houses, of which £41 trillion are due to mature after March 2019. In the absence of new legal and operational guidelines, EU corporates and banks could lose market access to cleared derivatives, potentially disrupting cross-border financial services. This could constitute a major shock to financial systems in the EU, with contagion effects on other regions, given the prominence of European banks in driving global cross-border financial flows. Shim and Shin (2018) showed that financial stress in developed-country banks is a key driver of capital outflows from the emerging economies, regardless of the strength of the economy's macroeconomic fundamentals.

A further risk stems from the state of fiscal accounts in the EU. Italy, which already has an elevated level of public debt, has openly stated its intention for increased fiscal spending. This creates the potential for an open clash between the limits and guidelines on fiscal policy set by the EU and national fiscal policy stances. As a consequence, the EU may face a renewed need to refine and strengthen its fiscal policy framework.

Domestic financial turmoil in several countries could lead to more widespread contagion to other emerging economies

While the turmoil in Argentina and Turkey is mostly due to idiosyncratic issues, concerns over contagion effects to other economies persist. During the year, the sharp depreciation in the Turkish lira had a knock-on effect on European financial markets, contributing to higher currency and equity volatility. Based on BIS data, Spanish banks have the largest exposure to Turkish borrowers, amounting to over 6 per cent of GDP. Banking sector exposure of other European countries is relatively limited, thus exemplifying the importance of investor confidence, regardless of fundamentals, in influencing financial market movements. Importantly, while financial market pressures were most severe in Argentina and Turkey, several large emerging economies, including Brazil, Indonesia, and South Africa, also experienced considerable financial market turbulence during the year. For these economies, the deterioration in growth prospects, large macroeconomic imbalances and high external financing needs contributed to the sharp deterioration in investor risk appetite. With rising interest rates and a strengthening dollar, an abrupt tightening of global financial conditions could exacerbate domestic fragilities and financial difficulties in some countries, potentially leading to higher risk of sovereign and corporate distress. Furthermore, the risk of a "sudden stop" in capital flows has increased, particularly for emerging economies with weak macroeconomic fundamentals, large external imbalances and low policy buffers.

High indebtedness is a cause for concern in the current environment of rising interest rates

High indebtedness has become a prominent feature of the global economy. Across many developed and developing economies, public and private debt levels have risen to historical highs in the post-crisis period (figure I.24). In the current environment of rising interest rates, high leverage in an economy is a cause for concern, as increasing debt service costs pose a risk to debt sustainability and financial stability.

In the emerging economies, BIS figures show that non-financial corporate debt continued to rise in the first quarter of 2018, amounting to 107.7 per cent of GDP. While the recent increase in corporate debt has been the most evident in China, other large emerging economies, including Brazil, Chile and Turkey, have also experienced a visible rise in cor-

Figure I.24
Breakdown of non-financial sector debt of developed and emerging economies

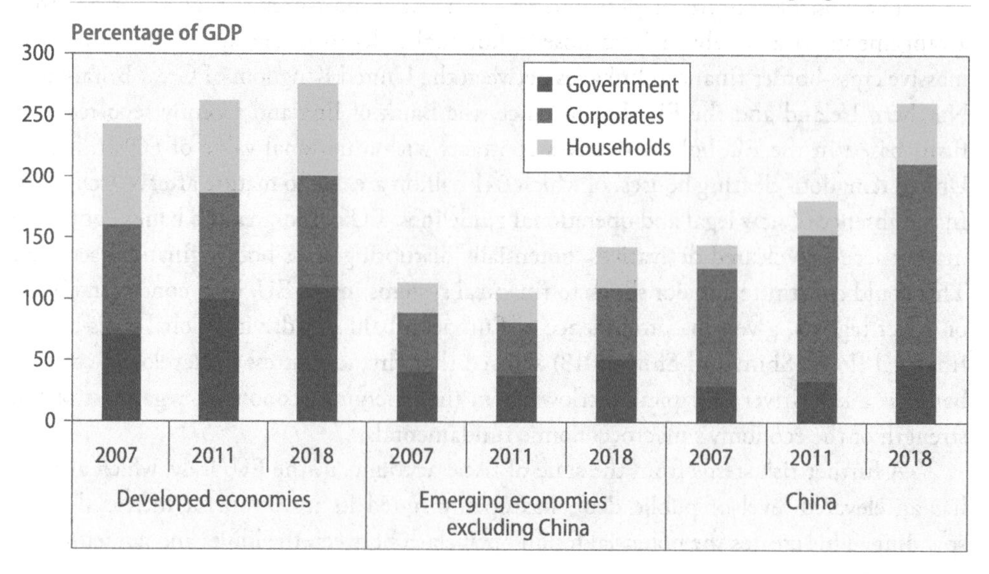

Source: Bank for International Settlements, Total Credit Statistics.

Note: 2018 refers to outstanding debt data as of 1Q 2018.

porate debt levels. In many of these countries, the prolonged period of excess of liquidity contributed to the "financialization" of the corporate sector to exploit carry trade opportunities, with a large part of corporate debt channelled neither to productive investments nor to high-productivity sectors.

In addition, the escalation in trade disputes adds to risks to corporate balance sheets, particularly those of export-oriented firms. The increase in tariffs are likely to result in a rise in input costs and lower product demand, eroding profits and potentially inducing a higher rate of corporate defaults or bankruptcies.

Countries with large external and foreign currency debt are more vulnerable to rising interest rates and a stronger dollar

The fragility of corporate and government balance sheets in several emerging economies has also been exacerbated by the rise in dollar-denominated debt, particularly in the post-crisis period (figure I.25). The Fed's continued tightening of monetary policy and elevated global risk aversion are factors that are likely to support a further strengthening of the dollar. In this aspect, countries with a substantial amount of dollar-denominated debt are particularly vulnerable to rising interest rates and an appreciation of the dollar, given their high exposure to refinancing and currency mismatch risks.

Rising public debt and government interest burdens are a growing source of risk to financial stability for many developing countries

In many developing countries, rising public debt and government interest burdens represent a growing source of risk to financial stability. In 2018, rising fiscal sustainability concerns prompted several governments—including Argentina, Barbados, Pakistan, and Sri Lanka—to seek financial assistance from the IMF. For the commodity-dependent countries, particularly in Africa, Latin America and Western Asia, public finances have deteriorated rapidly over the past few years, due mainly to the collapse in commodity-related revenue. Consequently, many Governments in these regions have made cuts in social spending and SDG-related investment or resorted to ramping up borrowing in order to finance significant budget shortfalls.

Moreover, the extended period of low global interest rates has enabled Governments to increase debt levels with only a limited impact on debt-servicing costs. Several countries have even seen a decline in government interest burdens over the past decade despite ris-

Figure I.25
Dollar-denominated credit to non-bank borrowers in selected emerging economies

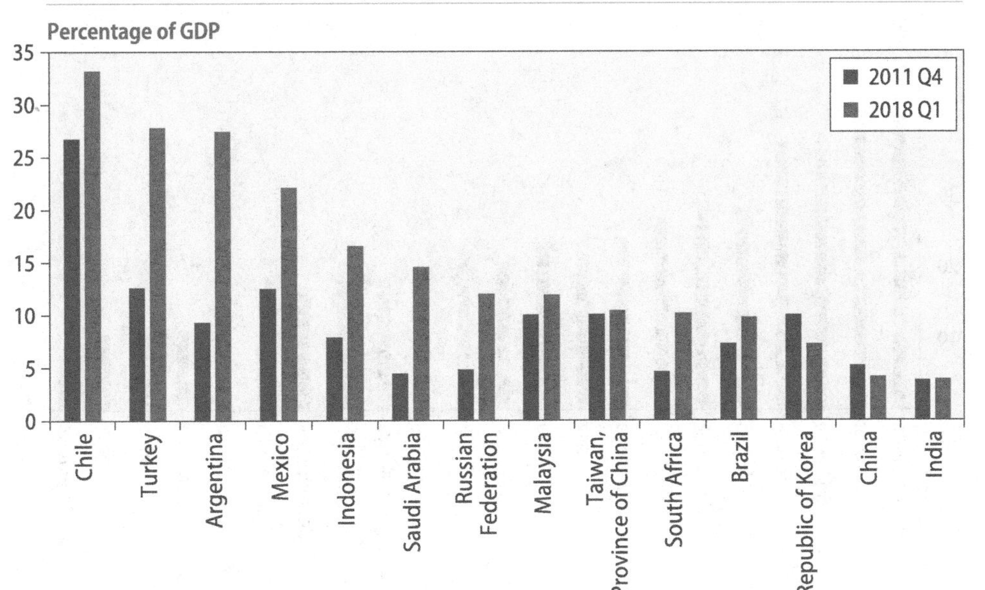

Sources: Bank for International Settlements, Total Credit Statistics.

Note: 2018 refers to outstanding debt data as of 1Q 2018.

ing debt levels, as maturing debt was reissued at a lower rate of interest. As the period of extremely loose global financial conditions draws to a close, debt-servicing costs are also likely to rise, potentially posing a threat to fiscal sustainability. The speed at which higher interest rates will feed into debt-servicing costs depends on the term structure of existing debt and related refinancing needs.

In several countries, high debt-service obligations already constitute a heavy burden on government finances. In 2017, interest payments alone exceeded 20 per cent of government revenue in several countries in Africa, Latin America and South Asia (figure I.26). A number of LDCs and heavily indebted poor countries are identified as being particularly vulnerable to financial shocks. The IMF recently warned that many low-income countries have experienced a substantial rise in both fiscal and interest burdens in recent years, placing them at high risk of debt distress (IMF, 2018b).

Policymakers are faced with the challenge of containing financial risks while supporting short-term growth

Policymakers in the developing economies are faced with the challenge of containing the build-up of financial risks while supporting short-term growth prospects. Deleveraging policies that are too aggressive could cause major disruptions to economic activity, while a focus on promoting growth, including through maintaining easy financial conditions, would induce further debt accumulation. A stronger policy focus on improving the composition and quality of investment is also important, given that raising investment in productivity-enhancing activities is key to improving the sustainability of growth prospects over the medium term.

Given the changing global financial environment, there is a need for many countries to enhance the resilience of the domestic financial system to external shocks, and to reduce the probability of the occurrence of a financial crisis. Crisis probabilities are influenced by many variables, including the availability of policy buffers and the strength of financial institutions. Barrell et al. (2018) shows that capital and liquidity buffers not only lower the probability of a crisis, but also limit the costs if a crisis occurs.

Figure I.26
Government interest payments as a share of general government revenue, 2018

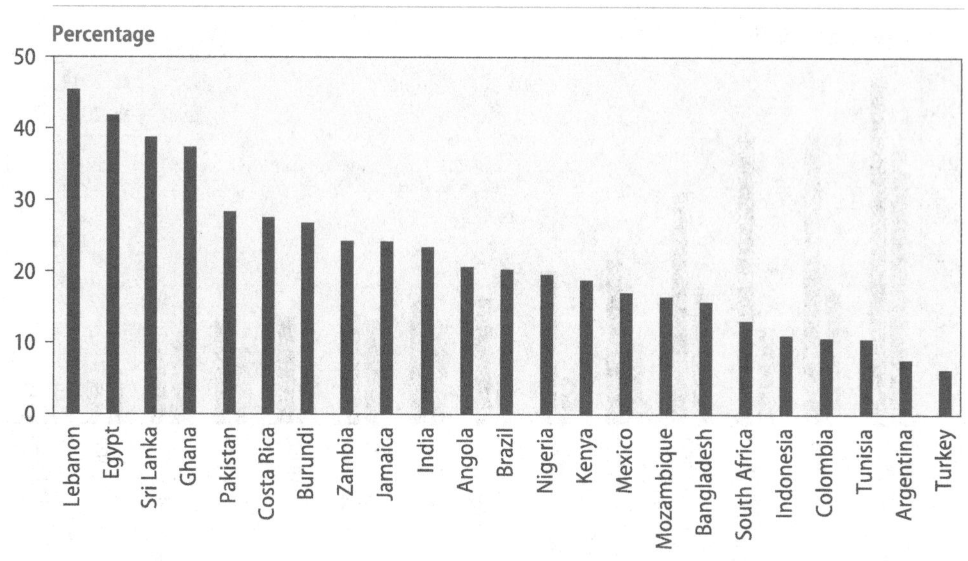

Source: UN/DESA, based on estimates from the IMF's World Economic Outlook October 2018 database.

Sound and prudent macroeconomic policies are needed to ensure sustained, inclusive and sustainable growth trajectories and to contain financial risks and vulnerabilities. Many policymakers are increasingly taking a proactive role in managing risks associated with debt and capital flows, through a wide range of policy tools. This includes monetary, fiscal, exchange rate, macroprudential policies and capital flow management measures. There is a need to ensure policy consistency when utilizing the various instruments, as well as to clearly communicate policy strategies, in order to sustain confidence. In addition, policymakers should also be cognizant of the significant trade-offs that could exist. For example, Ayyagari, et al. (2017) found that small firms were disproportionately affected by macroprudential policies given that they have limited access to non-bank financing, thus illustrating the trade-off between the objectives of preserving financial stability and promoting greater financial deepening.

Appendix
Baseline forecast assumptions

This appendix summarizes the key assumptions underlying the baseline forecast, including recent and expected developments in major commodity prices, the monetary and fiscal policy stance for major economies, and exchange rates for major currencies.

Commodity prices

Recent developments and the short-term outlook for key commodities are reported in table I.A.1. With the exception of crude oil, commodity prices generally weakened in the first three quarters of 2018. In particular, a strong US dollar and rising global trade tensions have weighed on demand for base metals and other commodities. Some individual commodities have seen price increases driven by fundamentals. For example, wheat prices rose in 2018, mainly driven by unfavourable weather conditions in the Russian Federation and some other producer countries. The price of cocoa beans has also risen, after falling to the lowest level in a decade in December 2017. Further upward cocoa price pressures remain weak, as a healthy crop in the primary producer, Cote d'Ivoire, is expected. Overall, commodity prices remain significantly below their 2011 peak levels (figure I.A.1).

Figure I.A.1
Selected commodity prices, January 2011–September 2018

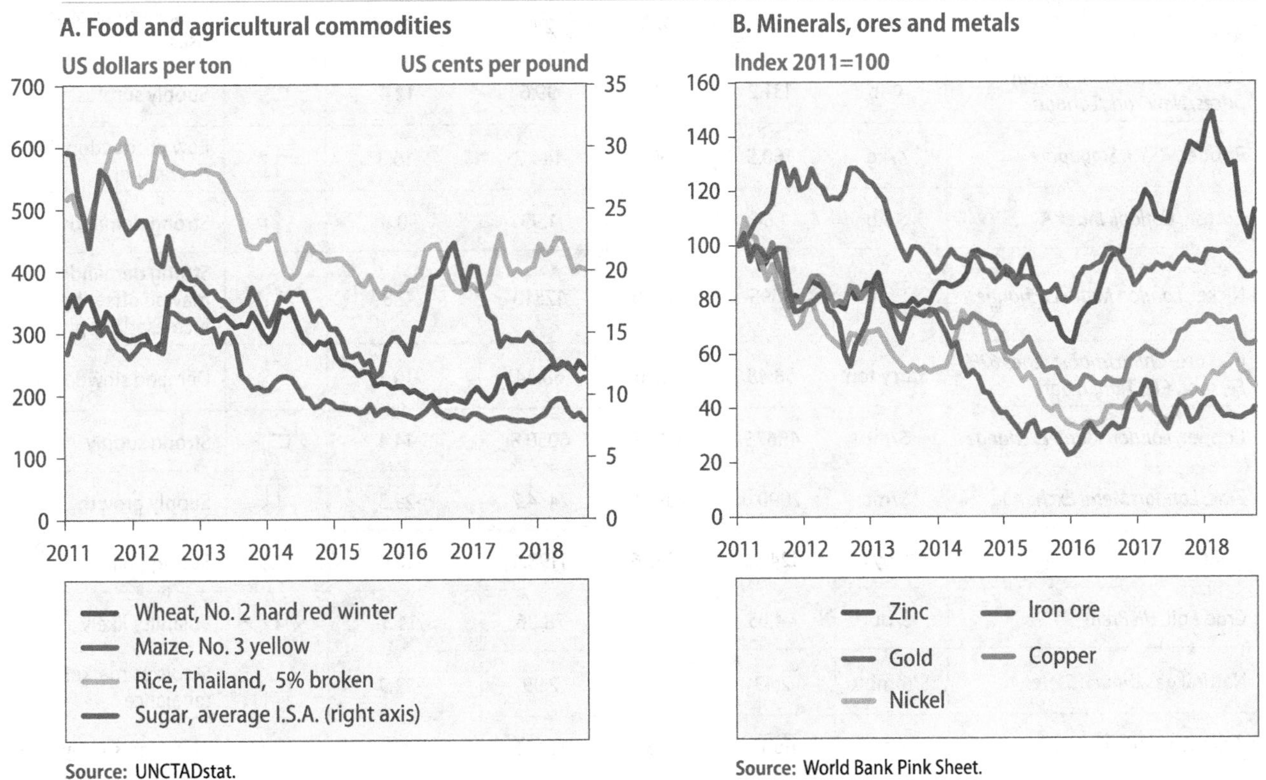

In the outlook, high inventories and supply prospects are likely to keep prices in check for commodities such as sugar, coffee, cocoa beans, and copper. Strong demand and lower supply levels are expected to exert upward pressure on wheat, maize and cotton prices. Rubber supply is likely to be restricted by unfavourable weather conditions in India, Malaysia, Sri Lanka and Viet Nam. The metals markets remain sensitive to global trade tensions and demand. In particular, the price of iron ore may decline if a slowdown of Chinese steel demand materializes. The ongoing expansion of the electric vehicle market (see box I.3) may add upward pressure to nickel prices in the medium to long term, although supply increases from Indonesia, which has eased its export ban on nickel, will exert an attenuating effect on prices. The price of Brent crude is assumed to average $71.9 per barrel in 2019 and $74.6 in 2020, but is expected to exhibit significant volatility.

Table I.A.1
Key commodity prices

	Unit	2016	2017	Sep 2018	Jan–Sep 2018 (% change)	Outlook	Key influencing factors
Sugar, *average I.S.A. daily prices*	¢/lb	18.06	16.02	11.37	-19.3	⇨	High inventories and supply surplus
Rice, *Thailand, white milled, 5% broken*	$/mt	386.17	398.92	402.00	-9.0	⇧	Stock level decline
Wheat, *Hard Red Winter No. 2*	$/mt	196.42	211.84	241.01	6.0	⇧	Strong demand and lower supply
Maize, *Yellow Maize No. 3*	$/mt	168.21	160.81	157.8	-3.4	⇧	Strong demand and lower supply
Coffee, *International Coffee Organization composite indicator*	¢/lb	127	127	98	-15.1	⇨	Supply surplus
Tea, *Mombasa/Nairobi auctions, African origin*	¢/kg	242	245	241	-18.3	⇨	Subject to weather risks
Cocoa beans, *average daily prices, New York/London*	¢/lb	131.2	92.0	99.6	12.4	⇨	Supply surplus
Rubber, *RSS 3, Singapore*	¢/kg	160.5	199.5	144.2	-16.3	⇧	Low production due to weather
Cotton, *Cotlook Index A*	$/kg	1.64	1.84	1.99	-0.8	⇧	Strong demand
Nickel, *London Metal Exchange*	$/mt	9595	10410	12510	-2.8	⇧	Strong demand may be offset by increased supply
Iron ore, *China import, fines 62% Fe, spot, CFR Tianjin port*	$/dry ton	58.48	71.76	68.44	-10.3	⇩	Demand slowdown
Copper, *London Metal Exchange*	$/mt	4867.9	6169.9	6050.8	-14.4	⇨	Strong supply
Zinc, *London Metal Exchange*	$/mt	2090.0	2890.9	2434.7	-29.3	⇩	Supply growth
Gold	$/troy oz	1249.0	1257.6	1198.4	-10.0	⇨	Strong dollar
Crude oil, *UK Brent*	$/bbl	44.05	54.39	78.86	14.3	⬂ ⬀	Volatility likely
Natural gas, *United States*	$/mmbtu	2.49	2.96	2.99	-22.9	⇨	Stable as market rebalance
Coal, *Australian*	$/mt	66.12	88.52	114.16	7.2	⇧	Declining supply

Sources: UNCTADstat, International Coffee Organization, World Bank Pink Sheet, UNCTAD and UN/DESA assessments.

Figure I.A.2
Price of Brent crude: recent trends and assumptions

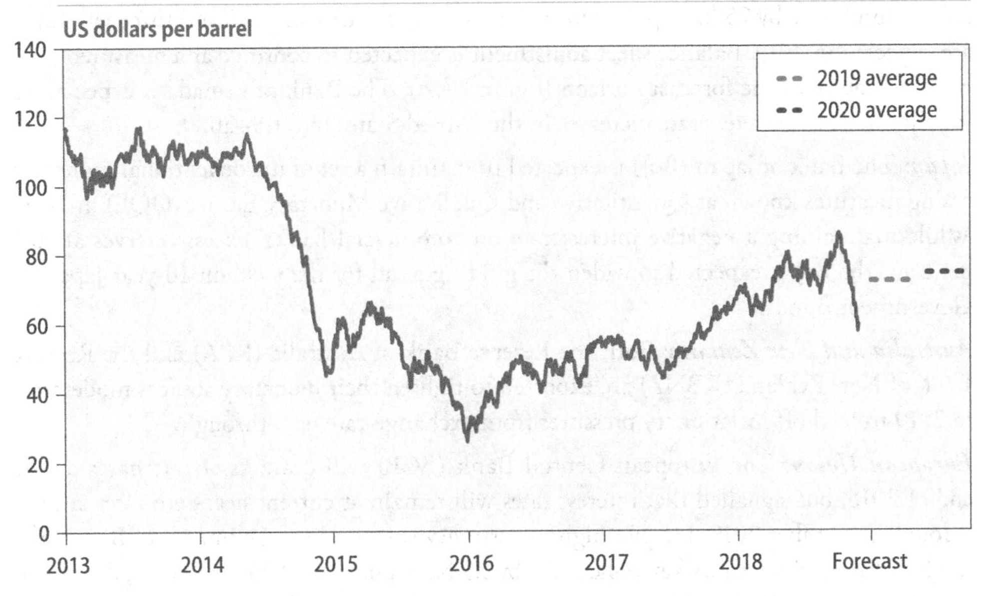

Sources: Energy Information Administration and UN/DESA forecast assumptions.

Monetary policy

In the developed economies, the monetary policy normalization process is expected to continue at a measured pace, as inflation rises closer to central bank targets. Interest rates will continue to diverge between the United States of America, Japan, and the euro area (figure I.A.3), reflecting differences in the timing and pace of withdrawal.

Figure I.A.3
Key central bank policy rates: recent trends and assumptions

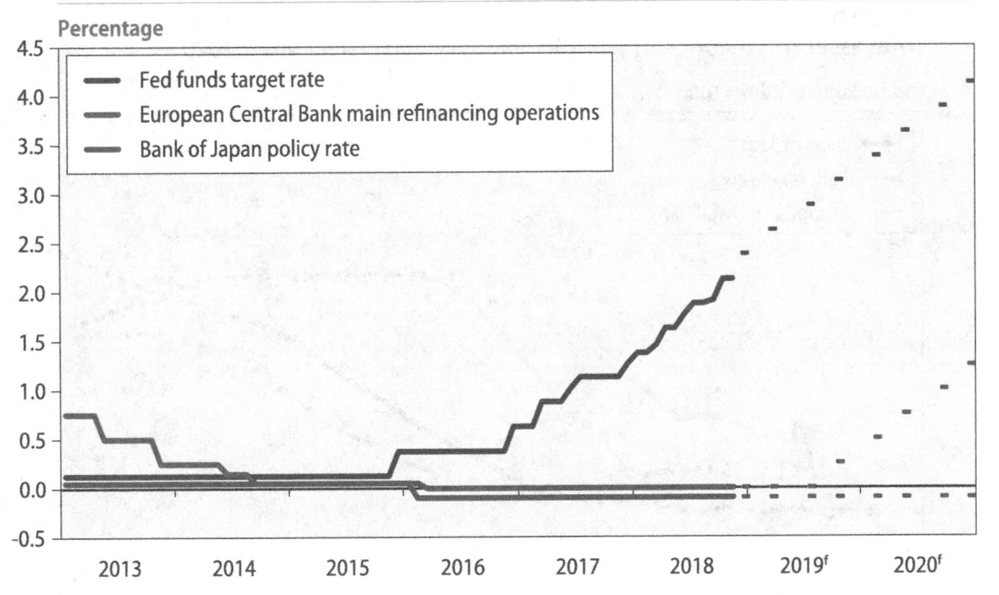

Sources: National central banks and UN/DESA forecast assumptions.

Note: f = forecast.

North America: The United States Federal Reserve (Fed) is embarking on a slightly faster pace of monetary adjustment than earlier expected. The Fed raised the target range for the federal funds rate by 25 basis points four times over the course of 2018 and three rate hikes are expected in 2019. Balance sheet adjustment is expected to continue at a measured pace over the course of the forecast horizon (figure I.A.4). The Bank of Canada is expected to roughly track the interest rate increases in the United States in 2019–2020.

Japan: The Bank of Japan (BoJ) is expected to maintain a set of unconventional monetary easing measures known as Quantitative and Qualitative Monetary Easing (QQE) in 2019. While maintaining a negative interest rate on commercial banks' excess reserves at -0.1 per cent, the BoJ is expected to widen the guiding band for the yield on 10-year Japanese Government Bonds.

Australia and New Zealand: Both the Reserve Bank of Australia (RBA) and the Reserve Bank of New Zealand (RBNZ) are expected to tighten their monetary stances moderately in 2019 to fend off inflationary pressures from exchange-rate pass-through.

European Union: The European Central Bank (ECB) will cease asset purchases at the end of 2018, but signalled that interest rates will remain at current near-zero rates at least through September 2019. Despite high uncertainty surrounding the impact of Brexit, the Bank of England raised its key policy rate by 25 basis points to 0.75 per cent in August to contain inflation. Rates are expected to remain on hold until the central bank can assess the impact of Brexit after March 2019.

A growing number of countries tightened monetary policy or reduced the degree of monetary accommodation in 2018 (figure I.A.5). Many developing economies and economies in transition have increased rates alongside the Fed to stem capital outflows. By contrast, in response to escalating trade tensions and volatile commodity prices, several central banks have loosened or maintained accommodative monetary policy stances.

CIS and Georgia: In the Commonwealth of Independent States (CIS), amid rising inflationary expectations and increased uncertainty, monetary accommodation has started to

Figure I.A.4
Total assets of major central banks, January 2007–December 2020

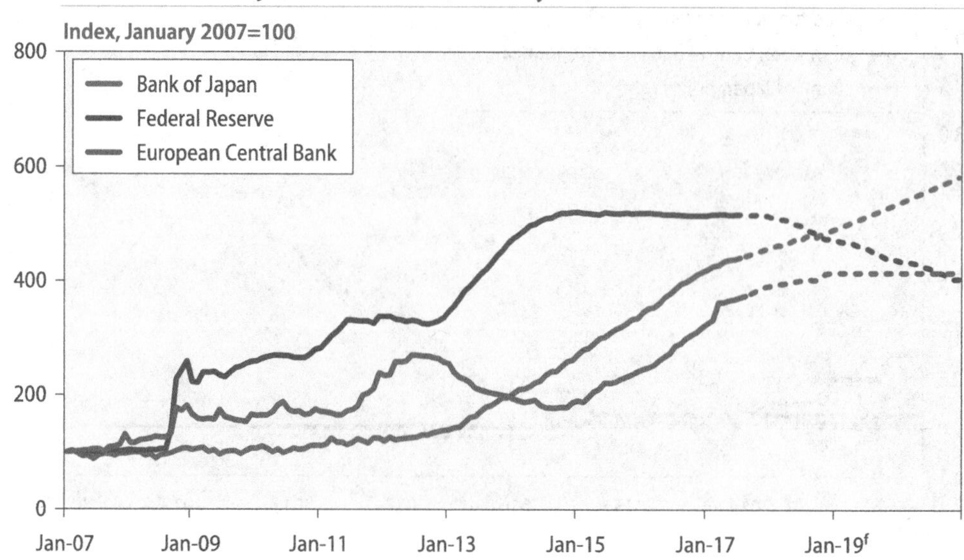

Sources: National central banks and UN/DESA forecast assumptions.
Note: f = forecast.

Figure I.A.5
Monetary policy stances

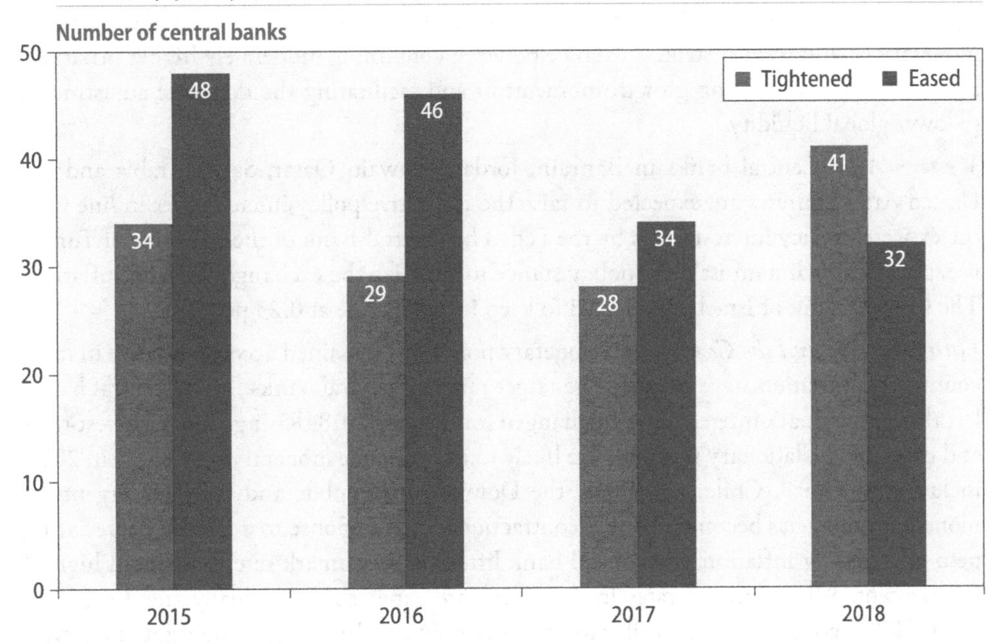

Source: Central Bank News.

Note: As of 30 November 2018. Sample covers 95 central banks across developed and developing economies, as well as the economies in transition.

be withdrawn. In the Russian Federation, depreciation of the rouble and increasing uncertainty led to the first rate hike since 2014 in September. In Ukraine, monetary authorities delivered a number of interest rate increases, prompted by rising inflation expectations—as labour shortages caused strong wage growth—and increases in economic uncertainties. Monetary policy was also tightened in Kazakhstan and Uzbekistan, due to rising inflationary risks and currency pressures. By contrast, in Azerbaijan, rapid disinflation allowed for a series of rate cuts, and the National Bank of Georgia marginally reduced its policy rate in August. Overall, policies remain relatively tight, with high real interest rates limiting the growth of private credit.

South-Eastern Europe: In South-Eastern Europe, monetary policy remains accommodative, despite the modest acceleration in inflation. Albania saw rapid appreciation of the currency in the first two quarters of 2018, which, according to the central bank, steered the exchange rate away from its long-term equilibrium, and undermined export competitiveness. In response, the central bank in June lowered its policy rate to a historically low level of 1 per cent. The National Bank of Serbia also cut its policy rate to a record-low level of 3 per cent in April 2018.

East Asia: Given moderate inflationary pressures and rising downside risks to growth, monetary policy is expected to remain accommodative in most East Asian economies. However, as the developed countries normalize monetary policy, central banks are faced with the risk of managing stronger capital outflow pressures. In China, rising trade tensions in 2018 prompted the People's Bank of China (PBoC) to announce several easing measures during the year. In the outlook period, the PBoC is expected to continuously fine-tune its policy mix in order to support short-term growth, while containing domestic financial vulnerabilities.

South Asia: After several years of accommodative monetary policy, South Asia has gradually moved into a more neutral stance. Some countries have even implemented a more aggressive tightening, amid financial and economic turbulences. In the current conditions, monetary decisions must strike a balance between containing moderately higher inflationary pressures, maintaining growth momentum and facilitating the domestic adjustments to lower global liquidity.

Western Asia: Central banks in Bahrain, Jordan, Kuwait, Qatar, Saudi Arabia and the United Arab Emirates are expected to raise the respective policy interest rates in line with the expected policy interest hikes by the Fed. The Central Bank of the Republic of Turkey is expected to maintain its tight policy stance to stabilize the exchange rate and inflation. The Central Bank of Israel is projected to keep its policy rate at 0.25 per cent.

Latin America and the Caribbean: Monetary policy has remained accommodative in most countries as inflation stayed within the target range of central banks. Many central banks left their benchmark interest rates unchanged for most of 2018. Rising global interest rates and increased inflationary pressures are likely to lead to some monetary tightening in 2019, including in Brazil, Chile, Colombia, the Dominican Republic and Peru. In Argentina, monetary policy has become strongly contractionary. In response to a rapidly depreciating peso and soaring inflation, the central bank lifted its benchmark rate to a record high of 60 per cent. While interest rates in Argentina are expected to gradually trend down in 2019–2020, monetary policy will remain contractionary. In Mexico, the tightening cycle that began in 2016 continues, and the policy rate reached the highest level since 2008. With upside and downside risks to both inflation and growth, there is a high degree of uncertainty over the direction of Mexico's monetary policy during the forecast period.

In countries that are fully dollarized (Ecuador, El Salvador and Panama) or operate a peg to the dollar (e.g., Antigua and Barbuda, Dominica, Bahamas and Barbados), local interest rates are projected to rise in line with those of the Fed.

Africa: In many parts of Africa, monetary policy remains tight, given weakened exchange rates and elevated inflation rates. However, as inflationary pressures have eased, several countries, including Angola, Gambia, Ghana, Kenya, Mozambique and Zambia, lowered interest rates in 2018 to support the economy. For 2019, monetary policy is expected to remain tight in several countries, including Egypt, Sudan and Tunisia, aiming to stabilize foreign exchange and inflation. In Algeria, Libya, Morocco and Mauritania, monetary policy stances are expected to stay neutral.

Fiscal policy

Most developed-country Governments have adopted a broadly neutral or mildly expansionary fiscal policy stance for 2018–2020. The main exception is the United States, which has introduced a major fiscal stimulus programme, adding at least 0.5 percentage points to gross domestic product (GDP) growth in 2018. Fiscal deficits are expected to remain sizeable in most commodity-dependent economies, with public debt-to-GDP ratios expected to rise further in the outlook period. Globally, the fiscal stance is easing in the most number of countries since 2009 (figure I.A.6).

United States: The United States is following a highly expansionary fiscal programme, with steep cuts in both household and corporate taxes, and increases in expenditure. The debt ceiling is suspended until March 2019, after which the budgets for the fiscal years

Figure I.A.6
Fiscal policy stances

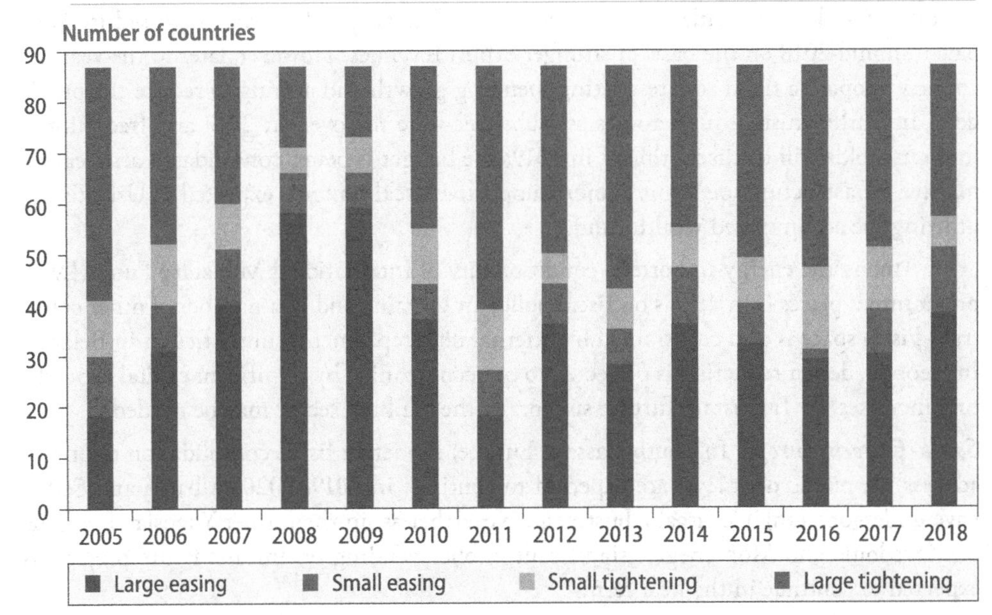

Source: IMF Fiscal Monitor Database.

Note: Small easing/tightening defined as a change in the cyclically adjusted fiscal balance of less than 0.5 per cent of GDP. Large easing/tightening is greater than 0.5 per cent of GDP.

2019/20 and 2020/21 are likely to be neutral to mildly contractionary, to stem the ongoing rise in debt.

Japan: The fiscal policy will likely be tightened slightly over the 2018 and 2019 fiscal years. While health- and social-welfare-related expenditures are expected to increase moderately, other current expenditures are subject to fiscal consolidation. The consumption tax rate is planned to be raised from 8 per cent to 10 per cent on October 2019 with an introduction of the invoice method.

Australia and New Zealand: The fiscal deficit is projected to narrow moderately over 2019 and 2020 in Australia despite planned personal income tax cuts. New Zealand is forecast to maintain a fiscal surplus with prudent management on expenditures.

European Union: Fiscal policy in the European Union is expected to have a neutral impact on growth in 2018–2019, with many countries shifting away from austerity in recent years. Across the region, stronger GDP growth and significant labour market gains have driven cyclical improvements in budget balances, by boosting tax revenues and reducing welfare expenditures. While almost all European countries are projected to record a primary balance surplus in 2019, the region's aggregate public debt-to-GDP ratio remains high and is expected to decline only slowly.

CIS and Georgia: A higher oil price has eased budget constraints for CIS energy exporters. Some countries have also benefited from privatization proceeds. Nevertheless, fiscal policy remains moderately conservative. In the Russian Federation, public spending is constrained by a fiscal rule, aimed at reducing the sensitivity to oil price fluctuations and building net sovereign assets. The planned budget for 2019–2021 maintains a fiscal surplus and increases non-hydrocarbon revenues, including a rise in the value added tax rate in 2019 and an increase in the pension age. The net effect of fiscal measures on growth in 2019 is expected to be negative; later, higher spending to meet recently adopted social and economic development targets may add to growth. In Kazakhstan, significant funds were used in 2017 to bail out the banking sector; stronger economic activity in 2018 helped to consolidate the budget and a fiscal rule has been introduced. Fiscal spending was increased in Azerbaijan in mid-2018 on the basis of stronger export revenues. However, later in the year the country adopted a fiscal rule restricting spending growth and aiming to reduce the public debt. In Turkmenistan, numerous state subsidies were removed in 2017 and free utilities for households will be discontinued in 2019; the budget is being consolidated after earlier massive infrastructure spending. A more supportive fiscal stance is expected in Uzbekistan, utilizing the accumulated wealth fund.

Among the energy importers, conditionality of International Monetary Fund (IMF) programmes places restrictions on fiscal policy in Ukraine and in a number of other countries. Fiscal space is also constrained by external debt repayments, in particular in Belarus. In Georgia, deficit reduction is projected to be accompanied by significant capital expenditure increases. In Tajikistan, further support to the banking sector may be needed.

South-Eastern Europe: In South-Eastern Europe, moderate fiscal consolidation efforts to address the public debt level are expected to continue in 2019–2020. Albania and Serbia have undergone tangible fiscal adjustment. Nevertheless, in the former Yugoslav Republic of Macedonia and Montenegro, significant public spending on infrastructure projects is expected to continue in the near term.

East Asia: As monetary policy space narrows, most East Asian economies are likely to maintain expansionary fiscal stances to support domestic demand. The Republic of Korea plans to increase fiscal spending significantly in 2019, with a focus on job creation and expanding social welfare. China has also introduced several pro-growth fiscal measures such as lowering personal income taxes and accelerating infrastructure investment. Several other economies, including the Philippines and Thailand, will also continue to embark on large infrastructure projects.

South Asia: South Asia's fiscal policies have gradually moved to a moderate expansionary stance. Thus, fiscal deficits are projected to remain elevated. To avert sustainability concerns, some countries will need medium-term consolidation plans, especially those with a fragile tax base and elevated levels of debt.

Western Asia: Due to the recent recovery in oil prices, fiscal stances in Cooperation Council for the Arab States of the Gulf (GCC) economies are expected to be more accommodative. Following Saudi Arabia and the United Arab Emirates, other GCC economies are expected to introduce the value added tax over 2018 and 2019. Iraq is expected to increase fiscal expenditures for public investment projects and public service provisions. Further fiscal consolidation measures are expected to be taken in Jordan, Lebanon and Turkey. The fiscal policy stance is forecast to be accommodative in Israel, given its strong fiscal position.

Latin America and Caribbean: Many Governments will face significant fiscal adjustment pressures during the outlook period. Despite some improvements in 2018, primary fiscal deficits often exceeded debt-stabilizing levels. Government debt-to-GDP ratios are high in several countries, especially in South America (Argentina, Brazil, Uruguay) and the Caribbean (Barbados, Jamaica). Rising global interest rates, a strong dollar and capital flow volatility add to pressures for fiscal consolidation. Most Governments will continue to pursue a gradual approach to minimize the negative impact on economic activity. In Argentina, fiscal policy will remain strongly contractionary in 2019–2020, with both large spending cuts and tax increases in efforts to eliminate the primary deficit by 2019. In Brazil, the new Government faces strong pressures to consolidate public finances, including comprehensive reform of the pension system. In 2018, Brazil's deficit in the general government overall balance is estimated to have risen to about 8.5 per cent of GDP and general government gross debt to 88 per cent of GDP.

Africa: In aggregate, fiscal deficits narrowed slightly in Africa in 2018, reflecting ongoing fiscal consolidation efforts in many countries that nonetheless allow for higher levels of investment in infrastructure. However, in East Africa, deficits have continued to widen, as domestic resource mobilization remains insufficient to finance expenditure needs. In aggregate, the fiscal position in Africa is forecast to remain stable in 2019, supported by rising export revenues, particularly from natural resources. Under the IMF Extended Fund Facility arrangement, Egypt and Tunisia are projected to implement further measures to reduce budget deficits.

Exchange rates

The dollar/euro exchange rate is assumed to average 1.183 in 2018, and to depreciate marginally in line with the widening differential between ECB and Fed interest rates to 1.120 in 2019 and 1.117 in 2020 (figure I.A.7).

The yen/dollar exchange rate is assumed to average 110.41 in 2018, 116.55 in 2019 and 118.4 in 2020.

The renminbi/dollar exchange rate is assumed to average 6.61 CNY/dollar in 2018 and 6.96 in 2019 and 7.03 in 2020.

Figure I.A.7
Major currency exchange rates: recent trends and assumptions

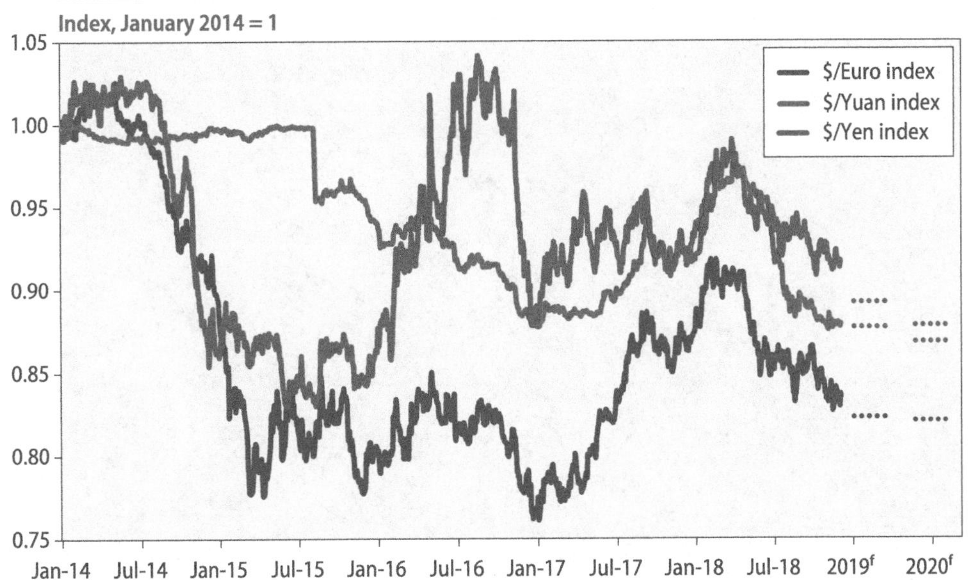

Sources: IMF Exchange Rate Query Tool and UN/DESA forecast assumptions.

Note: f = forecast,
A rise indicates an appreciation.

Chapter II

Macroeconomic prospects and the implementation of the 2030 Agenda for Sustainable Development

Global progress on the SDGs is not keeping pace with the ambitions of the 2030 Agenda for Sustainable Development

In tandem with the solid global growth performance over the past two years, countries have continued to advance efforts towards attainment of the Sustainable Development Goals (SDGs). Three years into the implementation of the 2030 Agenda for Sustainable Development, many countries are in the process of aligning their national development plans and strategies with the SDGs. At the 2018 High-level Political Forum (HLPF), 47 countries presented their voluntary national reviews (VNRs), which took stock of their achievements and challenges, as well as identified the next steps in implementing the Agenda.

Nevertheless, for most countries, the pace of progress has not been rapid enough to keep up with the ambitions of the Agenda. The *Sustainable Development Goals Report 2018* highlighted that countries continue to face daunting challenges to the successful transition towards more sustainable and resilient societies by 2030 (United Nations, 2018b). While global economic conditions have remained strong since 2017, a large number of developing countries are struggling to achieve sustained growth in per capita incomes and productivity. Moreover, even within countries that are expanding at a strong pace or have reached high standards of living, there are marginalized and disadvantaged groups that are not benefiting from improved economic conditions. Rising inequalities, conflict and climate change pose additional challenges, contributing to growing numbers of people facing hunger and displacement in several parts of the world.

Several of the goals to be reviewed at HLPF 2019 are strongly linked to current macroeconomic conditions

Several of these challenges will be at the heart of discussions in the upcoming sessions of the HLPF, under the auspices of the Economic and Social Council (ECOSOC) in July 2019 and at the Heads of State level during the General Assembly in September 2019 under the theme "Empowering people and ensuring inclusiveness and equality". During this forum, six out of the seventeen SDGs will be reviewed in depth, many of which are strongly linked to the current macroeconomic conditions. These include Goal 8 on economic growth and productive employment, Goal 10 on reducing inequality, Goal 13 on combating climate change, and Goal 17 on revitalizing global partnerships.[1]

Strengthening multilateralism is indispensable for advancing sustainable development

Several of the SDGs are also global by nature and require collective and cooperative action. In today's closely integrated world economy, internationally agreed rules and institutions are vital for ensuring smoothly functioning markets, resolving disagreements and preserving stability. Strengthening multilateralism is therefore an indispensable element needed to advance sustainable development across the globe. What is required is a more inclusive, flexible and responsive multilateral system that helps tackle existing and emerging global challenges.

1 The other two Sustainable Development Goals (SDGs) to be reviewed at the 2019 High-level Political Forum on Sustainable Development (HLPF) are Goal 4 on inclusive and equitable quality education and Goal 16 on peaceful and inclusive societies.

In recent years, however, support for a multilateral approach to global policymaking has been waning. The global financial crisis of 2008/09 and the subsequent slow economic recovery have put the spotlight on some of the unintended consequences of trade and financial liberalization.[2] There has been a growing perception that the benefits of globalization have not been equitably shared—both across and within countries.[3] Many of the rules adopted to promote free trade have not created a system that is inclusive, transparent and development friendly. Trade and financial liberalization are now more widely seen as exacerbating income and wealth inequality within countries, limiting policy space and, in some cases, even undermining national sovereignty. As the backlash against globalization gained momentum and an increasing number of countries adopted more inward-looking policies, the institutions at the heart of global governance have been facing increased pressure.

As macroeconomic trends have significant implications for the implementation of the 2030 Agenda for Sustainable Development, this chapter is intended to analyse the interlinkages between a few selected macroeconomic issues and the achievement of the SDGs, organized in two parts.

The first part is focused on the greater-than-ever need for international cooperation and multilateral solutions in order to achieve shared goals in the three main areas of sustainable development: international trade, international finance and climate change.

The second part is focused on a few domestic structural challenges that are perceived as major obstacles to the achievement of the SDGs for many countries, namely, excessive dependence on commodities with volatile prices and persistently high levels of inequality.

Strengthening international cooperation and multilateralism

International trade policy

Trade tensions escalated in 2018, posing a threat to growth in international trade and output as well as to the very foundations of the rules-based multilateral trading system (MTS). As discussed in chapter I, the United States has implemented a series of unilateral measures in the form of tariff hikes since early 2018, triggering retaliatory measures by affected countries. This development is unprecedented in the history of the contemporary international trading system, where unilateral measures are precluded except under exceptional circumstances.

Rising trade tensions and the multilateral trading system

There are significant uncertainties over the international trading system

The ongoing trade disputes have created tremendous uncertainty over the evolution of the international trading system. Systemically, a spiral of unilateral trade barriers and retaliations goes directly against the very spirit of multilateral cooperation and challenges the integrity of the MTS. Furthermore, in heightened trade tensions, there are no winners, but only losers, especially among developing countries, while in bilateral negotiations the dominant trading partner tends to gain the most (Alschner et al., 2017). Thus, a move away from multilateral agreements is likely to herald less-favourable arrangements for small de-

2 Before the global financial crisis, trade and financial liberalization—and globalization, more generally—had already been criticized for being unfair to developing countries (see, for example, Stiglitz, 2002).

3 Globalization is defined here as the integration of countries through increased flows of trade, capital, technology, ideas and peoples.

veloping countries. Strengthening multilateralism and international cooperation is crucial in supporting least developed countries (LDCs) in their pursuit of strong and sustained export growth (see box II.1 that discusses SDG target 17.11 on doubling the LDC share of global exports).

Unilateral measures and countermeasures pose a challenge to the multilateral trading system

The unilateral measures and countermeasures represent a major challenge to the rules-based MTS. In the current context of trade tensions, some 27 cases (as of November 2018) were brought to the World Trade Organization (WTO) dispute settlement mechanism (DSM).[4] Figure II.1 shows that the total number of active trade disputes has been rising in recent years. This demonstrates the continued legitimacy and authority enjoyed by the system underpinning the rules-based MTS. On the other hand, adjudication of complex and large-scale cases could confront the DSM with significant challenges. These measures raise difficult legal questions of a systemic nature, and how the cases are handled could have wider institutional implications.

The dispute settlement mechanism ensures enforcement and compliance of the rules-based MTS...

The rules-based MTS requires an effective enforcement system. This role is assured by the WTO DSM, which, unlike many other international courts, guarantees automaticity in panel proceedings and remedial actions through suspension of trade concessions in case of non-compliance. This system has been widely used by WTO members. Since its establishment in 1995, the DSM has received 572 requests for consultations. It has facilitated amicable resolution of disputes, and when they reach litigation stage, compliance to rulings has been secured in 90 per cent of the cases. However, the process can be lengthy, as the DSM cannot prevent the parties involved in the dispute from maintaining disputed measures until all procedural requirements, including review by the Appellate Body, are completed. This can take several years. Implementation of rulings in some complex cases by large countries has proven to be difficult in the past.

Figure II.1
Total number of active trade disputes, 1996–2018

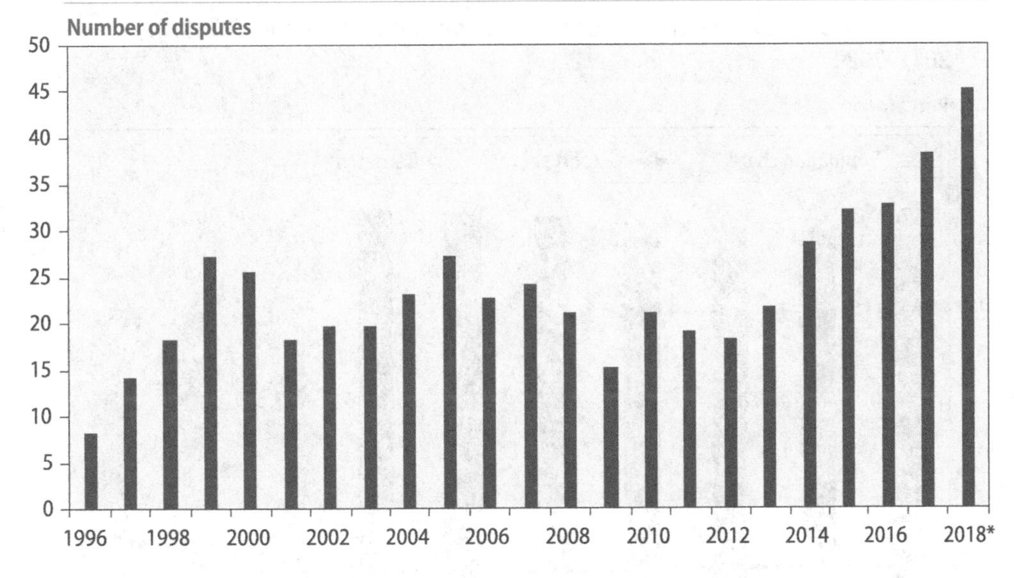

Source: World Trade Organization (WTO).
Notes: Several disputes are counted as one if they deal with the same subject matter. Data for 2018 are UN/DESA estimates based on information up to 28 September 2018.

4 These include cases raised against the US Section 232 tariff measures on steel and aluminum by China, India, Canada, Mexico, Norway, the Russian Federation, Switzerland, Turkey and the European Union (EU); by the United States of America against the countermeasures to the US Section 232 tariffs taken by Canada, China, Mexico, the Russian Federation, Turkey and the EU; against US safeguard measures on washing machines by the Republic of Korea and on solar panels by China and the Republic of Korea; against China's measures affecting intellectual property rights by the United States and transfer of technology by the EU, and against US Section 301 tariffs by China.

Box II.1

Strengthening multilateralism and international cooperation to achieve SDG target 17.11

Doubling the global share of least developed countries' (LDC) exports by 2020 (Sustainable Development Goals (SDGs) target 17.11) remains elusive. As of 2017, the share of merchandise trade not only remained well under the 2.06 per cent target, but has remained below the 2011 benchmark year value since 2013 (figure II.1.1). Similarly, the LDC share in global services exports remains broadly unchanged at about 0.7 per cent. The fall in merchandise trade share was mainly driven by declining LDC export prices: export volume grew by about the same rate as total global trade while prices declined by 6 per cent annually.

Several obstacles are impeding the progress towards the SDG target, including the high degree of export concentration in low value added activities, insufficient resources to support structural transformations, and barriers to market access. For example, top 10 goods account for 61.8 per cent of merchandise exports of the LDCs in 2017—more than double the world average.[a] Moreover, primary and resource based manufactured goods account for 58.8 per cent while low technology products capture 29 per cent of exports—again, about twice the global average.[b]

Structural issues, among others, lie behind these challenges. LDCs often have insufficient domestic productive capacities in activities generating high value addition and industries requiring advanced technologies, know-how and diverse human skills. Structural transformation requires carefully crafted and coordinated development polices as well as financial resources. In contrast to some oil-rich countries, LDCs are also lacking financial resources for development in crucial areas such as infrastructure, education and access to technologies.

Insufficient international collaboration to support access to markets still poses a barrier to the trade performance of LDCs. Issues such as non-tariff measures (NTMs), logistics, connectivity and trade facilitation can represent larger hurdles to exports than tariffs. Eliminating the distortionary trade effects of NTMs, for example, could increase LDC exports to Group of Twenty countries by $23 billion, equivalent to a more than 10 per cent rise in total exports and more than twice the impact of tariff-free market access (Nicita and Seiermann, 2016).

a UNCTADstat. 3-digit SITC classification, Rev. 3, available from http://unctadstat.unctad.org/EN/Classifications/DimSitcRev3Products_Official_Hierarchy.pdf.

b UNCTADstat. Lall classification, available from http://unctadstat.unctad.org/EN/Classifications/DimSitcRev3Products_Ldc_Hierarchy.pdf.

Figure II.1.1

LDC share of world merchandise exports, population and the SDG target, 2011–2020

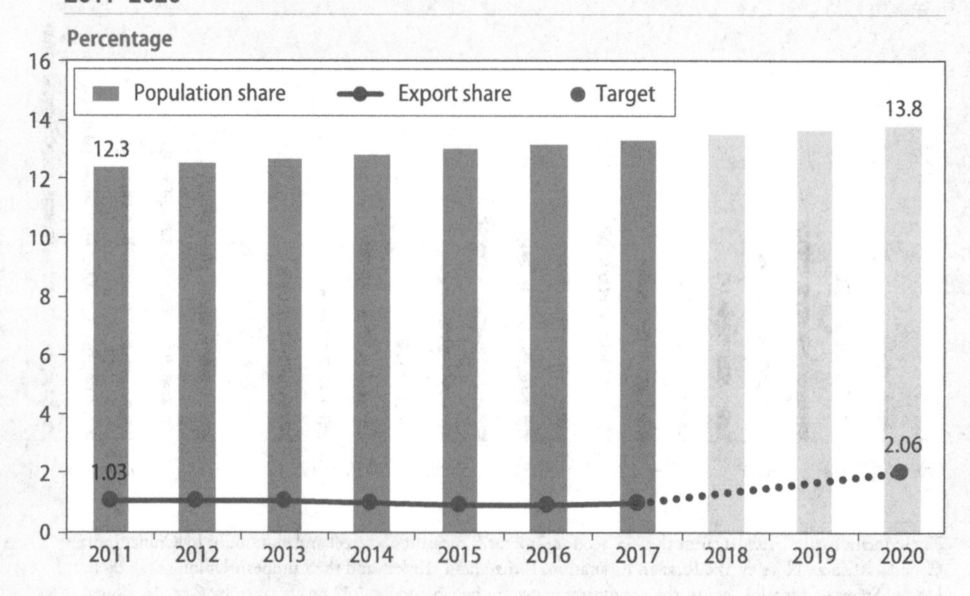

Source: UNCTADstat.

Note: 2018–2020 population figures are UNCTAD projections.

(continued)

Box II.1 (*continued*)

New risks are also emerging as global tensions build up. Some developed countries are trying to replace the existing trade preferences favouring the LDCs by bilateral trade agreements based on reciprocity. Research by UNCTAD shows that trade agreements are often recycled from previous treaties, and powerful countries act as "rule makers" whereas poorer ones become "rule takers". While the asymmetric bargaining power allows the former to get internally consistent and beneficial treaties, the latter accepts the deals that are closer to their trade partners' interests. Thus, rule makers on average experience a larger increase in exports once the agreement enters into force than rule takers (Seiermann, forthcoming).

In contrast to bilateral agreements, the preferential trade arrangements for LDCs are often unilateral and extend the product coverage beyond the Generalized System of Preferences. Their substitution by bilateral agreements when negotiation powers are asymmetric may damage prospects for achieving SDG 17.11, impose losses on many LDCs and hamper trade among developing countries, which plays a vital role in fostering local production in high value added activities. Intra-African trade, for example, has a larger share of manufactured goods, and medium and high technology content, than the continent's exports to the rest of the world (UNCTAD, 2018d).

Strengthening regional integration among developing countries is a strategy for enhancing domestic markets and boosting trade in an uncertain global trade context. In this respect, the African Continental Free Trade Area (see Box III.3) and other South-South initiatives can help to achieve sustained export growth in the LDCs.

Authors: Mesut Saygili and Julia Seiermann (UNCTAD/DITC/TAB).

In 2018, the United States introduced global tariffs on steel and aluminium products. The tariffs were imposed on the grounds of national security concerns under Section 232 of the US Trade Expansion Act of 1962, which gives large discretion to the United States President in taking measures for national security reasons. This has been contested by several affected countries. Under General Agreement on Tariffs and Trade (GATT) Article XXI on security exception, any action could be taken in cases of substantial national security concerns such as "war or other emergency in international relations". This clause has, in practice, rarely been used. Affected countries argue that the current political situation in the United States does not warrant such emergency measures, while the United States holds the view that the issue of national security is not subjected to review by the DSM.

The United States has also recently imposed a wide range of tariffs on goods imported from China, under Section 301 of the US Trade Act of 1974, which allows the United States President to take actions against trade practices by its trading partners considered to be "unfair". Section 301 of the US Trade Act of 1974 was widely used as a trade policy instrument in the 1980s and 1990s. This often led to grey-zone policy arrangements such as voluntary export restraints (VERs). The inception of the WTO in 1995 has significantly reduced its relevance, as the new WTO rules on the DSM have prohibited unilateral measures without first going through the WTO dispute settlement procedures. Sections 301–310 of the US Trade Act of 1974 were challenged in the late 1990s. The panel in the case ruled, in essence, that the law was not in itself incompatible with WTO rules, but needed to be implemented in a manner consistent with them. Until now, the United States had refrained from taking recourse to Section 301 since the creation of the WTO. The tariff measures against China marked a departure from this practice.

...but handling current trade disputes poses a challenge to the dispute settlement mechanism

In view of their systemic implications, handling these cases could place the DSM under tremendous strain. If the recently imposed unilateral tariff measures were judged to be justified, this might open the door to far greater use of unilateral measures by other countries, which risks eroding the disciplines of the world trade regime. If the measures were deemed incompatible with WTO agreements, securing compliance could prove to be a daunting challenge. Either way, the effectiveness of the DSM may suffer and the integrity of the MTS in general could be negatively affected, which constitutes a key challenge ahead.

The increase in trade tensions comes at a time when the WTO DSM has already been under pressure owing to the blockage of the appointment of new Appellate Body members (judges) due to the lack of consensus among WTO members. Four out of seven seats were vacant as of October 2018 leaving only three judges in the roster, the minimum number required to hear an appeal. In December 2019, another seat will become vacant at which time the Appellate Body would cease to function. Paralysis in the DSM would critically weaken the rules-based MTS.

Implications for multilateral negotiations

Unilateral and bilateral trade policy responses partly reflect limited multilateral progress...

Recourse to unilateral actions and bilateral approaches rather than multilateral approaches can be partly attributed to the limited and slow progress made in the MTS in key areas. This includes the inducement of market-opening trade liberalization, rule-making on modern trade issues and market-oriented trade policy reforms abroad, particularly in emerging economies, and the overall lack of progress in the Doha Round negotiations launched in 2001. WTO rules and the Doha negotiating agenda are considered by some to be outdated, given the rapid and drastic changes in the way trade is conducted within global value chains, enabled by a vibrant digital economy and services activities.

...as the negotiations under the Doha Round were complex and inefficient

The Doha Round was expected to redress imbalances inherent in the WTO architecture by placing development at its heart and vigorously tackling agriculture, services and the development agenda across negotiating issues. However, the negotiations struggled with single issues and consensus rule. Some developed economies have increasingly questioned the adequacy of treating large developing countries with a growing share of global trade in the same way as other smaller and more vulnerable developing countries. They advocate reforms to ensure that each country undertakes commitments in a manner commensurate with its share in global trade.

Given the deadlock, more pragmatic and flexible approaches have been suggested

The incapacity to continue negotiations on the sole basis of the existing Doha mandates became apparent at the Tenth WTO Ministerial Conference (MC10) in 2015. Developed countries did not reaffirm the existing Doha mandates and stressed the need for new approaches, including plurilateral ones, and new issues in achieving meaningful results. It was overtly argued that inclusion of new issues would be required to secure a balance of trade-offs across different negotiating areas. Most developing countries underscored the importance of the Doha mandate, the multilateral process and the development dimension.

Despite some ambiguity of mandates, significant efforts are being made to revitalize multilateral trade negotiations through a more pragmatic, incremental and flexible approach. Proposals for new approaches and new issues appear to have been partially taken on board in the latest Ministerial Conference (MC11) held in 2017. This includes plurilateral initiatives to discuss "new issues" relevant to twenty-first century trade, most notably on electronic commerce, as well as investment facilitation; micro, small and medium enterprises (MSMEs); and domestic regulation of services.[5]

This leaves open the possibility of new approaches, while also addressing traditional Doha negotiating issues on an issue-by-issue basis where feasible. This approach has already

5 The proponents of these initiatives emphasized that new ways of doing business would allow "willing countries" to move faster on specific issues. The critics expressed concerns over the possible implications for core WTO principles, including multilateralism and consensus rule.

borne fruit in delivering specific negotiated outcomes in respect of trade facilitation and food security in 2013, and elimination of agricultural export subsidies in 2015. On this basis, negotiations aimed at eliminating harmful fishery subsidies are being pursued with a view to finalization by MC12, now scheduled for June 2020. This is expected to contribute to delivering on SDG target 14.6 for prohibiting certain forms of fisheries subsidies.

The way forward

International trade is a crucial dimension of the 2030 Agenda for Sustainable Development...

The 2030 Agenda for Sustainable Development recognizes the role of trade as a powerful enabler of sustainable development. Goal 17 of the SDGs defines trade as a means of implementation, and it calls for revitalizing the Global Partnership for Sustainable Development, including on trade. The central element is to "promote a universal, rules-based, open, non-discriminatory and equitable multilateral trading system" under the WTO (target 17.10 of the SDGs). A robust MTS, and meaningful progress in a revitalized multilateral process, are therefore essential for the achievement of Goal 17 while accelerating progress towards other SDGs. Furthermore, every effort must be made to protect the integrity and viability of the MTS. In fact, the WTO continues to attract new members with 36 countries having acceded since 1995, demonstrating its legitimacy.[6] While there is strong support for the rules-based MTS, it is essential to also recognize and address its shortcomings.

...as trade integration remains a major driver for progress

Agreement on the case for economic integration is widely shared, as evidenced by continued engagement of economies in regional integration processes. Integration at the regional level could enhance countries' readiness for further trade policy reforms and multilateral cooperation at a later stage. In March 2018, the eleven members of the original Trans-Pacific Partnership, other than the United States, signed the Comprehensive and Progressive Agreement for Trans-Pacific Partnership. A web of large-scale bilateral free trade agreements is emerging, such as those between Canada and the European Union (EU), or Japan and the EU. Negotiations are underway for the Regional Comprehensive Economic Partnership Agreement in Asia and the Pacific. The case for developmental integration has also been acknowledged in Africa through a historic signing in March 2018 of the agreement establishing the African Continental Free Trade Area (AfCFTA) (see box III.3).

Action at national, bilateral and multilateral levels is required

To sustain the viability of the MTS, actions at bilateral and multilateral levels as well as at national levels are necessary. The resolution of trade tensions arising from US tariff measures and countermeasures would need to be left in large part to bilateral discussions between the countries concerned. In the light of the primacy of the rules-based MTS, any bilateral solutions that may be sought could include a renewed commitment to multilateral rules, processes and institutions. This could also include the commitment to abide by the primacy of dispute settlement processes, and de-link bilateral trade tensions from ongoing multilateral Doha round negotiations, such as on fishery subsidies, so that the existing Doha negotiations could advance on a stand-alone basis where possible.

At the multilateral level, the system requires adaptation and modernization, addressing concerns over the possible limitations of the MTS, including delivering negotiated outcomes and securing compliance. Discussions could include ways to strengthen and modernize the MTS through reforms in its modus operandi to make the system more relevant and effective in dealing with twenty-first century trade realities and delivering results that will be conducive to inclusive and sustainable development. In the current context, various initiatives have been taken to examine possible reform options, for example, in the areas

6 Since 2008, 13 countries have become member of the WTO.

of subsidies, technology transfer, digital trade and the special and differential treatment (SDT) principle.[7]

WTO members have different views with regard to the future direction of the MTS. For instance, the developing countries stress the need for an MTS that does not undermine their efforts to pursue development, including industrial development. Hence, any reform efforts should take different interests and concerns on board in a balanced manner and prioritize practical and actionable solutions that will work for all members.

The MTS must be aligned with the SDGs

The backlash against the MTS also calls for strengthening policy responses at the national level. These responses need to focus specifically on the consequences of trade and trade agreements for domestic labour markets. In this context, trade adjusted assistance programmes play an important role by providing financial support, facilitating skills development and helping workers find new jobs. Trade policy and liberalization approaches within the framework of the strengthened MTS should aim at economic growth that is sustainable in all three dimensions.

Revenue mobilization for sustainable development

The investment needs associated with implementing the 2030 Agenda for Sustainable Development are immense. Currently mobilized domestic public resources are insufficient to meet these needs. The situation is most extreme in the LDCs: total tax revenues in about half of them fall below the 15 per cent of gross domestic product (GDP) level that recent research suggests is the minimum necessary to fund basic state functions (Gaspar et al., 2016). This is especially the case in countries that are experiencing or have recently experienced conflict. Within this context, the Addis Ababa Action Agenda on Financing for Development, adopted by the United Nations in 2015, provides comprehensive guidance to Member States of the United Nations and sets out policy options for enhancing the financing of sustainable development, including domestic revenue mobilization. The Addis Agenda recognizes the critical role to be played by development-oriented and progressive tax policies, modernized tax systems, and more efficient tax collection procedures in developing countries. At the same time, it promotes improved multilateral approaches, especially in the form of strengthened international tax cooperation and efforts to combat illicit financial flows.

Global trends in tax revenues

Tax-to-GDP ratios have risen in most developing regions since 2000

Increases in the nominal level of domestic public resources are primarily generated by economic growth. In general, developing countries have increased their tax revenue over the last 15 years both in nominal terms and as a share of GDP.[8] Median tax revenue excluding social contributions as a proportion of GDP has gone up in most groups of countries since 2000, but large regional disparities in tax revenue generation persist (figure II.2 and table

7 See for instance, European Commission (2018a) and United States Trade Representative (2018). At the Trade Negotiating Committee and Heads of Delegations meeting in the WTO on 16 October 2018, many developing country members stated their positions on the WTO reform.

8 Generating consistent, comparable revenue data and measuring revenue as a percentage of GDP is a complex undertaking. For example, there are changes and unevenness in the implementation of the system of national accounts in some countries, differences between federal and non-federal systems, and differences between budgetary and other central government information. These challenges create difficulties in aggregation, as well as in measuring trends over time.

Figure II.2
Median tax revenue by country groupings, 2000, 2010 and 2015

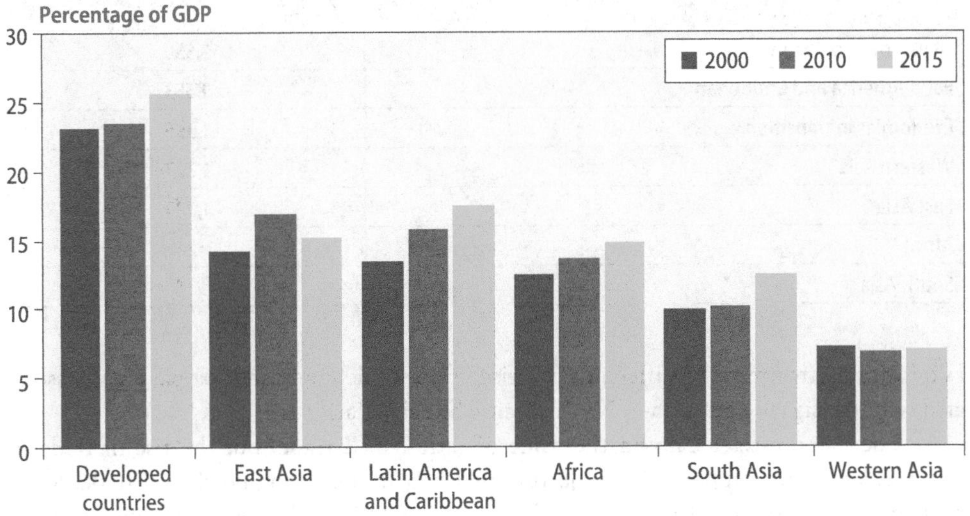

Source: UN/DESA calculations, based on the IMF 2017 World Revenue Longitudinal Database (WoRLD).

Note: Only countries that have observations for all three years have been included.

II.1). These stem from a number of factors, including differences in national economic structures, tax administration capacity and policy choices. Developed countries continue to have the highest shares of taxation, recording an increase in the median tax revenue from 23.4 per cent in 2010 to 25.5 per cent in 2015. On the other side of the spectrum, South Asia and Western Asia have the lowest tax-to-GDP ratios. Positive trends have recently been observed in Africa and in Latin America and the Caribbean. In these regions, the median tax-to-GDP ratio has risen considerably since 2000. From 2010 to 2015, 36 African countries saw increases (gaining on average 2.7 percentage points), while 14 countries recorded a decline. Of those, the biggest declines were registered in countries that are hydrocarbon exporters, such as Algeria, Angola, Chad and Nigeria, reflecting the effect of lower oil prices in commodity-dependent economies.

International tax cooperation

The need for international tax cooperation is increasing

In a world of significant cross-border trade, investment and financial flows, there are also limits to what countries can do on their own through domestic taxation policies. The speed and ease of financial transfers, and the increasing importance of non-tangible assets (which can easily be shifted between countries) in modern economies, underline the need for international tax cooperation. For many years, international tax cooperation focused on the conclusion of bilateral tax treaties, which had the principle aim of reducing double taxation. Recently, international tax cooperation has increasingly looked at closing loopholes, preventing tax avoidance, increasing the exchange of information between tax authorities to limit tax avoidance by all types of taxpayers, and curbing illicit financial flows.

Debates have escalated regarding the most appropriate way to allocate taxing rights on the profits of multinational enterprises (MNEs), as well as about the tax treatment of cross-border services and digital transactions. Attention is focused on transfer pricing between branches or subsidiaries of MNEs located in different tax jurisdictions; on appropriate tax treatment of the provision of intellectual property, such as trademark usage; on technical services, such as management functions between parts of the same MNE; as well

Table II.1
Per capita tax revenue by region, 2015

Region	Per capita tax revenue, dollars
Developed countries	9,550
Latin America and Caribbean	1,553
Economies in transition	1,395
Western Asia	1,327
East Asia	1,233
Africa	287
South Asia	247

Sources: UN/DESA calculations, based on data from the IMF 2017 World Revenue Longitudinal Dataset; IMF World Economic Outlook October 2018 database; United Nations World Population Prospects 2017.

as on varying treatment in different tax jurisdictions of debt and interest payments associated with the significant intra-MNE financing by subsidiaries.

There is no exact data on the value of intra-MNE trade, but the rise of trade in intermediate goods supports the conjecture that it is an increasing portion of trade. Some estimates put the total at 30 per cent of all international trade.[9] While there is international consensus that taxes should be paid where economic activity occurs and value is created (United Nations, 2015, para. 23), the value of trade in intangibles and the location of value creation are hard to define and measure.

Tax challenges are compounded by digitalization and other emergent technologies

The existing challenges in determining the appropriate tax base related to MNE activity are compounded by the transformation of many economies through digitalization and other emergent technologies. Greater access to information and enhanced digital systems and processing capabilities opens new options for tax authorities to improve collection and compliance. At the same time, the digitalization of business models makes the determination of the appropriate jurisdiction for taxation more difficult. Digitalized companies may be able to generate large sales with little or no physical presence in an economy. They may also generate value by monetizing the data obtained from the use of their services by end consumers. There are many different views on how to adapt international tax rules to the digitalization of the economy. While norm changes are currently being discussed within the EU, the Organization for Economic Cooperation and Development (OECD), the Inclusive Framework for BEPS Implementation (a Group of Twenty (G20)/OECD initiative), and at the United Nations Committee of Experts on International Cooperation in Tax Matters, a number of countries are moving ahead with measures such as digital services taxes. In setting new norms related to taxation of digitalized economic activity, policymakers need to think carefully about the implications, especially as the rules are likely to affect an increasing portion of their tax base over time. New rules may imply different allocations of taxing rights, and these rights may be distributed in ways that are counter-productive to achieving greater convergence and equity in international taxation.

Multilateral approaches must leave space for effective national tax policies

Given the challenges surrounding the allocation of tax bases for an increasingly complex array of intra-firm and digital transactions, international tax cooperation and inclusive norm setting have become even more important. International tax discussions are usually dominated by sovereignty concerns, as tax policies define the relationship between citizens and the state and undergird the social contract and the provision of public services. Furthermore, as markets for many new digital services are frequently dominated by a few firms,

9 For a deeper discussion, see UNCTAD (2013) and UNCTAD (2018a, box 2.1).

their power to influence policymaking should be considered. To guard against international tax norms that may disadvantage some countries, Member States have agreed that efforts in international tax cooperation should be universal in approach and scope and should fully take into account the different needs and capacities of all countries. In the digitalized era, a multilateral approach to taxation is important. Nevertheless, this approach needs to leave space for countries to adopt effective tax policies that enhance domestic public finance for sustainable development.

Significant progress has been made in several areas of tax cooperation...

The strengthening and scaling up of international tax cooperation is still a work in progress. New multilateral legal instruments are being developed, which represents a fundamental change of direction for tax cooperation away from bilateral approaches. Considerable progress has been made in several areas: exchanging information about the assets held in accounts in financial institutions; preparation and exchange of country-by-country reports of multinational enterprises; mutual assistance among tax administrations for sharing information and resolving disputes; and instruments to implement changes to international tax norms agreed by the OECD and G20 in 2015 to cut down on base erosion and profit shifting (BEPS).[10]

...but the lack of a fully multilateral system creates challenges

A key milestone was passed in 2017, as 49 jurisdictions began exchanging information for the first time under the Global Forum on Transparency and Exchange of Information for Tax Purposes' Automatic Exchange of Information standard. This requires tax authorities to automatically exchange financial account information of non-residents with the tax authorities of the account holders' country of residence based on a common reporting standard (CRS). A further 53 jurisdictions are starting such exchanges in 2018. However, there is a systemic imbalance in application of these norms, as many developing countries either find it difficult to participate or choose not to for a variety of reasons, often because of a lack of capacity of tax authorities to meet the reciprocity demands of the systems. For example, out of over 100 participating jurisdictions in the Automatic Exchange of Information standard, only one is an LDC. The lack of a fully multilateral system will undermine the prospects for those that want to use such cooperation to crack down on undeclared offshore wealth and other forms of tax evasion. Two types of challenges emerge: those resulting from countries opting out, and those from countries excluded from participation. First, non-participation of some jurisdictions will provide options for tax evaders to continue to hide wealth. Although the CRS is based on the United States Foreign Account Tax Compliance Act, the US Government has not yet signed on to the international standard and is not participating in reciprocal exchanges under the multilateral system set up at the Global Forum. This leaves a major economy, which is both a source and destination of wealth, out of the primary international system for tax-information exchange. Second, many smaller and poorer countries with limited capacity in their tax administrations are excluded. As a result, some of those that are furthest behind in tax collection are unlikely to benefit from increased multilateralism.

Exchange of country-by-country information on MNEs, which will start in 2019, is another example of the importance of multilateralism. At present, the exchange will be done through a bilateral process. MNEs will file a full set of country-by-country reports in their home jurisdictions. Jurisdictions that host MNE branches or subsidiaries will only gain access to those reports through exchanges with the host-country tax authority. Countries have submitted expressions of interest for exchange to the OECD, and when jurisdictions

10 For a longer description of the BEPS Action Plan and its potential implications, see United Nations (2016), pp. 103–106.

have expressed reciprocal interest, there is a bilateral match for exchange. More than 1400 of these matches have now been activated. However, of these, only 477 involve middle-income countries, and no LDCs have any matches (United Nations, 2018a). Although some LDCs have requested matches, no developed country has prioritized them in the process. This leaves opportunities for tax avoidance and evasion, harming the efforts of excluded countries to mobilize revenue. More work needs to be done to enable all developing countries to benefit from new tax norms, especially the poorest ones.

At the same time, reforms to international tax norms, which have been agreed in bodies that are not inclusive of all countries, will impact sustainable development across all jurisdictions. Further analysis is needed on the impact of these reforms, especially for the poorest countries, given that the ability to effectively tax relevant transactions must be maintained. Unfortunately, the data that is needed to complete this analysis—such as complete aggregate information from the country-by-country reports of multinational enterprises—is not yet available in the public sphere. This hampers the capacity of international organizations and researchers to assess the consequences and make relevant policy recommendations. Ultimately, more inclusive multilateralism in the tax sphere will ensure that no countries are left behind, and that the world can achieve shared progress on securing public revenue that is vital to sustainable development-oriented investment.

Illicit financial flows

Illicit financial flows are a major obstacle for domestic resource mobilization

While improved tax administration, better national tax policies, and strengthened international tax cooperation are essential factors in mobilizing domestic resources for sustainable development, illicit financial flows (IFFs) represent a major obstacle to these efforts. Member States expressed their deep concern about IFFs and have repeatedly called for greater international cooperation to combat illicit financial flows.[11] However, there remains no universally agreed definition of what constitutes IFFs, although there are some parameters for identifying IFFs that are frequently referenced. First, illicit financial flows are often defined as constituting money that is illegally earned, transferred or used and that crosses borders. Second, there are generally three categories of IFFs, although these are not mutually exclusive or comprehensive: IFFs originating from transnational criminal activity; corruption-related IFFs; and tax-related IFFs. Even within the above parameters, controversies remain, particularly on how to treat tax-related IFFs. Tax practices such as BEPS are sometimes challenging because of differences in legal standards across countries, the absence of legal frameworks, and different interpretations and acceptance of norms on international taxation. Figure II.3 shows a schematic representation of components and channels of IFFs, noting that multiple components and channels can be combined in specific transactions. As the different components of IFFs are not comparable, aggregation across channels and components could result in double counting, and analysis of channels or components separately is more beneficial in designing policy responses to prevent illicit flows.

Tackling IFFs more effectively will not only bolster domestic resource mobilization but also help build trust and confidence in the fairness of the tax, legal and financial systems, the efficiency of law enforcement, and in government as a whole. The lack of agreement on the definition of IFFs need not curtail or constrain the important work of countries on strengthening existing institutions and policies for combatting IFFs in both source and destination countries. Efforts can be directed at both the ultimate owners of the resources involved

11 General Assembly resolution 72/207 of 20 December 2017.

Figure II.3
Schematic representation of components and channels of illicit financial flows

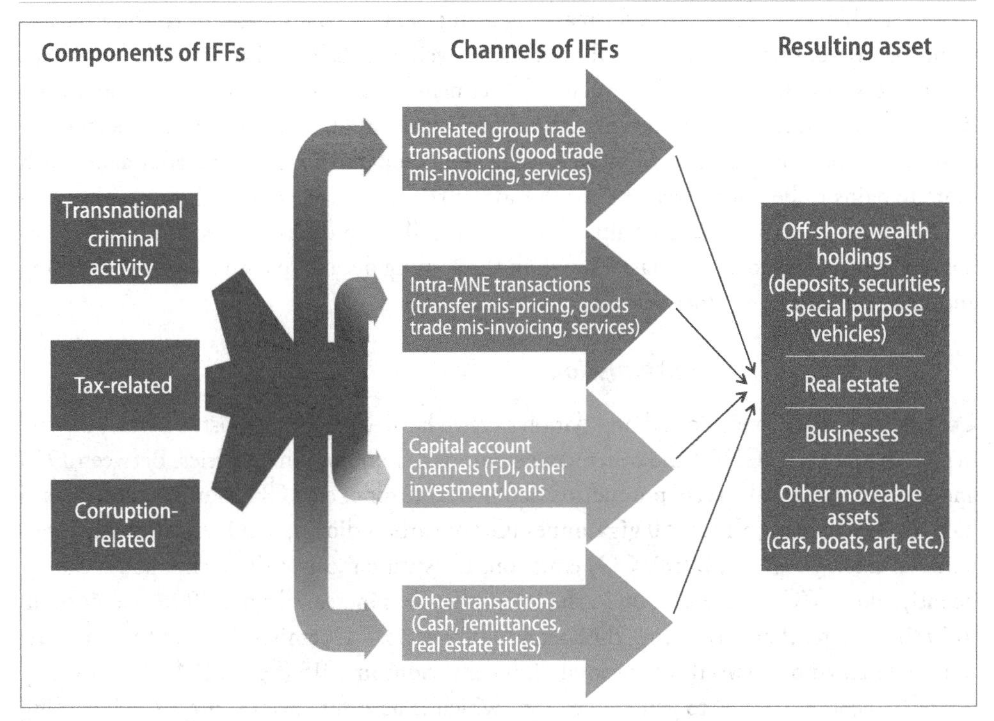

Source: United Nations (2018a).

in IFFs as well as at the enablers of transactions, including financial institutions, accountants and other professional service providers.

Multilateral approaches for sharing beneficial ownership information are required

One critical area of work is tackling the anonymity of transactions, which is facilitated by shell companies and trusts. New international standards have been agreed, that keep beneficial ownership information in a manner available to country authorities. However, except for a few efforts in Europe, initiatives for the publication or sharing of beneficial ownership information have faltered. Further consideration should be given to advancing the exchange of beneficial ownership information among tax authorities, but no standard or multilateral accord has yet been developed. Deeper cooperation to develop such standards and greater financial transparency would facilitate efforts towards encouraging tax compliance, containing BEPS and combatting IFFs.

Macroeconomic conditions and climate change

The baseline outlook points to continued robust growth of economic activity in 2019–2020 at the global level. However, the adverse impact of modern economic activity on the environment is apparent. This includes loss of biodiversity and ecosystems, deforestation, water pollution, deterioration of air and soil quality, and emissions-driven climate change. Economic activity continues to be powered by fossil fuel, which in turn leads to rising greenhouse gas emissions and climate change.

The current scientific consensus indicates that a fundamental shift in the way the global economy produces goods and services is necessary in a short period of time to avert further serious damage to our natural and human systems and avoid "tipping points"—

thresholds beyond which certain impacts can no longer be avoided. Steep emissions reductions, and a decoupling of economic growth from equivalent increases in resource use, are required in all sectors, as are far-reaching changes in the energy sector, land use, urban planning, agriculture and industrial systems, as well as substantial mitigation and adaptation measures (IPCC, 2018).[12] Such a fundamental transformation requires policy action on many fronts, acceleration of technological innovation, and significant behavioural changes. While some progress has been achieved compared to a few decades ago, much more remains to be done given the magnitude of the transitions required. Strong international cooperation and a scaling up of countries' collective efforts is necessary for greenhouse gas emissions to decline fast enough in the coming decade to confine global warming and meet the Paris Agreement targets.

Economic growth and emissions

Continued global economic and population growth have driven the persistent, worrying rise in greenhouse gases (GHG) and other gases stemming from human activities. Between 1990 and 2015, as the global level of production doubled, anthropogenic GHG emissions increased 45 per cent, reaching almost 50 gigatonnes (Gt) of carbon dioxide (CO_2) equivalent (International Energy Agency, 2018). CO_2 emissions constitute most of these emissions. Consequently, global CO_2 concentration in the atmosphere has increased since 2000 at a speed up to 10 times faster than any during the past 800,000 years. CO_2 emissions from fuel combustion represented over two thirds of total GHG emissions in 2015 (figure II.4). The primary use of fuel combustion is to generate energy, which is used for various purposes, including engine power, heat and electricity. The energy sector is thus the largest contributor to global anthropogenic GHG emissions.

CO_2 emissions have likely reached a record high in 2018

After three years of remaining flat, global energy-related CO_2 emissions increased 1.5 per cent in 2017, reaching a historical high of 32.5 Gt. This resulted from the acceleration of global economic growth, supported by the relatively low cost of fossil fuels and weaker energy efficiency efforts, according to the International Energy Agency (IEA). Preliminary evidence of global energy-related CO_2 emissions suggests a further increase in 2018. At this rate, the IEA warns, current efforts to combat climate change are insufficient to meet the objectives of the Paris Agreement.

Insufficient energy efficiency gains and unchanged carbon content of energy prevent decoupling

Growth in GDP and emissions remains closely linked (figure II.5). A decomposition analysis of global CO_2 emissions into the contributions from economic activity, offset by gains in energy efficiency—defined as the global consumption of energy (in terms of oil equivalent) per unit of output—and emissions intensity of the global energy mix shows that the decline in emissions per unit of output produced has been insufficient to halt the rise in total carbon emissions. In 2017, a 1.0 per cent increase in world gross product was associated with a 0.5 per cent increase in global CO_2 emissions.

Nonetheless, the level of emissions per unit of output produced has declined substantially since 1990. This reflects reductions in the energy intensity of production of approximately 1.5 per cent per year between 1990 and 2017. The pace of efficiency gains has accelerated in recent years, averaging 2.3 per cent in 2014–2016, but slowed to 1.7

12 This section focuses on climate change, but environmental and social sustainability is also under increasing threat from the unfettered rise in natural resource use. Sustainability will require reducing both the carbon- and resource-intensity of our production and consumption patterns.

Figure II.4
Global anthropogenic GHG emissions, 2015

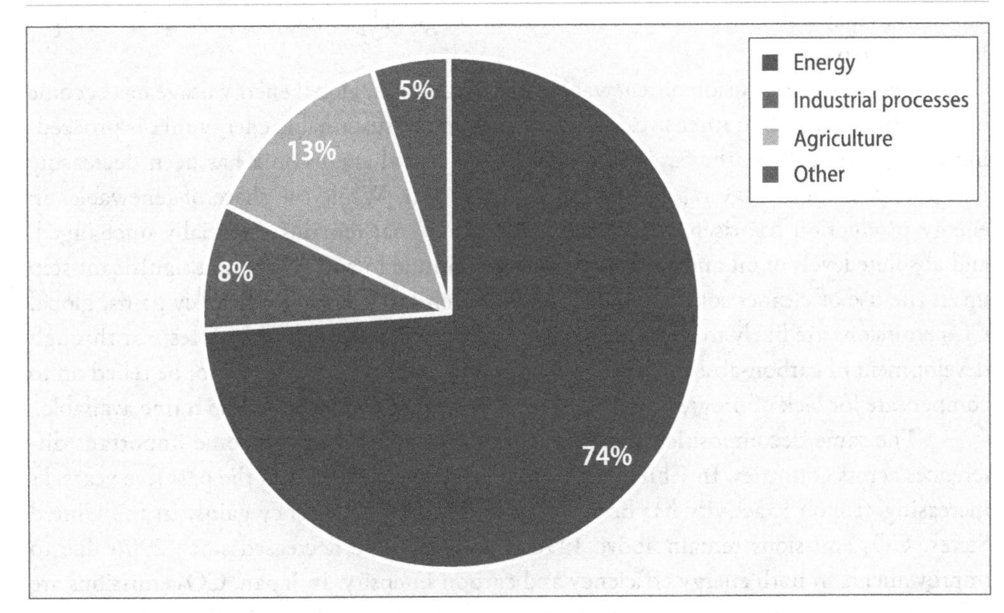

Source: International Energy Agency (IEA).

Note: "Energy" includes IPCC categories Fuel Combustion and Fugitive. "Other" includes large-scale biomass burning (excluding CO_2), post-burn decay, peat decay, indirect N_2O emissions from non-agricultural emissions of NOx and NH_3, waste, and solvent use.

Figure II.5
GDP and emissions growth

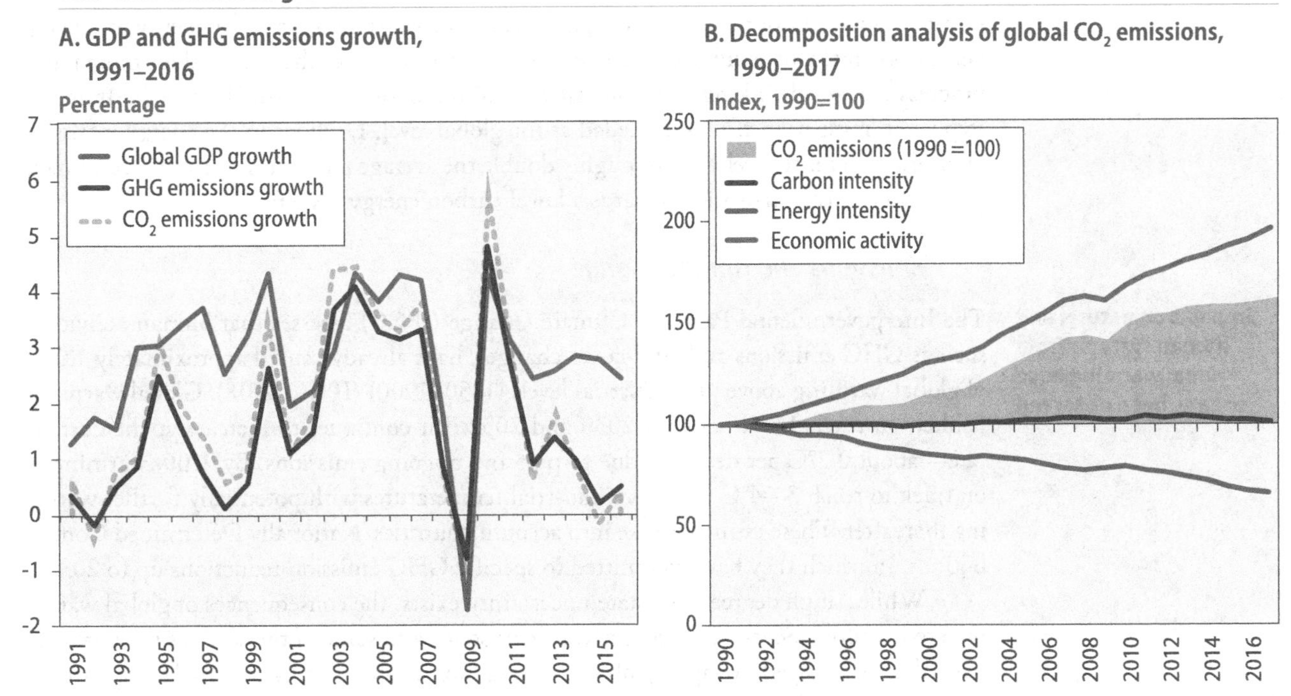

Sources: UN/DESA calculations, based on data from the United Nations Statistics Division (UNSD) and PBL Netherlands Environmental Assessment Agency (left) (2013–2016 emissions are estimates) and UN/DESA staff estimations, based on data from European Commission, IEA and UNSD (right).

Note: Carbon intensity is total emissions divided by global consumption of energy. Energy intensity is global consumption of energy divided by world gross product. Economic activity is world gross product in 2010 market prices.

per cent in 2017 due to the low fossil-fuel price environment and weaker improvement in efficiency policy coverage and stringency (IEA, 2018). Declines in the energy intensity of production may also reflect shifts in the structure of global production, towards less energy-intensive sectors.

Stronger emissions reduction requires tangible progress in lowering carbon intensity

Despite the expansion of renewables and natural gas, global energy usage has become only slightly less carbon intensive. Transition to a more sustainable energy mix is proceeding slowly. Since 2014, the carbon content of the global energy mix has been decreasing marginally, at an average rate of 0.6 per cent per year. While the share of renewables in energy production has risen, global consumption of coal remains essentially unchanged, and absolute levels of oil and gas consumption continue to rise. Without a significant step up in the use of cleaner sources of energy and much faster energy efficiency gains, global CO_2 emissions are likely to continue to rise. Any uptake of emissions by forests or through development of carbon-absorbing technologies is uncertain. Thus, it cannot be relied on to compensate for lack of progress on these fronts within the very short time frame available.

CO_2 emissions did not rise everywhere

The same decomposition analysis at the country level reveals some important differences across countries. In China, CO_2 emissions have stabilized in the past five years, as increasing economic activity has been matched by energy efficiency gains. In the United States, CO_2 emissions remain above 1990 levels, but have decreased since 2006 due to improvements in both energy efficiency and carbon intensity. In Japan, CO_2 emissions are decreasing as a result of improved energy efficiency per unit of GDP. Carbon intensity was also decreasing until 2011, but the nuclear power phase-out following the 2011 Fukushima nuclear disaster increased the carbon content of the energy produced. Similarly, in Germany, CO_2 emissions have stabilized, but the carbon intensity has increased mildly since 2011, possibly as a result of nuclear power phase-out. The substantial gains in energy efficiency and carbon intensity exhibited by some countries demonstrates the potential for more rapid progress towards delinking emissions growth from economic growth. However, a dramatic step up in mitigation efforts is needed at the global level. Declines in the energy intensity of production must accelerate to roughly double the average rate seen since 1990, combined with a much faster transition towards a lower carbon energy system.

Emissions and climate change

Impacts on natural and human systems from global warming have already been observed

The Intergovernmental Panel on Climate Change (IPCC) assesses that human activities, such as GHG emissions and land-cover changes, have already caused approximately 1.0°C of global warming above pre-industrial levels (1850–1900) (IPCC, 2018). Global warming is likely to reach 1.5°C between 2030 and 2052 if it continues to increase at the current rate—about 0.2°C per decade—due to past and ongoing emissions. By 2100, warming is on track to reach 3°–4°C above preindustrial temperatures with potentially further warming thereafter. These estimates take into account countries' Nationally Determined Contributions, in which they have committed to specific GHG emission reductions up to 2030.

While a high degree of climate uncertainty exists, the consequences of global warming are manifold. Several land and ocean ecosystems and some of the services they provide have already changed owing to global warming. Some impacts may be long lasting or irreversible, such as the loss of ecosystems.

Over the past few decades, the world has observed an increasing number of extreme weather events. According to Munich Re's NatCatSERVICE database, the number of registered weather-related loss events has more than tripled since the 1980s (figure II.6). The year 2017 ranks among the top five years in terms of number of natural catastrophes. While attribution of any given weather event to climate change alone is difficult, climate change is expected to increase the likelihood and intensity of extreme weather events, such as catastrophic floods, droughts and storms (IPCC, 2013). Furthermore, scientists have found that climate change was a significant driver of 65 per cent of 131 weather events examined in the last 6 years (Herring et al., 2018). Three of these events were considered to be beyond the bounds of natural variability, which means these events were not possible in a preindustrial climate, before human-induced greenhouse gases were changing the climate.

Negative growth effects are likely to be strongest in developing countries

Climate change already poses serious threats to communities. In 2017, there were 18 million new internal displacements in 135 countries due to weather disasters (Internal Displacement Monitoring Centre, 2018). Estimates of financial losses related to relevant[13] natural events reached $335 billion globally, of which less than half were insured ($140 billion) according to Munich Re's NatCatSERVICE database.[14] An alternative estimate puts the reported direct economic losses between 1998 and 2017 due to climate-related disasters at $2,245 billion (United Nations International Strategy for Disaster Reduction, 2018). Overall, reported losses from extreme weather events rose by 151 per cent between 1978–1997 and 1998–2017. However, these figures may underestimate actual loss value, as data is not available for nearly 90 per cent of disasters in low-income countries. Importantly, while absolute economic losses might be concentrated in high-income countries, the human cost of disasters falls overwhelmingly on low- and lower-middle-income countries (ibid.).

Climate change is expected to substantially dampen economic growth in many developed and developing economies. Warming is projected to be the highest in the Northern Hemisphere, where several of the world's largest economies are located. One study finds that limiting global warming to 1.5°C as opposed to 2.0°C would substantially reduce eco-

Figure II.6

Number of registered weather-related loss events worldwide, 1981–2017

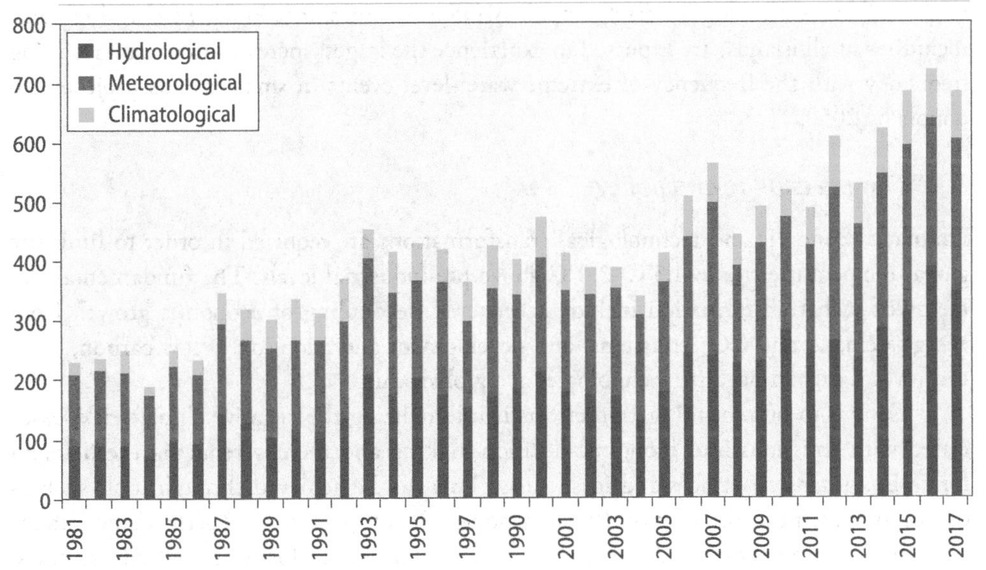

Source: NatCatSERVICE.

Note: Hydrological events include flooding (river floods, flash floods and storm surges) and wet mass movements (rock fall, landslides, avalanches and subsidence). Meteorological events include storms (tropical, extratropical and local windstorms). Climatological events include extreme temperatures (heat waves, freeze and extreme winter conditions), droughts and wildfires.

13 Relevant events are considered those where fatalities exceeded one person and normalized overall loss is equal to or higher than $100,000, $300,000, $1,000,000 or $3,000,000 (depending on assigned World Bank income group of each affected country).

14 Database was accessed on 7 December 2018.

nomic losses associated with climate change in China, Japan and the United States (Burke et al., 2018). Another study estimates that the economic damage in the United States from climate change would be roughly 1.2 per cent of GDP per 1.0°C increase on average under a scenario where GHG emissions continue to rise throughout the twenty-first century (Hsiang et al., 2017). Still, it is the developing economies in the tropics and Southern Hemisphere subtropics that are projected to experience the largest economic losses due to climate change.

Climate risks in SIDS and LDCs threaten infrastructure and tourism revenues

Small island developing States (SIDS) and LDCs are among those facing the highest risks of adverse consequences from climate change, as they are exposed to multiple interrelated climate risks. For example, drought is found to significantly increase the likelihood of sustained conflict, particularly for vulnerable countries or groups dependent on agriculture, which includes several LDCs. Additionally, many SIDS and LDCs derive a substantial proportion of national income (more than 15 per cent of GDP) and foreign exchange from tourism, which is threatened by climatic change. In SIDS, increasing global temperatures, intensifying storms and elevated thermal stress cause loss of tropical coral reefs and associated recreational services, while increasing the risk of wave-driven coastal flooding. A recent study found that an eventual one-metre sea level rise could partially or fully inundate 29 per cent of 900 coastal resorts in 19 Caribbean countries, with a substantially higher proportion (49–60 per cent) vulnerable to associated coastal erosion (Scott and Verkoeyen, 2017 and box II.2). A global vulnerability index covering 181 countries found that among those with the highest risks of climate-related losses are SIDS in the Caribbean, and Indian and Pacific Oceans (Scott and Gössling, 2018). In the case of 1.5°C warming, the Caribbean is expected to see higher temperatures, with longer warm spells and longer hot and dry spells. The effects would be more severe in the case of a 2°C increase (Taylor et al., 2018). Even at 1.5°C warming, several atoll islands might become uninhabitable due to increases in aridity, decreases in freshwater availability, and sea level rise. Changes in availability and quality of freshwater may adversely impact SIDS economies, too. Finally, tropical regions, including small islands, are expected to experience the largest increases in coastal flooding frequency with the frequency of extreme water-level events in small islands projected to double by 2050.

Climate change and policy

Dramatic economic and technological transformations are required in order to limit the global temperature rise to 1.5°C–2.0°C above pre-industrial levels. The fundamental elements of such transformation include accelerated decoupling of economic growth from energy demand and CO_2 emissions, and development and adoption of low-carbon, zero-carbon and carbon-negative technologies at a global scale.

Establishing a price for emissions could limit warming in a cost-effective way

Central to prompt mitigation efforts is internalizing the negative climate risks associated with emissions into economic decision-making and thereby reducing the demand for carbon-intensive services and fossil fuels. This can be achieved through tools such as carbon pricing measures, energy efficiency policies (such as minimum performance standards and building codes) and reduction of socially inefficient fossil-fuel subsidy regimes. Carbon pricing can serve as an incentive for low-carbon technology innovation, as well as generate an additional source of government revenue, which could be redistributed in the form of social transfers to ease the transition to the low-carbon economy or used to subsidize the development of low-emissions technology and infrastructure. Carbon pricing would also incentivize deployment of carbon removal practices such as natural climate

Box II.2

Climate change adaptation for coastal infrastructure in Caribbean small island developing States

Seaports and coastal airports are critical infrastructure assets that serve as catalysts of economic growth and development in the Caribbean. Compelling scientific studies (IPCC, 2014a and b; IPCC, 2018) project that climate change will increase the hydro-meteorological hazards for the coastal transport infrastructure of the Caribbean, one of the most disaster-prone regions worldwide. Significant socioeconomic consequences (e.g., for tourism and trade) are expected as these vital international transportation facilities are threatened by climate change. Climate-related extreme events affecting coastal transport infrastructure are likely to exacerbate existing challenges, making effective adaptation action an urgent imperative (UNCTAD, 2014).

The Caribbean might face climate-related losses of $22 billion annually by 2050. In terms of infrastructure damages due to sea level rise alone (exclusive of hurricane damage), the cost of inaction has been projected to amount to about $16 billion annually by 2050 (Bueno et al., 2008). The significance of threats associated with extreme weather events has been highlighted by the impacts of the 2017 hurricane season that wreaked havoc on several Caribbean islands, including coastal airports and seaports. Global economic losses in relation to extreme weather-related events in 2017 were estimated at $330 billion (MunichRe, 2018). Dominica's total damages and losses from hurricane Maria alone have been estimated at 224 per cent of the country's GDP (Government of the Commonwealth of Dominica, 2017), whereas losses from hurricanes Irma and Maria in Anguilla, the Bahamas, British Virgin Islands, Saint Maarten, and Turks and Caicos Islands have been estimated at $5.4 billion, with infrastructure-related costs representing a significant percentage of the total (ECLAC, 2018b). Economic implications of hurricanes Harvey, Irma and Maria also include, inter alia, reported losses by airlines serving the Caribbean (e.g., $75 million by American Airlines and $40 million by Spirit Airlines (Barrow, 2017)); at the disruption

Figure II.2.1

Projected flooding of George F.L. Charles International Airport and Port Castries, Saint Lucia

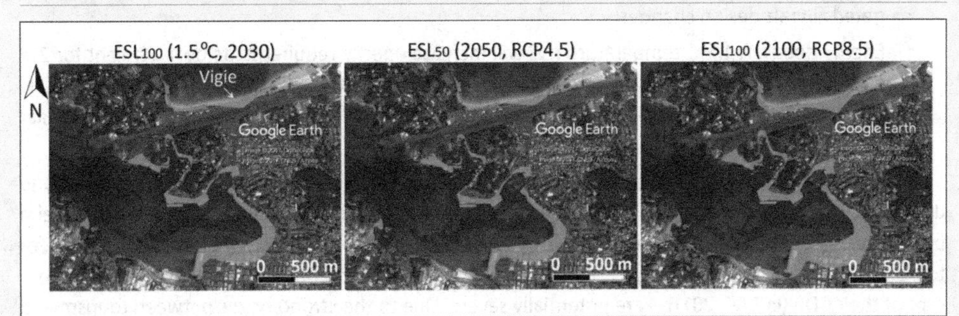

Source: Monioudi et al., 2018.

Note: Under 1.5°C warming compared with the pre-industrial times (2030), GCIA appears vulnerable to the one in 100 years extreme sea level (ESL100) mostly at its northern side (Vigie beach). As the century progresses, its vulnerability will increase. In addition, Vigie beach, located only 30 metres away from the airport fence, has been projected to face significant beach erosion that will further increase coastal flooding. Under a 50-year ESL by 2050 (under the moderate IPCC RCP 4.5 scenario) the runway will be flooded from Vigie beach. Given that Port Castries is only about 1.5 metres above mean sea level, there will be significant damage to the port and the capital city of Saint Lucia. Later in the century, and under both RCP scenarios tested, flooding is projected to deteriorate in the absence of effective adaptation measures.

(*continued*)

Box II.2 (*continued*)

peak, revenue losses for the industry were estimated at $75 million to $85 million per day (International Air Transport Association, 2017).

A recent assessment by UNCTAD (2017b) of the climate change induced impacts on the seaports and coastal airports of two Caribbean small island developing States (SIDS) (Jamaica and Saint Lucia)—an assessment that focused on the risk of coastal flooding and of potential operational disruptions under different climate scenarios (Monioudi et al., 2018; IPCC, 2018)—highlights the importance of climate change adaptation for critical international transportation assets. The study projected severe impacts on coastal transport infrastructure and operations that could cause major disruptions to the connectivity of SIDS to international markets, as well as to related economic sectors such as tourism.

Projections show that the coastal transportation assets of both Jamaica and Saint Lucia will face rapidly increasing coastal flooding in the twenty-first century. Flooding is projected for the airport runways of some of the examined airports and for most seaports from as early as the 2030s. Tests that consider the resilience of infrastructure in the face of a once-in-one-hundred-years extreme event (in terms of sea level and waves) under the 1.5°C specific warming level (which will be reached by the early 2030s) indicate flooding for the airport runways of some of the examined airports (the George Charles International Airport and Hewanorra International Airport in Saint Lucia, for example, as well as Sangster International Airport in Jamaica) and for most of the seaports. The exposure of these assets to coastal flooding is projected to deteriorate as the century progresses (figure II.2.1).

Results of the study (Monioudi et al., 2018) also suggest that air transport operations will be affected in Jamaica and Saint Lucia due to future climate variability and change. The projected increases in the frequency of hot days will likely affect the ability of airport staff to work safely outdoors, require reductions in aircraft payloads, and increase energy costs. Projected operational disruptions include the following:

- Outside working conditions. By the early 2030s, staff working outdoors at the Jamaica and Saint Lucia international transportation assets could be at high risk for 5 and 2 days per year, respectively. By 2081–2100, such days could increase to 30 and 55 days per year, respectively;
- Aircraft take-off. By 2030, Boeing 737-800 aircraft that serve all studied airports will have to decrease their take-off load for 65 days per year at Sangster International Airport (SIA) and 24 days per year at Norman Manley International Airport (NMIA)—both in Jamaica—whereas by the 2070s, such days could increase at least twofold for SIA and fourfold for NMIA, assuming no targeted aircraft design changes;
- Energy needs. A 1.5°C temperature rise will increase energy requirements by 4 per cent for 214 days per year for Jamaican seaports, whereas a 3.7°C rise (2081-2100) will increase energy requirements by 15 per cent for 215 days per year. Saint Lucia seaports are projected to experience similar trends.

Finally, the dominant 3S (sea-sand-sun) tourism model of Saint Lucia and other Caribbean island destinations is projected to be challenged by increasing beach erosion, which, by 2040, may overwhelm between 11 and 73 per cent of Saint Lucia's beaches (UNCTAD, 2017b). The negative ramifications for tourism—the main driver of many Caribbean SIDS economies, accounting for between 11 and 79 per cent of their GDP (ECLAC, 2011)—are potentially severe. Due to the strong nexus between tourism and the facilitating transport infrastructure, this will also have negative impacts on transportation demand.

It should be noted that important gaps remain in terms of data availability, as well as current levels of resilience and preparedness among seaports worldwide, as revealed by the UNCTAD Port Industry Survey on Climate Change Impacts and Adaptation (UNCTAD, 2017c). Given the potential economic implications of climate-related damage, disruption and delay, relevant information and adequate climate adaptation efforts are urgently required, especially for ports in developing regions and SIDS.

Authors: Regina Asariotis and Viktoria Mohos-Naray (Policy and Legislation Section, UNCTAD/DTL/TLB).

solutions (reforestation, land-use change and other ecosystem-based approaches). These measures could also accelerate efforts towards economic diversification in countries that remain highly reliant on fossil-fuel production. However, care must be taken to ensure a fair transition for communities adversely affected by climate change policies.

Limiting global warming requires mobilizing finance and shifting investment patterns

Such radical transformations require a major shift in investment patterns and a financial system aligned with mitigation challenges. According to the IPCC, limiting global warming to 1.5°C will require an annual average investment in the energy system of about $2.4 trillion (constant 2010 dollars) between now and 2035, representing about 2.5 per cent of world GDP (IPCC, 2018). More broadly, climate risks must be more readily integrated into investment decisions. For example, plans for development in hazard-prone locations (e.g., flood plains, vulnerable coasts, earthquake zones) must reflect the perceived disaster risks in those areas (United Nations International Strategy for Disaster Reduction, 2018). To this end, some progress is being made by the G20 Financial Stability Board Task Force on Climate-related Financial Disclosures (TCFD), which seeks to improve the quantification and disclosure of the financial impact of weather events in private and public entities. Climate-related disclosure can contribute to an orderly transition to a low-carbon economy by allowing investors to better evaluate their financial risk exposures (Batten et al., 2016).

International cooperation on technology transfer can decrease the cost of mitigating emissions

Besides demand-side management, Governments can also act on the technology supply side via "technology push" policies, such as research and development subsidies, to stimulate the technology market, in particular in regions with well-developed institutional and technological capabilities such as developed and emerging economies. Where technical capacities are insufficient, international cooperation on technology, including technology transfer, is needed to decrease the costs of global emissions mitigation and enhance the contributions of developing countries to mitigation efforts (IPCC, 2018). The current international technology transfer landscape has important gaps, especially in reaching out to LDCs, where institutional and technology capabilities are limited (ibid.). By the same token, lack of international cooperation and delayed short-term mitigation policies and measures increase total economic mitigation costs because stronger efforts will be required to counterbalance the higher emissions in the near term (ibid.).

Acting on the side of caution means acting urgently

As the world moves fast into a new era defined by the influence of human activity over climate and environment, countries must intensify efforts to preserve the planet as we know it, especially in the face of incomplete information. Climate data bears a significant degree of uncertainty. For example, measurements of the Earth's response to climate change continue to be updated. The IPCC warns of several uncertainties, such as the size of the remaining carbon budget,[15] the exact climate response to CO_2 and non-CO_2 emissions, and the feasibility of some unconventional solutions. However, the greater the uncertainty, the more likely it is that we may have already exceeded human and planetary limits with existing carbon emissions, and the greater the urgency to act. Given the prevalence of knowledge gaps and uncertainties, the difficulty of fine-tuning the emissions from complex and interconnected economic sectors, and the long duration and irreversibility of some impacts, it is essential that Governments act on the side of caution. The potential for co-benefits, such as reducing pollution and improv-

15 A carbon budget is the cumulative amount of carbon dioxide emissions permitted over a period of time to stay within a certain temperature threshold.

ing health and social outcomes, can additionally incentivize climate action and facilitate cooperation.

Governments must act collectively to correct the current global emissions trajectory and aim for global CO_2 emissions to begin to decline well before 2030. Such an ambitious goal can only be achieved through coordination and cooperation at the global level, made even more necessary considering the need to deal with the transboundary impacts of climate change. Scaling up efforts to reduce national emissions beyond the pledged targets should remain a priority. All countries and non-state actors need to strengthen their contributions without delay, through sharing of efforts based on bolder and more committed cooperation, with support for those with the least capacity to adapt, mitigate, and transform (IPCC, 2018). Societal lifestyle and behaviour transformation will also be required, supported by non-state actors such as industry, civil society and scientific institutions.

Time is of the essence. If institutional capacity for financing and governing the various transitions that are required is not urgently built, many countries will lack the ability to change pathways from a high-emission scenario to a low- or zero-emission scenario (ibid.). Strong international cooperation will be decisive in rapidly decreasing greenhouse gas emissions in the next decade.

Overcoming domestic structural challenges

Excessive commodity dependence

Growth laggards and reliance on natural resources

Notwithstanding rising cross-border challenges on multiple fronts, many countries continue to face persistent domestic structural issues that are hindering their sustainable development prospects. The recent strong global growth figures mask some worrying trends in the underlying pattern. Notably, there are a significant number of countries that have not been part of this global upturn and are at risk of falling further behind. If this trend continues, many of the SDGs, including eradicating poverty and hunger, creating decent jobs for all, and ensuring access to affordable and clean energy, will become increasingly out of reach.

In 2017–2018, 29 countries, with a combined population of 610 million, experienced a decline in GDP per capita. In a further 25 countries, GDP per capita expanded at a weak pace of between 0 and 1 per cent. These 54 countries are home to 1.4 billion people, representing about 15 per cent of the global population. Africa hosts 20 of these growth laggards, while the rest are mainly located in Western Asia and Latin America and the Caribbean.

In many of these cases, the low growth seen in the past two years is a continuation of a longer-run trend of weak economic performance. Figure II.7 suggests a positive correlation between a country's recent GDP per capita growth and its historical average growth rates. In 37 of the 54 growth laggards in 2017–2018, GDP per capita growth averaged less than 1 per cent over the period 1980 to 2016 (lower left quadrant of figure II.7). This suggests the existence of significant growth barriers—and in some cases even growth traps—for certain developing and transition economies (Arias and Wen, 2015).

The group of 37 growth laggards contains a heterogeneous mix of countries, with vastly different levels of development. Cross-country growth literature has shown that there is no single factor or set of factors that fully explains why some countries continue to fall behind

Figure II.7
GDP per capita growth 1980–2016 vs 2017–2018

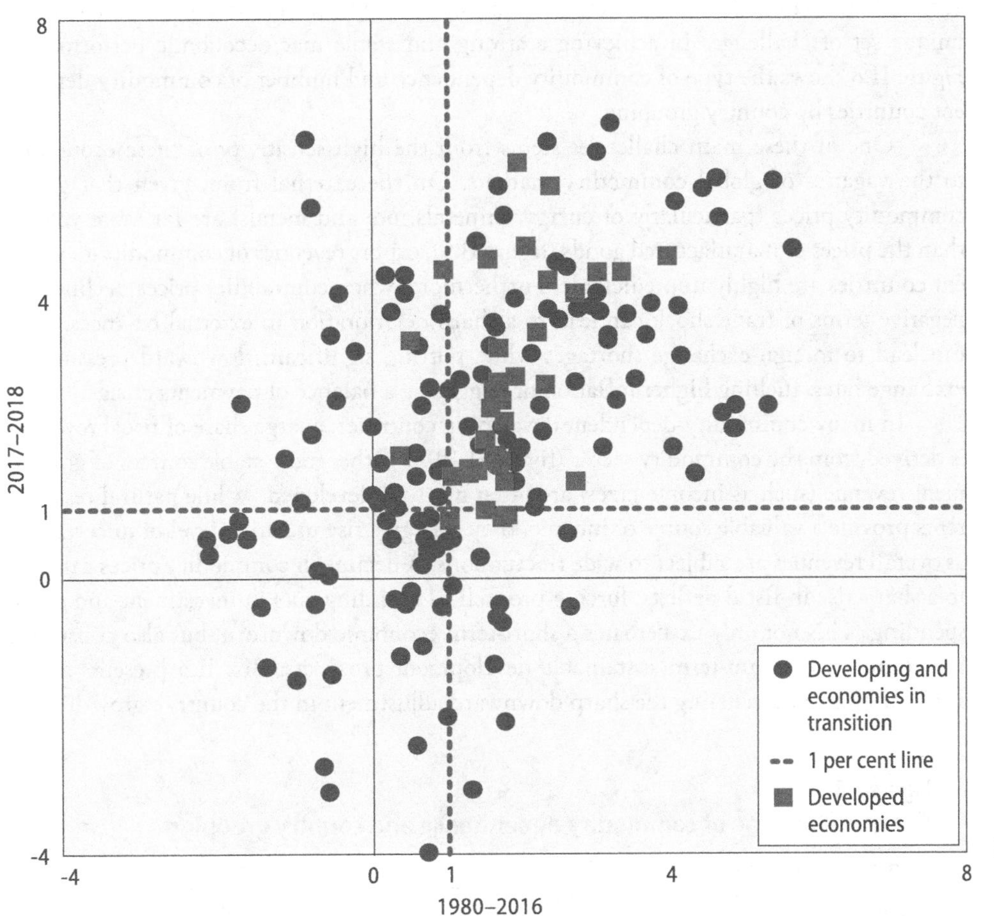

Source: UN/DESA.

others (see, for example, Ciccone and Jarocinski, 2008.)[16] Nevertheless, a closer look at these countries reveals several common features that are posing critical domestic policy challenges. These include high commodity dependence, conflict, weak institutions, as well as widespread poverty and elevated inequality. The following sections focus on analysing some of these characteristics, namely, commodity dependence and poverty and inequality, while also highlighting their close interlinkages with other domestic structural vulnerabilities.

Many of the developing economies that are falling behind depend on natural resources

Based on the United Nations Conference on Trade and Development (UNCTAD) definition,[17] 30 out of the 37 countries that are falling behind[18] are considered commodity dependent, with commodity exports accounting for more than 60 per cent of total merchandise exports. For several oil-producing countries, commodity dependence is particularly acute, with fuel exports constituting more than 90 per cent of merchandise exports.

16 In the words of Durlauf (2009), "[…] there is no a priori reason to expect cross-country growth behavior differences to reduce to a single major determinant or a very small set of determinants".

17 UNCTAD defines a country as commodity dependent when at least 60 per cent of merchandise export earnings are derived from primary commodities such as minerals, ores, metals, fuels, agricultural raw materials and food. For more information, please see the UNCTAD State of Commodity Dependence Report 2016.

18 This group of countries includes those with GDP per capita growth below 1 per cent in 1980–2016 and below 1 per cent in 2017–2018.

Commodity-dependent countries are subject to volatile global commodity prices

Past empirical studies of the relationship between resource dependence and growth have yielded mixed results (for a recent overview, see Venables, 2016). However, it is widely accepted that countries with an excessive economic dependence on commodities face a unique set of challenges in achieving a strong and stable macroeconomic performance. Figure II.8 shows the type of commodity dependence and number of commodity-dependent countries by country grouping.

One of these main challenges stems from the high sensitivity of these economies to the vagaries of global commodity markets. On the external front, given that global commodity prices (particularly of energy, minerals, ore and metals) are far more volatile than the prices of manufactured goods (figure II.9), export revenues of commodity-dependent countries are highly unpredictable. Furthermore, when commodity prices decline, the negative terms of trade shock can lead to a sharp deterioration in external balances. This can lead to foreign-exchange shortages while putting significant downward pressure on exchange rates, fuelling higher inflation or triggering a balance of payments crisis.

In many commodity-dependent developing countries, a large share of fiscal revenues is derived from the commodity sector (figure II.10).[19] Other more stable sources of government revenue (such as income taxes) are often not well developed. While natural resource rents provide a valuable source of income, they also give rise to a high level of uncertainty, as overall revenues are subject to wide fluctuations. A decline in commodity prices can lead to a sharp rise in fiscal deficits, forcing procyclical spending cuts in investment and social spending. This not only exacerbates a short-term economic downturn, but also constrains the country's medium-term sustainable development prospects. Box II.3 presents a case study of Nigeria, discussing the sharp downward adjustment in the country's growth pros-

Figure II.8

Countries by type of commodity dependence and country grouping

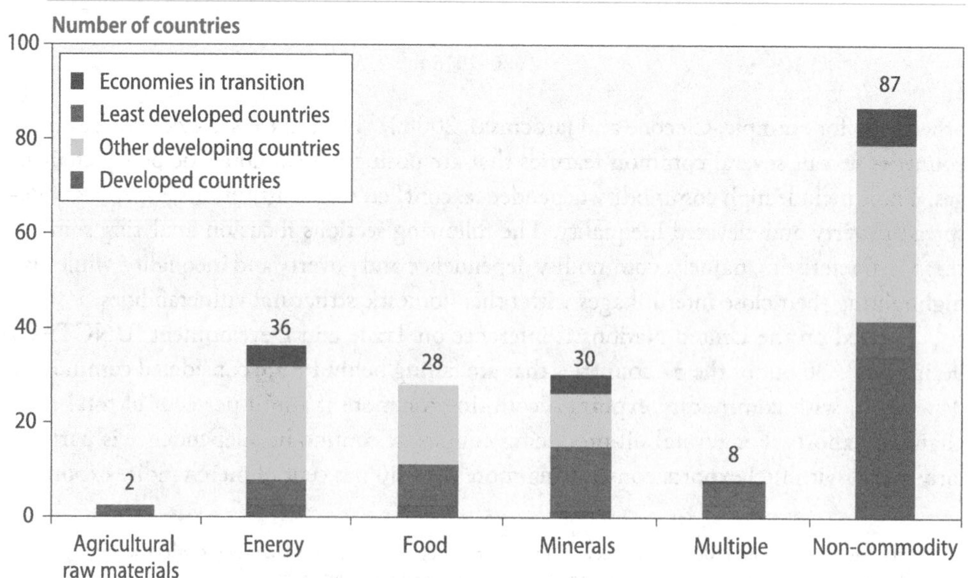

Source: UNCTAD.

19 In fuel-exporting least developed countries, the energy sector generally provides more than half of all central government revenue (UNCTAD, 2017d).

Figure II.9
Commodity price volatility between 2000–2017

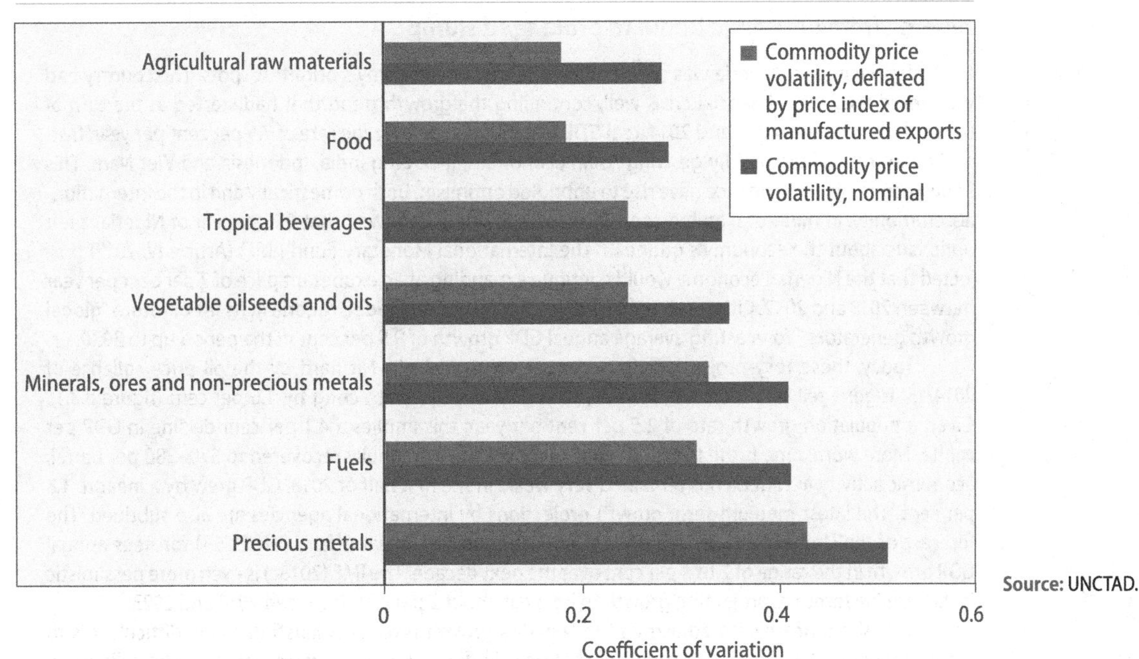

Source: UNCTAD.

pects in the wake of the commodity price collapse of 2014/15. Furthermore, a deterioration of both current account and fiscal positions is likely to worsen credit ratings, leading to higher borrowing costs and restricting access to finance. In such an environment, risks to debt sustainability are also higher. This often causes a vicious cycle that is only broken when commodity prices increase again.

Negative effects of high commodity dependence are exacerbated by weak institutions

The combination of high volatility of export and fiscal revenues often translates into high volatility of economic activity. In fact, high commodity price volatility has been shown as an important explanatory factor of low long-term growth in many commodity-dependent economies (Van der Ploeg and Poelhekke, 2009; Bleaney and Halland, 2014). Large swings in commodity prices are also associated with macroeconomic instability, which in turn generates high uncertainty and negatively affects investment and development planning.

In several countries, commodity sectors, particularly in the extractive industries, operate as "enclave" projects, which produce raw commodities for export. These projects create only a limited number of local jobs, without generating many domestic linkages or positive spillovers to the rest of the economy. In such economies, the returns from natural resource wealth are often not shared broadly across society. This is also related to the Dutch Disease phenomenon, where a strong focus on natural resource extraction because of high returns results in the displacement of other productive sectors. The negative effects of high commodity dependence on long-term growth prospects are exacerbated in countries with weak governance and poor institutional quality. In these countries, a larger exposure to corruption and rent-seeking behaviour to gain control of resources not only hinders investment, but also diverts scarce public resources and reduces the availability of resources that are channelled towards development purposes. For example, Mehlum et al. (2006) found a significant negative impact of resource abundance on growth only for countries with poor institutional quality.

Box II.3
Nigeria: from economic boom to prolonged slump

Only a few years ago, Nigeria was seen as one of the world economy's brightest spots. The country had weathered the global financial crisis well, continuing the growth trend that had started at the turn of the century. Between 2000 and 2014, real GDP expanded at an average rate of 7.5 per cent per year, faster than in most of the rapidly growing Asian economies, including India, Indonesia and Viet Nam. This strong economic performance gave rise to unbridled optimism, both domestically and in the international community. In mid-2012, an index of consumer confidence showed that 95 per cent of Nigerians felt optimistic about the economy's outlook.[a] The International Monetary Fund (IMF) (Article IV, 2012) projected that the Nigerian economy would continue expanding at an exuberant pace of 7 per cent per year between 2018 and 2032. Citigroup Global Markets (2011) even included Nigeria in its list of future "global growth generators," forecasting average annual GDP growth of 9.5 per cent in the period up to 2030.

Today, those rosy projections look completely unrealistic. Hit hard by the oil price collapse of 2014/15, Nigeria fell into recession in 2016, with annual GDP contracting by 1.6 per cent (figure II.3.1). Given a population growth rate of 2.5 per cent per year, this implies a 4.1 per cent decline in GDP per capita. More worrisome is the fact that while oil prices have gradually recovered to $70–$80 per barrel, economic activity in Nigeria has remained very weak. In the first half of 2018, GDP grew by a meagre 1.8 per cent. The latest medium-term growth projections by international agencies are also subdued. The forecast of the United Nations Department of Economic and Social Affairs (UN/DESA) foresees annual GDP growth in the range of 2 to 4 per cent over the next decade. The IMF (2018c) is even more pessimistic in its baseline forecast, projecting growth to hover at about 2 per cent between 2018 and 2023.[b]

This sharp downward adjustment in Nigeria's growth prospects illustrates how difficult it is to forecast medium-term trends in countries that heavily depend on a single commodity. The collapse in global oil prices in 2014/15 exposed major structural weaknesses in Nigeria's economy, triggering significant fiscal and balance of payments pressures. Several factors help explain why the downturn in economic activity has been so severe and the recovery prospects are so weak.

First, the dependence on a single commodity rendered Nigeria's economy highly vulnerable to external price shocks. In 2014, oil and gas accounted for 91 per cent of merchandise exports and 62 per cent of fiscal revenues. Non-oil revenues stood at only 4 per cent of GDP, one of the lowest rates in the world, due to a narrow tax base, low tax compliance and weak tax administration.

Second, Nigeria's fiscal policy stance was strongly procyclical in the pre-crisis period as high oil prices and the electoral cycle drove spending pressures up (IMF, 2016).[c] In 2013, when oil prices were close to an all-time high, the fiscal deficit reached 2.3 per cent of GDP. While the country had mechanisms for countercyclical fiscal policy—an oil-price-based fiscal rule, a savings fund (Excess Crude Account) and a newly established Sovereign Wealth Fund—partisan interests and myopic decision-making hindered the build-up of buffers. As a result, the Government did not have fiscal space to mitigate the downturn in 2015/16 and instead had to tighten fiscal policy.

Third, persistent political uncertainty and violence have been weighing heavily on Nigeria's economy in recent years. In 2016, the country experienced major disruptions to its oil production as militant groups attacked pipelines. Average daily crude oil production fell by 20 per cent between November 2015 and September 2016, amplifying the pressure on fiscal and current account balances.[d] Security concerns and political uncertainty (general elections are scheduled for February 2019) remain a significant impediment to investment.

Fourth, Nigeria's initial monetary and exchange-rate policy responses to the balance of payments difficulties were highly ineffective. The combined shock to oil price and oil production put strong downward pressure on the naira and weighed on economic growth. Nigeria's monetary authorities responded by implementing exchange-rate restrictions to maintain the de facto peg to the dollar, while easing monetary policy to support growth. These measures, however, failed to revive economic activity and restore investors' confidence. Instead, they exacerbated the downward pressure on the naira, causing the black-market rate to soar and fuelling inflation. In mid-2016, the central bank changed course, devaluing the naira and lifting interest rates. However, the central bank maintained the system of multiple exchange rates, which lacks transparency and deters foreign investment.

(continued)

a MasterCard, Worldwide Index of Consumer Confidence.

b In the IMF baseline scenario, Nigeria would see GDP per capita decline for eight consecutive years.

c During 2010–2014, many discretionary, adhoc withdrawals were made from the Excess Crude Account that receives excess oil revenues (or funds shortfalls) relative to the budgeted reference oil price.

d Saudi Arabia, in contrast, increased its daily oil production by 7 per cent in the same period.

Box II.3 (*continued*)

Fifth, during the boom period of the 2000s, only very limited progress was made in tackling Nigeria's structural obstacles to growth, including significant governance deficits, large gender and regional inequalities, high rates of underemployment (particularly among young people) and severe shortages of infrastructure and energy.

If nothing is done to correct these short- and long-term weaknesses, Nigeria faces the risk of being stuck on a protracted low-growth path. This would have far-reaching implications for the country's pros-

Figure II.3.1
Nigeria's macroeconomic indicators

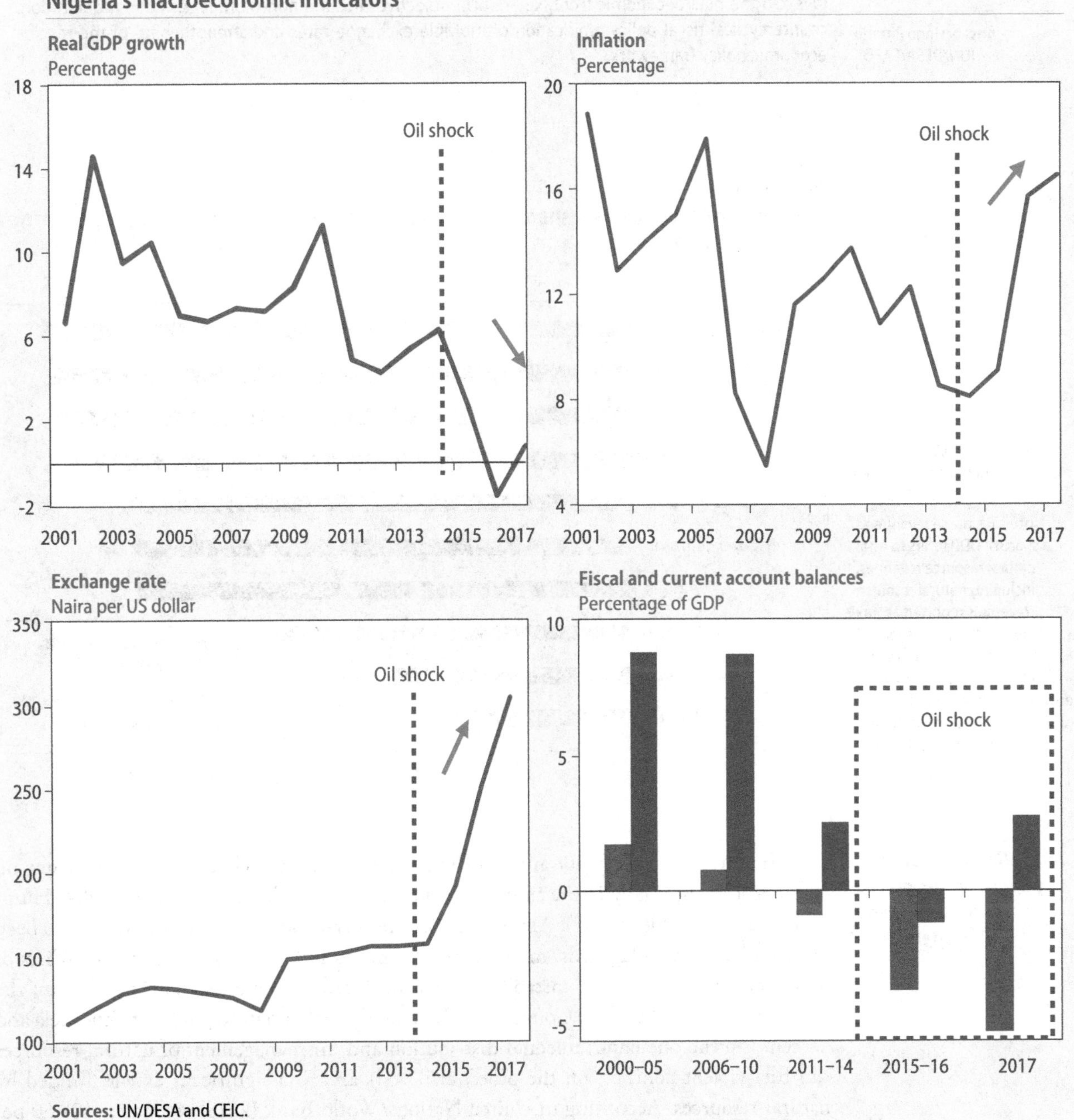

Sources: UN/DESA and CEIC.

(*continued*)

Box II.3 (*continued*)

pects to achieve the Sustainable Development Goals. Most importantly, it would make poverty reduction a daunting task. The World Bank estimates that in 2017, almost half of Nigeria's population lived below the PPP-adjusted $1.90 per capita per day poverty line (World Bank, 2018). The socioeconomic challenges are further magnified by continued strong population growth, which will place immense strains on infrastructure and public services. According to the latest United Nations projections (2017), Nigeria's population will increase from 191 million in 2017 to 264 million in 2030 and 410 million in 2050.

Unleashing Nigeria's immense economic potential and lifting more people out of poverty requires a firm commitment to wide-ranging macroeconomic and structural reforms. The objective must be to strengthen inclusive growth by raising the economy's potential and tackling the existing large inequalities. On the macroeconomic front, key reform objectives include non-oil fiscal revenue mobilization, countercyclical fiscal policy, unification of multiple exchange rates and strengthening of the macroeconomic policy framework.

Author: Ingo Pitterle (UN/DESA/EAPD).

Figure II.10
Government revenue as a share of GDP in selected commodity-dependent countries, average 2010–2016

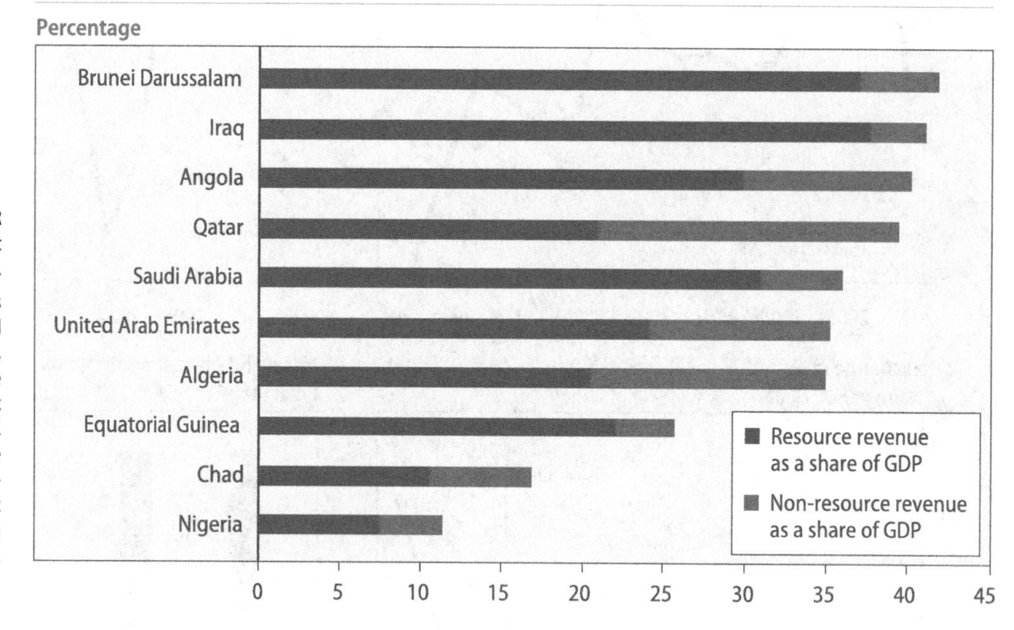

Source: ICTD/UNU-WIDER Government Revenue Dataset 2018: Merged.

Notes: Resource revenue as a share of GDP refers to total natural resource revenues, including natural resource revenues reported as "tax revenue" or "non-tax revenue". Non-resource revenue as a share of GDP refers to total non-resource revenues from both tax and non-tax sources, including social contributions.

Instability and conflicts appear to be correlated with commodity dependence

Importantly, instability and conflicts appear to be correlated with dependence on commodities, especially in the case of oil and minerals (Collier and Hoeffler, 2004; Humphreys, 2003; Collier, 2007). Among the commodity-dependent countries that have been identified as growth laggards, many have been mired in long-standing armed conflicts or have faced civil unrest and instability in recent decades. These include Afghanistan, the Democratic Republic of the Congo, Iraq, Liberia, the Bolivarian Republic of Venezuela and Yemen. On the one hand, unequal distribution and mismanagement of natural resources can fuel violent conflict; on the other, civil wars are, to a significant extent, funded by natural resources. According to United Nations/World Bank (2018) estimates, 40–60 per cent of intrastate conflicts in the past 60 years have been triggered, funded or sustained by natural resources.

Harnessing natural resource wealth

Through effective policy strategies, natural resource wealth can create vast development opportunities

Countries that are well endowed with resources are not necessarily stuck in a low-growth trap. On the contrary, an abundance of natural resource wealth has the potential to create vast opportunities in an economy. Returns from primary commodity production can provide revenue to support economic diversification, broader access to education and health care, investment in vital infrastructure, and provision of crucial social safety nets. Natural resources can also act as collateral to secure investment finance in many countries that face difficulties in accessing international capital markets.

Overcoming the challenges of commodity dependency and harnessing the development potential of natural resources require a comprehensive long-term development strategy, careful management of resource revenues, and firm policy commitments. In the recent past, several resource-rich countries have developed successful policy strategies that have allowed their economies to benefit immensely from resource wealth (see box II.4 for case studies of Botswana and Costa Rica). Drawing on the experiences of these countries highlights three key policy objectives that commodity-dependent countries need to address, namely, building resilience against volatility, expanding linkages from the commodity sector to the rest of the economy, and developing necessary human and physical capital.

Well-tailored fiscal policies help build resilience against volatility

Given the high volatility of commodity prices, commodity-dependent countries should adopt fiscal strategies to build resilience against price shocks. Fostering countercyclical policies—saving windfall commodity revenue when prices are high and raising expenditures to support the economy when commodity prices are low—is an important element. In this aspect, many countries have established revenue stabilization funds as buffers against commodity price fluctuations. Importantly, countercyclical rules must be transparent and institutionalized, so that they are not subject to changes in government, the electoral cycle or other political pressures that may arise. In addition, it is vital to ensure that the returns from natural resources are widely shared across society and directed towards promoting development objectives and productive investment.

Greater diversification of fiscal revenue sources is also an important element of building resilience against volatility. This can be politically challenging in countries with little or no cultural history of direct taxation but is an important aspect of long-term sustainability that includes adequate provision of public services and social safety nets. Clearly, greater economic diversification will also help protect economies against commodity price volatility. This is closely associated with developing linkages between the commodity sector and the rest of the economy.

Forward and backward linkages from the commodity sector should be expanded

To create stronger positive spillovers from the commodity sector to the broader economy, countries should prioritize investment geared towards vertical and horizontal diversification. Vertical diversification would include, for example, developing natural resource processing industries, such as smelting and refining of metals and processing of fossil fuels, and industries that use the abundant natural resource as an input to production. Botswana, for example, is pursuing the objective of developing its downstream diamond industry. This includes sorting and valuing of rough diamonds, selling and marketing of diamonds to local companies, and supporting and developing the cutting and polishing industry (Intergovernmental Forum on Mining, Minerals, Metals and Sustainable Development, 2018).

Vertical diversification allows more of the value added associated with the global use of raw materials to be internalized by the commodity-producing countries themselves. However, even after successfully developing refining and processing industries, an economy may still be exposed to commodity price volatility and shifts in global demand. Horizontal

Box II.4

Case studies of successful natural resource management: Botswana and Costa Rica

Botswana

Botswana offers one of the best examples of an economy that has been able to exploit its natural resource sector to advance its development objectives. The passing of the Mines and Minerals Act following independence in 1966 vested subsoil mineral rights in the Government. The Government also renegotiated diamond-mining agreements with foreign investors, thus securing a large share of the revenues. The proceeds were channeled into developing other industrial ventures, as well as into investments in the areas of infrastructure, health and education. To smooth the effects of diamond price fluctuations on the economy and stabilize the planning and execution of investment projects, Botswana has been pursuing a countercyclical policy, for which three funds are crucial: the Stabilization Fund for accumulating assets during boom periods; the Public Debt Service Fund (PDSF) for servicing public debt and extending loans to public enterprises; and the Domestic Development Fund (UNCTAD, 2017e). According to Transparency International (2017), Botswana is the least corrupt country in Africa and has been ranked comparably to several OECD and European countries for decades. Strong and effective legal and policy frameworks have enabled the diamond industry to become an important driver of growth. As a result, the country managed to achieve one of the highest rates of per capita growth in the world (figure II.4.1), developing from one of the poorest countries into a middle-income country within just half a century.

Figure II.4.1

Real GDP per capita trends in Botswana and selected regions

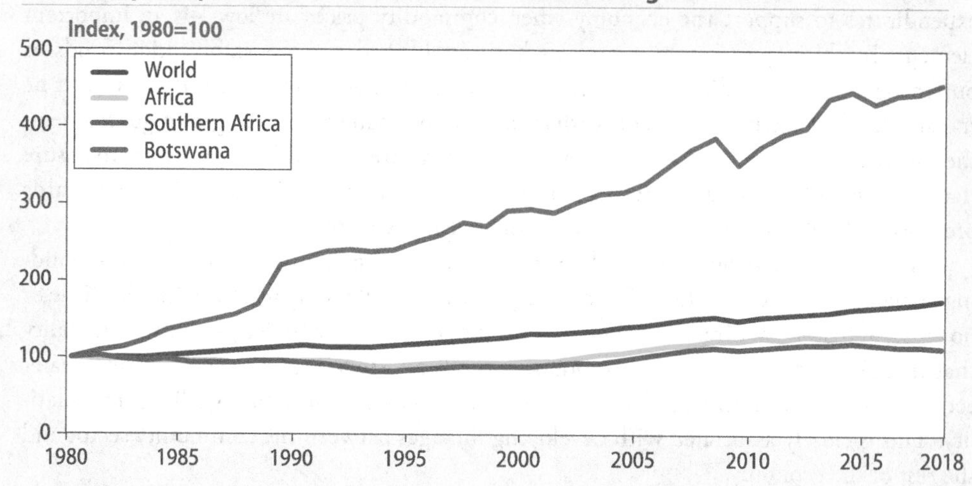

Source: UN/DESA.

Costa Rica

Costa Rica provides an example of a resource-rich country that successfully transformed and diversified its economy. Until the 1980s, the country was heavily dependent on coffee and bananas, with the majority of the workforce employed in agriculture. This implied a strong exposure to market fluctuations and unanticipated drops in commodity prices. To address these resulting challenges, the Costa Rican Government undertook major efforts to diversify its economy both vertically and horizontally: it provided financial incentives to develop non-traditional agricultural export products such as pineapples, of which Costa Rica now is the biggest producer in the world; it created export processing zones (EPZs); it implemented proactive foreign direct investment (FDI) policies to ensure that the strategies of multinational companies are aligned with the country's development priorities, facilitating technology transfer and productive linkages (Mortimore and Vergara, 2004); it supported development of manufacturing and high-tech industries that allowed the country to enter completely new sectors such as chips manufacturing and medical instruments; and it promoted the domestic service sector, in particular the tourism industry, capitalizing on its well-established system of national parks and conservation areas.

diversification can be supported by channelling a fraction of resource revenue to support investment in unrelated sectors.

Natural resource management can be improved through investing in human and physical capital

Developing natural resource industries and enabling economic diversification requires significant investment in both human and physical capital. This poses an important challenge for countries that lack the capacities for this investment, and often rely on foreign investors and companies to undertake costly exploration activities and establish the foundations of such industries. There is often a tendency to offer incentives and tax breaks in order to attract foreign investors who seek short-term returns from resource exploitation. But these short-term gains risk becoming enclave projects and may be to the detriment of a longer-term strategy to maximize the development potential of nascent industries. Expertise in procurement and contract negotiation is critical to ensuring an equitable long-term relationship with foreign or domestic private sector partners. In the example of Botswana in box II.4, one of the keys to the country's success was the renegotiation of contractual arrangements with foreign partners at an early stage. Also essential is the development of labour force skills that are needed to maintain and develop the industry, so that the returns can be more broadly shared.

Despite the potential for natural resource wealth to promote economic growth and development, excessive commodity dependence, for the most part, remains an obstacle to development. Releasing this potential requires a comprehensive approach to commodity management embedded within a broad development strategy. Key elements include strengthening institutions, increasing transparency, developing countercyclical policies, economic and fiscal diversification, and targeted investment in human capital.

Poverty and inequality

The goal of eradicating poverty by 2030

More than 700 million people worldwide currently live in extreme poverty

The upturn in global economic growth since mid-2016 presents an opportunity to accelerate progress towards the SDGs. However, faster GDP growth alone will not lead to broad-based improvements in living standards and shared prosperity. The mantra that "a rising tide lifts all boats" has been widely refuted (see, for example, Stiglitz, 2002). In many countries around the globe, widening socioeconomic inequalities since the 1980s have hindered progress in poverty reduction and shared prosperity.

Thanks to the successful experiences in China and other Asian countries, the share of people living in extreme poverty has declined steadily and significantly over the past few decades. However, despite this progress, there are currently more than 700 million people worldwide who live below the extreme poverty line of $1.90 per day (in 2011 purchasing power parity). More than half of them live in sub-Saharan Africa, which has experienced only a moderate decline in poverty rates since the 1990s.

Achieving the goal of eradicating poverty by 2030 (SDG 1) will require a combination of strong and sustained growth in average incomes and significant reductions in inequality. While developing countries have made some headway against inequality, much more fundamental transformations are needed going forward. Baseline scenarios, using the World Economic Forecasting Model (WEFM) and extending the current short-term forecasts, vividly illustrate the magnitude of the challenges that lie ahead. The results underscore the necessity of combining rapid economic growth with strong declines in income inequality.

Nearly 30 per cent of the population in Africa and in LDCs may remain in extreme poverty in 2030

The scenarios for poverty headcount ratios illustrated in figure II.11 rely on two key inputs: a projection for the total level of household income in the economy, and the way

Figure II.11
Extreme poverty headcount ratios, scenarios for 2030

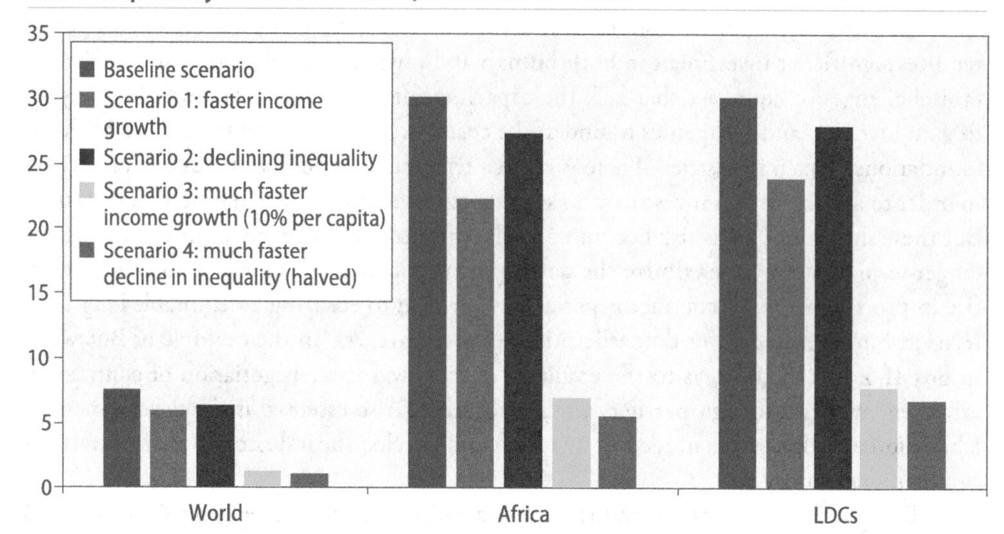

Source: UN/DESA, based on projections and scenarios produced with the World Economic Forecasting Model.

that income is distributed across the population.[20] In the baseline scenario—which can be viewed as the most likely outcome in the absence of a significant shift in productivity, economic policy or consumer behaviour—the first input is derived as a model-based extension of the current short-term forecasts underpinning this report. The second input assumes that the distribution of income—or the degree of inequality—remains constant within a country over the forecast horizon to 2030. These baseline projections suggest that more than 7 per cent of the global population may remain in poverty by 2030. About 30 per cent of the population in Africa and in the LDCs would be expected to remain in extreme poverty under this scenario, constituting a serious shortfall in global ambitions.

What needs to change to achieve the goal?

Prospects for poverty rates under some alternative scenarios for growth and inequality are also illustrated in figure II.12. The first scenario considers a more rapid rise in incomes relative to the baseline projections. Average income growth is increased to at least 4 per cent per year (where the baseline projections exceeded 4 per cent, the growth rate is left unchanged). This benchmark figure of 4 per cent is derived as an "optimistic" scenario based on the distribution of growth rates across countries in the period 2000–2015. Over this period, in half of the countries in the sample consumption per capita[21] expanded at an average annual rate of between 0.8 and 3.9 per cent (figure II.12.A). Holding inequality constant, raising per capita growth to at least 4 per cent would bring poverty rates in Africa and the LDCs down to 22–23 per cent by 2030—still considerably off target.

20 Additional technical assumptions: (i) following the World Bank methodology to estimate poverty rates in non-survey years, the mean of the income distribution is assumed to evolve in line with aggregate consumption per capita, adjusting for the historical discrepancy between the two; (ii) the distribution of income is approximated as lognormal, which holds relatively well for most countries, but in some cases the actual data is more skewed or erratic.

21 Consumption per capita is used as a proxy for average household income. In practice, household surveys underlying Gini coefficients and other inequality measures are often derived from consumption expenditure distributions rather than income distributions.

Figure II.12
Distributions of per capita consumption growth and inequality change across countries

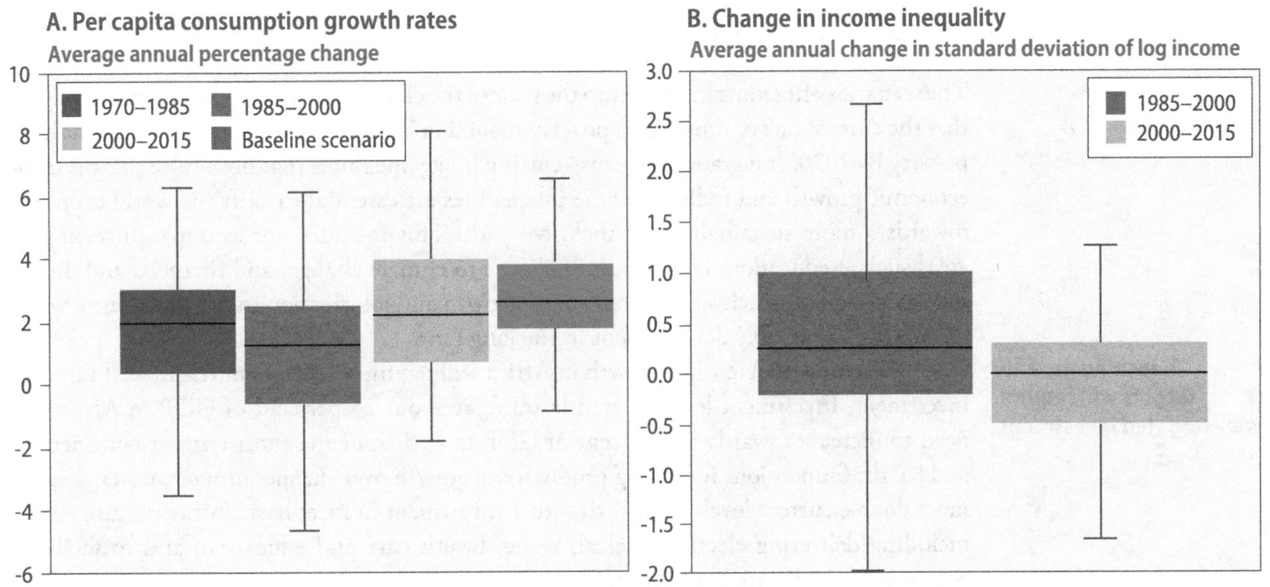

Source: UN/DESA calculations, based on data from Global Consumption and Income Project.

Note: Distributions across 176 countries (panel A) and 145 countries (panel B). Central lines indicate the median, boxes indicate range of 50 per cent of observations around the median, and endpoint of whiskers indicate the range of 95 per cent of observations.

The second scenario maintains income growth from the baseline scenario but allows inequality to decline. The magnitude of decline is calibrated as an optimistic scenario, based on historical changes in inequality over the period 2000–2015, as illustrated in figure II.12.B. The measure of inequality used—the standard deviation of the log of income—is allowed to decline by 0.5 per cent per year. Under this scenario, poverty rates decline to about 27 per cent in both Africa and the LDCs—a significant but nonetheless limited improvement. Combining scenarios one and two (consumption per capita growth of at least 4 per cent per year and an annual decline in inequality of 0.5 per cent) would bring poverty rates in Africa below 20 per cent. While this would mean that 240 million fewer people would remain in extreme poverty compared to the baseline scenario, it nonetheless falls well short of the goal to "leave no one behind".

Eradicating poverty by 2030 will require both double-digit growth in Africa and steep reductions in income inequality

The third and fourth scenarios consider more radical departures from historical behaviour. Scenario 3 illustrates the prospects for poverty reduction when average income growth rises to 10 per cent per year. Scenario 4 illustrates the prospects under a dramatic decline in inequality that essentially halves the level of inequality in each country.[22] Under both scenarios, global poverty rates fall to close to 1 per cent, while in Africa and the LDCs rates of extreme poverty drop to 5–8 per cent. Reaching progress on this scale demands a step change in both the rate of economic growth and the level of income inequality. In Africa, where the population is expanding at a rate of more than 2 per cent per year, GDP growth needs to rise to double-digit levels to ensure per capita consumption rates reach the levels needed. This is well beyond growth rates recorded over the last 50 years. Historical changes in inequality—which averaged 0 over the 15 years from 2000 to 2015 in the major-

22 Median income growth in the scenario is the same as in the baseline scenario.

ity of countries and deteriorated over the previous 15-year period—are also clearly woefully inadequate as a guide for the improvements needed over the coming decade.

How do we get there?

The scenarios offer some insights into the scale of the challenges ahead. The crucial message is that the current rate of progress in poverty reduction is far below what is needed to eradicate poverty by 2030. Integrated and cross-cutting policy measures that both raise prospects for economic growth and reduce income inequalities are essential to shift the world economy towards a more sustainable and inclusive path. This includes, for example, investing in areas such as education, health care, resilience to climate change, and financial and digital inclusion—all of which support economic growth and job creation in the short-term, while promoting sustainable development in the long term.

Reaching growth targets will require well-targeted investment

Reaching double-digit growth in Africa will require a significant rise in well-targeted investment. Investment levels currently stand at about 25 per cent of GDP in Africa but need to increase towards 30 per cent of GDP to both spur the short-term growth needed and lay the foundations for strong productivity growth over the medium term. Many states must double current levels of infrastructure investment to meet basic infrastructure needs, including delivering electricity, clean water, health care and education, and to facilitate economic diversification and trade.

Securing the finance to sustain a steep escalation in investment poses an enormous challenge. Debt levels are high and rising. As of 1 November 2018, 30 low-income countries were considered in or at high risk of debt distress, according to the methodology established by the World Bank and IMF.[23] Mobilizing resources via private sector involvement, tax revenues, remittances, and tapping into excess liquidity in commercial banks must be complemented by strengthened international tax cooperation and efforts to combat illicit financial flows, as discussed above. Above all, long-term strategic planning is needed to make the most valuable use of limited resources.

Faster GDP growth alone will not be sufficient to meet SDG targets

Faster GDP growth alone will not be sufficient to deliver the improvements in living standards and shared prosperity envisaged in the 2030 Agenda for Sustainable Development. Substantial declines in socioeconomic inequality are also needed. The period 1980–2000 was characterized by a broad-based increase in within-country inequality. The picture has since become more heterogeneous. This is illustrated in figure II.13, which depicts the income share held by the bottom 40 per cent in 2000–2004 and 2010–2016, using World Bank data. In most developed countries, income inequality has continued to widen further. By contrast, disparities appear to have narrowed in the majority of developing countries—albeit often only modestly and from very high levels, well above those prevailing across developed countries.

It is important to note that the World Bank's data on inequality is based exclusively on national income or expenditure household surveys. Such surveys often fail to adequately capture the incomes at the top of the distribution, leading to an underestimation of income inequality (Atkinson, 2007; World Inequality Lab, 2018). In an effort to correct this shortcoming, the *World Inequality Report* uses a new dataset that combines household survey data with fiscal data coming from taxes on income.[24] As expected, the report finds significantly higher levels of inequality than analyses based on World Bank data, but the qualitative trends are

23 See https://www.imf.org/external/Pubs/ft/dsa/DSAlist.pdf.

24 While this approach allows for a more complete and accurate picture of the incomes at the top, the country coverage is much more limited compared to the World Bank.

Figure II.13
Income share held by the lowest 40 per cent of the population in income distribution, 2000–2004 vs 2012–2016

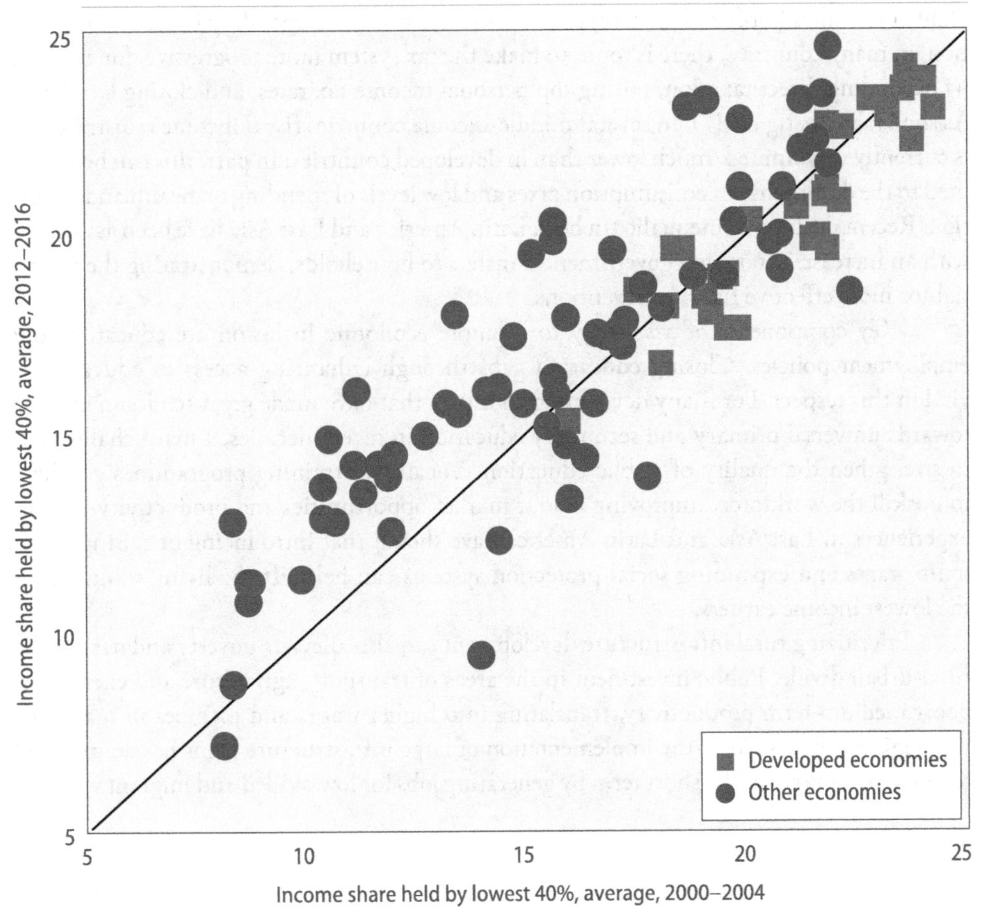

Source: UN/DESA, based on data from World Bank's World Development Indicators database.

Note: The sample includes 109 countrries for which data is available.

largely the same. Although there have been modest improvements since the turn of the century in parts of the Middle East, Latin America and the Caribbean, and sub-Saharan Africa, inequality levels remain very high.

Fiscal policy plays a crucial role in inclusive development

Given that high levels of inequality are a major barrier to achieving the SDGs, urgent policy action is needed. There are no one-size-fits-all recommendations, but the recent experiences in various developing regions offer valuable lessons and can help identify key areas of reform.[25] From a macroeconomic perspective, the experiences in Latin America and the Caribbean and sub-Saharan Africa in particular underscore the importance of macroeconomic stability and a strong development-oriented policy framework, including a well-functioning and robust financial system (see box II.5 for a discussion of the linkages between financial sector development, growth and inequality). Fiscal policies play a particularly important role in promoting inclusive development, not only by helping to smooth the business cycle, but also by providing public goods, correcting market failures and directly

25 Several recent studies by international organizations have examined inequality trends and policy responses from a global, regional and national perspective. See for example, World Bank, 2016; ESCAP, 2018; United Nations Development Programme, 2017; ECLAC, 2018c; Inter-American Development Bank, 2016.

influencing the income distribution. While more efficient tax collection and administration can help generate additional revenues, it is equally important to improve the efficiency and quality of public expenditure. In this context, moving away from regressive and inefficient blanket subsidies (for fuel, for example) towards better targeted spending is needed. In addition, in many countries, there is room to make the tax system more progressive, for example by expanding direct taxation, raising top personal income tax rates, and closing loopholes. As shown by Lustig (2017), in several middle-income countries fiscal income redistribution is currently very limited, much lower than in developed countries. In part, this can be attributed to the dominance of consumption taxes and low levels of spending on health and education. Recent declines in inequality in both Latin America and East Asia have been associated with an increase in targeted government transfers to households, demonstrating the potential for more effective fiscal interventions.

Education, employment policies and rural infrastructure are central to reducing inequality

Key components of a strategy to promote economic inclusion are education and employment policies. Closing education gaps through enhancing access to education is vital in this respect. For many developing countries that have made great strides in moving towards universal primary and secondary education in recent decades, a main challenge is to strengthen the quality of public education. Vocational training programmes can help to upskill the workforce, improving labour market opportunities and productivity. Recent experiences in East Asia and Latin America have shown that introducing or raising minimum wages and expanding social protection systems can help lift the living standards of the lowest income earners.

Prioritizing rural infrastructure development can also alleviate poverty and narrow the rural-urban divide. Public investment in the areas of transport, agriculture and energy can boost medium-term productivity, translating into higher wages and incomes in marginalized regions. In East Asia, the implementation of large infrastructure plans has contributed to reducing poverty in the short term by generating jobs for low-skilled and migrant workers.

Box II.5

Finance, growth and inequality

The primary function of the financial sector is to intermediate funds from savers to investors. By allowing savers to diversify risk, financial systems should facilitate productive investment, which can boost growth prospects. The linkages between financial sector development and GDP growth have been established in the literature since the 1990s.[a] Since then, the size of the financial sector has grown significantly in both developed and developing countries, often much more rapidly than the overall economy (UNCTAD, 2017f).

Recently, there have been an increasing number of discussions about the negative effects that can result from an overly developed financial sector. In this context, there is a need to distinguish financial depth (the size of the financial sector relative to the economy) from financial breadth (the population's access to different segments of the financial sector). While an improvement in access to financial services should benefit the poor, there are concerns over whether the benefits of greater financial deepening eventually level off. There are also growing concerns over whether high levels of "financialization"—defined as the increase in size and influence of financial markets and institutions in the overall economy—could exacerbate inequality.

Figure II.5.1 illustrates this nonlinear relationship between further financial sector development and economic growth,[b] while holding other growth determinants constant. Based on data from 128 countries in the period 1980–2013 (Sahay et al., 2015), there is a bell-shaped relationship between financial development and economic growth. The results show that for countries at a low stage of financial sector development, further financial deepening has strong positive effects on growth.

Figure II.5.1

Relationship between financial development and economic growth

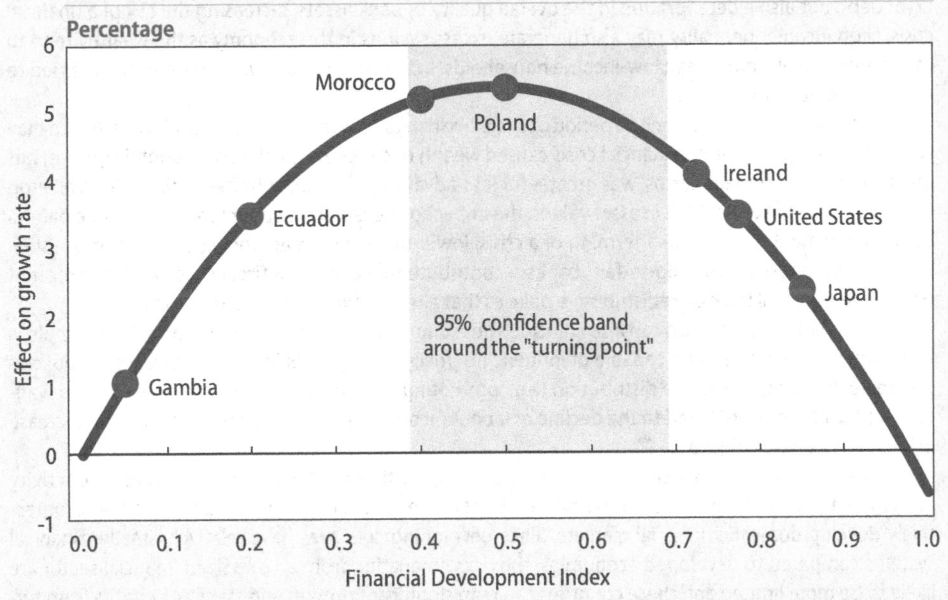

Source: Sahay et al. (2015).

However, the data show that at higher stages of financial sector development, the gains to growth from further financial development reach a plateau, and eventually start to decline. Although there is not a single inflection point that applies to all countries, one study found that when private credit reaches about 100 per cent of GDP, the impact of further financial sector development on growth can turn negative (Berkes, Panizza and Arcand, 2012), alongside an increase in volatility (Easterly, Islam and Stiglitz,

(continued)

a See for instance, Levine (2005).

b Financial development is measured by an index that combines data on financial institutions and financial markets in terms of depth, access and efficiency. See Čihák et al. (2012).

Box II.5 (*continued*)

2000). Greater financial deepening, rather than financial access, has been identified as the driver of this weakening effect on growth. This can be due to several factors, including financial crises preceded by credit booms (Jordà, Schularick and Taylor, 2011); funds allocated to speculative bubbles instead of productive assets; or diversion of talent towards financial services and away from other economic sectors (Tobin, 1984).

Such limits to growth depend, inter alia, on the quality of a country's regulatory framework. High-quality regulation can help broaden access to credit without jeopardizing financial stability. Financial development that occurs at a pace that is too rapid may also generate higher instability. Likewise, the composition of finance is important. Credit to businesses has been found to be more growth friendly than credit to households (Sahay et al., 2015).

Financial sector development also affects income distribution, although empirical studies have produced mixed results surrounding the nature of this relationship. On one hand, there is evidence that financial development, measured as private credit to GDP, benefits the poor disproportionally and reduces income inequality. This is because a more developed financial system can better address market imperfections, such as information asymmetry between lenders and borrowers. For the poor, this helps alleviate credit constraints that may be imposed because of their lack of collateral and credit history (Beck et al., 2007). Better access to financial services also helps people escape poverty by encouraging savings while lessening the effects of financial shocks, such as job losses and crop failures. Realizing these benefits, countries have tried to promote greater financial inclusion.[c] Considerable progress has been made in this area, notably due to the proliferation of mobile banking technology. Yet, 1.7 billion adults remain unbanked compared to 2.0 billion in 2014 (Demirgüç-Kunt et al., 2018).

On the other hand, the 2008/09 global financial crisis highlighted the role of excess financialization in generating higher instability and widening inequality. For example, high inequality can lead to the build-up of financial vulnerabilities.[d] Workers with stagnant wages may be willing to take on more credit to maintain or improve their standards of living. This may result not only in an unsustainable build-up of debt, but also a deterioration in the overall quality of bank assets, increasing the risk of a financial crisis. High income inequality may also generate excess savings in the economy as the wealthy tend to save proportionally more than low-income households. In the past, these savings have sometimes led to excessive risk-taking.

A widespread and prolonged period of excessive risk-taking can lead to financial crises, which may widen inequality. The global financial crisis caused wealth declines across all socioeconomic groups, but the decline, in percentage terms, was greater for less-advantaged groups (Pfeffer et al., 2013). While top earners experience a sharp fall in asset values, the impact of a crisis on the poor tends to be more painful as unemployment rises. In the aftermath of a crisis, lower tax revenues and policy interventions—such as measures to rescue "too-big-to-fail" banks—contribute to a decline in fiscal space and may prompt Governments to roll back on redistributive policies that aim to address income inequality.

Greater financialization can also coincide with some degree of regulatory capture. For example, a larger financial sector may be capable of influencing policymaking in its favour and weakening policies that foster more equal income distribution (e.g., promoting fiscal austerity and limiting minimum wages). This may have contributed to the decline of labour income shares in many countries and an increase in income inequality (figure II.5.2).

Well-functioning financial systems are vital in supporting capital accumulation and productivity growth. Nevertheless, countries need to be cognizant of the risks of over-financialization as they progressively develop domestic financial markets. Since developing countries have relatively smaller financial systems compared to developed economies, the risks emanating from an oversized financial sector are likely to be more limited and these countries can reap significant growth and stability benefits from further financial sector development. More developed countries, by contrast, may, benefit from a smaller financial sector.

Importantly, financial supervision and regulation must keep up with efforts to deepen or liberalize financial systems. Effective and appropriate regulation and supervision is critical for all countries, notably to identify and contain systemic risks. This is challenging, especially for countries with limited capacities. Investment incentives also need to change to avoid rewarding short-termism and speculation.

c For example, at least 58 developing countries have adopted or are in the process of developing national strategies to accelerate the level of financial inclusion. See Alliance for Financial Inclusion (2015).

d See UNCTAD (2017f) and Kumhof et al. (2015).

(*continued*)

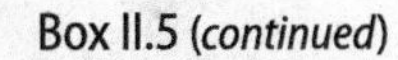
Box II.5 (*continued*)

Figure II.5.2
Share of pre-tax national income in the United States and the world

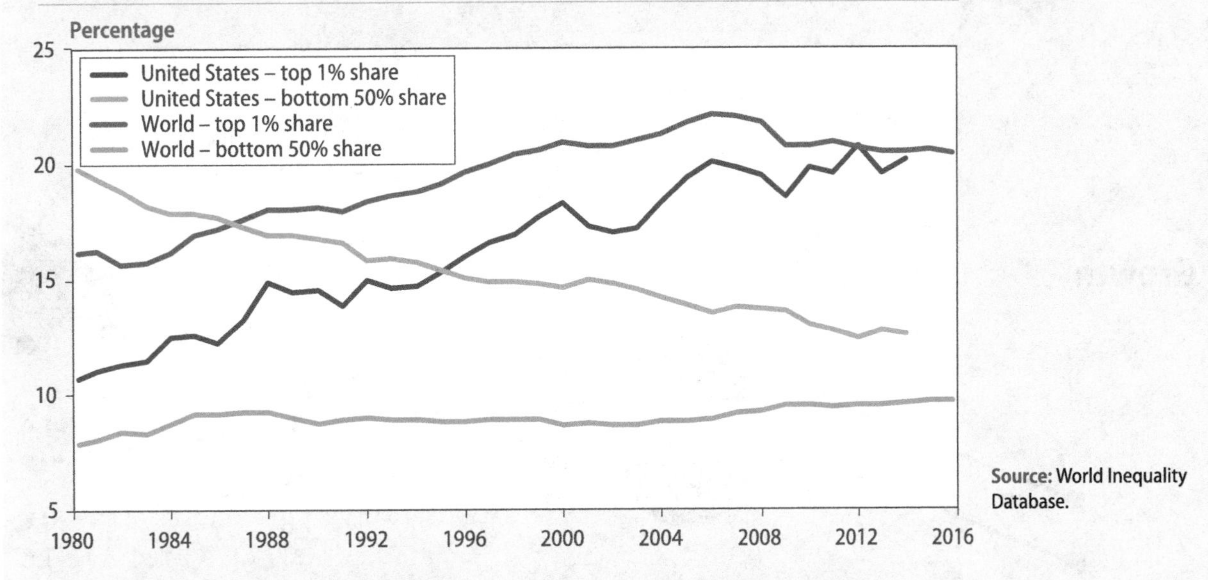

Source: World Inequality Database.

In addition, policymakers need to have a deeper understanding of the linkages between inequality, financial stability and crisis. Reducing inequalities, through enhancing social protection systems for instance, may reduce the risk of future crises, while ensuring financial stability can mitigate future inequalities.

Authors: Mathieu Verougstraete and Shari Spiegel (UN/DESA/FSDO).

Developed economies

GDP Growth

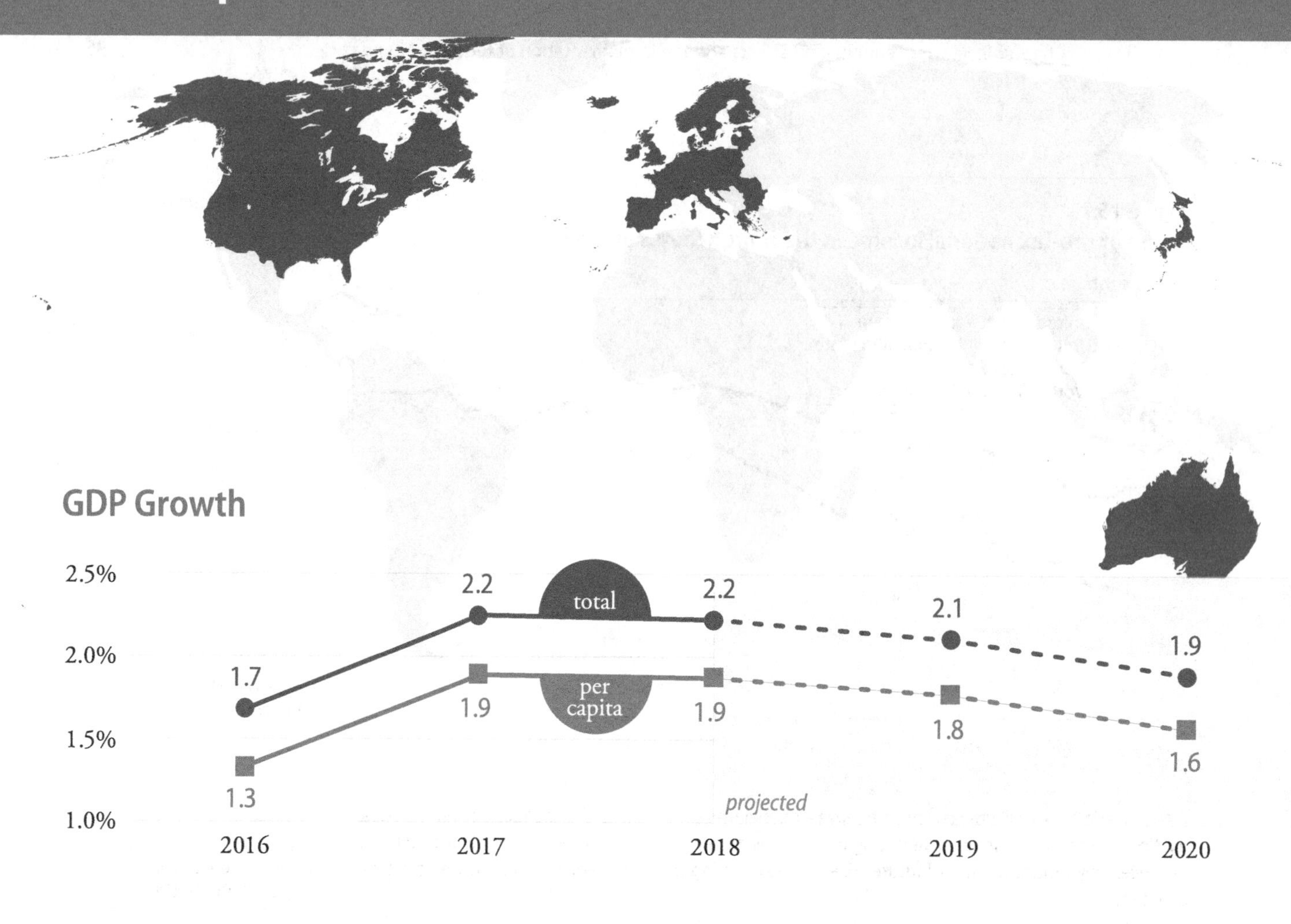

GDP per capita

2018

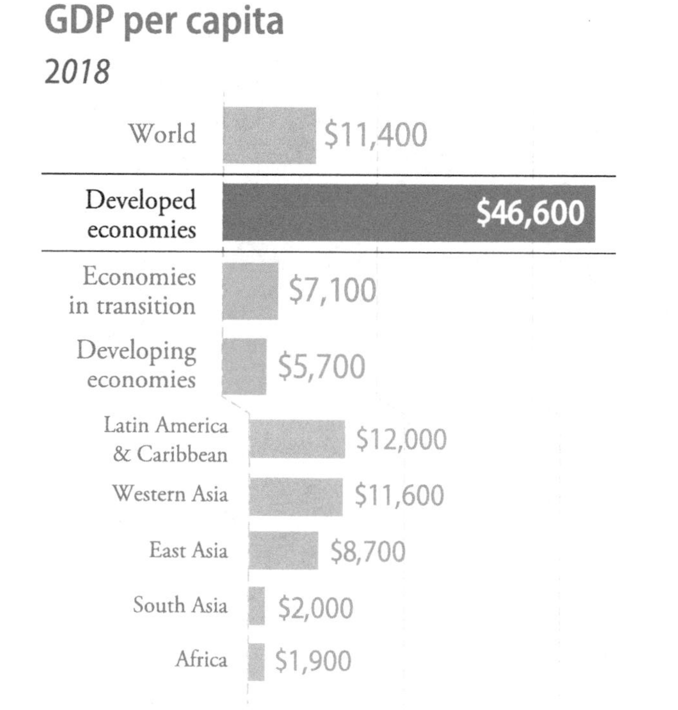

Exports structure

2016

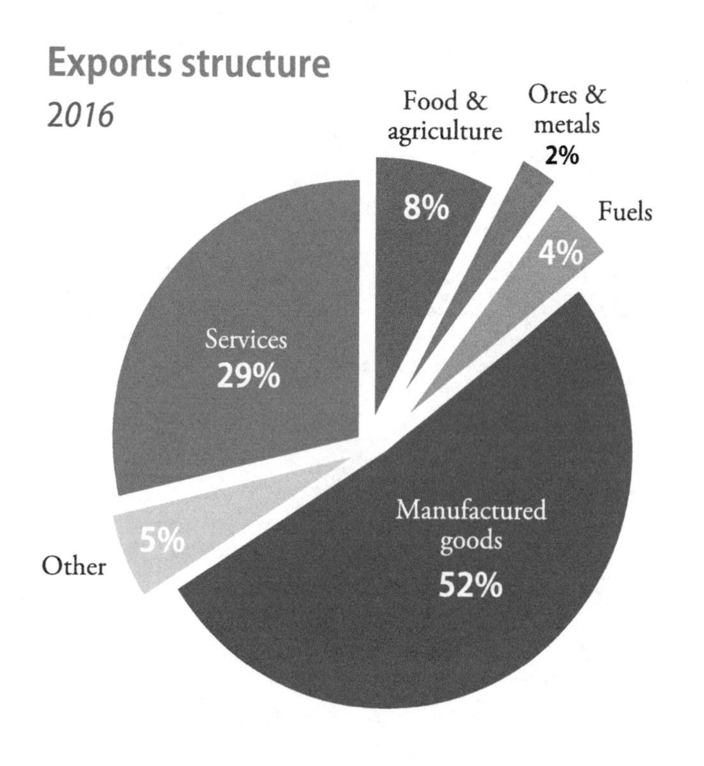

The boundaries and names shown and the designations used on this map do not imply official endorsement or acceptance by the United Nations. The map represents countries and/or territories or parts thereof for which data is available and/or analysed in *World Economic Situation and Prospects 2019*. The shaded areas therefore do not necessarily overlap entirely with the delimitation of their frontiers or boundaries.

Chapter III
Regional developments and outlook[1]

Developed economies

- Capacity constraints are restraining economic growth in several developed economies
- Fiscal policy remains procyclical in the United States, while underpinning institutional challenges in Europe
- Monetary policy may need to be tightened faster than expected in the United States and Europe

United States: GDP growth to moderate as impact of fiscal stimulus wanes amid rising capacity constraints

The impact of ongoing trade disputes on the domestic economy has been offset by major fiscal stimulus measures

Economic confidence and sentiment indicators in the United States of America are near to historical highs, despite the wide range of tariff hikes and the build-up of trade tensions that intensified over the course of 2018. The impact of ongoing trade disputes on the domestic economy has been offset by major fiscal stimulus measures introduced in 2018, including a two percentage point drop in income tax rates, a steep decline in the corporate tax rate and a rise in federal government consumption spending, especially on defence. This has supported strong jobs growth and buoyant economic activity. In the first three quarters of 2018, gross domestic product (GDP) was 2.8 per cent higher than a year earlier. The expansionary fiscal stance has accelerated the pace of interest rate rises by the United States Federal Reserve (Fed), sparking episodes of turbulence in global financial markets and asset price adjustments. The federal deficit is expected to widen to about 5 per cent of GDP by 2019, and government debt will continue to rise relative to GDP for the next decade.

Capacity limits in rail transport and increasing labour shortages restrain prospects for 2019

There is growing evidence that firms in the United States are facing capacity constraints, which will restrain growth in 2019 despite the continued support of fiscal stimulus measures. Internal freight transportation costs have risen sharply—up 8.3 per cent year on year to September 2018—reflecting labour shortages in the trucking sector and capacity limits in rail transport. The unemployment rate is at its lowest level since 1969, and the ratio of job seekers to job openings is also at historical lows. While pockets of unemployment persist in certain sectors and regions of the country, and labour force participation rates of workers over the age of 55 have declined significantly since the global financial crisis, labour market conditions have clearly tightened (figure III.1). Firms have reported difficulties in finding qualified workers in several sectors, including highly skilled engineers, finance and sales professionals, construction and manufacturing workers, and information technology professionals. Recent changes in immigration policy, which are likely to restrict inward migration, will also act as a restraint on labour force expansion. Since 2000, immigration has contributed roughly half of the expansion of the United States labour force.

1 For underlying forecast assumptions, refer to the appendix to chapter I. Country-level forecast detail is reported in the Statistical annex.

Figure III.1
Job openings in the United States by sector, relative to unemployment, 2001–2018

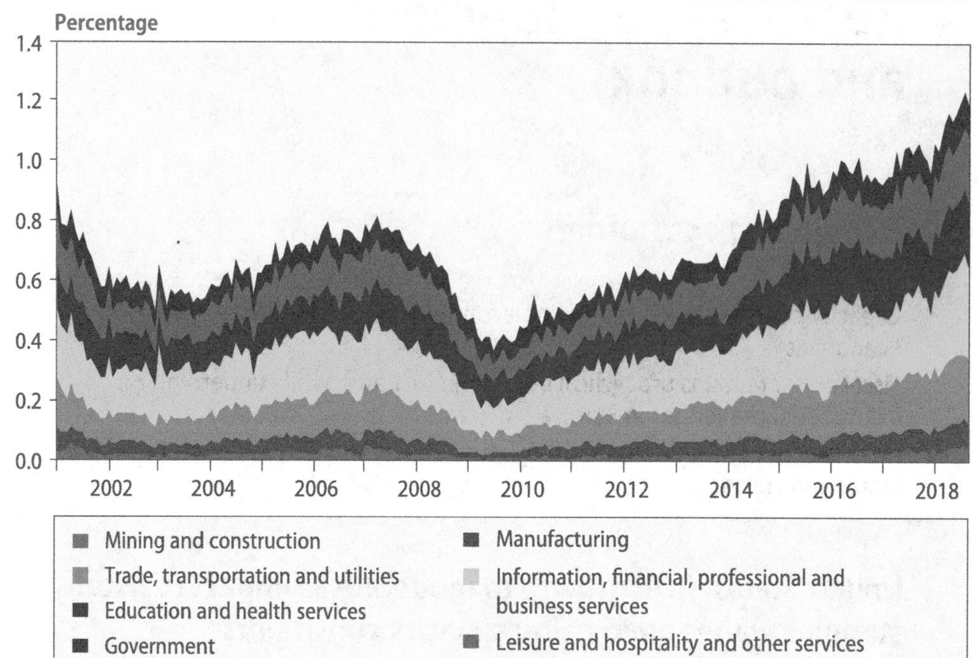

Source: UN/DESA, based on data from United States Bureau of Labor Statistics.

As capacity constraints tighten, the economy will rely on an expansion of imports to meet demand. This will cause the current account deficit to deteriorate, in contrast to the stated objectives of ongoing changes in United States trade policy. Increased reliance on imports, coupled with the upward impact of rising import tariffs and tightening capacity constraints, will also add to domestic price pressures. Input price pressures are already evident, particularly for construction materials and freight transportation. So far, higher input costs have largely been absorbed by firms, although headline consumer price inflation has exceeded 2.0 per cent since November 2017. Core inflation, closely monitored by the Federal Open Market Committee (FOMC) of the Fed, has also hovered at about 2 per cent for most of 2018. Wage pressures have started to build, and average hourly earnings growth has reached its highest level since 2009. Inflation is forecast to average 2.5 per cent in 2019.

Rising inflationary pressures have accelerated interest rate increases by the Fed

The rise in inflationary pressures has accelerated the pace of interest rate increases by the Fed, which raised rates four times in 2018. If capacity constraints persist, a greater share of rising costs will be passed on to customers, exerting further upward pressure on inflation. Interest rates are expected to rise by a cumulative 75 basis points in 2019, and the Fed will continue to reduce the size of its balance sheet. As monetary stimulus is withdrawn, GDP growth is expected to moderate to 2.5 per cent in 2019 and will revert towards 2 per cent when the temporary impact of fiscal stimulus measures dissipates in 2020.

Corporate tax cuts supported a strong rise in business investment in the first half of 2018, continuing the upturn seen in 2017. Some signs of moderation in the pace of investment activity emerged in the second half of the year, although investment in intellectual property products, which includes software, computers and research and development (R&D) activity, continued to expand rapidly. More moderate investment growth may partly reflect the impact of uncertainty regarding future trade relationships and rising interest rates, while upgrading of computing equipment may be a reaction to rising capacity constraints. Residential investment contracted in 2018 and is expected to continue to act as a drag on GDP growth as interest rates rise further in 2019.

Fossil fuel sectors are expanding in North America

Shifts in environmental policy in the United States—which include easing of restrictions on drilling, coal use and new car emissions standards—have helped support an expansion of activity in fossil fuel sectors. Real private fixed investment in mining exploration, shafts and wells increased by over 30 per cent in the first three quarters of 2018 compared to a year earlier, while the mining industry added 60,000 jobs in the year through end-September 2018. This short-term support to economic activity has also slowed progress towards an environmentally sustainable economy.

Canada: housing market has cooled, but household debt may pose a risk as interest rates rise

In Canada, the economy registered exceptional growth of 3.0 per cent in 2017, driven by fiscal stimulus measures and strong gains in housing wealth. In 2018, the pace of growth moderated towards a more sustainable level of 2.0 per cent. Household consumption and investment growth slowed, largely reflecting more moderate activity in the buoyant real estate sector. This was partly offset by accelerating business investment, especially in mining and oil extraction industries. Higher oil prices will continue to support activity in the energy sector. While Canada continues to make important strides in its climate policy, including the Pan-Canadian Framework on Clean Growth and Climate Change, it is among the world's largest oil producers and has the world's third-largest proven oil reserves. Further expansion of the fossil fuel sector will slow progress towards environmentally sustainable economic growth.

Looking ahead, surveys point to strong investment growth in Canada in 2019, and economic activity is expected to continue to expand at the more moderate but healthy pace of 2.0–2.2 per cent in 2019–2020.

The United States-Mexico-Canada Agreement eases some downside risks for the Canadian economy

About two thirds of Canada's goods and services trade is conducted with the United States. This dependency was laid bare during the prolonged renegotiation of the North American Free Trade Association (NAFTA) between May 2017 and October 2018, which was the source of huge uncertainty regarding future trade relations, amid threats of high tariffs on key Canadian exports such as automobiles. The new United States-Mexico-Canada Agreement (USMCA) lifts a significant degree of uncertainty regarding relations with Canada's largest trading partner and eases some downside risks for the Canadian economy. The new agreement gives the United States greater access to the Canadian dairy market, which may cause some temporary disruption in this sector. The agreement also left open the removal of tariffs on steel and aluminium exports to the United States that were imposed in May 2018. While on the whole USMCA offers a stable framework under which firms will operate for the next 16 years, many firms may seek greater diversification in their export markets to protect against excessive dependence on a single market.

Household mortgage debt may pose a risk as interest rates rise

A key area of vulnerability in the Canadian economy is the high level of household debt, which stands well above the level of many other developed economies (figure III.2). House prices in Canada increased sharply from late 2015, with particularly strong gains in cities such as Toronto and Vancouver, partly reflecting strong speculative demand from foreign investors. This prompted policy measures to cool housing demand in major cities. By mid-2017 these measures had already helped to curb housing starts, and house prices stabilized in late 2017.

Figure III.2
Total credit to households, selected developed economies

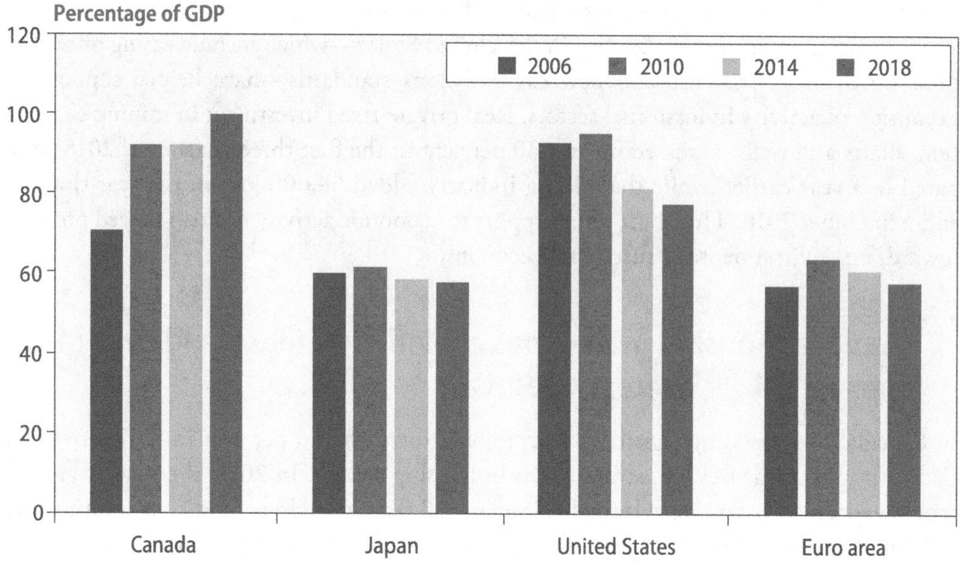

Source: Bank for International Settlements.

While mortgage arrears remain very low, the outstanding stock of residential mortgages has doubled in size since 2006. Strong gains in housing wealth have also fuelled debt-driven consumption spending. The Bank of Canada is expected to continue to withdraw monetary stimulus from the economy, with interest rate rises likely to broadly track those of the Fed. With an increasing number of borrowers linked to variable rate loans, this exposes many households to interest rate risk. This will act as a constraint on household spending over the forecast horizon, with potential for a sharper slowdown if interest rates rise more rapidly than anticipated.

Japan: economy at capacity despite a slower expansion

In Japan, real GDP growth slowed to 1.0 per cent in 2018 from 1.7 per cent in 2017. Rising corporate profits have resulted in robust growth in corporate capital investments, particularly in R&D. Solid growth of the world economy and a stable exchange rate resulted in resilient growth in external demand. However, a rapid decline in private housing investments has weighed on the aggregate investment level. The growth in private consumption has decelerated as consumer confidence waned over the year as a result of stubbornly weak real wage growth.

Labour markets remain tight. While unemployment came down to 2.3 per cent in September, the quarterly Tankan Survey of the Bank of Japan (BoJ) indicated a deepening labour shortage for business enterprises. The Tankan Survey also implied that capital equipment of business enterprises was operating at levels close to capacity limits (figure III.3). However, the situation did not give rise to significant inflationary pressure in 2018. The consumer inflation rate is estimated to have risen to 1.2 per cent in 2018 from 0.5 per cent in the previous year. However, the rise in the price level reflected mostly the rise in fuel prices. The core inflation rate (all items, less fresh food and energy) is estimated to be 0.4 per cent in 2018, only slightly higher than 0.1 per cent in the previous year.

Figure III.3
Diffusion indices on employment and production capacity in Japan, 2000–2018

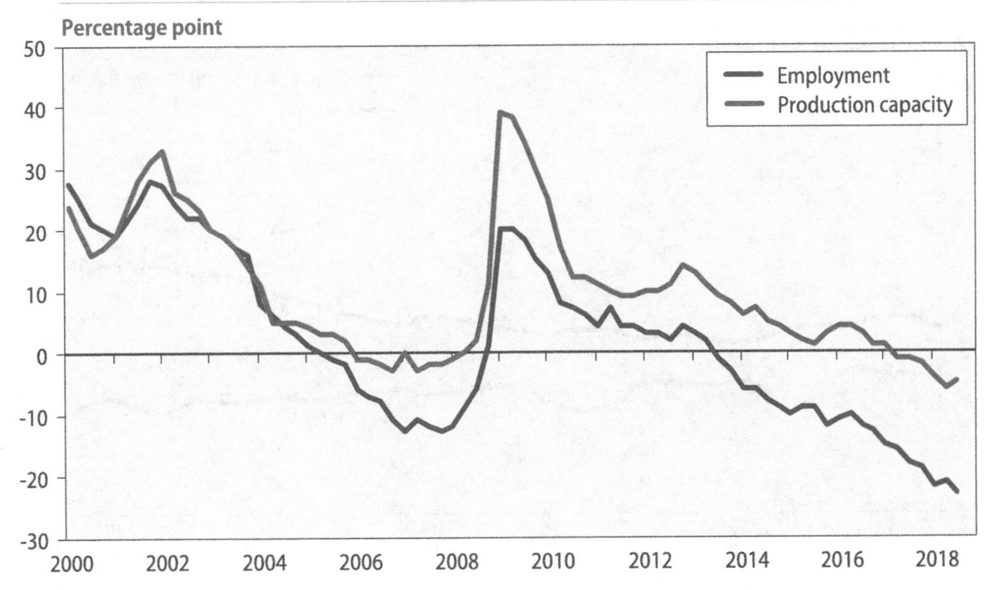

Source: Bank of Japan's Tankan Survey.
Note: Figures are for large enterprises. Negative values indicate a shortage of labour and production capacity in the majority of businesses.

Quantitative and qualitative monetary easing continues

The BoJ has maintained a set of unconventional monetary easing measures, known as Quantitative and Qualitative Monetary Easing (QQE). The BoJ has continued to use its balance sheet to expand the monetary base, but the pace of the asset expansion slowed down in 2018. Meanwhile, the year-on-year growth rate of the broad money stock (M2) decelerated from its peak of 4.0 per cent in October 2017 to 2.8 per cent in September 2018, at the same time, given the Government's commitments to lowering its debt dependency, the fiscal policy stance shifted to neutral in 2018.

Growth of GDP is forecast at 1.4 per cent for 2019 and 1.2 per cent for 2020. The consumer inflation rate is forecast at 1.5 per cent in 2019 and 2020 due to upward pressures on wage levels as well as the proposed hike of the sales tax rate in October 2019. Nevertheless, the inflation rate is forecast to remain well below the BoJ inflation target of 2 per cent.

An abrupt appreciation of the Japanese yen remains the main downside risk for the Japanese economy. A substantial appreciation of the yen would be deflationary and erode business sentiment reducing corporate profits of exporting industries. Labour shortages also pose a risk. An increased number of small businesses have already shut down, after failing to hire the necessary number of employees.

Australia and New Zealand: robust economic growth continues despite emerging uncertainties

In Australia, real GDP growth is estimated to be 3.2 per cent in 2018. A consistent but more moderate economic expansion is forecast in 2019 at 2.7 per cent and in 2020 at 2.4 per cent. Investment in large mining projects peaked in 2012/13, at 9 per cent of GDP, and subsequently declined rapidly. In 2018, however, a rise in new dwelling construction allowed total real fixed capital formation to increase by more than 5 per cent. Housing-related investment is expected to moderate in 2019. As wage growth remains persistently slow, the inflation rate is estimated at 2.1 per cent in 2018, and forecast to be 2.2 per cent in 2019 and 2020.

Figure III.4
Sectoral share of gross value added in Australia, 2000–2018

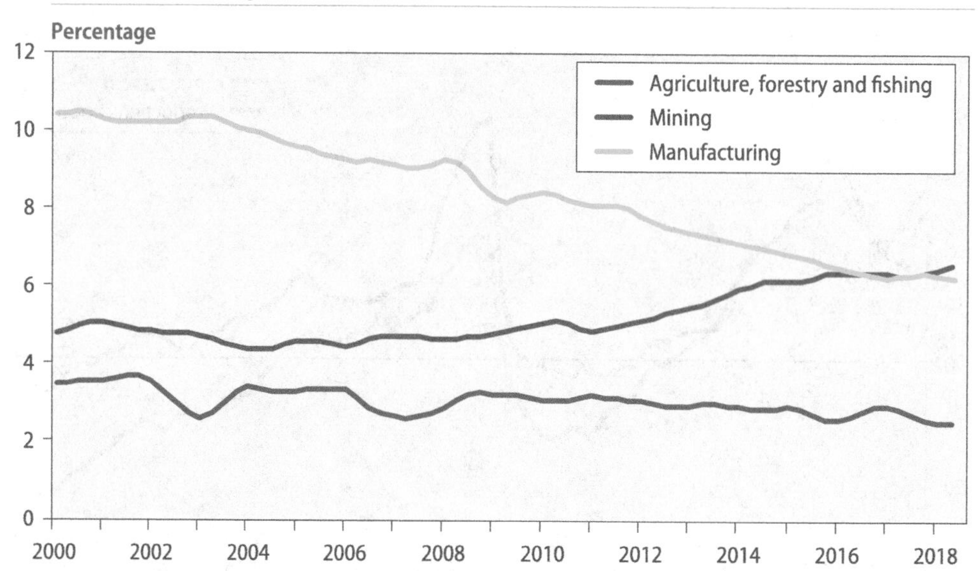

Source: Australian Bureau of Statistics.
Note: Figure shows percentage share of chain volume measure.

Australia faces international pressures to curb coal production

Australia remains dependent on commodity exports. The share of primary products in merchandise exports in 2017/18 edged up to 61 per cent from 59 per cent in the previous year. Despite the stagnating price of iron ore, coal prices rose significantly in 2018, strengthening Australia's balance of payments position. The gross value added share of the mining industry surpassed that of the manufacturing industry in 2018 (figure III.4). As coal-burning power generation is one of the major sources of carbon dioxide (CO_2) emissions, Australia is expected to face increasing international pressures to curb coal production.

House prices moderate in New Zealand

In New Zealand, real GDP growth is estimated at 2.9 per cent in 2018, and forecast to be 2.7 per cent in 2019 and 3.0 per cent in 2020. A mild deceleration in 2019 is expected, due to slower fixed capital investment growth and a cooling housing market. However, private consumption is forecast to be robust over 2019 and 2020; as economic fundamentals remain strong and the Government maintains its healthy fiscal position, robust growth is forecast to continue over 2019 and 2020. An abrupt downward adjustment of house prices is the main downside risk for the economy.

Europe: robust growth ahead, but risks to the outlook are shifting

Europe will continue to see robust growth

Europe will continue to see robust growth of 2.0 per cent in both 2019 and 2020. The main drivers of this performance remain intact, notably solid household consumption propelled by lower unemployment, rising wages and the continued accommodative monetary policy stance. On the business side, companies, especially in the construction sector, also continue to benefit from the expansionary monetary policy stance.

Downside risks include increased trade tensions, a shift in policy stance, and Brexit

However, the risk profile of the outlook has markedly changed for a number of reasons. First of all, numerous countries in the region find themselves on a decelerating growth trend, which is one symptom of the uncertainty created by the increase in global trade tensions. Second, the European Central Bank (ECB) faces the challenge of exiting its accommodative policy stance, which holds the potential for major ramifications along the way, such as heightened financial market volatility. In the area of fiscal policy, the euro area will be faced with the unresolved problem of how to achieve and maintain a common policy stance in the absence, at least so far, of a more institutionalized policy framework. Tensions has arisen over the restrictions on fiscal policy imposed by EU policy guidelines. The European Commission has indicated that Italy's fiscal plans for 2019 are not in compliance with recommendations, while the Italian Government stands firm on the plans. Uncertainty over the credibility of the EU's fiscal framework has the potential to lead to sharp financial market reactions. Finally, the uncertainty created by the looming exit of the United Kingdom of Great Britain and Northern Ireland from the European Union (EU)—Brexit—has already led to increased tangible economic consequences, such as companies moving assets or diverting investment from the United Kingdom to the EU. In the case of a disorderly exit from the EU, the British economy runs the risk of even more domestic disruptions because of the lack of a broad legal framework for its future trade relations with the EU, while the European financial sector could face severe disruption.

Growth in Germany and France will remain slightly lower

The overall regional growth profile traces the performance of the largest economies in the region. In Germany, growth will remain moderately lower at 1.8 per cent in 2019 and 2020, as the external environment is becoming less supportive and the important car industry is facing disruption and pressure through new technologies, new competitors and significant legal and financial consequences from past sales practices related to the diesel technology. By contrast, private consumption remains a major driver of growth, given a strong employment picture that is increasingly feeding through to higher wages. In various regions in Germany, employment conditions are equivalent to full employment, with companies being held back in their operations by the lack of qualified workers. France will see a similar growth profile, with growth staying at 1.8 per cent in 2019 and 2020. Weaker exports will be offset by economic reforms that are expected to provide additional growth impetus going into 2020.

Italy will see the slowest growth rate, while the exit from the EU casts a shadow on growth in the United Kingdom

The lowest growth rate in the region will materialize in Italy, with the economy forecast to expand by just 1.2 per cent and 1.0 per cent in 2019 and 2020, respectively. The generally weakening external environment combines with significant constraints on private consumption in view of political uncertainty, the fragility of the banking system, and only limited growth in employment and wages. In the United Kingdom, economic growth will reach 1.4 per cent in 2019 and 1.7 per cent in 2020. The uncertainty related to the exit from the EU remains a major drag on the economy, with firms taking precautions against a hard exit without a clear agreement on future trade relations, while higher inflation and monetary policy tightening have negatively impacted consumer purchasing power. On the flip side, these factors are partially offset by stronger exports due to the increase in competitiveness stemming from the depreciation of the pound.

Policy space in the euro area is limited

A major risk of wider significance for the global economy stems from limited policy space in the euro area. In the wake of the financial crisis, countries followed a path of procyclical fiscal consolidation, with monetary policy playing the role of stimulating economic activity. Monetary policymakers repeatedly emphasized the need for individual countries to complement the extremely accommodative stance with necessary economic reforms to revitalize their economies. Today, with a turn in monetary policy imminent and by some measures even overdue, the window of opportunity provided by the extraordinarily loose monetary policy stance to undertake further-reaching economic reforms is about to start closing. In many cases, countries still find themselves in fundamentally challenging policy positions: Belgium, Greece, Italy and Portugal feature public debt-to-GDP ratios above 100 per cent, while in Cyprus, France and Spain, the ratio is only slightly less than 100 per cent (figure III.5).

Faster tightening of monetary policy may be needed

In terms of monetary policy, the ECB has signalled that it will maintain the current level of near-zero interest rates at least through the summer of 2019, and that after ending its net asset purchases at the end of December 2018, it will continue to reinvest the principal payments from maturing assets for an extended period of time. With respect to its policy interest rates, the ECB has made any move also conditional upon the convergence of inflation to a level of less than but close to 2 per cent over the medium term. The reinvestment of maturing assets will last as long as required in order to ensure favourable liquidity conditions.

Figure III.5
Public debt in the European Union, 2017

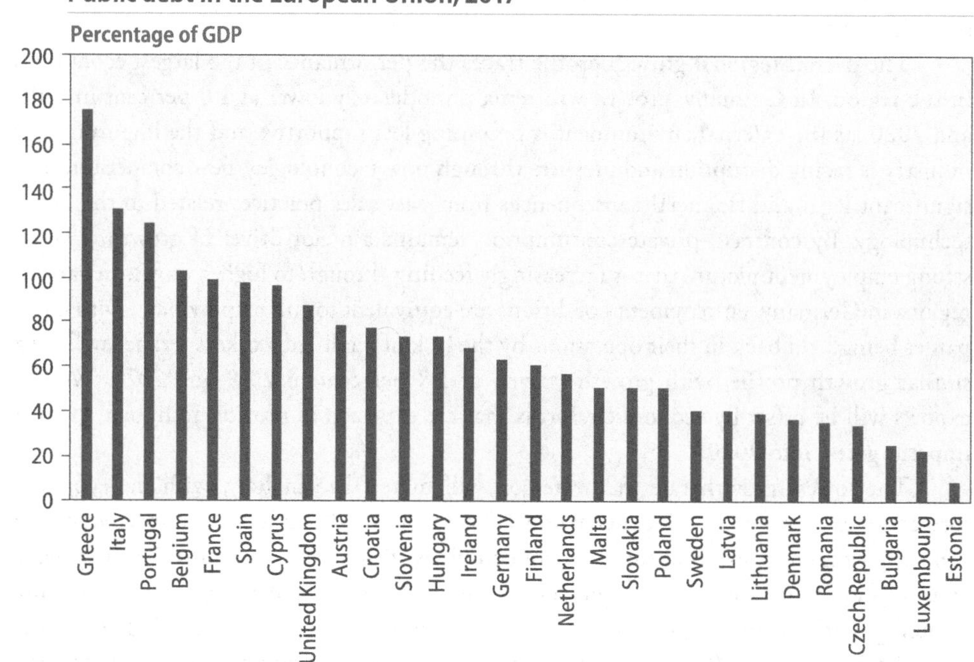

Source: Eurostat.

Assessing this monetary policy stance against the business cycle in the euro area shows that there is significant risk that monetary policymakers might fall behind the curve, in the sense of maintaining extraordinary crisis measures at a time when they are not needed anymore. In the case of upside surprises in inflation data, the ECB could be induced to tighten monetary policy faster than expected, accompanied by the resulting volatile readjustment in financial market expectations and financial asset prices.

A renewed crisis would pose a significant policy challenge

High levels of debt, the prospect of rising interest rates with the associated jump in the costs of servicing these debt levels, and the EU budget rules on debt levels and deficits all serve to limit the scope for fiscal policy to offset the withdrawal of monetary stimulus. These conditions also leave very limited policy options in case of a renewed economic slowdown, stemming, for example, from an escalation of global trade frictions. Under one scenario, it would fall again to monetary policymakers to manage the economy, but from a starting position that is already akin to crisis modus, pinning them to the zero bound of interest rates for much longer and with much fewer normalization options than anticipated. In the other scenario, national Governments could respond to a renewed slowdown by initiating more expansionary fiscal policy stances; this, in many cases, would be in open violation of EU rules, casting doubt on the validity of EU agreements and testing the tolerance of financial markets for further increases in debt levels.

Aggregate GDP of EU members from Eastern Europe and the Baltics expanded

During most of 2018, the EU members from Eastern Europe and the Baltics have sustained the buoyant economic dynamism of 2017, with GDP growth often exceeding earlier forecasts. The aggregate GDP of these countries has expanded by 4.2 per cent, well above the EU average; in the largest economy in the group, Poland, growth is estimated at 5.0 per cent.

Industrial exports, consumption and investment propel growth...

Export performance of the Eastern European industrial sector remains one of the key growth drivers. Output of the automotive industry, after reaching record highs in 2017, remained strong, and the sector is attracting massive new investments despite rising wage costs. Private consumption, boosted by tight labour markets and the surge in nominal wages and mostly loose monetary policy, has also notably contributed to growth, becoming the main engine of the Polish economy. Investment has also increased rapidly, thanks to the higher rate of absorption of EU funds. The construction sector significantly contributed to growth in Hungary.

...but labour shortages are holding back expansion

Labour market conditions have continued to tighten (box III.1), with the unemployment rate at record lows in several countries. For example, the Czech Republic has the lowest in the EU, at 2.3 per cent, while the unfilled vacancies rate in the country has exceeded 5.0 per cent in 2018. Those conditions—exacerbated in certain countries by outward migration, skills shortages and demographic trends—exerted upward pressure on wages.

There are signs that some of those economies may be operating above potential. This raises questions about growth sustainability, as consumption-driven expansion and the rising private debt burden are masking numerous risks. The climbing house prices across Eastern Europe and the increased exposure of the financial sector to housing loans may indicate the emergence of another housing bubble. Concerns about overheating—along with currency pressures linked to the stronger dollar and the announced tapering of the ultra-loose ECB stance—and accelerating inflation have prompted a few central banks to tighten monetary policy (the Czech National Bank lifted policy rates several times, for example). By contrast, in Hungary and Poland, where wage pressures have yet to feed into inflation (perhaps because of higher saving rates and remittance outflows), the monetary stance remained loose.

Some moderation in economic activity is expected in 2019–2020

Economic activity in the group is expected to moderate in 2019–2020 as global trade tensions may negatively affect exports, and the consumption boom should slow in response to inflation. The EU funding from the 2014–2020 budget cycle has apparently passed its peak. The aggregate growth of this group of countries should nevertheless exceed the EU average, as they are still catching up, with capital accumulation, technology transfers and productivity gains. However, both external and internal constraints are emerging. The outflow of labour to the richer EU counterparts is curbing capacity output and has reached dangerous levels of depopulation in certain cases. The decision of the United Kingdom to leave the EU may affect future migration flows, although a mass return of migrants from the United Kingdom to their countries of origin in Eastern Europe and the Baltic States is unlikely. The proposed reduction in EU cohesion funds in the 2021–2027 EU budget cycle may curb further progress in infrastructure development and construction; however, some countries that attained fiscal surpluses, such as the Czech Republic, intend to carry on with publicly funded infrastructure projects.

Box III.1

Emerging labour shortages in Eastern Europe

Since the beginning of the transition to market economies in the late 1980s, high unemployment has persisted as one of the most serious macroeconomic and social problems in the countries of Eastern Europe and the Baltic States (EU-11). Privatization and restructuring of the formerly State-owned enterprises—often involving massive layoffs, modernization of the industrial sector and the resulting skills mismatch, the shift from manufacturing to services sector with smaller-sized companies, and reductions in the public sector, along with other factors—contributed to persistently high structural and long-term unemployment in the region. The situation improved in the early 2000s, as significant job gains were seen in the region. However, most of the new jobs created were in the construction and manufacturing industries, which were hit very hard by the global economic and financial crisis in 2008–2009. According to the World Bank, nearly half of the jobs created during the period 2002–2008 were subsequently lost in the crisis (World Bank, 2013); in some countries the unemployment rate jumped to 20 per cent. The post-crisis recovery in employment was sluggish, as fiscal austerity policies often involved further cuts in public sector employment and restrained aggregate demand, the construction industry was slow to recover, and gains in labour productivity allowed firms to postpone hiring decisions.

Since 2014, however, the situation has been changing quite steadily (figure III.1.1). In many of the EU-11 countries, the unemployment rate declined to record lows in 2018, with the Czech Republic having the lowest unemployment rate in the EU, at 2.3 per cent. Persistent labour shortages emerged as one of the most serious constraints on economic growth, including in Poland, which has seen noticeable labour migration from Ukraine since 2014. About 75–80 per cent of surveyed firms in the Czech Republic, Hungary and Poland in 2018 indicated labour shortage as a constraint to capacity expansion.

Several factors contributed to the dramatic decline in unemployment in the region. Economic growth and expansion of output capacity in response to the stronger external and domestic demand have definitely played an important role. Activity rates in the region have been steadily increasing, exceeding 76 per cent in the Czech Republic in 2018. A simple ordinary least squares (OLS) regression based on a version of Okun's Law, which links cyclical unemployment dynamics to economic growth, identifies

Figure III.1.1

Unemployment rate, selected countries in Eastern Europe

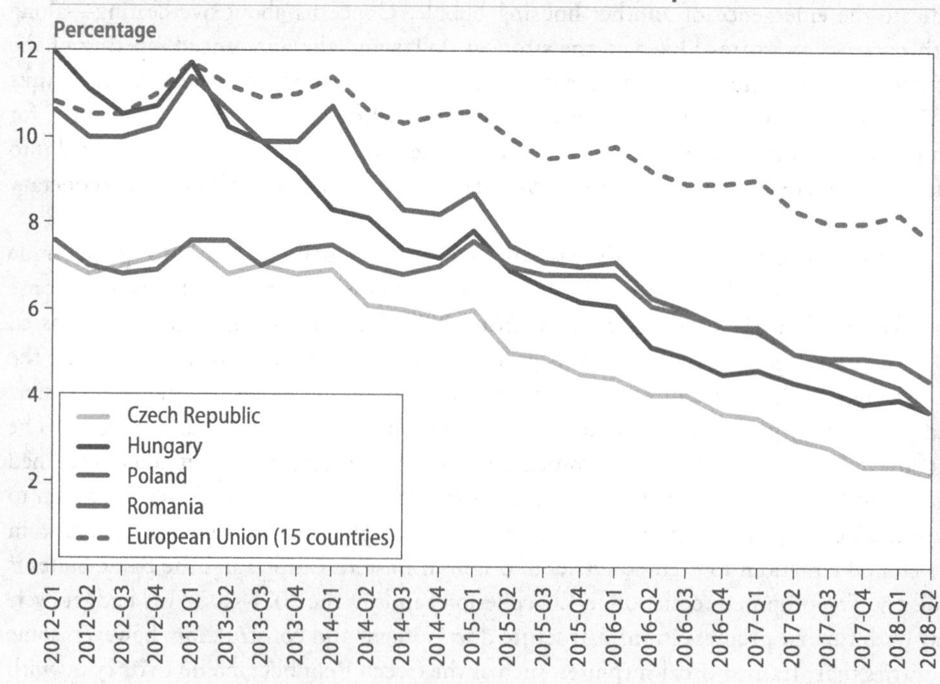

Source: Eurostat.

(continued)

Box III.1 (*continued*)

a correlation between GDP growth and movement in the unemployment rate.[a] However, this relationship can only partially explain the steep decline in unemployment rates in recent years, which may partly reflect the shadow economy not captured by the labour force surveys and large outward migration. Meanwhile, many countries in the region have also been experiencing unfavourable demographic trends over the last decade, including population ageing and decline, and gradual withdrawal from the labour force by those heavily impacted by the transition process.

High levels of outward labour migration to the EU-15, especially from Poland and the Baltic States, may also help explain the decline in unemployment. Outward migration was important for alleviating labour market pressures in the region, as many migrants came from the pool of workers with a higher probability of unemployment at home, belonging to medium-skill groups but with limited work experience. On the other hand, in the Czech Republic, which has the lowest unemployment rate in the region, net inward migration has been positive since the early 2000s; in Poland, the net migration balance has also turned positive since 2016.

The current labour market situation in most of the EU-11 can be characterized as quantitative labour shortages—a mismatch between the total supply and demand for labour affecting virtually all sectors of the economy. The tightness of the labour market in the Czech Republic is illustrated in figure III.1.2A. The Beveridge curve plots the vacancy rate against the unemployment rate; moving up the curve and to the left indicates increasing tightness of the labour market. This is clearly different from the qualitative labour shortages observed in some of the EU-15 countries (European Parliament, 2015), which are reflecting skill mismatches or reluctance to accept wages/working conditions. In this case, a high unemployment rate often coexists with a high number of unfilled positions (figure III.1.2B).

The observed record-low unemployment rates in Eastern Europe, combined with labour shortages across sectors, have driven rapid real wage growth, which is starting to outpace productivity gains. The shortage of workers has also influenced the magnitude of foreign direct investment outflows from those countries, in particular to South-Eastern Europe. Since encouraging immigration remains a politically contentious issue, companies may expedite automation and robotization in production to increase productivity. But there is also emerging evidence that workers from the EU-15 countries, although in small numbers, are increasingly moving to Eastern Europe in search of employment. Data from Eurostat points to steadily increasing numbers of working-age EU-15 citizens residing in the EU-11. If this trend persists, it may constitute a further important step towards the integration of the European labour markets.

a Estimation of a relationship $U_t - U_{t-4} = \beta_0 + \beta_1 * \left(\frac{Y_t}{Y_{t-4}} - 1\right) + \varepsilon_t$ was carried out for 8 countries in the region, using Eurostat's quarterly seasonally adjusted output and unemployment rate data for 2010 Q1–2018 Q2, producing statistically significant regression coefficients for the economic growth variable and R^2 values for the equations ranging from 0.11 in the case of Poland to 0.71 in the case of Croatia.

Author: Grigor Agabekian (UN/DESA/EAPD).

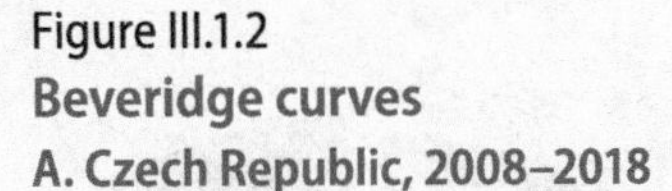
Figure III.1.2
Beveridge curves
A. Czech Republic, 2008–2018

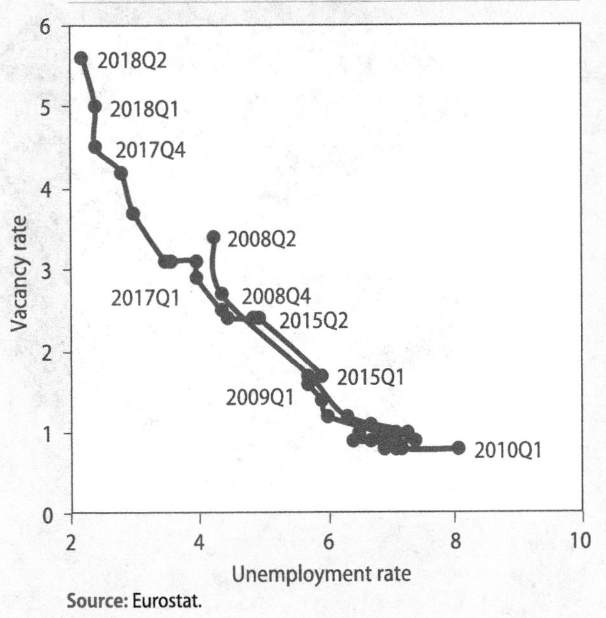

B. Finland, 2012–2018

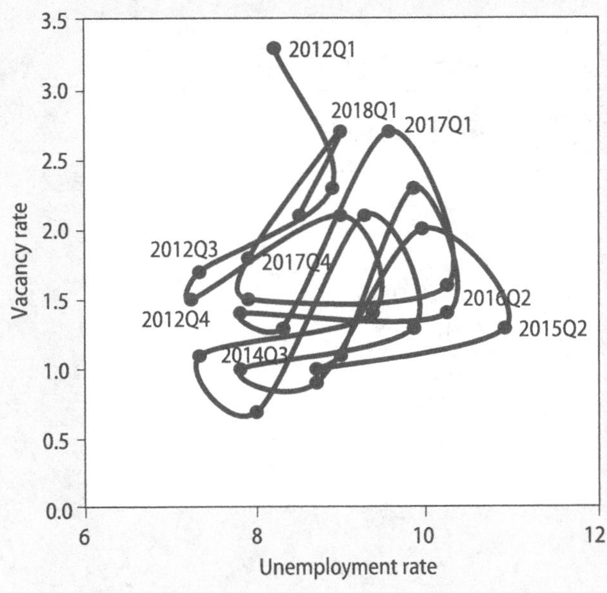

Source: Eurostat.

Economies in transition

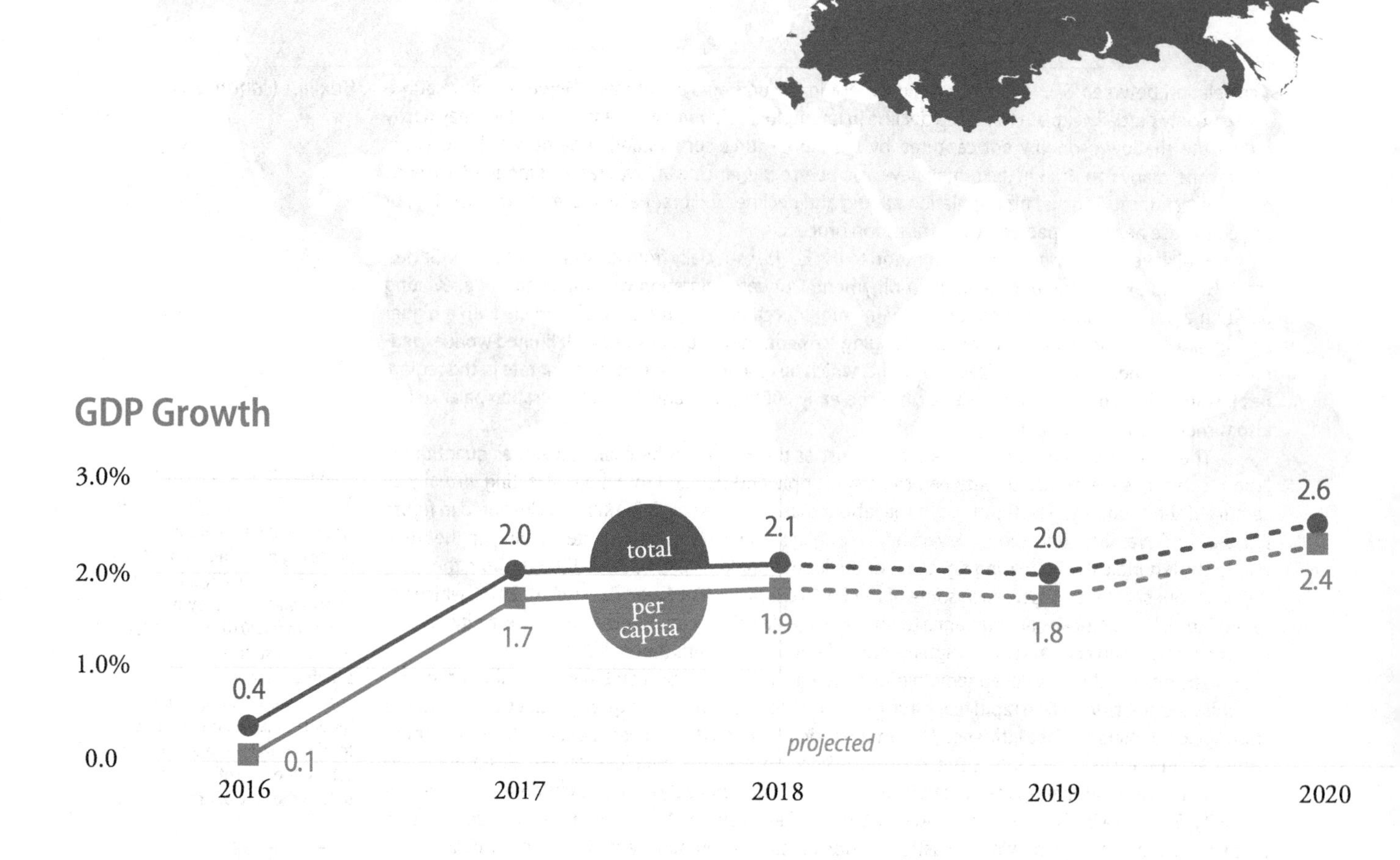

GDP Growth

GDP per capita

2018

Exports structure

2016

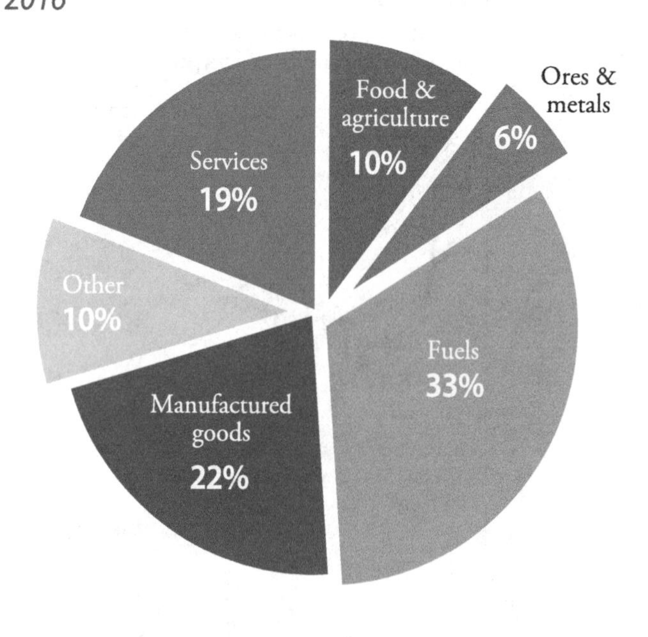

The boundaries and names shown and the designations used on this map do not imply official endorsement or acceptance by the United Nations. The map represents countries and/or territories or parts thereof for which data is available and/or analysed in *World Economic Situation and Prospects 2019*. The shaded areas therefore do not necessarily overlap entirely with the delimitation of their frontiers or boundaries.

Economies in transition

- Economic trends both in the CIS and South-Eastern Europe are broadly positive
- Commodity dependence and tighter access to external funding pose risks for the CIS economies
- Despite strong growth in South-Eastern Europe, many structural problems still have to be addressed

The Commonwealth of Independent States and Georgia: commodity price increases and remittances sustained growth

Most economies of the Commonwealth of Independent States (CIS) saw favourable economic outcomes in 2018, with accelerating growth and tapering inflation, as external conditions were generally supportive. Commodity prices increased, including not only oil but also other commodities such as aluminium or cotton, which are important for non-energy-exporting CIS countries. The recovery in the Russian Federation has supported activity across the region via trade and remittance channels. After two years of improvements, however, the dynamics in the terms of trade are likely to be less favourable in 2019. The aggregate CIS growth is expected to decelerate modestly in the outlook, as the strong expansion recorded by some of the smaller economies in 2018 may not be sustainable, fiscal policies are growth-neutral at best and monetary tightening is on its way in several countries.

Risks to the outlook persist

Aggregate GDP of the CIS and Georgia is expected to increase by 2.0 and 2.5 per cent in 2019 and 2020, respectively. The region—the Russian Federation in particular—continues to show a lack of economic dynamism, since structural impediments to growth remain despite the improved macroeconomic frameworks. In the presence of adverse demographic trends in the European part of the CIS, increased attention is required to productivity-enhancing factors. A sudden downturn in commodity prices remains the main downside risk for the region, given the slow progress in output diversification. Other risks include banking sector weaknesses, which have not been eliminated despite numerous bailout efforts, geopolitical conflicts, and also tightening of access to external funding and debt refinancing.

Russian economy to remain on a low-growth trajectory

The Russian economy expanded by an estimated 1.5 per cent in 2018, mostly driven by private consumption, while a higher oil price has allowed rebuilding of fiscal buffers. The FIFA 2018 World Cup, whose preparations contributed to fixed investment earlier, provided a large boost to the tourism industry. Meanwhile, consumer spending gradually recovered at the beginning of the year thanks to a stabilized currency, sharp disinflation and the pick-up in household borrowing. However, geopolitical tensions have led to several rounds of additional economic sanctions in 2018, including the possibility of freezing several large Russian banks' assets abroad and restricting their dollar transactions, and targeting Russian sovereign debt. This has complicated activities of Russian companies and exerted downward pressure on the rouble. The central bank has temporarily suspended foreign-exchange purchases conducted in accordance with the budget rule and reversed monetary loosening by lifting policy interest rates in September. Meanwhile, business lending remains supressed. The depreciation of the rouble also had regional spillover effects, particularly to Kazakhstan (figure III.6).

Figure III.6
Exchange rate vs the US dollar in the Russian Federation and Kazakhstan, January–October 2018

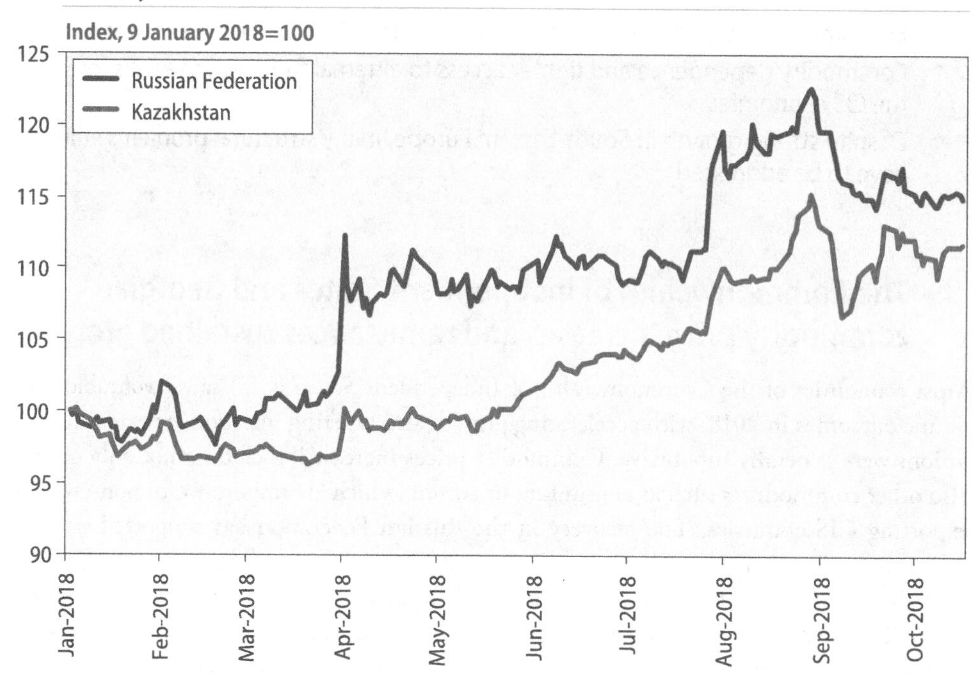

Source: UN/DESA, based on data from the IMF Exchange Rate database.

The Russian economy is expected to remain on a low-growth trajectory, at about 1.5–2.0 per cent in 2019–2020. Constraints to growth prospects include insufficient business lending; weak investment; banking sector vulnerabilities and moderately conservative fiscal policy; and prioritizing the build-up of protective buffers. Lifting the value added tax (VAT) rate in January 2019 may add to inflationary pressures in 2019, curb consumer spending, and prevent monetary relaxation. International sanctions remain a source of uncertainty, deterring investment and raising financing costs. For example, the share of non-residents in the domestic bond market has started to decline while yields have increased. Full implementation of the proposed United States sanctions may push the Russian economy into a protracted stagnation with negative regional spillovers, as the scope for import substitution is largely exhausted. On the positive side, however, the country has a large current account surplus, low public debt and has massive foreign-exchange reserves. The implementation of the social and economic development programmes for the period until 2024 will improve infrastructure and add to GDP growth, especially beyond 2019.

Other energy-exporting economies of the CIS should maintain a positive growth trajectory in 2019–2020, thanks to relatively high oil prices and prudent macroeconomic policies. In Kazakhstan, growth reached 4 per cent in 2018, reflecting the rising oil and gas output and investment in transport infrastructure. As oil output at the giant Kashagan field is approaching full capacity, growth is expected to come from the non-energy sector in 2019–2020. Escalation of trade disputes between China and the United States may affect some of Kazakhstan's exports of intermediate goods (chemical products and metals). In Azerbaijan, the planned rise in natural gas output should accelerate growth in 2019 above the low levels seen in 2018. In Turkmenistan, efforts are on the way to diversify natural gas export markets and develop the non-energy sector.

Belarus and Ukraine face large external debt repayments

Among the CIS energy importers, the economy of Ukraine has expanded by about 3.2 per cent in 2018 and this trend is likely to continue. However, further progress is hampered by mass emigration, which is also driving up wage costs. The sharp increase in remittances has mitigated external financing needs, but tough policy choices remain, as large external debt repayments are looming in 2019. The possible downscaling, or even suspension, of the Russian natural gas transit beginning in 2019 presents a serious risk. Belarus, which is also facing external debt repayments, benefited in 2018 from the improved Russian demand and strong expansion of industrial exports to non-CIS countries. However, emerging new disputes with the Russian Federation on the terms of oil imports may seriously damage the economy in 2019, and the country remains reliant on oil subsidies and credits from the Russian Federation in the absence of alternative sources of financing.

Some smaller CIS economies expanded strongly

In 2018, remittances to the smaller CIS countries remained robust, increasing in dollar terms by over 15 per cent in the first half of the year. This bolstered private spending, although the weakening of the Russian rouble may undermine the purchasing power of those transfers. In the Caucasus, strong economic activity was recorded in Armenia, driven by construction, mining, manufacturing and services. In Central Asia, growth was robust in Tajikistan, thanks to larger aluminium and gold exports and Chinese investment in metals processing. The series of economic reforms in Uzbekistan attracted foreign investment and spurred interregional trade. Growth in these countries may slightly decelerate in 2019 if higher inflation erodes purchasing power.

Looking forward, the Central Asian region should benefit from the implementation of the Belt and Road Initiative (BRI), through upgrades of the railway, road and energy infrastructure, improved connections with China and Europe, and better market access. However, in some cases, funding of the BRI project has driven up external debt, giving rise to longer-term financial stability risks. The signing of a convention determining the legal status of the Caspian Sea in August 2018 by the littoral States may in the longer run encourage investment and exploration of new oil and gas fields in the Caspian basin. The delimitation of the seabed is still unclear and remains a limiting factor.

Additional inflationary pressures are possible in 2019

Inflation in early 2018 has been on a declining trend throughout the region. The observed deceleration was particularly large in Azerbaijan, as the impact of past exchange-rate depreciation wore off. However, some price pressures are emerging. In the Russian Federation, inflation has been accelerating, driven by the recent bout of exchange-rate weakness; the planned VAT hike in 2019 will push inflation further. In Ukraine, increases in gas prices will boost inflation in 2019.

Labour market performance has been positive. The unemployment rate continued to decline to record-low levels in the Russian Federation. By contrast, in Kazakhstan, the unemployment rate remained practically unchanged, although employment levels continued to grow. For the smaller CIS economies, seasonal migration to the Russian Federation is alleviating labour market pressures.

Amid rising inflationary expectations and increased uncertainty, earlier loosening of monetary policies has been halted or reversed. The depreciation of the rouble and increasing uncertainty put further interest rate cuts on hold in the Russian Federation early in the year and, in September 2018, led to the first hike since December 2014. The National Bank of Ukraine delivered a number of interest rate increases, prompted by concerns regarding (i) inflation expectations, (ii) the expected risks caused by a decreasing appetite for emerging assets and (iii) uncertainties around International Monetary Fund (IMF) programmes. Monetary policy was also tightened in Kazakhstan and Uzbekistan, reflecting

Box III.2

New fiscal rules in energy-exporting countries of the Commonwealth of Independent States

Managing the output, inflation and currency volatility created by fluctuating oil prices has been an ongoing challenge for energy-exporting economies in the Commonwealth of Independent States (CIS). The decline that began in 2014 ushered a new environment of persistently lower prices. This shock was initially partially absorbed by countercyclical spending, which, at different speeds, was replaced by fiscal consolidation. Foreign currency assets that accumulated in existing oil funds were depleted, although the depreciation of national currencies has partly offset the losses in domestic currency terms. In a context of restricted access to external finance, due to the sanctions against the Russian Federation and a worsened environment for emerging markets, the importance of rebuilding fiscal buffers to reduce vulnerability to external shocks has increased.

Fiscal rules, which impose quantitative constraints on government finances, have been used to reduce the impact of changes in commodity prices on the domestic economy. In the Russian Federation, a new fiscal rule was introduced in 2017 and slightly modified in 2018. A structural non-oil primary balance of the federal budget is calculated using a $40 per barrel oil price benchmark (in 2017 prices, with annual indexation to account for inflation). This balance should be zero or positive, although allowances are made for a transitory period; plans for 2019–2021 envisage an annual deficit of about 0.5 per cent of GDP. Revenues derived from oil prices exceeding $40 per barrel are set aside to buy foreign currency in the domestic market, fuelling the growth of international reserves under current price levels. The rule also sets limits on the use of National Welfare Fund resources, depending on the level of accumulated resources.

In Kazakhstan, according to the current fiscal rule, all hydrocarbon revenues accrue to the National Oil Fund of the Republic of Kazakhstan (NFRK), with the exception of customs duties, which are directly allocated to the budget. Annual guaranteed transfers flow from the NFRK to the budget. There are plans to reduce these transfers from 4.5 per cent of GDP in 2018 to 3.0 per cent of GDP by 2020. At the same time, the rule also targets the non-oil deficit. In Azerbaijan, a fiscal rule will be implemented as of 2019 setting limits on the use of oil revenues and overall expenditures. The impact of these fiscal rules

Figure III.2.1

Oil price and exchange rate in the Russian Federation, 2014–2018

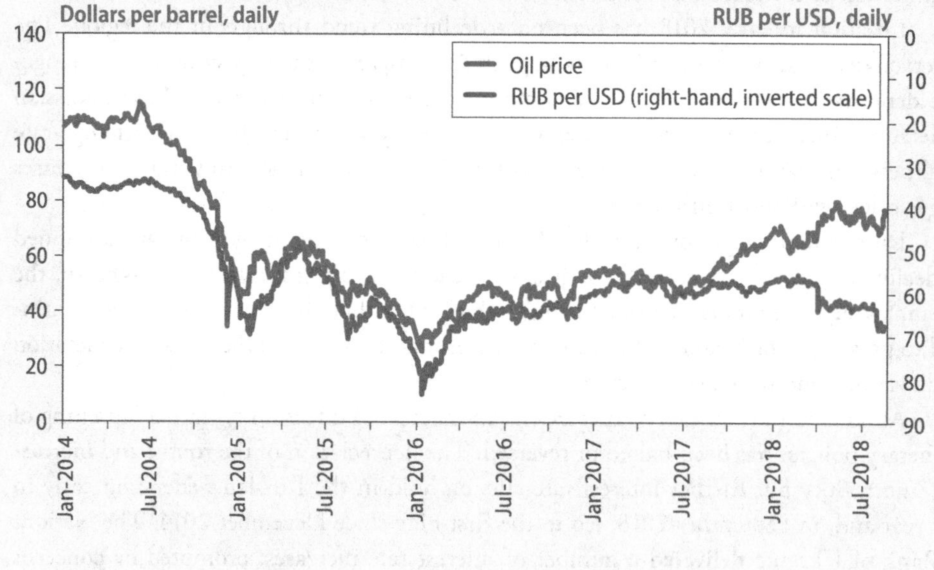

Sources: Central Bank of Russia, US Energy Information Administration (via FRED).

(continued)

Box III.2 (*continued*)

is to weaken the link between oil price dynamics, on the one hand, and economic performance, budget revenues, inflation and the exchange rate on the other. The design of the new fiscal rule in the Russian Federation has indeed broken the traditional correlation between the exchange rate and the oil price (figure III.2.1). This has also increased the profitability of energy companies. In the past, higher oil prices increased revenues but also local costs, given the accompanying appreciation of the exchange rate.

The current design of fiscal rules also presents some limitations. In Kazakhstan, guaranteed transfers from the NFRK are not linked to changes in revenues due to oil prices, while discretionary transfers persist, thus undermining the credibility of the fiscal framework. In the Russian Federation, the rule does not cover off-budget expenditures and therefore does not constrain procyclical spending per se. In both countries, State-owned enterprises may be a source of contingent fiscal risks.

Oil and gas reserves horizons are relatively long in the region. As a result, macro stabilization concerns, rather than intergenerational considerations, have dominated the design of fiscal rules. Typical price-based rules, such as the one adopted in the Russian Federation, provide an anchor for fiscal policy but do not address the fact that resources are exhaustible. However, demographic trends and rising pension liabilities point to the need for a long-term savings target for the National Welfare Fund.

The recovery of oil prices since mid-2017 will allow a more rapid rebuilding of buffers. However, there is the danger that this may undermine fiscal consolidation efforts. These efforts should also pay attention to the need to preserve growth-enhancing spending in key areas such education, health or infrastructure.

Author: José Palacín (UN/ECE).

rising inflationary risks and currency pressures. By contrast, in Azerbaijan, rapid disinflation allowed for a series of rate cuts, and the policy rate was marginally reduced in Belarus, Georgia and Kyrgyzstan. Overall, policies remain relatively tight, thus limiting the growth of private credit.

Fiscal policies are expected to stay largely conservative

Continued economic recovery and higher oil prices have boosted public finances, narrowing fiscal deficits. Fiscal policy in the Russian Federation is constrained by the fiscal rule introduced in 2017 (box III.2). To boost budget revenue, particularly for programmes aimed at the social and economic targets announced in May 2018, the Russian Government has decided to lift the VAT rate in January 2019 and increase the pension age. The planned budget for 2019–2021 assumes maintaining the estimated surplus of 2018 and increasing reliance on non-hydrocarbon revenues. Building a massive net sovereign asset position remains a priority and public spending may stagnate in real terms if inflation accelerates. In Kazakhstan, significant funds were used in 2017 to bail out the banking sector; stronger economic activity in 2018 helped to consolidate the budget and a tighter fiscal rule has been introduced. Azerbaijan has also adopted a fiscal rule restricting spending growth and aiming to reduce the public debt. In Turkmenistan, numerous state subsidies were removed in 2017 and free utilities for households will be discontinued in 2019; the budget is being consolidated after earlier massive infrastructure spending. A more supportive fiscal stance is expected in Uzbekistan, utilizing the accumulated wealth fund.

Among the energy importers, conditionality of IMF programmes—requiring, in some cases, a reduction in the size of the public debt—places restrictions on fiscal policy in Ukraine and in a number of other countries. Fiscal space is also constrained by external debt repayments, particularly in Belarus. In Georgia, deficit reduction is projected to be accompanied by significant capital expenditure increases. In Tajikistan, further support to the banking sector may be needed.

South-Eastern Europe: positive economic trends set to continue

The countries of South-Eastern Europe saw accelerated economic growth in 2018, reflecting robust domestic demand, both consumption and investment, in the context of a favourable external environment. Serbia, the largest economy, bounced back strongly from the past slowdown, bolstered by agriculture and construction sectors, with a double-digit growth in investment. Solid economic performance was also recorded in Albania, as exports and domestic demand remained strong and investment was boosted by foreign interest in the energy sector. Growth in the former Yugoslav Republic of Macedonia picked up from nearly zero last year. A surge in investment boosted growth in Montenegro, but the completion of some infrastructure projects will moderate the growth in the outlook.

Labour markets improve, but structural unemployment remains a drag on the economies

Labour markets in the region continued to improve in 2018, with the unemployment rate falling to a record low in Albania, although persistently high unemployment in Bosnia and Herzegovina and the former Yugoslav Republic of Macedonia remains a sustained drag on the outlook, with damaging implications for labour quality. Inflation has somewhat accelerated, fuelled by stronger domestic demand and higher energy and food prices. However, price increases remained moderate and inflation is largely below central banks' targets. Among the countries with flexible currencies, monetary policy was relaxed in Albania and Serbia.

Stronger growth is constrained by structural unemployment and inadequate infrastructure

The region's aggregate GDP is expected to expand by 3.7 per cent in both 2019 and 2020, supported mostly by investment and exports. Stronger growth is needed to address the region's diverse problems, including the need for reindustrialization and a low labour force participation rate. However, the longer-term capacity expansion is constrained by structural unemployment, improving but still inadequate infrastructure, dependence on foreign financing, and a still challenging business environment. High levels of outward migration and increasing dependency ratios are becoming policy challenges, in particular in Serbia. The region is attracting large foreign direct investment (FDI) inflows; a significant part of these inflows target sectors such as financial services, telecommunications, real estate and retail trade. The recent investment financed by loans from China has driven up external debt.

Joining the EU remains a policy anchor

The prospect of EU accession, confirmed by the European Commission (2018b) strategy paper, and the decision by the Council of the EU to open accession negotiations with Albania and the former Yugoslav Republic of Macedonia in 2019 (if they meet certain conditions) remain important macroeconomic policy anchors. The pre-accession assistance provided by the EU has a tangible developmental impact. However, Brexit may lead to about a 10–15 per cent decline in funding available to EU accession countries. Given the importance of trade, investment and remittance links with the EU, any deterioration in the economic performance of the EU will have negative consequences for the region. Some countries are strongly exposed to Greece and Italy and would suffer spillovers from possible deterioration in those countries.

GDP Growth

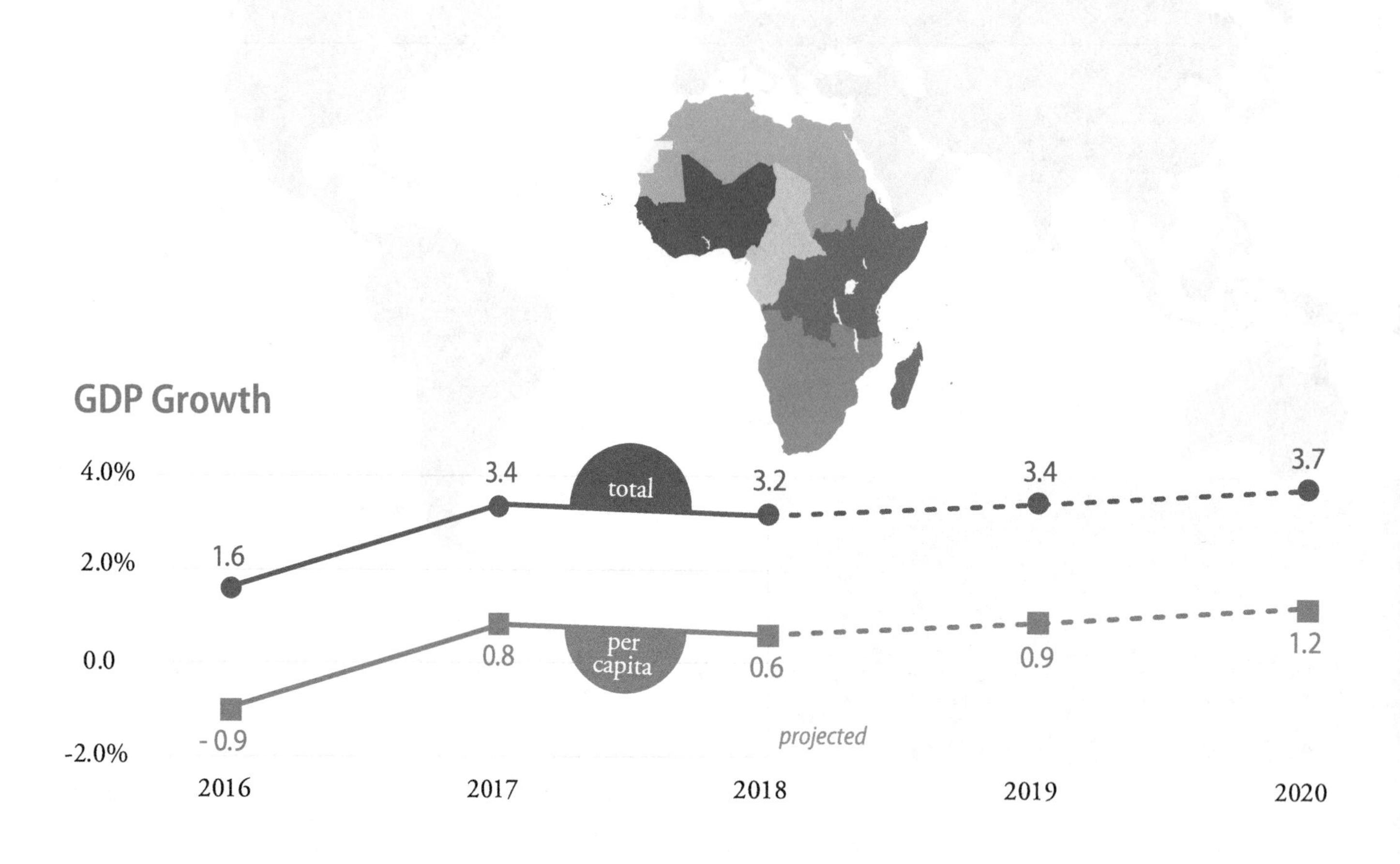

GDP per capita

2018

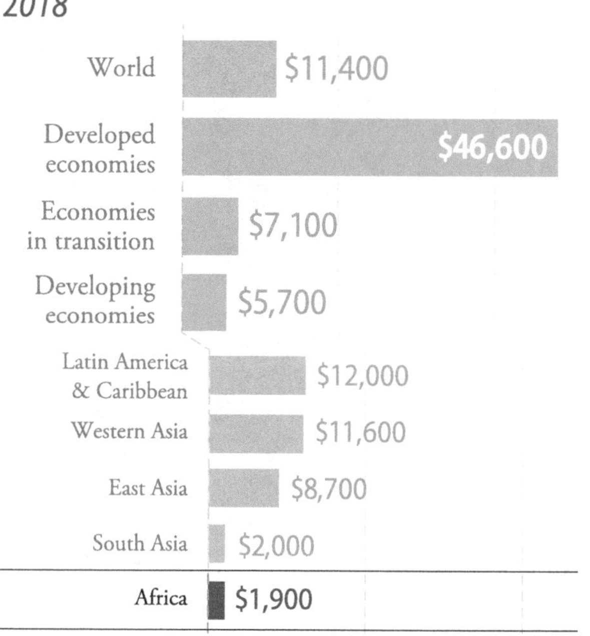

Exports structure

2016

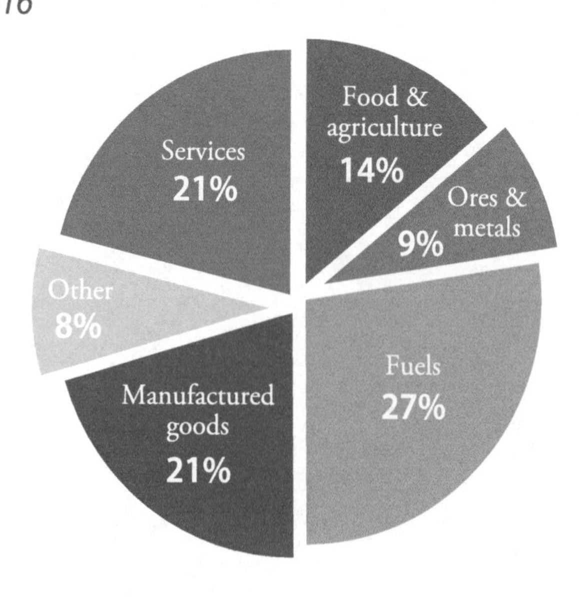

Developing economies

Africa: improving short-term outlook but with significant medium-term vulnerabilities

- Growth in Africa is expected to strenghten
- The outlook is clouded by downside risks, while substantial structural vulnerabilities remain unresolved
- Medium-term prospects remain too weak to reach many targets of the Sustainable Development Goals

Growth is modestly improving and inflationary pressures have eased

Africa's economic growth is projected to increase slightly from 3.2 per cent in 2018 to 3.4 per cent in 2019 and 3.7 per cent in 2020 (figure III.7). This moderate acceleration is expected to be supported by external factors, including a strengthening of global demand for Africa's products, and domestic factors, such as robust private consumption, sustained investments in infrastructure, and rising oil production, particularly due to new field development. Inflation is estimated to have declined in 2018 and should fall further in 2019 due to improving agricultural and food production as well as stable exchange rates in most countries.

Despite a robust investment-to-GDP ratio of about 25 per cent, GDP growth in Africa remains well below what is needed to reach many Sustainable Development Goals (SDGs) targets and keep pace with rapid population growth. Per capita income growth for the continent has modestly improved from the contraction in 2016; however, at only 0.6 per cent in 2018 and 0.9 per cent projected in 2019, it remains insufficient to significantly improve living standards of large segments of the population. Overall, Africa needs to at least double the current growth rate in order to make significant progress towards achieving the SDGs. Furthermore, inequality levels in the continent remain high and slow moving. Only a few African economies have achieved significant improvements in income distribution between 2000–2004 and 2012–2016. Out of 25 economies for which data is available, only 4 countries (located in West Africa) have seen the share of those in the bottom 20 per cent of income distribution increase by 2 percentage points or more (figure III.8.A). By contrast, over the same period, the income share held by those in the top 20 per cent of income distribution has risen by at least 2 percentage points in 7 economies (figure III.8.B). In Zambia, this share jumped by almost 9 percentage points. This implies that the gains from GDP growth will likely remain very unequally distributed in many countries.

There is some progress in fiscal consolidation…

The overall fiscal position continued to improve, with the fiscal deficit narrowing slightly in 2018, mainly due to ongoing fiscal consolidation efforts in many countries. The fiscal position is forecast to remain stable in 2019, supported by rising export revenues, particularly from natural resources.

…while the current account strengthens

Africa's overall current account deficit narrowed in 2018. The improvement was underpinned by several factors, such as improvements in commodity prices and production, but counterbalanced by, inter alia, capital and food imports.

Gradually rising economic growth is seen in all subregions

The economic performance varied significantly across the five subregions in 2018 (figure III.9). East Africa continues to be the fastest-growing subregion in Africa with a 6.2 per cent growth rate driven by government spending on infrastructure and domes-

Figure III.7
GDP growth and inflation in Africa, 2010–2020

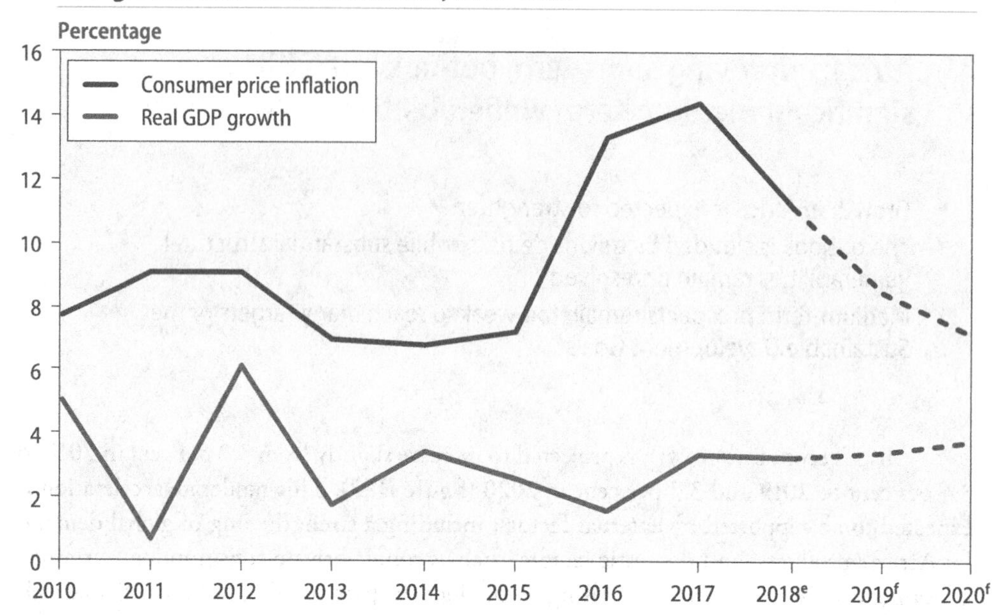

Source: UN/DESA.

Note: e = estimate, f = forecast.

Figure III.8
Income distribution by population quintiles, Africa

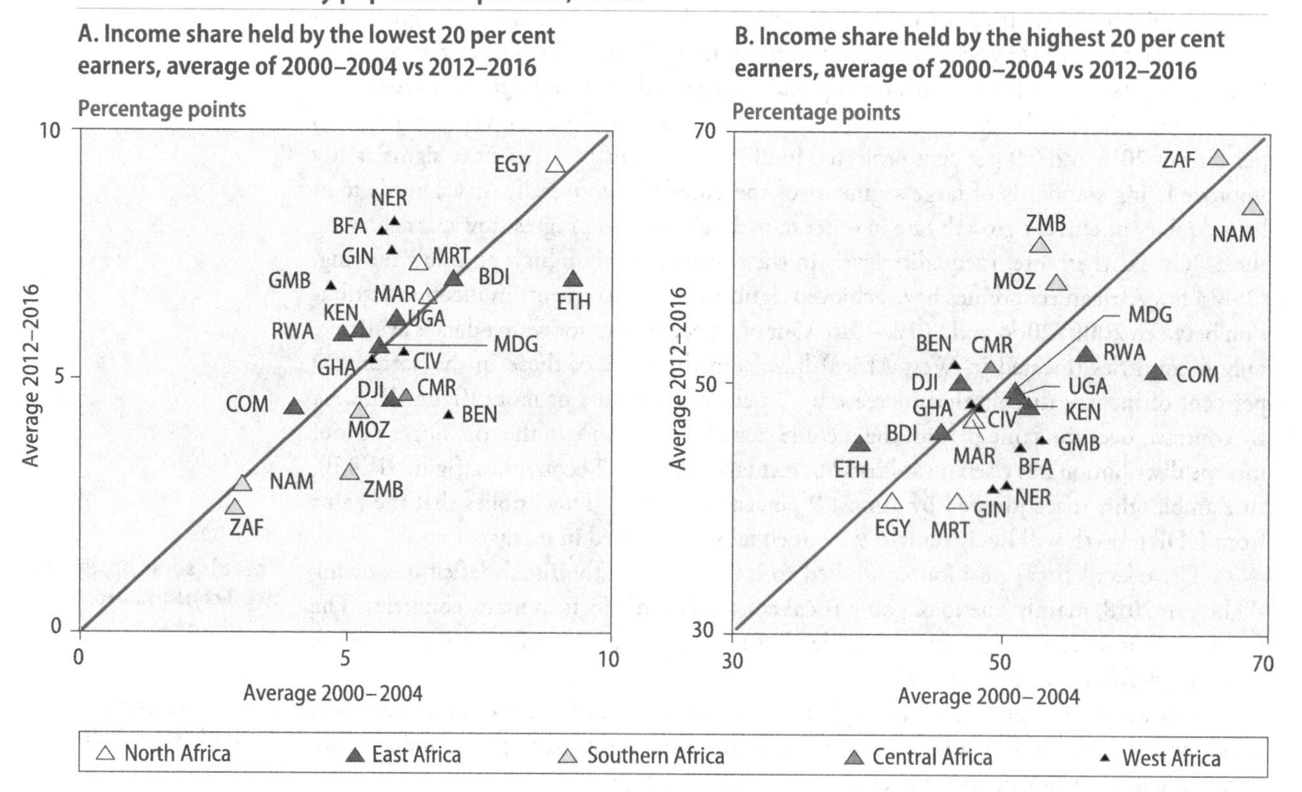

Source: UN/DESA, based on data from World Bank's World Development Indicators database.

tic demand. North Africa expanded by 3.7 per cent, with economic activity driven by improvements in tourism revenues and rising agriculture production. West Africa, led by the Nigerian economy, grew by 3.2 per cent due to the increase in oil revenue. Meanwhile, economic growth of the Southern African subregion deteriorated slightly from 1.5 per cent in 2017 to 1.2 per cent in 2018, and remains adversely affected by the economic performance of South Africa. After two challenging years, Central Africa achieved a 2.2 per cent growth rate in 2018, exiting recession of -0.2 per cent in 2017.

Figure III.9
GDP growth rates by African subregions, 2016–2020

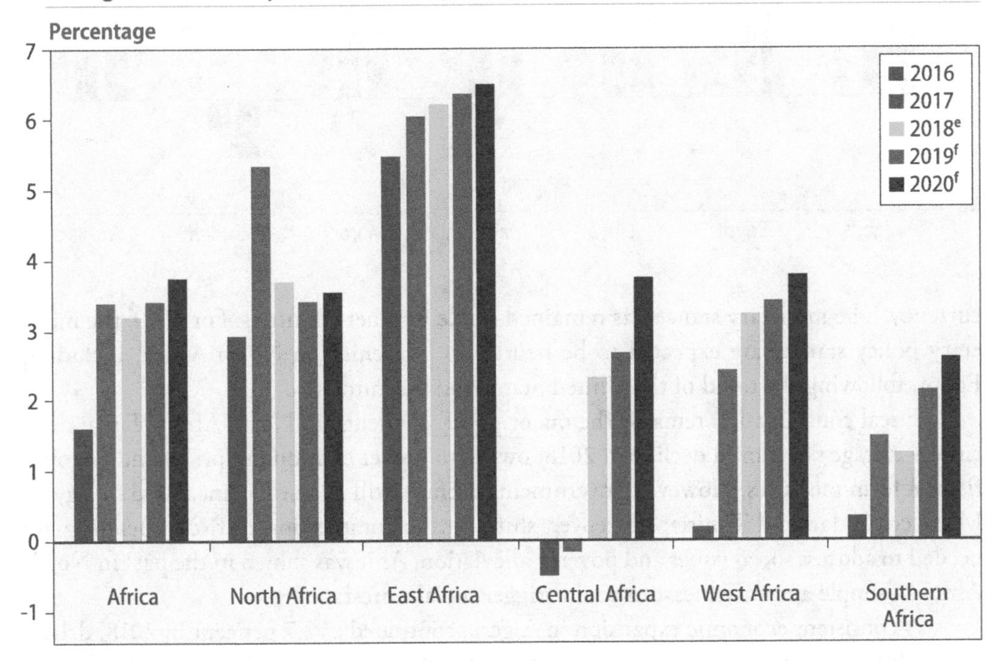

Source: UN/DESA.
Note: e = estimate, f = forecast.

North Africa: growth supported by favourable external conditions

North Africa is estimated to have grown by 3.7 per cent per cent in 2018. The recent economic expansion reflects improving external conditions with higher commodity prices and strong growth in European economies, the largest export destination. The economic growth of North Africa is forecast to moderate slightly to 3.4 per cent in 2019 and 3.5 per cent in 2020 (figure III.10). While external conditions are forecast to stay mostly favourable, structural vulnerabilities, including weak fiscal and balance of payment positions, are projected to weigh on growth prospects, particularly in Egypt, Sudan and Tunisia. Political instability and social unrest also remain a downside risk factor in North Africa.

Balance of payment conditions contribute to different economic performances

In 2018, balance of payment constraints on Egypt and Libya eased, which resulted in declining inflation rates and policy space to support domestic demand. Meanwhile, Tunisia and Sudan remain under severe balance of payment constraints, resulting in rapid inflation with limited space for domestic demand expansion.

Egypt eased its monetary stance for the first time since 2015

These balance of payment constraints dictate monetary policy stances. While the Central Bank of Egypt eased its stance for the first time since 2015, the Central Bank of Tunisia further tightened its stance by raising its policy interest rate. The Central Bank of Sudan took a tightening measure through a series of drastic devaluations of the national

Figure III.10
GDP growth in North Africa, 2018–2020

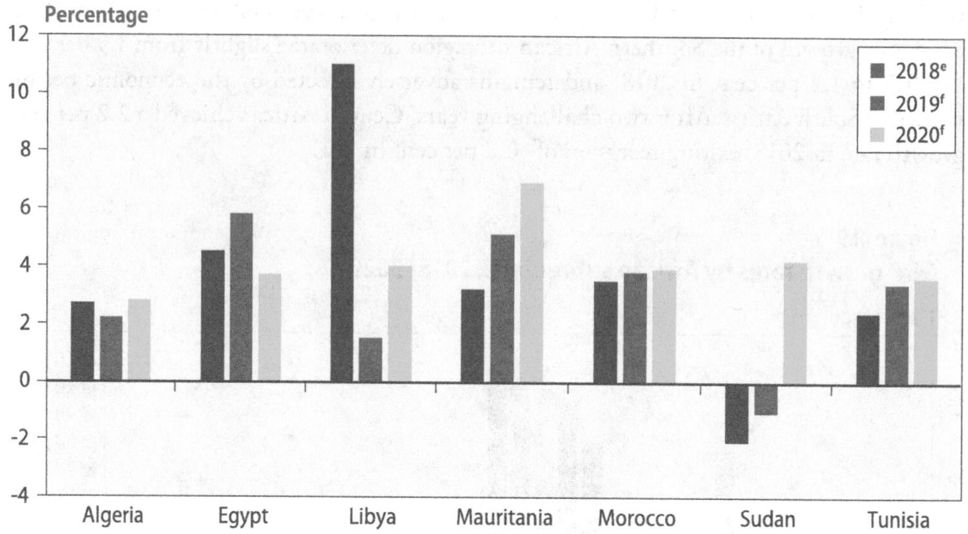

Source: UN/DESA.
Note: e = estimate, f = forecast.

currency. The monetary stance has remained stable in other countries. For 2019, the monetary policy stances are expected to be neutral to tightening in North Africa, including Egypt, following the trend of the United States and the euro area.

Fiscal consolidation remains challenging

Fiscal consolidation remains the major policy challenge in North Africa. Fiscal deficits on average saw a mild decline in 2018, owing to higher commodity prices and ongoing fiscal reform measures. However, government revenues still need to be increased in Egypt, Morocco, Sudan and Tunisia. Moreover, shifts in the composition of fiscal spending are needed to address social issues and poverty alleviation. As it was shown in the past in North Africa, a simple austerity measure could trigger social unrest.

A consistent economic expansion in Algeria continued at 2.7 per cent in 2018, driven mainly by higher oil and gas production. As private consumption remains subdued, however, the growth rate is forecast to decline to 2.2 per cent in 2019. In Egypt, external demand drove the growth rate to 5.8 per cent in 2018. A recovery in domestic demand, particularly private consumption, is forecast to sustain economic growth at 5.2 per cent in 2019. The Libyan economy continues to expand rapidly, by 11.0 per cent in 2018, as the crude oil production has recovered to reach 1.2 million barrels per day. However, domestic demand remains weak as a result of the unstable security situation. As the impact of increasing crude oil production tapers off, the Libyan economy is forecast to grow at 1.5 per cent in 2019.

Healthy expansion continues in Morocco while a challenging situation remains in Tunisia

Morocco's healthy economic expansion continues, albeit at a slightly reduced pace, estimated at 3.5 per cent in 2018. While a slower phosphate production and modest agricultural production contributed to the slowdown, the domestic demand expansion remains robust. The Moroccan economy is forecast to expand by 3.8 per cent in 2019. In Tunisia, the growth in tourism and industrial production has contributed to a mild acceleration in GDP growth to 2.4 per cent in 2018. However, the Tunisian economy is constrained by balance of payment difficulties, witnessing insufficient foreign capital inflows to finance the current account deficits. The central bank's reserves continue to decline while the national currency, the Tunisian dinar, depreciates. However, the ongoing reform measures, particularly on the fiscal side, are expected to bring stabilization. The Tunisian economy is forecast to grow by 3.4 per cent in 2019.

Mauritania accelerates while Sudan suffers from high inflation

The mineral and fishery sectors, as well as foreign capital inflows to mining projects, continue to support a positive expansion of the Mauritanian economy. GDP has grown by 3.2 per cent in 2018 and is forecast to grow by 5.1 per cent in 2019. However, this rate of economic expansion is still insufficient to eradicate poverty, which is exacerbated by rapid desertification and the resulting urbanization. The Sudanese economy is under serious balance of payment constraints. The central bank's foreign reserves have been depleted, while the central bank actively purchases domestic government debt. The combination of a rapid expansion of the central bank's balance sheet and a rapid devaluation of the national currency resulted in an exceptionally high inflation rate, estimated to be 64.1 per cent in 2018. The severe price shock is expected to have caused a real contraction in 2018 of 2.0 per cent. The Sudanese economy is forecast to contract further in 2019 before resuming positive growth in 2020.

East Africa: growth remains robust although not inclusive

Stable and robust growth in East Africa

East Africa remains the fastest growing subregion of Africa, with 6.2 per cent GDP growth in 2018 and a minor further acceleration anticipated in 2019–2020. GDP per capita for the region expands at about half that rate, with growth of 3.3 per cent in 2018. With a population of over 100 million—one fourth of the entire region—Ethiopia is the largest economy in East Africa. Nevertheless, in GDP per capita terms, the country stands in sixth place after Dijbouti, Kenya, Comoros, Eritrea and the United Republic of Tanzania. Regarding GDP per capita growth, Dijbouti and Ethiopia both recorded growth in excess of 5 per cent in 2018. Kenya and the United Republic of Tanzania expanded by about 3.5 per cent in per capita terms in 2018. In contrast, after years of conflict and still submerged in sociopolitical crisis, Burundi recorded another year of decline in GDP per capita of 3.0 per cent in 2018. Since the progress towards stability remains sluggish, the economic outlook for Burundi remains negative until 2020. Similarly, growth prospects remain bleak in conflict-torn Democratic Republic of the Congo.

Growth does not close income inequalities

East African economies have observed a prolonged period of robust growth, outperforming their peers in the continent. The region benefits from improvements in stability, new investment opportunities, and incentives for development of new industries. Nevertheless, the situation remains almost unchanged regarding income distribution. In 2000, the estimates suggest that the bottom 20 per cent of earners received 6.5 per cent of the total income, while the top 20 per cent of earners received 48.0 per cent. In 2015, there was no statistically significant change to this picture, with shares at 6.3 and 48.0 per cent, respectively (figure III.11).

East African economies slowly diversifying towards services

Agriculture remains the dominant economic sector in terms of employment in the region, but many countries are increasing their economic diversification. The industrial sector is expanding in major economies, although the largest increase is observed in the services sector (figure III.12). The increased government expenditure on infrastructure and rapid expansion of the construction, real estate and retail sectors in Ethiopia and Kenya will continue to boost regional growth. Still, a large share of employment in agriculture remains one of the reasons for a low share of income at the bottom of the income distribution.

Fiscal deficits broaden amid insufficient savings and increasing external debt

All East African countries continue to experience relatively high fiscal deficits. Recent deteriorations generally reflect high infrastructure investment alongside weak domestic resource mobilization (figure III.13). The resulting savings gap is filled by external financing (e.g., the shift towards increased borrowing from China and the international bond

Figure III.11
Changes in income distribution, by income group, selected East African countries

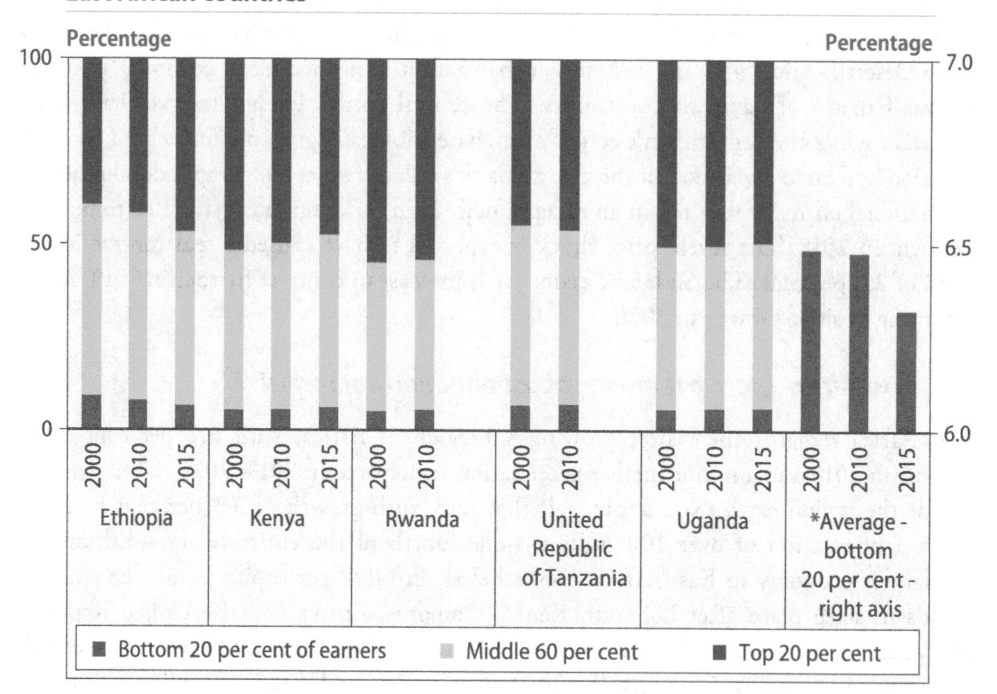

Source: UN/DESA, based on data from World Bank's World Development Indicators database.
*Unweighted average of the income share of the bottom 20 per cent among 5 presented countries.

Figure III.12
Labour market structure of selected East African countries, by sector

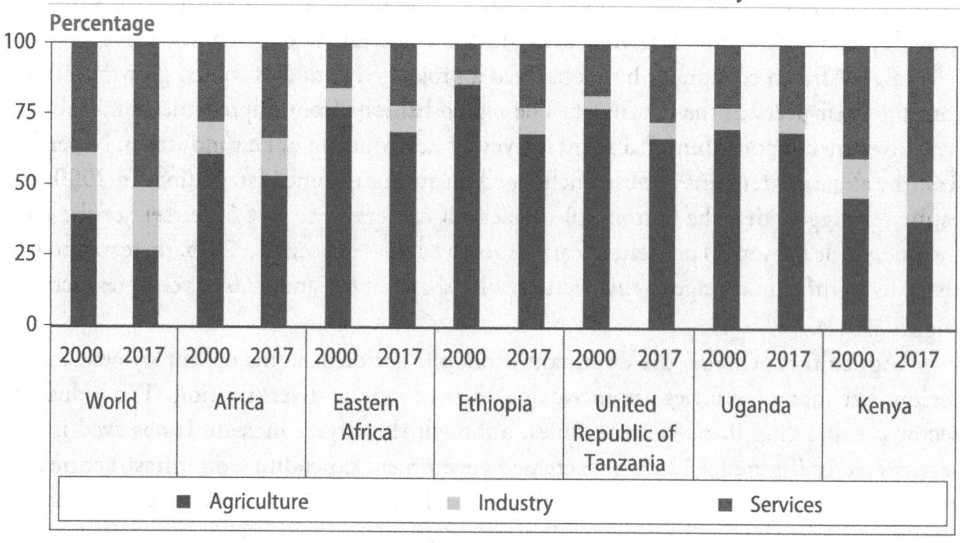

Source: World Bank's World Development Indicators database.

market). The debt position in the region is expected to deteriorate in the next few years, increasing the risk of external debt distress in a number of countries (Djibouti, Ethiopia, Kenya, Somalia and South Sudan) (IMF, 2018b). Furthermore, more pressure on debt-servicing is expected, due to tightening of the United States monetary policy and a stronger US dollar.

Figure III.13
Changes in savings and investment as ratios of GDP, 2000 and 2018

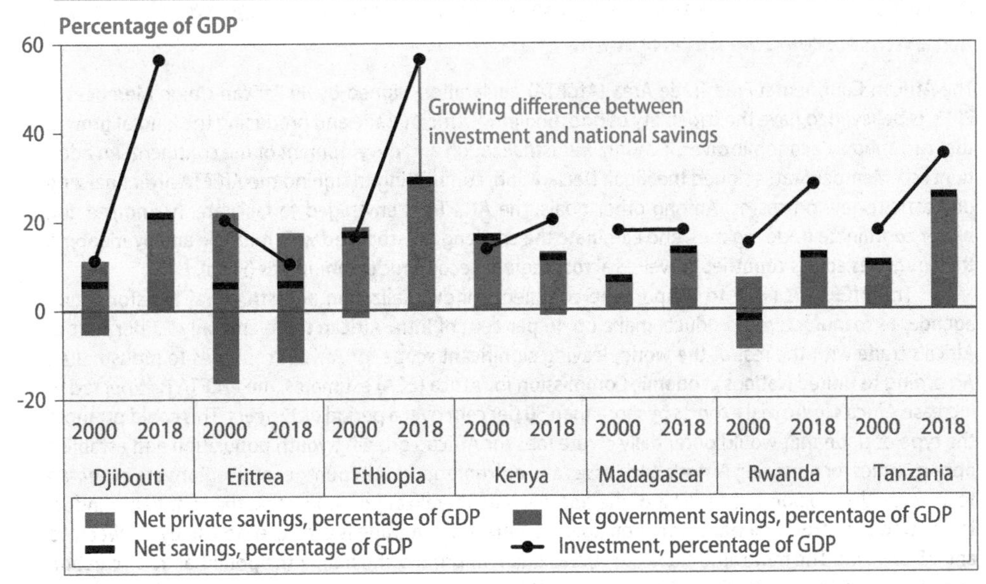

Sources: UN/DESA and IMF World Economic Outlook October 2018 database.

The macroeconomic environment is stable but under pressure

Inflation is expected to remain moderate in most countries in 2018, and decelerate further in 2019. South Sudan recorded inflation in excess of 100 per cent in 2018, but inflation should decelerate towards 20 per cent in 2019. Stability in the regional macroeconomic environment, driven by appropriate policy frameworks, should support stabilization of exchange rates, which depreciated only by about 2–3 per cent in 2018. The currencies of South Sudan, Ethiopia and Eritrea, might record stronger depreciations due to larger macroeconomic imbalances. External factors, in particular strengthening of the US dollar, might lead to cross-regional depreciations, especially between commodity exporters and other countries. Burundi, Djibouti, Ethiopia and Somalia are expected to have large deficits.

The outlook is positive but dependent on external factors

The outlook for the region remains largely dependent on external factors. Low coffee prices will weigh on the Ethiopian economy, while moderate tea prices will be beneficial for the Kenyan economy. Except for South Sudan, low oil prices would be a tailwind. Diaspora remittances will remain a supportive and stabilizing factor. The diminishing political uncertainties both in Ethiopia and Kenya are likely to boost investment and foreign capital inflows. At the same time, oil and gas explorations, favourable weather, and enhanced integration in regional economic communities and the African Continental Free Trade Area present substantial growth opportunities beyond the 2019–2020 outlook (box III.3).

Conflict leaves countries behind

The region faces considerable downside risks. These risks include conflicts, insecurity and rising political tension in Burundi, Democratic Republic of the Congo (with elections scheduled towards the end of 2018), Somalia and South Sudan. As witnessed throughout 2018, conflict does not only deter investment, thereby preventing growth in some regional economies, but also hinders international development assistance efforts. For example, conflict has been listed as one of the main factors undermining ongoing World Health Organization (2018) efforts in addressing the Ebola outbreak in the Democratic Republic of the Congo—efforts that would have had more impact on both the disease and the economy in a non-conflict environment.

Box III.3

African Continental Free Trade Area: opportunities and challenges for achieving sustainable development

The African Continental Free Trade Area (AfCFTA) declaration, signed by 49 African Union Members in 2018, is believed to have the capability of boosting intra-African trade and producing the kind of growth that can support economic diversification, industrialization and development of the continent. An additional six Member States signed the Kigali Declaration, committing to signing the AfCFTA after finalizing domestic review processes. Among other goals, the AfCFTA is envisaged to facilitate, harmonize and better coordinate trade regimes, and eliminate the challenges associated with multiple and overlapping trade regimes across countries as well as across regional economic communities (RECs).

The AfCFTA is likely to support the continent's industrialization and structural transformation agenda, as manufactured products make up 46 per cent of intra-African trade and only 22 per cent of Africa's trade with the rest of the world, leaving significant scope for African countries to industrialize. According to United Nations Economic Commission for Africa (ECA) estimates, the AfCFTA is expected to increase Africa's industrial exports by more than 50 per cent over a period of 12 years. This could promote the type of trade that would potentially create jobs for Africa's growing youth population and establish opportunities for nurturing Africa's businesses and entrepreneurs. All countries and regions are expected to increase their exports, regardless of the approach to liberalization, supporting the continent's industrialization and structural transformation agenda. Intra-African trade is projected to rise by between 15 and 25 per cent. The more ambitious the liberalization approach, the higher the potential trade creation and revenue gains within Africa. Estimates reveal the largest potential increases of over 40 per cent in textile, wood and paper, vehicle and transport equipment, other manufactures and wearing apparel industries (ECA, 2018).

The implementation of the AfCFTA has some fiscal policy implications through marginal losses in tariff revenue (ibid.). The small scale of the losses is mainly due to intra-African trade being a small share of Africa's total trade (only 18 per cent of total exports in 2016), and most intra-African trade is already liberalized under RECs. The AfCFTA is estimated to affect only about 7 per cent of Africa's total imports under current trade patterns. Nonetheless, there is widespread fear within participating countries that the revenue losses will prove significantly larger, which could delay implementation of the AfCFTA.

The resulting tariff cuts would lead to a redistribution of income from Governments to consumers and producers. Moreover, the AfCFTA is expected to produce additional welfare gains that surpass tariff losses significantly due to better allocation of resources (Saygili et al., 2018). Furthermore, countries will be allowed to exclude a certain number of tariff lines (e.g., tariff lines that are important for raising tariff revenues) from the liberalization process. Conveying these messages clearly to participating countries is crucial to accelerating the implementation of AfCFTA.

These tariff revenue losses may also be outweighed by the additional revenues from growth to be generated by the AfCFTA, which would broaden the tax base and boost revenue collection from other sources. Growth in Africa is expected to accelerate by 0.3–0.6 percentage points by 2040 (depending on the liberalization approach or scenario adopted), when compared to the baseline scenario. All African countries would experience an increase in their GDP with the AfCFTA reforms, whatever the scenario. Countries such as Zimbabwe are expected to increase by between 3.6 and 31.9 per cent, depending on the scenario.[a] However, these forecasts are likely to substantially underestimate the economic benefits of the AfCFTA, as they do not take into account the impact of liberalization in other areas such as services and investment (ECA, 2018).

The benefits of the AfCFTA would be further enhanced by maximizing the potential that comes with a fast-growing young population and the associated fast urbanization process occurring on the continent. This would be conducive for agglomeration economies providing major opportunities for industrialization through rising demand and shifting patterns of consumption (ECA, 2017). Through the AfCFTA, the growing middle class can be leveraged to stimulate industrial development to meet the rising demand domestically and regionally, leading to broader integration through value chains. However, for this to be achieved, Africa needs to take proactive steps to curb the associated risks that come with a rising and urbanizing population (ibid.).

a The wide difference tries to reveal the observed effects of the differences between approaches, which are more pronounced at country level (see ECA, 2018 for more details).

(continued)

Box III.3 (*continued*)

Implementation of the AfCTA may be delayed by the following circumstances: the multiple and overlapping trade agreements in Africa; fear of significant tariff revenue losses by countries; possible uneven distribution of other costs and benefits among member countries; and poor and inadequate domestic infrastructure. The role of payment systems in facilitating cross-border trade and the associated challenges and constraints of various payment arrangements, both at national and regional levels, need to be examined. There is a need, therefore, for policies to mitigate these challenges and help enhance the redistribution of potential benefits and costs of the AfCFTA.

The importance of infrastructure in enhancing regional integration cannot be emphasized enough. Recognizing the importance of efficient transport, communications, energy infrastructure and related services for trade and the pursuit of the continent's development goals, the African Union Heads of State and Governments, among others, reaffirmed the high priority accorded to infrastructure and launched the Plan for Infrastructure Development in Africa (PIDA) for its accelerated development (ECA, 2010). The objective of the PIDA is to help African leaders establish a strategic framework for creating regional and continental infrastructure based on a development vision, strategic objectives and sector policies. Accelerating this process is now all the more imperative for taking full advantage of the opportunities offered by the AfCFTA.

Authors: Hopestone Kayiska Chavula and Nadia S. Ouedraogo (UN/ECA).

Southern Africa: growth potential remains underutilized and hampered by lack of stability

Lack of stability curbs growth

Growth in Southern Africa decreased from 1.5 per cent in 2017 to 1.2 per cent in 2018. The outlook for 2019–2020 depends on developments in South Africa's economy, which contributes about 60 per cent to the economic output of the region. Despite some reported improvement, the outlook remains neutral to negative. South Africa fell into technical recession after two quarters of negative growth in the first half of 2018, with a widespread deterioration across sectors. The growth figures have been largely distorted by agriculture and forestry due to volatile weather in the last year. The second quarter recorded only a minor rebound in mining and quarrying, after a sharp decline in the previous two quarters. The economic situation is improving in Angola, the second largest economy of the region. GDP of Angola is estimated to have grown by 1.0 per cent in 2018. However, if the sharp decline in the oil price recorded at the end of 2018 persists, it will weigh down substantially on GDP forecasts for Angola. In aggregate, Southern Africa is forecast to grow by 2.1 per cent in 2019 and 2.6 per cent in 2020.

No improvement is seen in per capita growth in the largest economies amid deepening inequalities

Moving away from aggregates towards per capita numbers, the developments of Southern African economies present an even more alarming picture (figure III.14). In 2018, GDP per capita in South Africa declined to 2012 levels. Zimbabwe will also record a decline in GDP per capita, with a 3 per cent cumulative fall since 2013. The recent government change in Zimbabwe has so far not delivered. The GDP per capita is estimated to have grown by 3.5 per cent in Mauritius, driven largely by offshore financial services.

The inequalities in Southern Africa remain deep and are increasing. In the largest economy of the region, South Africa, the top 20 per cent of earners receives about two thirds of total income, while the bottom 20 per cent receives only 2–3 per cent. Although not as polarized, a similar scenario exists in other Southern African economies. Notably, the income of the bottom 20 per cent is on a long-term downward trend, and recent GDP per capita growth does not suggest short-term improvement in this area (figure III.15).

Figure III.14
GDP per capita growth in selected Southern African countries, 2015–2020

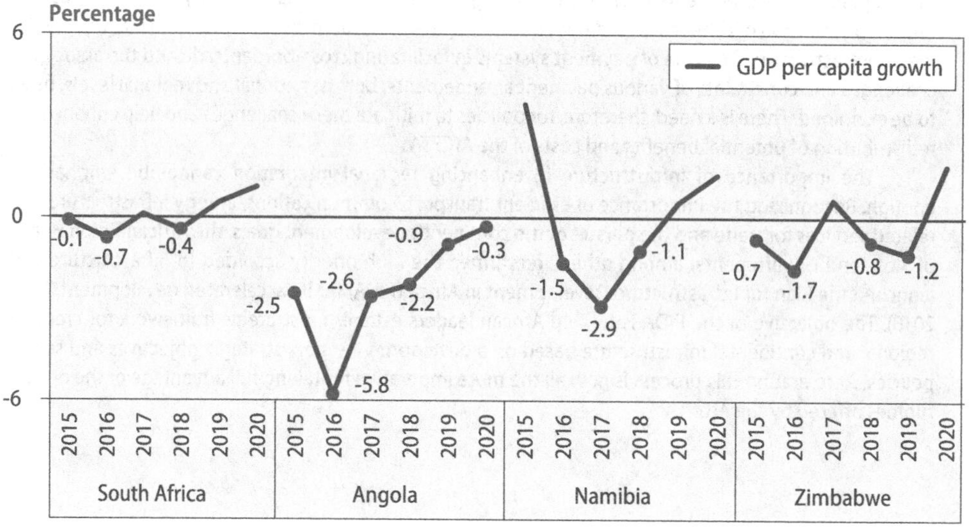

Source: UN/DESA.
Note: 2018 is estimated; 2019 and 2020 are forecasts.

Growth is dependent on commodity prices amid insufficient employment diversification

Growth in the subregion has been underpinned by increased commodity prices, leading to a strong mining sector, and improved energy supply, which have spillover effects to other sectors in the economies of the subregion. Efforts towards diversification are not substantial across the region, held back by lack of long-term government strategies, lack of local capital mobilization, narrow tax bases, and low levels of foreign investment. Since the agricultural sector contributes largely to the GDP of the region, bad weather conditions might significantly affect agricultural production and pose a serious risk for the 2019–2020 outlook (figure III.16).

Government debt-to-GDP ratios are expected to increase, with the exception of Angola, which managed to reduce government debt from 75 per cent of GDP in 2016 to 48 per cent in 2018 and is heading towards 30 per cent in 2020. Government debt remains very high in Mozambique, at 95 per cent of GDP, falling only a few percentage points a year. Meanwhile, government debt to GDP in Zimbabwe may rise to 94 per cent of GDP in 2018, and further up to 117 per cent in 2020. Monetary tightening in most developed economies and the associated rise in interest rates create doubts on the sustainability of debt dynamics in some countries.

The outlook for fiscal balances remains mixed. Botswana and Namibia are forecast to record improvement up until 2020. The fiscal deficit in South Africa is expected to remain largely stable, but is at risk of deterioration due to a challenging economic situation. Heightened political pressures to increase public sector wages and protect subsidies persist in Botswana, Malawi, Mauritius and Mozambique. Fiscal policy in the subregion continues to be guided by a commitment to fiscal consolidation aimed at reducing public debt and consolidating and rebalancing expenditure between capital investment and high recurrent expenditures. Malawi and Lesotho are particularly notable for their efforts to widen the tax base, introducing new consumer tax measures and automation of tax administration to increase revenues. The countries in the subregion have continued to maintain a relatively tight monetary policy stance in order to curb inflationary pressures—pressures that mainly

Figure III.15
Changes in income distribution, by income group, in selected Southern African countries

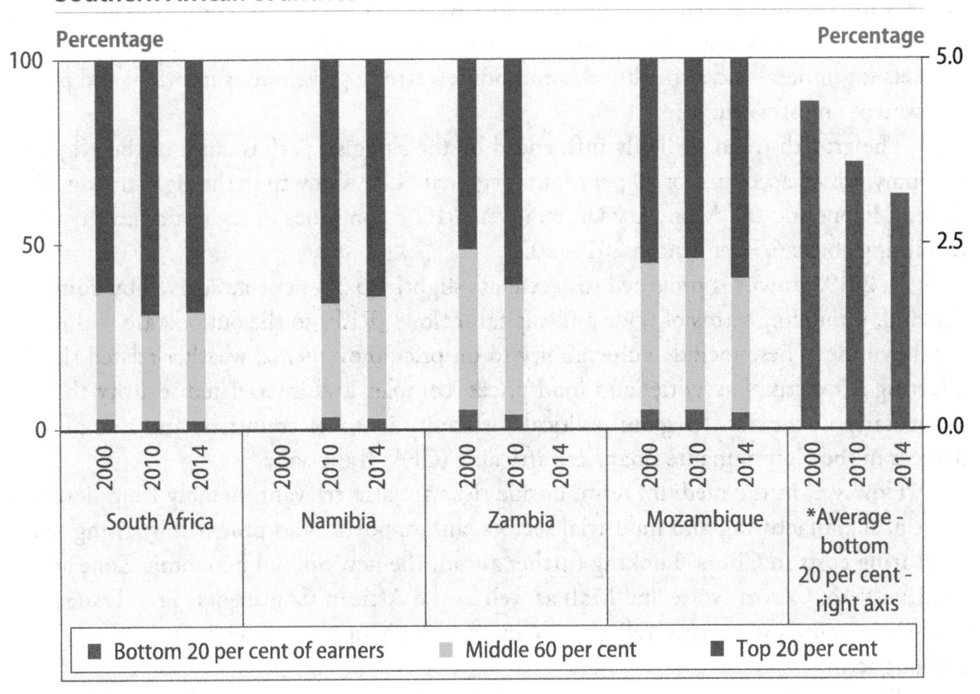

Source: UN/DESA, based on data from World Bank's World Development Indicators database.

Figure III.16
Labour market in selected Southern African countries, by sector

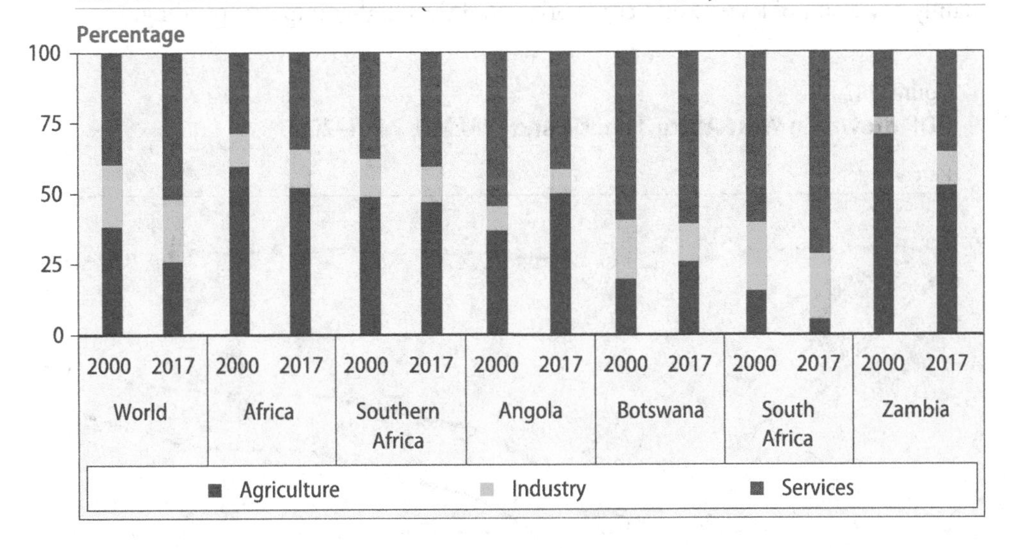

Source: World Bank's World Development Indicators database.

emanate from poor harvests caused by poor weather conditions. The current account deficit is expected to widen in 2018. High current account deficits in most of these countries are a result of high demand for capital imports, high food imports (as local food supply has been affected by adverse weather) and sluggish growth in export earnings.

West Africa: persistent vulnerabilities may jeopardize growth momentum

Real GDP in West Africa is estimated to have grown by 3.2 per cent in 2018, up from 2.4 per cent in 2017 (figure III.17), as a result of increased oil prices and production for Nigeria and Ghana; a strong and increasing services sector in most countries; relatively buoyant markets for mineral and agricultural commodities; strong private consumption; and public investment on infrastructure.

The growth trend is highly influenced by the sluggish performance of the Nigerian economy, which accounts for 70 per cent of regional GDP. Growth in the eight-nation West African Economic and Monetary Union (WAEMU)[2] continues to register a healthy pace, remaining above 6.5 per cent in 2018–2020.

In 2019, growth is projected to accelerate slightly to 3.4 per cent, driven by domestic demand, improving terms of trade and capital inflows. Risks to the outlook are mainly on the downside. These include vulnerability to oil price movements; weather-related shocks affecting agricultural activities and food prices; complex and interrelated security threats, particularly in the Sahel region; political instability in some countries; and risk of debt distress in the Communauté financière africaine (CFA) franc zone.

However, in the medium term, upside risks are also relevant, notably from development of manufacturing and industrial sectors, and opportunities provided by rising manufacturing costs in China. Looking further ahead, the new Special Economic Zone across Burkina Faso, Côte d'Ivoire and Mali as well as the African Continental Free Trade Area have the potential to boost GDP growth and economic opportunities across the region in the long term.

Commodity exports support current account surplus

The overall current account surplus of West Africa improved in 2018. The main drivers include improvements in oil prices, rising global prices of non-mining export commodities and rising cotton exports. However, in 2019, the current account surplus will narrow, mainly as a result of lower world crude prices and thus higher imports spending.

Figure III.17
GDP growth in West Africa, Nigeria and WAEMU, 2014–2020

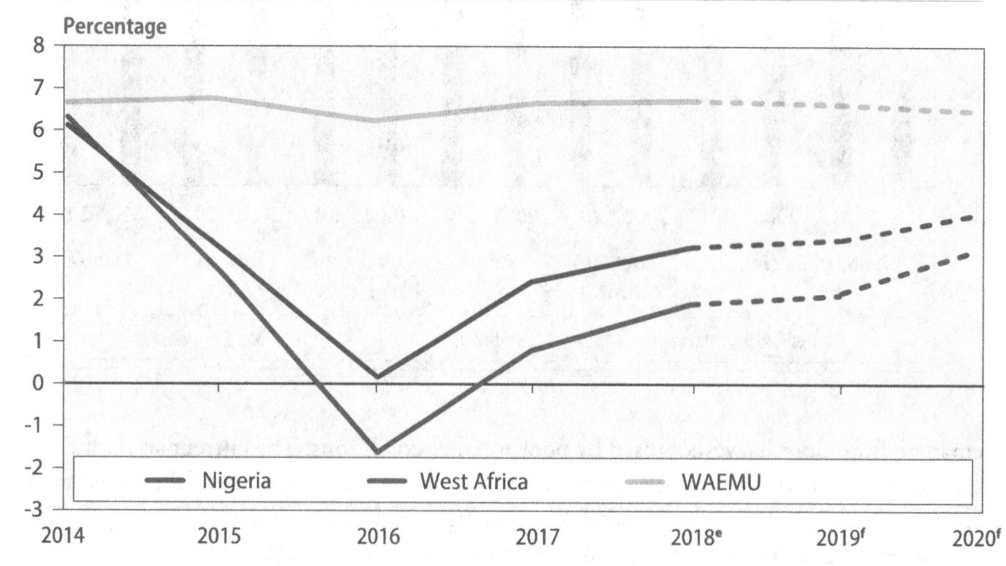

Source: UN/DESA.
Note: e = estimate, f = forecast.

2 Benin, Burkina Faso, Côte d'Ivoire, Guinea-Bissau, Mali, Niger, Senegal and Togo.

Tight monetary policy stances persist…

Monetary policy in the WAEMU has remained relatively tight since end-2016, reducing banks' appetite for government debt and contributing to Eurobond issuances. Further tightening is possible if pressures persist on the money market or foreign-exchange reserves. In Nigeria, monetary policy should remain tight to contain inflationary pressures and support the naira's exchange rate, while there is a slow move towards a uniform market-determined exchange rate. In Sierra Leone, monetary policy is tightening in order to curb rising domestic food prices, which have resulted from seasonal supply shocks, the depreciating leone, and rising international prices of fuel and rice. A more supportive situation exists in Ghana, where falling inflation allowed the Government to cut its benchmark interest rate in 2018. Interest rates are expected to decrease further in 2019.

…amid double-digit inflation

In 2018, West Africa's inflation was the highest across all subregions of Africa, at 13.4 per cent. Inflation remained high in 2018 due to inflationary pressures in Nigeria (16.2 per cent), Sierra Leone (11.7 per cent), Liberia (11.2 per cent) and, to a lesser extent, Ghana (8.3 per cent). Inflation was driven by a poor harvest in the Sahel region that led to an increase in food prices, higher import prices and an increase in production costs. In 2019 and 2020, inflation is expected to decrease but stay in double digits.

Depreciation is likely in many currencies

Despite regional dependence on primary commodities, exchange rates remained fairly stable in several of the francophone countries, cushioned by an appreciating euro that will continue in 2019. In Nigeria, exchange rates remained stable in 2018, supported by stronger oil prices, but are sensitive to political events. In the Gambia, the currency has remained stable due to improved macroeconomic fundamentals, although depreciation is also likely in 2019 due to moderation of external capital inflows. Exchange rates are forecast to depreciate in Ghana in connection with the sell-off in emerging market currencies and turmoil in local banking sectors. Likewise, depreciation is expected in Sierra Leone due to liberalization of the currency, and in Liberia due to poor terms of trade and reduced foreign currency inflows.

Fiscal consolidation efforts remain on the agenda for most West African Governments

Most countries in the subregion continue to undergo fiscal consolidation. Improved control of public expenditure and efforts to increase revenue have already caused some fiscal deficits to narrow, marginally decreasing the regional average—a trend that is expected to continue in 2019. Over the short to medium term, however, the fiscal deficit of the subregion is expected to widen again due to increased government spending (in Ghana, Nigeria and some WAEMU countries) and weaker revenue collection.

Central Africa: growth boosted by energy prices, but structural challenges remain

A fragile economic recovery is underway in Central Africa. After recession in 2016–2017, growth in 2018 reached 2.2 per cent, driven by a recovery in commodity prices, increased production from new oil and gas fields, and stronger performance in the agriculture, manufacturing and services sectors in different countries.

Growth in the Central African subregion is estimated to pick up to 2.5 per cent in 2019 and 3.8 per cent in 2020, supported by firming oil prices, rising investment, new oil and gas fields and consolidation of diversification measures in many countries. The remaining key downside risks include reversal in oil prices; weak fiscal reforms; deterioration in already precarious security situations (Cameroon's Anglophone region; Central African Republic, the Republic of the Congo Pool region, Lake Chad region); escalation of social tensions amid elections; and lower-than-expected donor budget support.

Furthermore, structural challenges hamper several economies in the subregion, including political instability and insecurity, fiscal dependence on commodity revenues, delayed public investment, vulnerability to weather shocks, difficult business environments, fragile state institutions and weak democracy.

A low and fragile level of foreign reserves...

The overall external account balance is estimated to keep improving, buoyed by several factors, most notably the improvements in commodity prices and exports. Support also stems from the partial lifting of a ban on exports of diamonds in the Central African Republic and relatively faster growth of services exports (mainly tourism earnings) compared to merchandise imports in Sao Tome and Principe. However, external reserves in the Central African Economic and Monetary Community (CEMAC)[3] remain below pre-crisis levels and fell short of targets in 2018, despite higher oil prices (figure III.18). Fiscal slippages by a few countries partly explain the lower-than-expected international reserve accumulation in 2018. Current medium-term predictions point to moderate levels of reserves, after international reserves deteriorated markedly from the start of the oil price shock in mid-2014 to end-2016. A higher level of reserves would strengthen the peg of the Central African CFA to the euro and contribute to a more sustainable external position.

...might prompt further monetary policy tightening

Under the direction of the Bank of Central African States (BEAC), monetary policy has remained relatively tight since 2017, which has contributed to narrowing the current account deficit and rebuilding reserve coverage, among other factors. Further tightening of monetary policy is expected in response to the withdrawal of monetary stimulus by the ECB or if reserves fall short of targets again. For Sao Tome and Principe—the only country outside the purview of BEAC, but whose currency is also pegged to the euro—the policy rate is unchanged since June 2017. The central bank will be constrained in 2019 to maintain the peg to the euro.

Figure III.18
Gross official reserves, Central African Economic and Monetary Community, end of period, 2011–2020

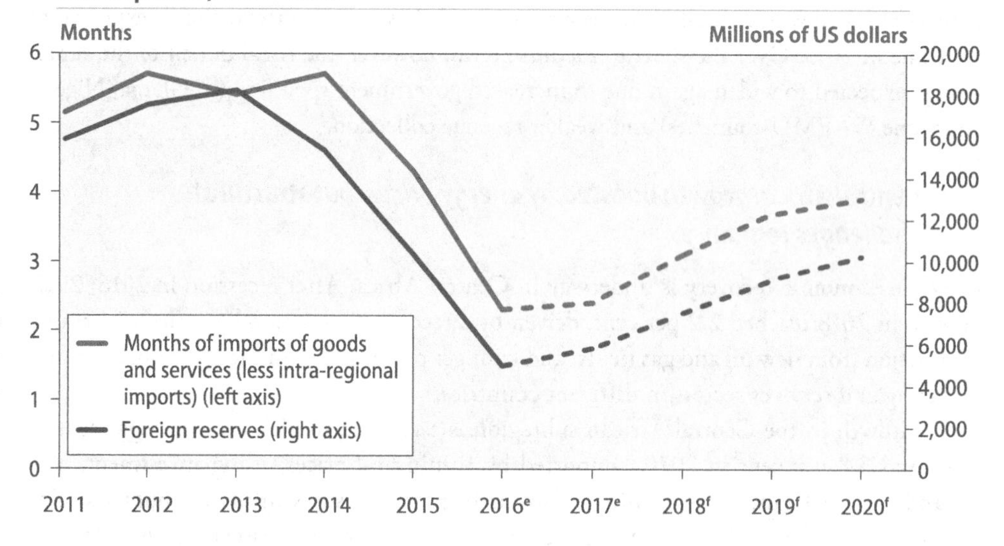

Source: UN/DESA, based on IMF (2018d) and de Zamaróczy et al. (2018).

Note: e = estimate, f = forecast.

3 The *WESP* Central Africa region comprises the CEMAC members (Gabon, Cameroon, Chad, the Central African Republic, the Republic of the Congo and Equatorial Guinea) and Sao Tome and Principe.

Inflation is close to CEMAC convergence criteria...

Inflation is expected to remain contained amid mild growth and continued tight monetary policy. In 2019–2020, inflation is projected to remain broadly close to the 3 per cent convergence criteria set by the CEMAC, barring spikes in food and oil prices, disruptions in agricultural production and general supplies due to insecurity, and removal of fuel price subsidies.

...while depreciation is possible, in line with euro currency developments

Since the currencies of this region (the dobra in Sao Tome and Principe and the CFA franc in the CEMAC) are pegged to the euro, the exchange rate in the region will weaken against the dollar in line with developments in the euro area. Sao Tome and Principe revalued its currency (dividing the currency by 1,000) in January 2018 and maintained its peg to the euro, with replacement of the old currency expected by the end of 2019, ostensibly to facilitate transactions but also to fight counterfeiting. Domestic currencies are expected to further depreciate slightly in 2019 as the monetary tightening continues in the United States.

Doubts over the CFA peg to the euro have resurfaced

Importantly, anti-colonialist sentiments and the depletion of foreign-exchange reserves since the 2014 oil price crash have reignited the debate on the merits of maintaining the CFA peg to the euro in some countries. In particular, there is a growing concern regarding the constraints in monetary policy that the peg imposes when asymmetric shocks affect individual countries.

Limited progress in fiscal consolidation

In terms of fiscal policy, all Central African economies, except Cameroon, have been pursuing successful fiscal consolidation. In Cameroon, irregular expenditures on elections and construction related to the Africa Cup of Nations caused the deficit to widen in 2018. In Chad and the Republic of the Congo, the fiscal balance is expected to turn into a surplus, due to higher global oil prices throughout most of 2018, cracking down on tax avoidance, and improvement in tax administration. The improving fiscal position in the subregion has also been helped by engagement with the IMF. However, although the subregion's fiscal deficit narrowed marginally in 2018, it remained outside the CEMAC convergence criteria of 3 per cent of GDP and is forecast to widen in 2019.

East Asia

GDP Growth

7.0%
6.0%
5.0%
4.0%

total: 5.7 (2016), 6.1 (2017), 5.8 (2018), 5.6 (2019), 5.5 (2020)

per capita: 5.0 (2016), 5.4 (2017), 5.2 (2018), 5.0 (2019), 4.9 (2020)

projected

2016 2017 2018 2019 2020

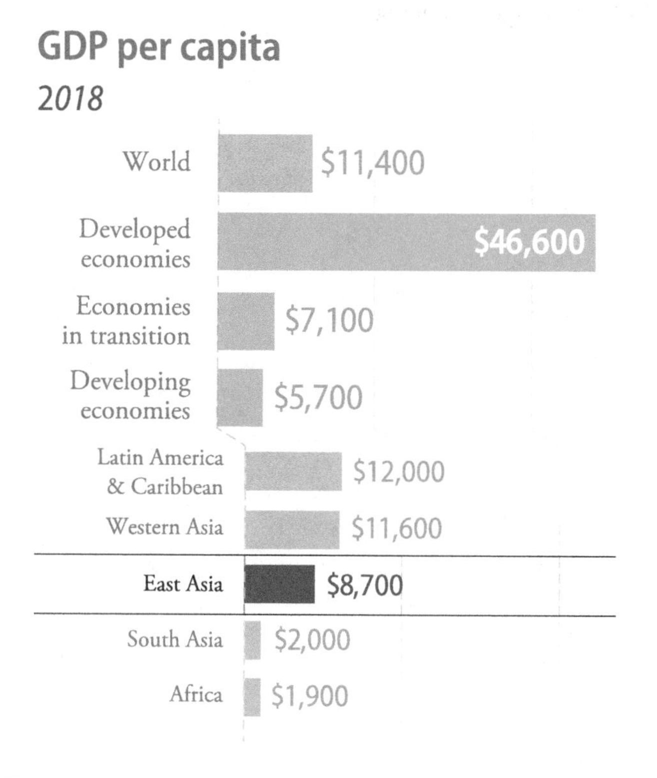

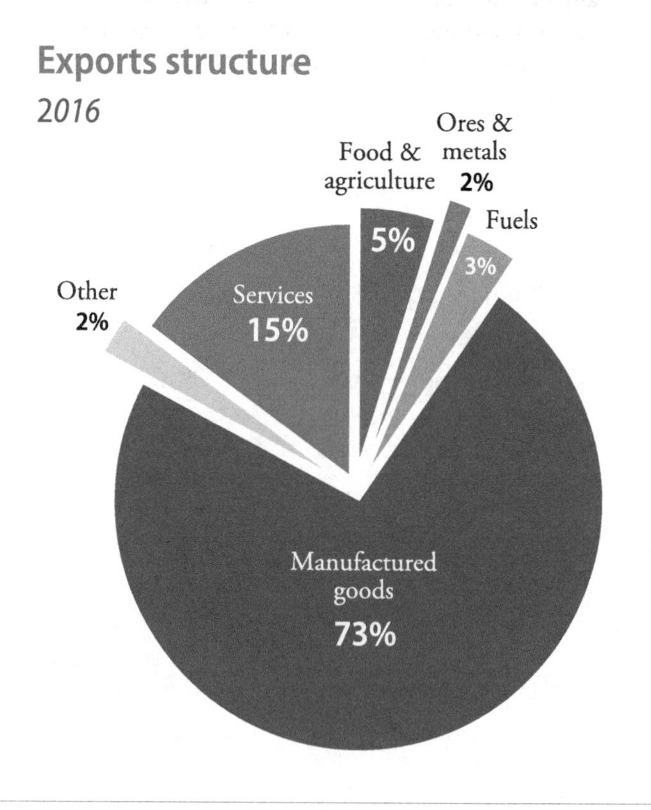

The boundaries and names shown and the designations used on this map do not imply official endorsement or acceptance by the United Nations. The map represents countries and/or territories or parts thereof for which data is available and/or analysed in *World Economic Situation and Prospects 2019*. The shaded areas therefore do not necessarily overlap entirely with the delimitation of their frontiers or boundaries.

East Asia: growth outlook remains robust, but downside risks are high

- Robust short-term growth characterizes the outlook, buoyed by resilient domestic demand and accommodative policies
- Escalation in trade tensions could disrupt existing supply chains, hurting the region's growth prospects
- East Asian economies have relatively stronger policy buffers to weather an external shock

The short-term growth outlook for East Asia remains robust, bolstered by resilient domestic demand and accommodative policies in most economies. On the external front, however, export growth is likely to slow, amid elevated trade tensions between China and the United States. Against this backdrop, regional GDP growth is projected to moderate to 5.6 per cent in 2019 and 5.5 per cent in 2020, from 5.8 per cent in 2018 (figure III.19). Downside risks to the region's growth outlook are high, arising mainly from a potential further intensification of trade disputes, which could disrupt existing regional supply chains. In addition, a sharp tightening of global financial conditions could lead to a large reversal of capital flows, posing a risk to financial stability. Nevertheless, compared to other developing regions, the East Asian economies are in a better position to weather an external shock, given relatively stronger macroeconomic fundamentals and policy buffers.

Robust private consumption growth is underpinned by healthy job creation and rising incomes

Private consumption remains the key driver of growth in East Asia, supported by healthy job creation, rising incomes, and moderate inflationary pressures. Despite some recent tightening in financial conditions, borrowing costs in the region remain relatively low. For several countries, including Myanmar, Thailand and the Republic of Korea, consumer spending will be lifted by substantial increases in the minimum wage in 2018.

Figure III.19
GDP growth and inflation in East Asia, 2006–2020

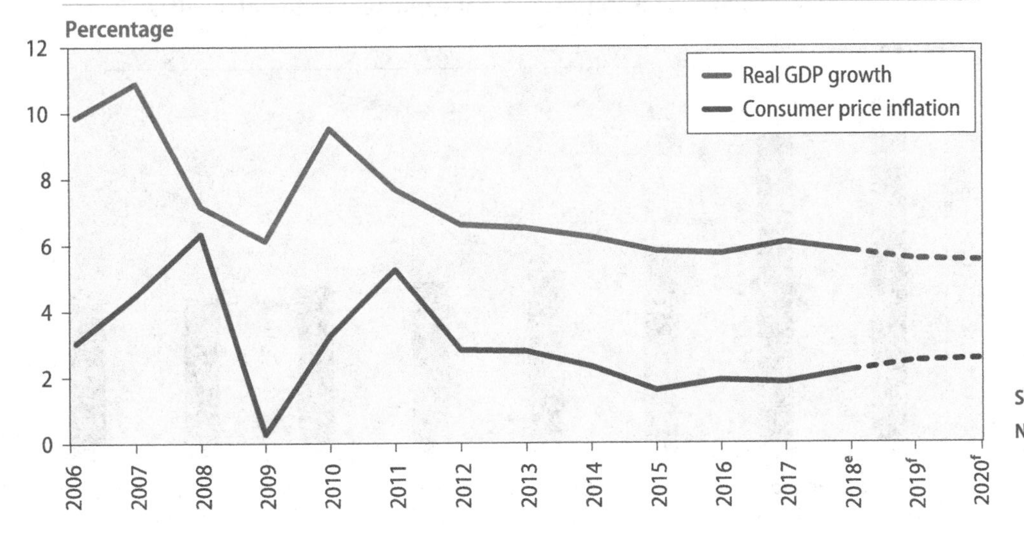

Source: UN/DESA.
Note: e = estimate, f = forecast.

Infrastructure investment remains strong in many countries

Public spending on infrastructure is likely to remain strong in most countries, as Governments continue to focus on easing critical structural bottlenecks and expanding productive capacity. In 2018, public investment growth accelerated in the Philippines and Thailand, driven mainly by the implementation of large transport development projects. The region's strong export performance since 2017 has also contributed to a pickup in private investment, particularly in the export-oriented sectors. However, persistently high uncertainty surrounding the imposition of tariffs may weigh on investor sentiment going forward.

The trade outlook in East Asia is clouded by elevated trade tensions between China and the United States

The region's strong export performance in 2017 extended into 2018, but the growth momentum moderated in most countries. In Malaysia, the Republic of Korea and Taiwan Province of China, exports remained driven by buoyant global demand for semiconductors and consumer electronics. In Brunei Darussalam, Indonesia and Malaysia, export revenue also benefited from the increase in global crude oil prices.

Recent indicators suggest that trade tensions are starting to weigh on the region's exports. In October, new export orders contracted in several economies, including China, the Philippines, the Republic of Korea and Taiwan Province of China. In 2019, exports are likely to provide less impetus to the region's growth, given a slower global growth momentum and a softening of the global electronics cycle. The protracted trade dispute between China and the United States is further weighing on the region's export outlook. In 2018, the United States imposed tariffs on more than $250 billion worth of Chinese goods, including solar panels, aluminium, steel, electrical and electronic (E&E) products, and a wide range of household items. These tariffs were met with retaliatory measures by China.

For China, exports to the United States account for almost 20 per cent of total merchandise exports. A decline in China's exports could have significant ramifications on the region, as many East Asian economies are deeply integrated into regional production networks, with China often at the centre of these networks. This is in part reflected in the high share of exports to China for many economies (figure III.20). Of note, the Republic of Korea, Singapore and Taiwan Province of China are particularly vulnerable to United States tariffs on Chinese E&E products and components, given the strong cross-border production linkages of these economies with the E&E industry in China.

Figure III.20
Share of selected East Asian countries' total exports sent to China, 2017

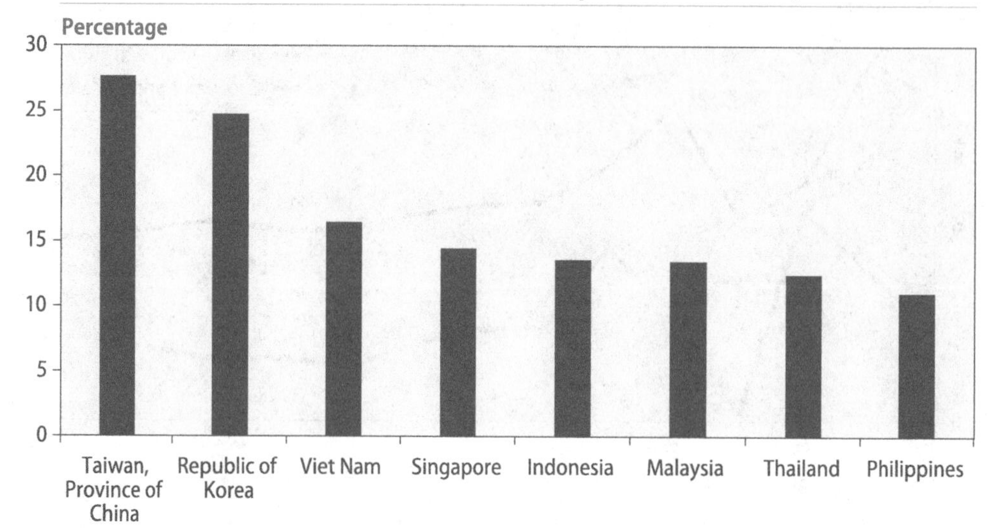

Source: National authorities, CEIC.
Note: Figure based on total merchandise exports.

Several Southeast Asian economies may benefit from some production diversion, as higher tariffs could potentially prompt firms to shift manufacturing operations away from China. However, any major relocation of production is unlikely in the short term, given that firms would need time to assess other aspects of operations in a new country, such as the availability of labour, infrastructure, and domestic regulations. Notwithstanding elevated China-United States trade frictions, the region has continued to progress on several initiatives to enhance intraregional trade activity. This includes the Regional Comprehensive Partnership Agreement (RCEP) and the Comprehensive and Progressive Agreement for Trans-Pacific Partnership (CPTPP).

East Asia remains subject to persistent, high volatility in international financial markets

Amid elevated policy uncertainty in the international environment, financial markets in East Asia will remain subjected to periodic episodes of heightened volatility in the outlook period. In 2018, expectations of a faster pace of monetary policy adjustment in the United States contributed to a significant rise in 10-year Treasury yields and a strengthening of the dollar. This induced some global portfolio rebalancing, which in turn drove short-term capital outflows from the emerging regions, including most East Asian economies. For China, however, the inclusion of Chinese stocks into the MSCI Emerging Markets Index contributed to strong foreign portfolio inflows during the year. MSCI also announced that it might raise the weight of Chinese stocks in its indices beginning in 2019, which is likely to support inflows in the near term.

Regional financial markets were also affected by escalating trade tensions between China and the United States, as concerns arose over the impact of higher tariffs on China's growth prospects and the potential spillovers to the region. Compared to the beginning of 2018, major stock markets in China have seen declines of more than 20 per cent while the renminbi has weakened by about 6 per cent against the dollar. Most other East Asian economies also experienced equity market losses and currency depreciations but to varying extents, as investors increasingly differentiated between countries based on their strength of macroeconomic fundamentals. Despite heightened financial market volatility, however, financial intermediation generally remained undisrupted in the region, supported by sufficient liquidity in domestic banking systems.

Inflationary pressures rise, amid higher global energy prices and weaker domestic currencies

Inflation is expected to pick up in the region, following higher global energy prices and weaker domestic currencies. Given limited capacity pressures, however, inflation is likely to remain moderate in most economies. In Indonesia and Malaysia, the reintroduction of fuel price subsidies will also mitigate the pass-through from higher global oil prices onto domestic inflation. In 2018, higher prices of oil and food contributed to rising inflation in several countries, including Cambodia, China, Singapore and Thailand. Meanwhile, in the Republic of Korea, inflation slowed, in part reflecting the lack of domestic demand pressures. In all these countries, inflation rates remained below their national targets. In contrast, the Philippines experienced a rapid increase in consumer prices, fuelled by agriculture supply bottlenecks, higher excise taxes on several goods, and an increase in the cost of oil imports. A key risk to East Asia's inflation outlook stems from a possible escalation of tariff measures, driving up the cost of intermediate inputs and exerting upward pressure on product prices.

Monetary policy is likely to remain accommodative, given high uncertainty in the external environment

Given moderate inflationary pressures and rising downside risks to growth, monetary policy is expected to remain accommodative in most East Asian economies. However, as the developed countries continue to normalize monetary policy, the region is likely to face stronger capital outflow pressures, making it more challenging for central banks to maintain low policy rates. Furthermore, several central banks have reiterated concerns over the need to reduce the degree of monetary accommodation, in order to prevent the further build-up of financial imbalances.

In 2018, Indonesia raised interest rates by a cumulative 175 basis points, in efforts to stem capital outflows and the sharp depreciation of the rupiah. Malaysia and Singapore tightened monetary policy earlier in the year, following strong growth and labour market conditions. Meanwhile, surging inflationary pressures in the Philippines prompted its central bank to increase rates at a sharp pace. In contrast, China loosened monetary policy during the year, to mitigate the effects of intensifying trade frictions on the economy. While likely to provide some support to short-term growth, this may contribute to a further increase in already high domestic debt levels, raising the risk of a disorderly deleveraging process in the future.

Fiscal policy will play a larger role in supporting domestic demand

As monetary policy space narrows, most East Asian economies are likely to maintain expansionary fiscal stances to support domestic demand. The Republic of Korea has announced plans for a sharp increase in fiscal spending in 2019, which will be focused on job creation and expanding social welfare. As risks to growth increase, China has also introduced several pro-growth fiscal measures, which include lowering personal income taxes and accelerating infrastructure investment. Boosting infrastructure spending has also been the focus of Governments in several other large economies, including the Philippines and Thailand. Meanwhile, in Indonesia, the authorities are focusing on reforms in order to enhance the efficiency and effectiveness of public expenditure on growth.

China's growth is projected to remain solid despite rising trade tensions

Amid rising external headwinds and ongoing economic rebalancing, China's GDP growth is projected to moderate at a gradual pace, from 6.6 per cent in 2018 to 6.3 per cent in 2019 and 6.2 per cent in 2020. Domestic demand growth is expected to remain solid, supported by a looser monetary policy stance and pro-growth fiscal measures. In 2018, China's growth momentum moderated from the previous year, due mainly to a deceleration in fixed asset investment. In particular, infrastructure investment growth was dampened by tighter regulatory restrictions aimed at reining in local government debt. Household spending remained robust in 2018, but expanded at a more moderate pace, amid a weakening of consumer confidence. Nevertheless, private consumption will remain the key driver of growth in the outlook period. Alongside healthy income growth, consumer spending will also be boosted by the increase in the minimum threshold for personal income tax exemption and several additional tax deductions, including on childcare and education.

China's export performance remained solid in 2018, buoyed by strong demand from the developed countries and intraregional trade activity. However, recent leading indicators suggest that the imposition of United States tariffs may have a more significant impact on the Chinese economy going forward. In October, China's manufacturing Purchasing Managers' Index weakened to its lowest reading in two years, as new export orders and business confidence declined.

As trade tensions with the United States intensified, the Chinese authorities announced a wide range of pre-emptive measures to support growth. On the financial front, the central bank reduced reserve requirement ratios for large banks and raised bank lending quotas in efforts to enhance domestic liquidity and stimulate credit growth. In addition, restrictions on local government bond issuances were eased to stimulate infrastructure investment. These measures, however, may exacerbate financial imbalances, thus increasing risks to domestic financial stability. At the same time, Chinese policymakers have announced several strategies geared towards lifting China's medium-term growth prospects. These include the easing of business regulation to foster stronger entrepreneurship and innovation. Ongoing plans to attract more high technology investment will also

Box III.4

China's economic transition and its potential impacts on Asia and the Pacific

In the last four decades, the Chinese economy has grown at an unprecedented speed, transforming from a predominantly agricultural economy to an industrial powerhouse, and is now increasingly services oriented. However, it is now confronting headwinds, including weakening external demand, rising import tariffs imposed by the United States of America, decelerating productivity growth along with high private debt, diminishing demographic dividends, increasing inequality and a deteriorating natural environment. Given such strains, a slowdown in China's economic growth is most likely to occur in the coming decade. However, different policy pathways could result in considerably different outcomes in terms of quality of economic growth.

Model simulation results, which consider different policy pathways, suggest that if China pursues a holistic approach to structural reforms that includes innovative, inclusive and sustainable growth paths simultaneously, the country could maintain relatively high rates of economic growth—even as external demand remains sluggish, the labour force shrinks and capital accumulation slows—and experience a decline in urban-rural income disparity and CO_2 emissions (figure III.4.1). However, the Government of China might still face difficult policy trade-offs. For example, policy priorities on technology and innovation could boost growth in GDP but might worsen inequality. Similarly, policy responses that address an increasingly uncertain external environment (especially trade) need to be carefully designed to avoid undermining longer-term social inclusiveness or environmental sustainability.

Due to closer regional economic integration, China's structural transformation is expected to have important ramifications for the Asia-Pacific region. Compared with a scenario wherein China continues to follow the current policy trends (baseline), a holistic structural reforms scenario generates positive impact on economic growth, exports and imports, and welfare gains in the Asia-Pacific economies (figure III.4.2). Japan, the Republic of Korea and South-East Asian countries are predicted to benefit the most from deepening trade links, while countries in the Pacific are expected to benefit the least. Growth in trade of heavy manufacturing products could outpace that of all other tradable goods between China and the rest of the region, thanks to China's manufacturing sector having moved up the value chain, whereas services exports to China could decline, as China develops its own services sector (e.g., health care or education). To maximize opportunities and mitigate risks arising from China's structural transformation, policymakers could consider policy options based on their economic conditions and degree of trade integration with China.

Figure III.4.1

Computable General Equilibrium (CGE) model simulation: the impact of China's economic transition on its development in 2030

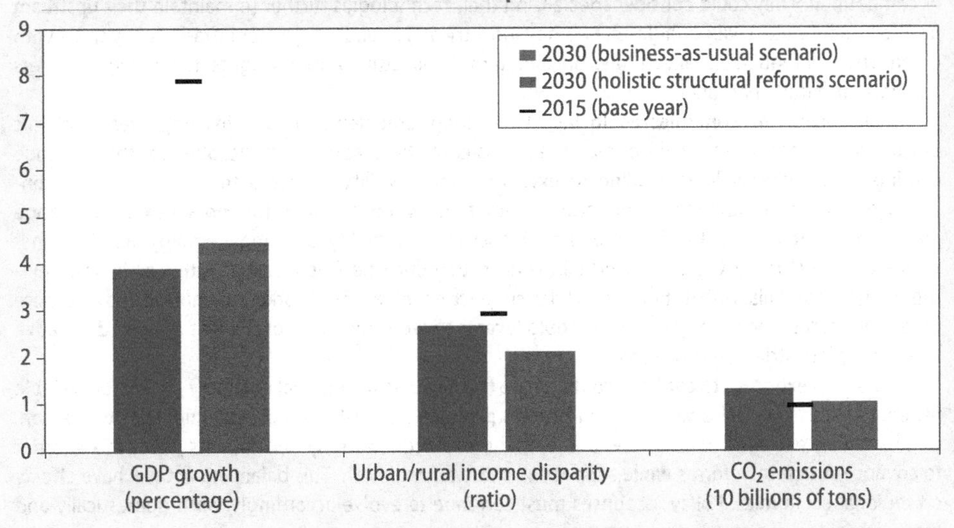

Source: ESCAP calculation.

Note: Urban/rural income disparity is measured by the ratio of urban income to rural income. If the ratio goes up, it indicates higher income inequality; if down, lower income inequality. Detailed assumptions for different scenarios are available in ESCAP (forthcoming).

(continued)

Box III.4 (*continued*)

Figure III.4.2
CGE model simulation: the impact of China's holistic structural reforms on the Asia-Pacific region in 2030

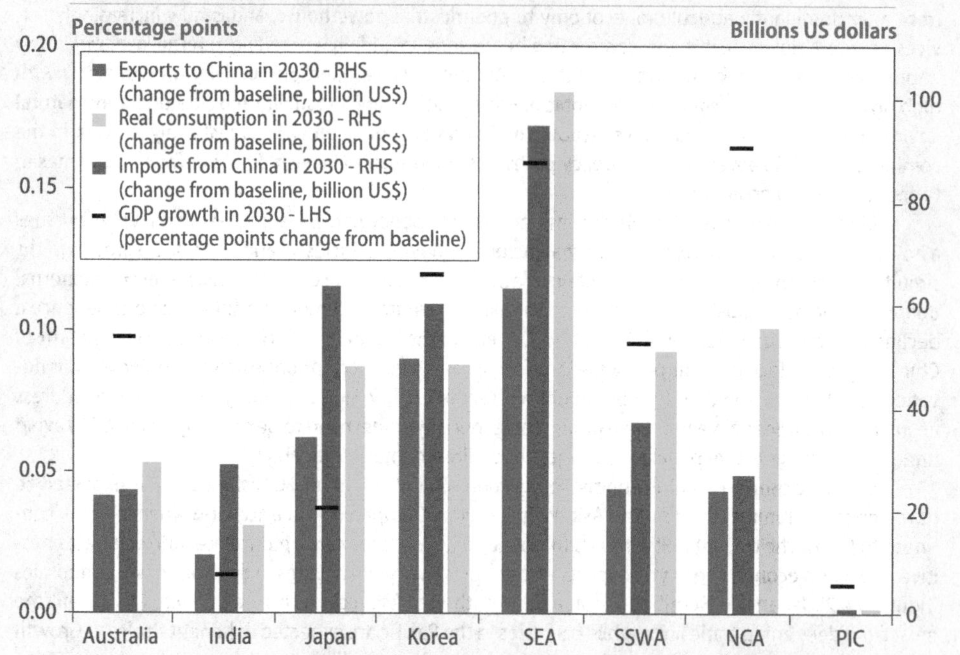

Source: ESCAP calculation.
Note: SEA = South-East Asia; SSWA = South and South-West Asia; NCA = North and Central Asia; PIC = Pacific; RHS = right-hand scale; LHS = left-hand scale. Regional aggregations are defined by ESCAP (http://data.unescap.org/escap_stat/#methodDefinition) and are not strictly comparable to regional definitions used elsewhere in the report. Baseline scenario assumes that China follows the current policy trends.

Countries with low labour costs, such as Cambodia and Nepal, will appear more attractive for labour-intensive manufacturing activities as wages rise in China. In order to further enhance their attractiveness to foreign investment, these countries need to strengthen domestic infrastructure and improve their business environments. Meanwhile, to continue to advance their transformation they will also need to promote the development and accumulation of new capabilities, promote a more diversified production and export base for more complex goods and services, and become more integrated into global value chains with access to a wider range of expanding suppliers and markets. For existing technology exporters, such as Japan and the Republic of Korea, China's industrial upgrading could lead to stronger competition. They could consider specializing their technologies further to maintain their upstream position in the value chain of high-technology industry and engage in greater intra-industry trade with China. This will require enhanced rules, including on intellectual property rights, technology transfers and non-tariff trade barriers.

Resource-rich economies could face lower long-term demand as China improves economic efficiency and reduces reliance on fossil fuels. This could have adverse implications for their revenue earnings and financial flows, leading to exchange-rate volatility. To avoid this, resource-rich economies may need to strengthen monetary policy frameworks to allow for more flexible exchange rates; diversify to lower risks of revenue and financial flow volatility; and boost employment in higher value-added sectors. As China is undertaking efforts to reduce inefficient and polluting activities, countries such as Mongolia, with its high export dependence on mining and markets in China, could face more urgent pressures. Commodity exporters could leverage investment links of the Belt and Road Initiative to enhance industrial diversification.

China is expected to continue to dominate the Asia-Pacific regional economy for the foreseeable future. China's structural transformation process presents new risks and opportunities for the region. Amid a rapidly evolving external environment, China will continuously fine-tune its policy mix in order to advance structural reforms while supporting short-term growth. This balancing act will have effects on regional economies. Policy responses must continue to evolve accordingly, both domestically and through regional cooperation efforts.

Authors: Zhenqian Huang and Daniel Jeong-Dae Lee (UN/ESCAP).

contribute to productivity and employment gains, while boosting competitiveness. China's gradual move up the value chain and ongoing structural transformation will have implications on the rest of the region (box III.4).

Exports will provide less support to growth in the Republic of Korea, Singapore and Taiwan Province of China

Growth in the Republic of Korea is projected to moderate from 2.6 per cent in 2018 to 2.5 per cent in 2019. An expected slowdown in export growth will be partly offset by a pickup in private consumption in the outlook period. Household spending will benefit from the significant increase in minimum wages, policy measures to boost employment and higher social spending. Following growth of 2.7 per cent in 2018, Taiwan Province of China is also expected to expand at a slower pace of 2.4 per cent in 2019, as export growth is tempered by a maturing global consumer electronics cycle and waning base effects. The current trade frictions are also likely to have a visible impact on trade, given that China and the United States account for almost 40 per cent of total exports. In Singapore, GDP growth is projected to ease from 3.2 per cent in 2018 to 2.6 per cent in 2019, as manufacturing activity expands at a more moderate pace. Growth in the domestic-oriented industries, including retail and food services, will remain robust, underpinned by improving labour market conditions and positive consumer confidence.

Domestic demand in the ASEAN economies will remain resilient

Growth in the large economies in the Association of South East Asian Nations[4] (ASEAN) will continue to be supported by resilient domestic demand. In the Philippines, GDP growth in 2018 was affected by a slowdown in household spending due to a rapid increase in inflation. Going forward, growth is projected to rebound slightly, from 6.3 per cent in 2018 to 6.5 per cent in 2019. Growth will be mainly driven by strong government spending and infrastructure investment. However, the economy faces the risk of persistently high inflationary pressures, prompting a more aggressive stance on monetary policy tightening, thus further constraining private consumption. Following growth of 4.6 per cent in 2018, Malaysia is expected to grow at a more moderate pace of 4.4 per cent in 2019. Private consumption will be supported by steady increases in wages and employment. Consumer spending will also benefit to some extent from the replacement of the Goods and Services Tax with the Sales and Services Tax, given that the latter is imposed on a narrower range of goods. Public sector spending will pose a drag on GDP growth as the new Government reprioritizes expenditure. The decision to cancel or suspend several large infrastructure projects will weigh on public investment growth.

Following exceptionally strong growth of 4.1 per cent in 2018, Thailand's GDP is projected to moderate to 3.8 per cent in 2019. Private consumption will be underpinned by a significant rise in non-agriculture wages and an improvement in consumer sentiments. Public investment growth will be driven by the implementation of large infrastructure projects. This includes the launch of the Eastern Economic Corridor, which aims to develop Thailand's eastern provinces into a manufacturing and services hub. In Indonesia, the economy is expected to continue expanding at a steady pace of 5.1 per cent in 2019. Private consumption will remain the key driver of growth, amid rising incomes in the formal sector and higher social welfare spending. However, recent policies to stabilize the rupiah, including interest rate hikes and the postponement of infrastructure projects to reduce capital imports, will weigh on the pace of expansion in domestic demand in the near term.

ASEAN LDCs will continue growing at a rapid pace

The least developed countries in ASEAN, namely, Cambodia, Lao People's Democratic Republic and Myanmar, will continue to expand at a rapid pace of between 6.5 to 7.5

4 Association of South East Asian Nations (ASEAN) member countries consist of Brunei Darussalam, Cambodia, Indonesia, Lao People's Democratic Republic, Malaysia, Myanmar, the Philippines, Singapore, Thailand and Viet Nam.

per cent in 2019 and 2020, as incomes rise from relatively low bases. Private consumption growth is expected to remain strong, while continued infrastructure investment, particularly in the energy and transportation sectors, will also boost economic growth in these economies. Nevertheless, low productivity levels—amid still poorly diversified economic structures and large infrastructure bottlenecks—remain a challenge to boosting competitiveness and achieving stronger medium-term growth prospects.

Meanwhile, growth in the Pacific Island countries, including Kiribati, Papua New Guinea, the Solomon Islands and Vanuatu, will be supported by rising tourist arrivals, higher commodity prices and stronger fishing revenues. The outlook, however, is highly susceptible to commodity price fluctuations and weather-related shocks.

Key downside risks to the region's growth outlook stem from a potential deterioration in global trade and financial conditions

Downside risks to East Asia's growth outlook have increased considerably over the past year. A further intensification of trade frictions between China and the United States will have adverse spillovers on regional growth through trade, investment, and financial channels. In addition, an abrupt tightening of monetary policy in the United States may trigger sudden and large capital outflows from the region, posing a risk to financial stability. On the domestic front, financial sector vulnerabilities, particularly high corporate and household debt, will continue to weigh on investment prospects in several countries.

Most East Asian economies have some degree of policy space to mitigate an external shock

Compared to other developing regions, the East Asian economies have a more optimistic growth outlook. This is in part due to stronger macroeconomic fundamentals as well as relatively less severe external and domestic vulnerabilities. Importantly, most economies in the region have some degree of policy flexibility and buffers to effectively mitigate an external shock. Foreign-exchange reserves in the region remain ample, with high import coverage ratios (figure III.21). Many countries have also been utilizing macroprudential tools as an additional policy instrument to manage financial stability risks. In addition, fiscal positions in East Asia are relatively stronger, attributed in part to robust GDP growth and more prudent fiscal management. Over the past five years, fiscal deficits in the region averaged only 1.8 per cent, while the region's public debt-to-GDP ratio is relatively low, amounting to 46 per cent of GDP in 2017. In a few countries, however, high government-contingent liabilities will likely constrain the Government's ability to embark on large fiscal stimulus measures.

Figure III.21
International reserves of selected East Asian economies, months of import coverage

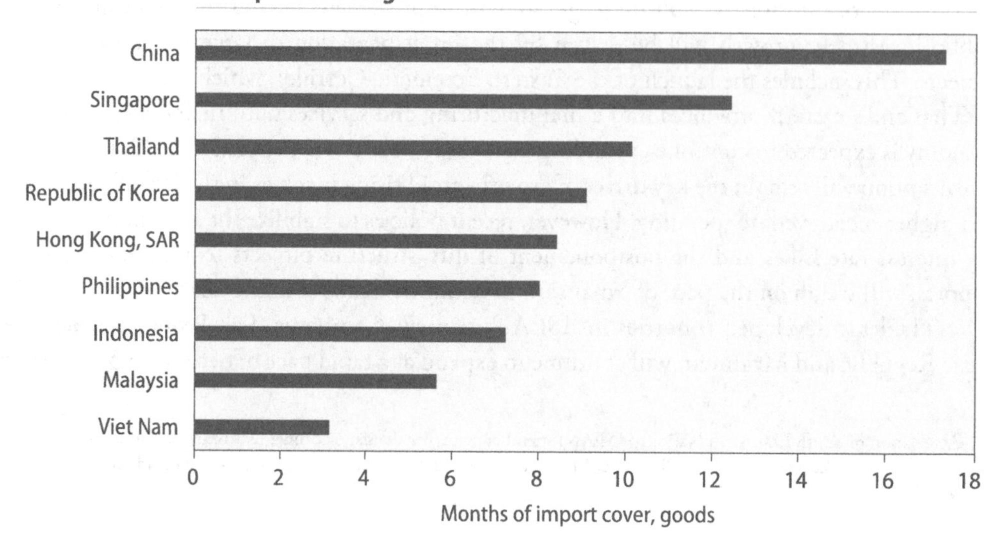

Source: World Bank's Global Economic Monitor database.
Note: A common rule of thumb used to guide reserve adequacy suggests that countries should hold reserves equivalent to more than 3 months worth of imports. Data on each country is based on latest available data in 2018.

South Asia

GDP Growth

8.0% 6.0% 4.0% 2.0%

total: 2016 8.0, 2017 6.1, 2018 5.6, 2019 5.4, 2020 5.9

per capita: 2016 6.6, 2017 4.8, 2018 4.4, 2019 4.1, 2020 4.7

projected

2016 2017 2018 2019 2020

GDP per capita

2018

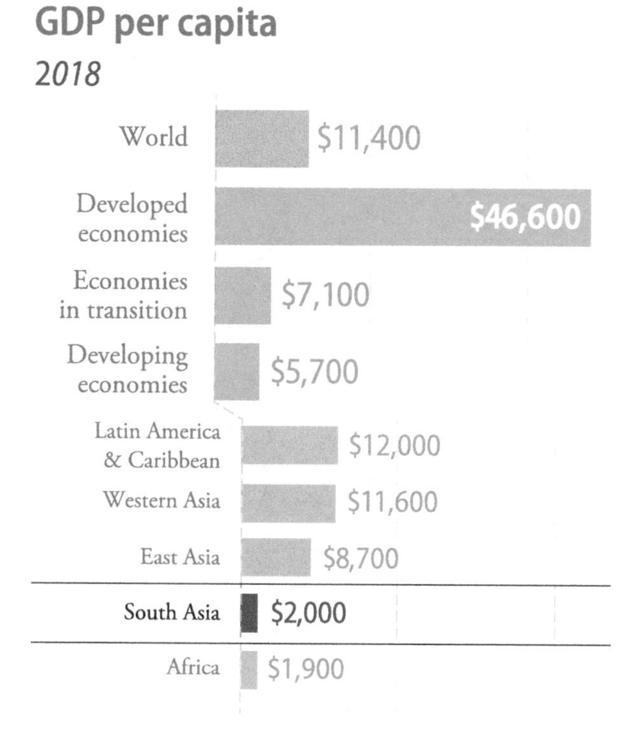

Exports structure

2016

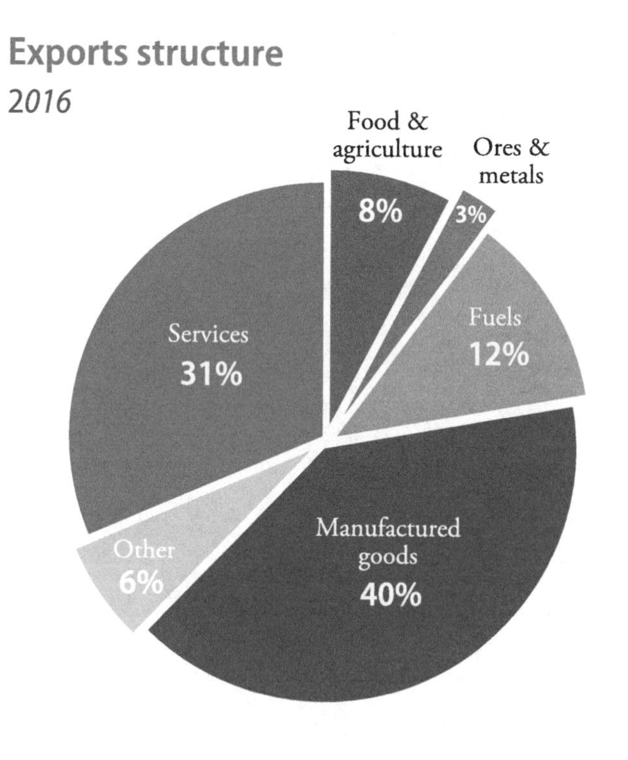

The boundaries and names shown and the designations used on this map do not imply official endorsement or acceptance by the United Nations. The map represents countries and/or territories or parts thereof for which data is available and/or analysed in *World Economic Situation and Prospects 2019*. The shaded areas therefore do not necessarily overlap entirely with the delimitation of their frontiers or boundaries.

South Asia: economic outlooks diverge as short- and medium-term challenges remain

- **South Asia's outlook remains moderately favourable, but economic trends are highly divergent across countries**
- **The downside risks have increased in several economies in the short-term**
- **The region needs to strengthen productive capacities and international competitiveness to unleash its growth potential in the medium-term**

The economic outlook for South Asia is moderately positive...

The economic outlook for South Asia is highly divergent across countries. There are some economies, including Bangladesh, Bhutan and India, where economic conditions are largely positive, with GDP growth projected to remain robust in the near term. In contrast, the outlook in the Islamic Republic of Iran and Pakistan has visibly deteriorated. Consequently, regional GDP growth slowed down markedly in 2018. Yet, given the large size of the Indian economy, on the aggregate, the regional outlook is still moderately favourable, especially in comparison to other developing regions. Regional GDP is expected to expand by 5.4 per cent 2019 and 5.9 per cent in 2020, after an estimated expansion of 5.6 per cent in 2018 (figure III.22). Economic growth is expected to be supported by private consumption and, in some cases, investment demand, even as monetary policy stances tighten in some economies. Despite the increase observed for inflation figures throughout 2018 due to the depreciation of domestic currencies and higher oil prices, inflation is expected to accelerate only moderately or to remain stable in most economies in the near term, with the notable exception of the Islamic Republic of Iran.

Figure III.22
GDP growth in South Asia, 2018–2020

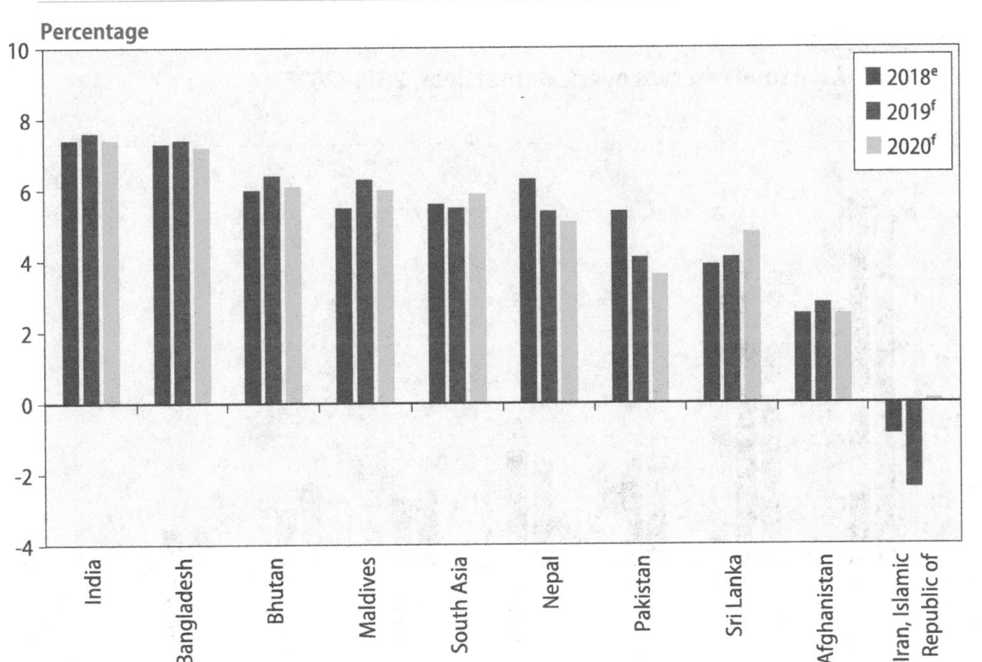

Source: UN/DESA.
Note: e=estimate, f=forecast. GDP growth numbers are based on a fiscal year basis for Afghanistan, Bangladesh, India, Iran (Islamic Republic of), Nepal and Pakistan, while on a calendar year basis for Bhutan, Maldives and Sri Lanka.

...but the domestic and external downside risks have increased across the region

The downside risks to the projections have recently increased across the region, because of domestic and external factors. On the domestic side, political uncertainties, setbacks in the implementation of reforms and, in some countries, security problems can affect investment prospects. This is a crucial issue, as the region needs to tackle the infrastructure bottlenecks for promoting productivity growth, encouraging further poverty reductions and adjusting to climate change. Also, natural disasters, including those associated with climate change, constitute a major source of risk to economic activity. On the external side, an abrupt tightening of global financial conditions, coupled with a further escalation of the ongoing trade disputes, is also a significant downside risk to the outlook. For example, more challenging external conditions can further expose macroeconomic imbalances and financial vulnerabilities associated with rising fiscal and current account deficits and elevated levels of debt in some economies. Notably, most economies have insufficient foreign-exchange reserves to face severe external shocks (figure III.23). In addition, given that South Asia is a net oil importer, a significant rise in oil prices could raise inflationary pressures and constrain economic activity in several economies.

Economic activity in India and Bangladesh remains vigorous

The Indian economy is expected to expand by 7.6 and 7.4 per cent in 2019 and 2020, respectively, after expanding by 7.4 per cent in 2018. Economic growth continues to be underpinned by robust private consumption, a more expansionary fiscal stance and benefits from previous reforms. Yet, a more robust and sustained recovery of private investment remains a crucial challenge to uplifting medium-term growth. The Bangladesh economy is also set to continue expanding at a fast pace in the near term, above 7.0 per cent per year, amid strong fixed investment, vigorous private consumption and accommodative monetary policy. Meanwhile, Sri Lanka's economy is recovering from the slowdown in 2017, but much more slowly than anticipated, amid weak business sentiment, feeble investment demand and political turbulences. Growth is projected to remain below its potential in the near term.

However, some economies are also experiencing significant difficulties, underscoring short-term macroeconomic and financial challenges. The economic outlook in the Islamic

Figure III.23
South Asia: total reserves over external debt, 2015–2017

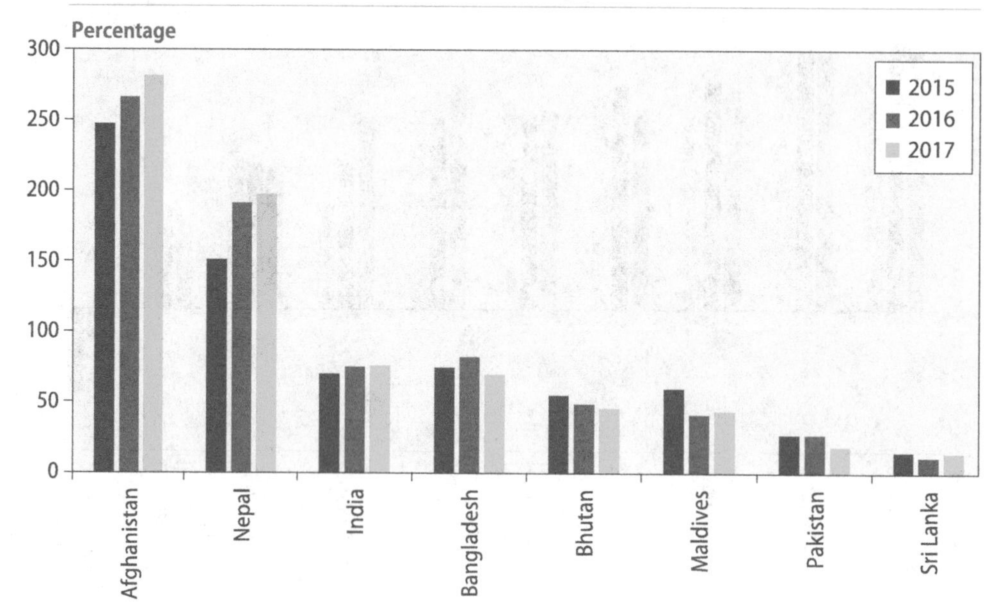

Sources: UN/DESA, based on data from World Bank's International Debt Statistics database.

Note: Data for Nepal correspond to 2014, 2015 and 2016, respectively.

Republic of Iran has deteriorated visibly, due to the re-imposition of trade, investment and financial sanctions by the United States, and structural domestic weaknesses. The sanctions have already exacerbated goods shortages and constrained productive capacity and oil export revenues. The depreciation of the domestic currency has also fuelled inflationary pressures: inflation reached record highs of more than 30.0 per cent by October and is projected to remain elevated in the near term. Against this backdrop, the Iranian economy is estimated to have entered into recession in 2018, which is projected to deepen throughout 2019. Importantly, weaknesses associated with severe underinvestment and lack of technology transfers for more than a decade will continue to constrain economic activity in the medium term.

Meanwhile, the economic outlook in Pakistan is challenging, and it encompasses significant downside risks. On the one hand, economic activity continues to be underpinned by robust private consumption, improvements in energy supply, and infrastructure initiatives of the China-Pakistan Economic Corridor. On the other, Pakistan's economy is facing severe balance of payment difficulties, amid large twin fiscal and current account deficits, a visible decline in international reserves and mounting pressures on the domestic currency. The level of public debt is also high—close to 70 per cent of GDP—with rising sustainability concerns. In fact, the Government is currently negotiating for official assistance from the IMF to address macroeconomic and fiscal challenges for the second time in the last five years. Against this backdrop, growth is projected to slow down markedly in 2019 and 2020 to below 4.0 per cent, after an estimated expansion of 5.4 per cent in 2018. The macroeconomic imbalances and financial fragilities pose significant risks of a further slowdown, which emphasizes the need for policy actions. This highlights some long-standing challenges for Pakistan's economy. To promote more sustainable medium-term growth, policymakers need to encourage much-needed infrastructure investment to alleviate chronic energy shortages while addressing external imbalances, particularly by promoting export growth.

Improving labour market conditions is a major challenge

Strengthening labour market indicators is a crucial aspect to forge a more inclusive development trajectory in South Asia. However, employment growth has recently slowed down in the region, and female labour force participation remains low and declining. In addition, youth unemployment is a major concern in several economies, especially given the growth of working-age populations. In India, for example, job creation rates in the formal sector have been feeble, leaving many workers underemployed or in low-salary jobs, with the situation for youth particularly worrisome. In fact, well-educated youths are struggling to find jobs in the formal sector, and most of them are absorbed into low-paying and vulnerable jobs in the informal sector.

Monetary policy stances are adjusting to more challenging external conditions...

The gradual tightening of global financial conditions is prompting the adjustment of monetary policy stances across the region. In the current context, policymakers face the challenge of maintaining growth momentum while containing inflationary pressures and facilitating domestic adjustments to lower global liquidity. Most domestic currencies across the region depreciated throughout 2018, while the current account deficits continued to rise in several countries, including Bangladesh, India and Pakistan.

Monetary policy stances have gradually and moderately tightened in several economies. In India, the central bank raised its policy interest rate by 25 basis points in both June and August, to reach 6.5 per cent, while the domestic currency depreciated to record lows in early October. Despite the depreciation, consumer price inflation moderated in the second half of 2018 and it is projected to remain within the central bank's target range. Given the currency peg of the Nepali rupee to the Indian rupee, Nepal Rastra Bank is expected to follow the same tightening path in the near term. During the first eight months of 2018, Pakistan's central bank raised its policy interest rates by 275 basis points to 8.5 per cent, and expectations are that the tightening will continue further in 2019. Despite this tightening, the significant depreciation of the domestic currency has increased consumer price inflation.

...while fiscal policies have recently become more expansionary

The fiscal policies across the region have gradually moved to a more expansionary stance; thus fiscal deficits are projected to remain elevated. To avert sustainability concerns, medium-term consolidation plans are required in some economies, particularly those with a fragile tax base and elevated levels of debt. For example, in India the size and composition of public budgets have been important in promoting growth, prioritizing public investments in infrastructure, subsidies and welfare payments, and the rural economy. This will prevent any reduction of the fiscal deficit in the near term. In the Islamic Republic of Iran, the fiscal deficit is expected to increase in 2019, amid significantly lower oil revenues and rising pressures to enhance social benefits. Meanwhile, the fiscal deficit in Bangladesh is at a record high, close to 5.0 per cent of GDP, as the country struggles to expand the tax base. In Pakistan, entering an IMF programme by 2019 would necessitate a sharp fiscal consolidation. In fact, rising expenditures and high debt repayment obligations have maintained a relatively high fiscal deficit, about 4.8 per cent of GDP. Overall, strengthening fiscal accounts remains a major challenge for the region, amid a low level of tax revenues, rigid public expenditures and persistent structural deficits. Improved tax revenues are a critical aspect in building fiscal buffers and in strengthening the capacity to implement countercyclical and redistributive policies.

Strengthening the productive and international competitiveness is a crucial challenge to unleash the growth potential

Beyond the short-term outlook, South Asia—which accounts for 25 per cent of the world population but only for 5 per cent of the world GDP—also needs to tackle medium-term challenges and structural constraints to unleash its enormous growth potential. A crucial challenge is the strengthening of its productive and international competitiveness, as the region is lagging in several competitiveness indicators, like attracting foreign investments, penetrating new markets, and diversifying and upgrading its export products. Also, the region shows a disappointing performance regarding technological capabilities, even in comparison to other developing regions, as measured, for example, by R&D investments, innovation activities, and other indicators, such as the Economic Complexity Index (figure III.24). Amid limited trade openness and regional integration, South Asia has an enormous

Figure III.24

Economic Complexity Index, selected countries and regions, 2016

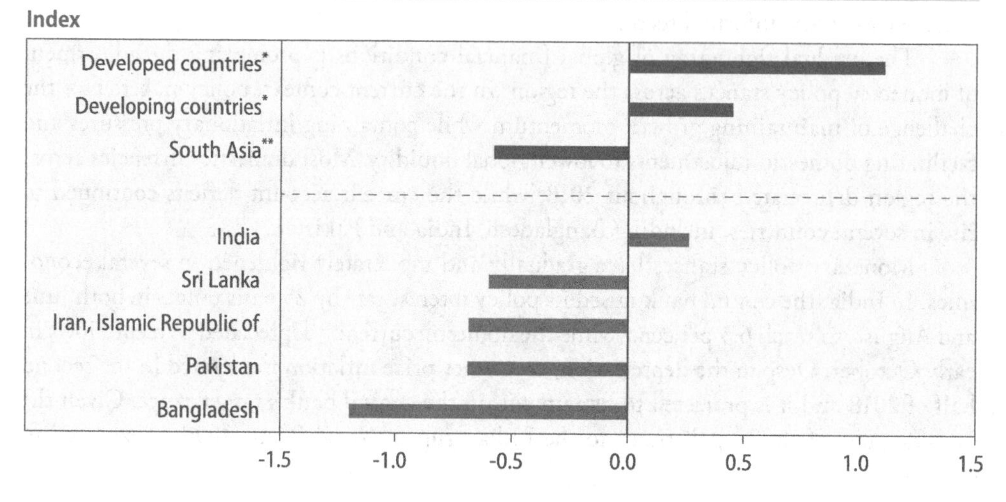

Source: UN/DESA, based on data from MIT Observatory on Economic Complexity, available from https://atlas.media.mit.edu/en/.

Note: The Economic Complexity Index measures the multiplicity of productive knowledge in an economy by combining information on the diversity of a country's exports (based on the number of its export products) and the ubiquity of its products (based on the number of countries that export a specific product); *average; ** average of the presented 5 countries.

potential to gain market share in foreign markets and to participate more decisively in global value chains (GVCs). In fact, while there are positive examples, such as the software and business outsourcing sectors in India, the garment sector in Bangladesh and Sri Lanka, and the Sialkot light manufacturing cluster in Pakistan, the positive effects of increased global integration have remained limited in most economies in the region.

South Asia needs to tackle this issue through a comprehensive policy approach. Policies to strengthen the business environment, with emphasis on industry-specific issues, can positively impact investment prospects. Also, trade policy changes can significantly reduce the elevated trade costs across the region, facilitate the access to foreign inputs to exporters and support the participation in GVCs. Meanwhile, policies regarding foreign direct investments and multinational firms can encourage not only financial flows but also productive linkages, technology transfers and training of the workforce. Public policies can also take a more proactive stance to promote innovation activities—for example, by uplifting public R&D interventions that can catalyse private R&D investments and by enhancing complementary factors, including infrastructure, labour skills and finance.

Western Asia

GDP Growth

4.0%
2.0%
0.0

3.1
2.5
3.0
2.4
3.4
total

1.1
0.6
1.1
0.6
1.7
per capita
projected

2016 2017 2018 2019 2020

GDP per capita

2018

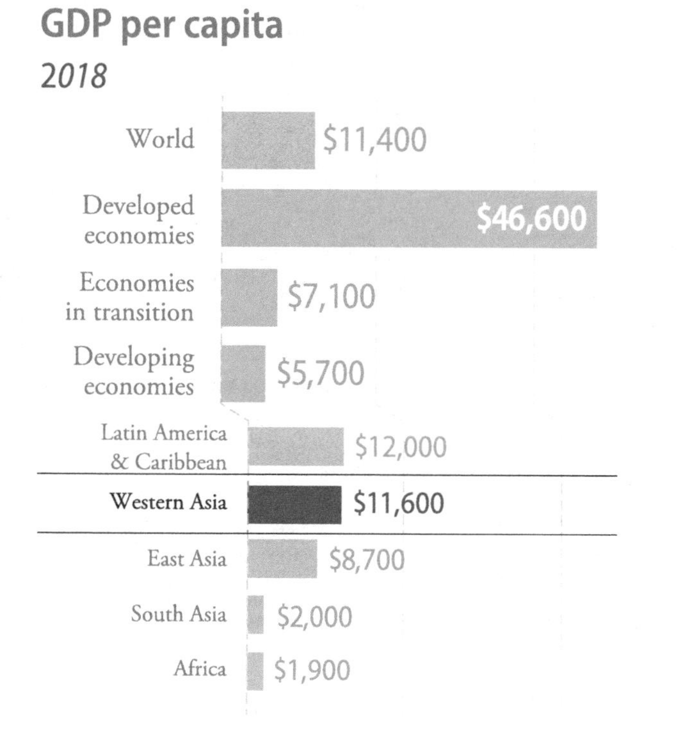

Exports structure

2016

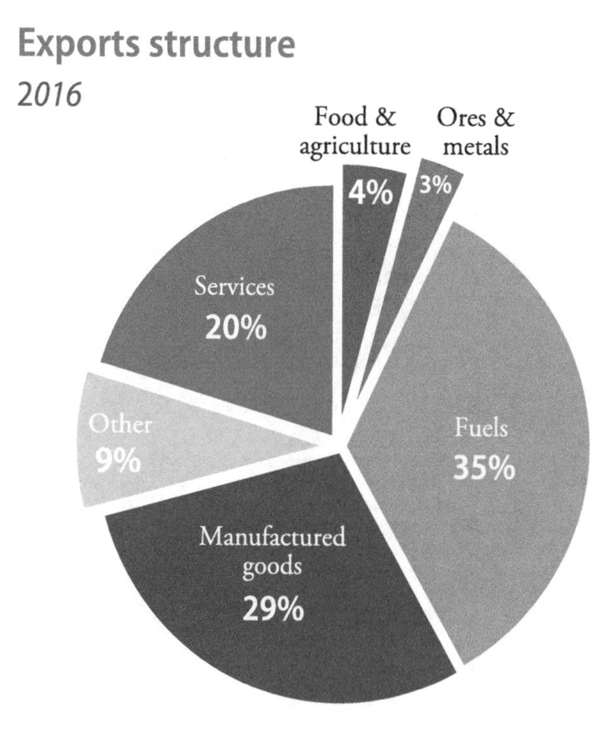

The boundaries and names shown and the designations used on this map do not imply official endorsement or acceptance by the United Nations. The map represents countries and/or territories or parts thereof for which data is available and/or analysed in *World Economic Situation and Prospects 2019*. The shaded areas therefore do not necessarily overlap entirely with the delimitation of their frontiers or boundaries.

Western Asia: gradual recovery as oil markets improve

- Higher oil prices improve business sentiments
- Geopolitical tensions continue to impact economies
- The policy environment remains a challenge for ongoing fiscal reform

Western Asian economies saw a gradual recovery in economic growth in 2018 as the rebalancing of oil markets has positively impacted the region's major crude oil producers (see chap. I). Higher oil prices have not only contributed to fiscal balance improvements but also buoyed economic sentiment in the region's major crude oil producers, namely, the member countries of The Cooperation Council for the Arab States of the Gulf (GCC): Bahrain, Kuwait, Oman, Qatar, Saudi Arabia and the United Arab Emirates. Moreover, the change in the Organization of the Petroleum Exporting Countries (OPEC) stance on the production ceiling in June 2018 has enabled the region's crude oil producers to moderately increase crude oil production over the previous year's level. On the other hand, growth in the energy-importing countries in the region (Jordan, Lebanon, and Turkey) has been mostly subdued, partly because of deteriorating terms of trade. Moreover, geopolitical uncertainty and high levels of public debt have negatively impacted these countries. The economic expansion in 2019 and 2020 is expected to be modest. Ongoing policy reforms and fiscal consolidation are expected to enhance macroeconomic resilience in energy-importing countries. The non-oil sector in GCC economies is projected to expand, deepening linkages to East and South Asian economies. However, the high reliance on hydrocarbon exports and geopolitical tensions weigh heavily on the region's growth prospects.

Figure III.25
GDP growth prospects of GCC countries

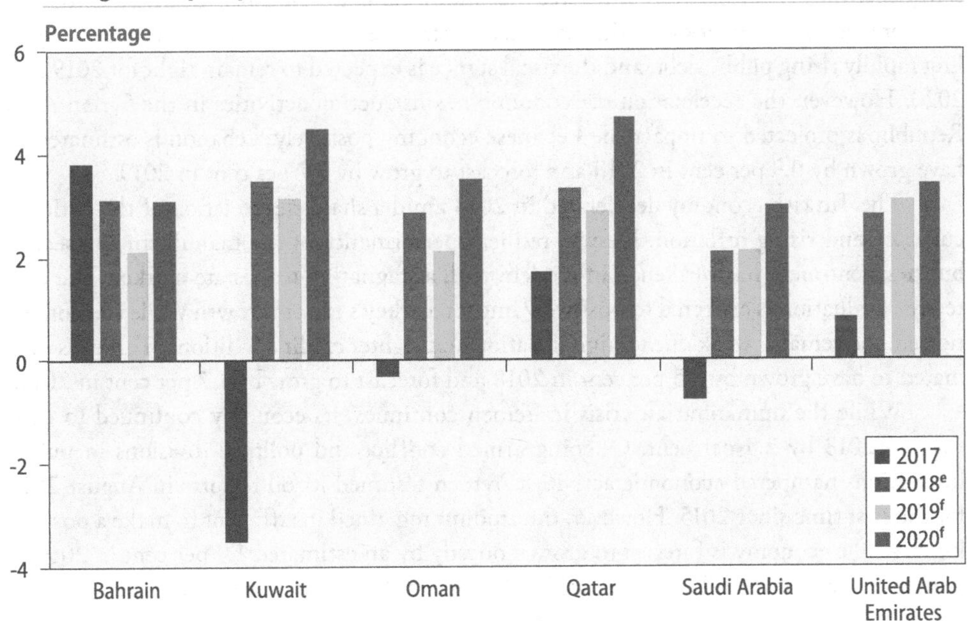

Source: UN/DESA.
Note: e = estimate, f = forecast.

The growth of GCC economies rebounded

The growth of GCC economies rebounded in 2018 from the weak growth performance in the previous year (figure III.25). The OPEC-led crude oil production ceiling resulted in a 4.5 per cent decline in crude oil production in GCC countries over the period between 2016 and 2017. Although domestic demand continued to expand consistently, the negative contribution of the oil sector halted the overall economic expansion in 2017. Economic growth rebounded in 2018 as both the oil and non-oil sectors positively contributed to growth. In addition to a modest increase in crude oil production, higher oil prices have improved business sentiment and stabilized financial and real estate markets. Ongoing reform measures to promote non-oil sectors also contributed to positive business sentiment. The efforts to diversify fiscal revenues, most notably through the introduction of the VAT, continued to improve fiscal frameworks and institutions. GCC economies are forecast to maintain steady growth over 2019 and 2020 as business sentiment is expected to remain mildly positive. Some acceleration may take place for large infrastructure projects such as World Expo 2020.

The recent decline in oil revenues has compelled the Government of Iraq to take fiscal consolidation efforts. Consequently, the reduction in public investment outweighed a pickup in non-oil economic activities. Moreover, inadequate public service provision, such as electricity, caused social unrest in the first half of 2018. With the formation of the new Government, public investment and public service provision are expected to strengthen. The Iraqi economy is estimated to have grown by 2.4 per cent in 2018 and forecast to grow by 2.3 per cent in 2019.

Geopolitical tensions and terms-of-trade deterioration impact Jordan, Lebanon and Turkey

Geopolitical tensions continue to negatively impact the economies of Jordan, Lebanon and Turkey. Moreover, rising energy prices caused terms-of-trade deterioration in those countries, resulting in tightening of balance of payment conditions. Robust growth in the mining sector and a pickup in tourism drove moderate growth in Jordan. However, fiscal austerity measures have weakened domestic demand growth. Ongoing reform is projected to stabilize the Jordanian economy over 2019 and 2020. Jordan is estimated to have grown by 2.1 per cent in 2018 and forecast to grow by 2.3 per cent in 2019.

Stagnant intraregional trade, a decelerating inflow of both workers' remittances and foreign investments negatively impacted Lebanon's economy in 2018. Business sentiment deteriorated with stagnation in the real estate sector. Lebanon faces the challenge of tackling rapidly rising public debt, and the fiscal stance is expected to remain tight for 2019 and 2020. However, the acceleration of economic reconstruction activities in the Syrian Arab Republic is projected to impact the Lebanese economy positively. Lebanon is estimated to have grown by 0.9 per cent in 2018 and forecast to grow by 1.7 per cent in 2019.

The Turkish economy decelerated in 2018 amid a sharp depreciation of the national currency and rising inflation. Despite resilient performance of the manufacturing sector, business sentiment has weakened in tandem with a stagnating real estate market. The currency devaluation is expected to positively impact Turkey's export growth while the domestic demand remains weak due to high inflation and tighter credit conditions. Turkey is estimated to have grown by 3.5 per cent in 2018 and forecast to grow by 1.7 per cent in 2019.

Yemen's economy contracts amid dire humanitarian conditions

While the humanitarian crisis in Yemen continues, its economy continued to contract in 2018 by 2.5 per cent. Ongoing armed conflict and political divisions in public institutions hampered economic activities. Yemen resumed its oil exports in August 2018 for the first time since 2015. However, the amount remained insufficient to make a positive impact. The economy is forecast to grow modestly by an estimated 1.9 per cent in 2019 as a slow recovery of the oil sector is projected. Despite this growth prospect, the population continues to face severe food insecurity as the agriculture sector was heavily damaged by armed conflict.

The Syrian economy has improved significantly as the intensity of conflict has eased. After five years of continuous contraction, the economy resumed expansion in 2017. While the stable exchange rate and monetary conditions stabilized economic conditions, increasing reconstruction activities contributed to the substantial recovery. Syria's economy is estimated to grow by 10.1 per cent in 2018 and forecast to grow by 11.3 per cent in 2019.

The economy of Palestine has been impacted by political tensions and instability. Industrial production declined while the economy was sustained by demand growth based on international aid and private sector transfers. The Palestinian economy is estimated to have contracted by 0.8 per cent in 2018 and forecast to grow by 1.3 per cent in 2019.

Robust economic growth continues in Israel

Robust economic expansion continued in Israel, supported by both strong external and domestic demand growth. While overheating domestic demand and upward pressure on wages have created inflationary pressures, consumer price inflation remained low in 2018. Weakening house prices are likely to lead to a gradual deceleration in domestic demand growth over 2019. The Israeli economy is estimated to have grown by 3.5 per cent in 2018 and forecast to grow by 3.2 per cent in 2019.

Mixed prospects in inflation

Inflationary pressures in GCC countries remained weak in 2018 except for Saudi Arabia and the United Arab Emirates where the introduction of the VAT impacted the price levels. Consumer price inflation for Iraq is also projected to remain low in 2018. This trend for GCC countries and Iraq is forecast to continue over 2019. The tax reform measures and rising energy prices resulted in rising price levels in Jordan and Lebanon. The inflation rate is forecast to decline in 2019 amid stabilizing energy prices in both Jordan and Lebanon. Due to the stable exchange rate, the high inflation rate in Syria is estimated to have come down to 4.3 per cent in 2018. However, as the economy is under severe foreign-exchange constraints, the rapid growth in reconstruction activities is forecast to push up inflation to 13.6 per cent in 2019. Yemen continues to face strong inflationary pressures that stem from the general shortage of supplies as well as monetary financing of a growing fiscal deficit, which is forecast to continue in 2019. Consumer price inflation in Turkey is estimated to be 16.1 per cent in 2018 due to the exchange-rate pass-through from a severe devaluation of the national currency. Despite a tight monetary stance, consumer price inflation is forecast to be high, at 10.2 per cent in 2019 as the impact of exchange-rate pass-through remains. Consumer price inflation is forecast to stay low in Israel through appreciation of the national currency and modest deceleration in domestic demand expansion.

The policy environment remains challenging

For the fiscal year covering 2018, GCC countries are expected to reduce budgetary deficits substantially. Although the improvement in fiscal positions is mostly attributed to increasing oil revenues from higher oil prices, the extensive efforts of fiscal consolidation—including subsidy reforms, revenue mobilization, and the introduction of the VAT—are forecast to positively impact the GCC countries' economic diversification strategy over the long term. Even though the impact of the VAT is modest regarding revenue increases, it is expected to improve the accounting system and business transparency. On the monetary side, the tightening monetary stance of the United States resulted in rising funding costs in the region as GCC countries, Iraq, Jordan and Lebanon sought a stable exchange rate of respective national currencies against the US dollar. Most of the central banks in the countries raised policy rates in tandem with the ongoing cycle of United States interest rate hikes. Moreover, the fast appreciation of the US dollar raised its funding costs in international capital markets for the region's borrowers. Although policy measures are in place to lessen liquidity pressures, which will enhance central banks' ability to supply credit to the private sector, the generally tightening monetary stance is expected to weaken domestic demand growth over 2019 and 2020.

Gradual social evolution continues amid grave challenges

Social evolution in the region was reflected in developments in Saudi Arabia, where women were allowed to obtain drivers' licenses in June 2018. Despite this indication of movement towards gender equality, the progress remains gradual. The Western Asia region witnessed remarkable progress in educational attainment for females over the last two decades, but the region on average is projected to experience only a modest increase in female labour force participation over 2019 and 2020. Moreover, the prolonged armed conflict caused a large-scale displacement of the population in Iraq, Syria and Yemen, resulting in a fragmented labour market for both the public and private sectors. The situation impeded policymakers' ability to intervene effectively and create job opportunities, particularly for women. As the labour market failed to recover, a significant gap between males and females is forecast to continue in the region's conflict-affected countries throughout 2019 and 2020.

Box III.5

Exploring exchange-rate misalignment in Arab countries[a]

Factors influencing the choice of exchange-rate regime vary across countries in the Arab region. About two thirds of Arab countries have a rigid exchange rate (i.e., currency board or conventional peg), while the remaining third operate more supple regimes by floating their currency and allowing for at least some flexibility in the exchange rate (table III.5.1). In effect, these choices are essentially concerned, inter alia, with the following: the degree of capital mobility; trade share with main partners; independency of monetary policy; flexibility and sustainability of fiscal policy; and the extent to which wages are sticky. However, the optimal choice of exchange-rate regime for a country is often widely debated.

In this context, assessing misalignment has been placed at the centre of academic and policy debate. A real exchange-rate misalignment refers to situations where the real exchange rate deviates from its long-run equilibrium path. Using an unbalanced data set for the period 2008–2016, Edwards' (1994) modelling specification is adopted to assess the degree of misalignment in five Arab countries with variables including real exchange rate, investment, government consumption, economic openness and terms of trade.

a This box draws on ESCWA, 2018.

Table III.5.1

Exchange-rate arrangements in Arab countries

	Rigid exchange rate				Supple exchange rate				Other
	Currency board	Conventional peg			Stabilized arrangement	Crawl-like arrangement	Floating	Free floating	Other arrangement
Country		USD	EUR	Composite					
Bahrain		■							
Kuwait				■					
Oman		■							
Qatar		■							
Saudi Arabia		■							
United Arab Emirates		■							
Egypt							■		
Iraq		■							
Jordan		■							
Lebanon					■				
Syrian Arab Republic									■
Algeria									■
Libya				■					
Morocco				■					
Tunisia						■			
Comoros			■						
Djibouti	■								
Mauritania						■			
Somalia								■	
Sudan					■				
Yemen					■				
Total	1	7	1	3	3	2	1	1	2

Source: IMF (2017), table 2, pp. 6-8.

(continued)

Box III.5 (*continued*)

Our empirical estimates of real exchange-rate misalignments show that there have been substantial misalignments in oil-exporting countries over this period (figure III.5.1). Bahrain and Saudi Arabia exhibit episodes of high levels of exchange-rate misalignment (above 15 per cent of deviation of the real exchange rate from its equilibrium level), which presents risks of distortion in relative prices and macroeconomic imbalances. On the other hand, our empirical evidence shows that in Morocco, the exchange rate appears to have only minor deviations, remaining close to its equilibrium level (less than 5 per cent deviation over the sample period). Since oil is the chief commodity in Bahrain and Saudi Arabia, the estimated high level of misalignment is mainly due to the impacts of swings in world oil prices on their currency valuations. In recent years, the decline in oil and commodity prices, growing fiscal imbalances, and geopolitical tensions have inspired reflections in many Arab countries on the most appropriate exchange-rate regime and triggered reforms concerning the way the exchange rate is managed.

Figure III.5.1
Modelling results on exchange-rate misalignment in Arab countries

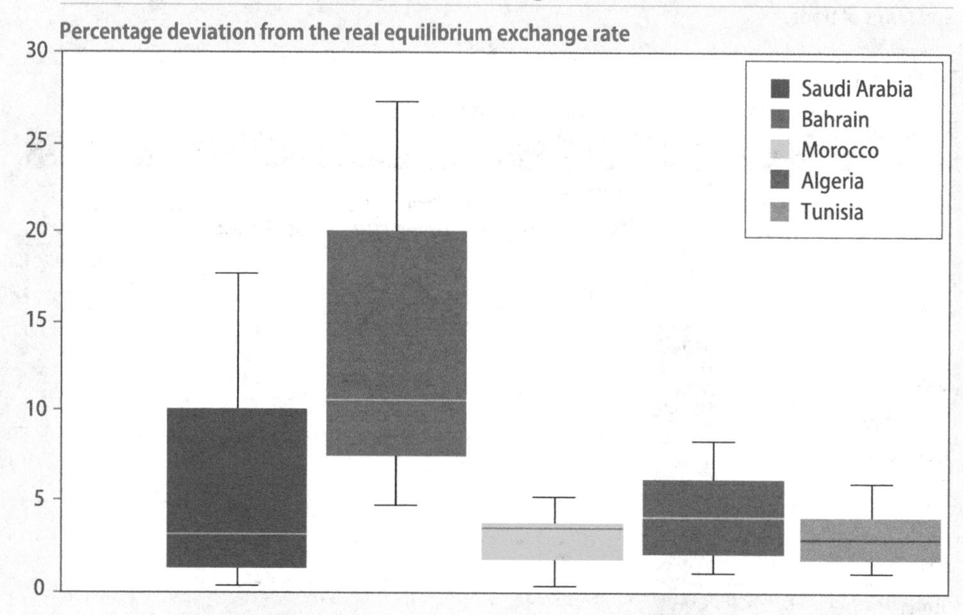

Source: ESCWA (2018).
Note: Figure illustrates the average deviation of the real exchange rate from real equilibrium exchange rate over the sample period 2008–2016, where the whiskers illustrate the range of misalignment over the entire period.

Mindful of misalignment testing, ten Arab countries have recently made adjustments to their exchange-rate regime. In particular, Egypt has opted for a hard landing policy by instantly adopting a floating exchange-rate system since November 2016. With the adoption of a floating exchange-rate regime, Egypt put forward an active monetary policy in order to reduce the high and persistent current account deficit, in addition to devaluing the currency. In a different approach, Morocco is opting for a soft-landing transition and implemented in 2018 the first step towards a long-term adoption of the floating regime, taking advantage of its relatively high-quality credit rating and solid economic performance.

Although switching to the appropriate exchange-rate regime allows a country to strengthen its competitiveness and promotes economic resilience, the transition requires a careful approach. In the case of Egypt, exchange-rate shocks have had immediate and high impacts on inflation, whereas Morocco may also face costs associated with losing the country's nominal anchor, in exchange for a more appropriate exchange-rate regime.

Transitioning from one form of exchange-rate regime to another has the potential to introduce greater stability in real exchange rates and reduce misalignments. However, policymakers should carefully consider the design and pace of transition to also preserve short-term macroeconomic stability. Modernization of monetary policy, including central bank reforms and gradual progress towards a transparent policy framework, could be a crucial aspect of reform efforts.

Author: Seung Jin Baek, UN/ESCWA.

Latin America and the Caribbean

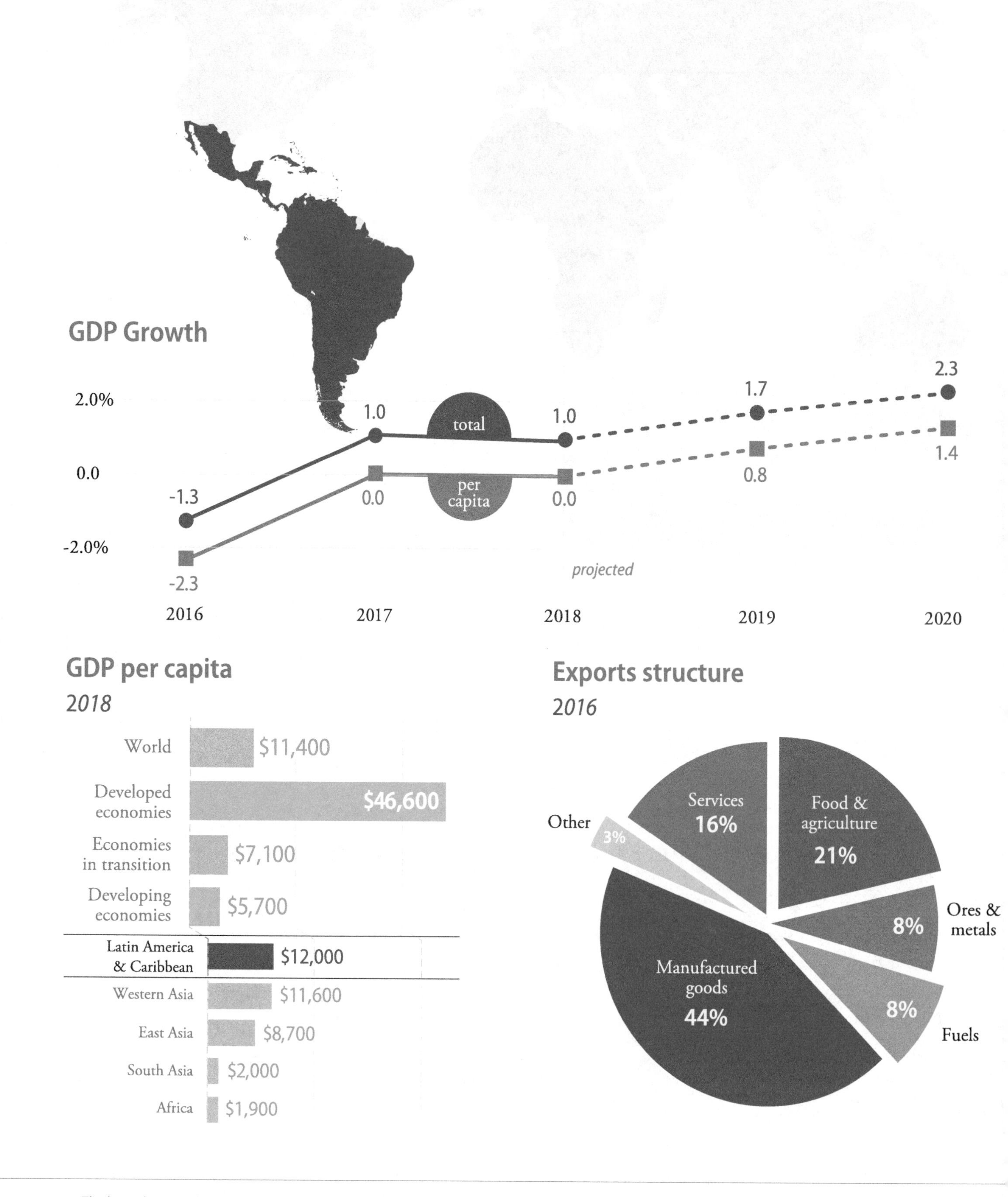

The boundaries and names shown and the designations used on this map do not imply official endorsement or acceptance by the United Nations. The map represents countries and/or territories or parts thereof for which data is available and/or analysed in *World Economic Situation and Prospects 2019*. The shaded areas therefore do not necessarily overlap entirely with the delimitation of their frontiers or boundaries.

Latin America and the Caribbean: growth is projected to gradually pick up, but major downside risks remain

- Weakness in several large economies weighs on the region's growth
- Macroeconomic policy space is limited, with some countries facing considerable need for fiscal adjustment
- Protracted poor economic performance creates serious risks for social progress

Economic recovery has lost momentum and become more uneven

Amid a more challenging external environment, the economic recovery in Latin America and the Caribbean[5] has lost momentum and become more uneven. Economic activity in some of the region's largest countries was much weaker than expected in 2018 as tighter global financial conditions exacerbated domestic vulnerabilities. This has resulted in a significant downward revision of regional growth. Aggregate GDP is estimated to have grown by only 1 per cent in 2018, the same rate as 2017. A moderate pickup in growth is projected for the next two years, with GDP in Latin America and the Caribbean forecast to expand by 1.7 per cent in 2019 and 2.3 per cent in 2020 (figure III.26). This recovery in regional growth will likely be supported by gradually improving economic conditions in Argentina and Brazil and a less severe contraction in the Bolivarian Republic of Venezuela. The risks to the outlook remain tilted to the downside. Many of the region's economies are vulnerable to a further tightening of global financial conditions, an escalation of international

Figure III.26
Annual GDP growth and consumer price inflation in Latin America and the Caribbean, 2010–2020

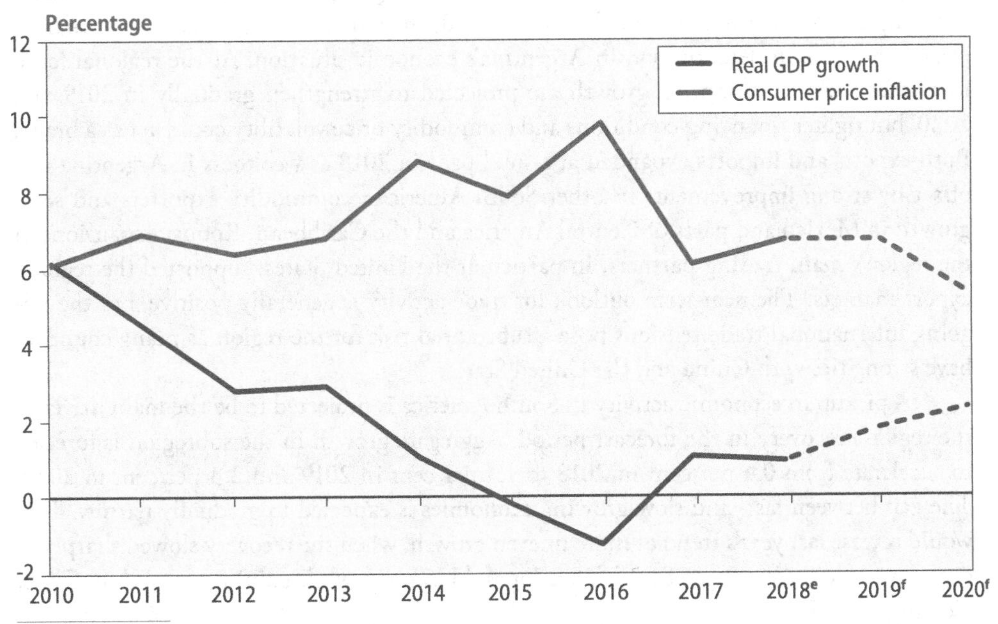

Source: UN/DESA.
Note: e = estimate, f = forecast. Consumer price inflation excludes the Bolivarian Republic of Venezuela.

5 The country classification is based on the United Nations Economic Commission for Latin America and the Caribbean (ECLAC). The region of Latin America and the Caribbean comprises three subregions: South America; Mexico and Central America (which includes Caribbean countries that are considered part of Latin America, namely, Cuba, the Dominican Republic and Haiti); and the Caribbean.

trade tensions and continued commodity price volatility. Macroeconomic policy space is generally limited because of significant fiscal deficits, elevated debt levels and considerable external financing needs.

Weak growth performance poses challenges for SDGs

Latin America and the Caribbean's economic performance over the past year fell well short of expectations. In per capita terms, the region's annual GDP stagnated in 2018. This means that GDP per capita has not grown for five consecutive years, underscoring the difficulty the region faces in returning to a robust growth path in the aftermath of the commodity price collapse. While the poor aggregate growth performance reflects a high degree of vulnerability to external and domestic shocks in parts of the region, it is also indicative of a long-standing and deep-rooted weakness in productivity. Between 2000 and 2015, increasing labour inputs accounted for the bulk of GDP growth, whereas rising productivity contributed relatively little. Lifting productivity growth is critical for strengthening economic growth going forward and for ensuring progress towards the Sustainable Development Goals, including the eradication of poverty by 2030. Recent United Nations Economic Commission for Latin America and the Caribbean (ECLAC) estimates highlight the urgency of this challenge: as per capita economic activity contracted from 2014 to 2016, the number of people living in poverty in Latin America and the Caribbean rose from 168 million to 186 million, with the poverty rate increasing from 28.5 per cent to 30.7 per cent (ECLAC, 2018c).[6]

Recovery in investment is expected to continue

Amid a relatively bleak economic picture, a positive development was the mild recovery of aggregate investment in 2018, following four consecutive years of contraction. The improvement was fairly broad based across countries (box III.6). In many cases, most notably Brazil, accommodative monetary policy supported private investment. Commodity exporters such as Colombia and Peru recorded significant gains, while Mexico benefited from reduced uncertainty as the new trade agreement with the United States and Canada was finalized. Reconstruction building, in the aftermath of severe hurricanes and natural disasters in 2017, has also increased investment spending in parts of the region. Household consumption growth decelerated slightly in 2018, in part reflecting weak labour market trends and a sharp deterioration in Argentina's economic situation. At the regional level, investment and consumption growth are projected to strengthen gradually in 2019 and 2020, but tighter financing conditions and commodity price volatility could act as a brake. Both exports and imports expanded at a solid pace in 2018 as weakness in Argentina was offset by strong improvements in other South American commodity exporters and solid growth in Mexico and parts of Central America and the Caribbean. Robust expansions in the region's main trading partners, in particular the United States, supported the region's export markets. The near-term outlook for trade activity is generally positive, but the ongoing international trade tensions pose a substantial risk for the region as many countries have strong ties with China and the United States.

Outlook for Argentina and Brazil remains challenging

A pickup in economic activity in South America is projected to be the main driver of the region's recovery in the forecast period. Aggregate growth in the subregion is forecast to accelerate from 0.4 per cent in 2018 to 1.4 per cent in 2019 and 2.3 per cent in 2020. The gap between fast- and slow-growing economies is expected to gradually narrow. This would reverse last year's trend of more uneven growth, when the recovery slowed sharply or came to a halt in Argentina, Brazil, Ecuador and Uruguay, while gaining strength in Chile, Colombia and Peru.

6 The rate of extreme poverty also increased from 8.2 per cent in 2014 (48 million) to 10.0 per cent in 2016 (61 million).

Box III.6

The determinants of investment and their relative importance

The dynamics and behaviour of investment are central to understanding the economic cycle and patterns of growth over the medium and long terms, as investment is one of the bridges between the economic cycle and trend growth. This box presents a quantitative analysis of the determinants of investment and their relative importance for six Latin American countries: Argentina, Brazil, Chile, Colombia, Mexico and Peru. This set of economies represents a significant share of the region's GDP and investment. The determinants of investment in the analysis include the rate of change of economic activity; a commodity price index; domestic real interest rates and external interest rates; an indicator of access to external credit (Emerging Market Bond Index (EMBI)); and the rate of change of the real exchange rate.[a]

The index of economic activity is included, as it has a strong statistical association with investment. For its part, the domestic interest rate is the main transmission channel from monetary policy to the real economy. The effect of the short-term rate on long-term rates—which are the basis for investment decisions—obviously depends on a number of other considerations, including the structure of financial markets, firms' balance sheets, and external conditions. The external interest rate and EMBI variables reflect the conditions of access to external financing.

A fourth variable that has gained importance as a determinant of investment is commodity price trends. Natural resources and natural-resource-based sectors represent a significant part of real activity in a number of countries of the region, primarily in South America. Finally, the real exchange rate is directly linked to investment through its impact on exports and imports. Improved external competitiveness can be an incentive to increase investment expenditure. At the same time, a real exchange rate that is favourable to imports can also boost investment since capital goods and imported machinery and equipment are an important component of imports.

The econometric estimates for this group of countries as a whole show that the most significant variables include the rate of variation in the index of economic activity, the monetary policy rate and the commodity price index (ECLAC, 2018d). A 1.0 percentage point increase in the rate of growth of economic activity results in a 1.7 percentage point increase in investment growth rates. This implies that investment has a more volatile cycle than GDP. By contrast, an increase of 1.0 percentage point in the monetary policy rate leads to a 0.24 percentage point slowdown in the rate of growth in investment. An increase of 1.0 percentage point in the commodity price index edges up investment growth by 0.38 percentage points.

In a second stage, the relative importance of each of these variables was assessed separately for each country by estimating their contribution to the explanation of the goodness of fit of the respective regression. This is reflected by the value of R^2: the greater the value of the R^2, the greater the goodness of fit of the regression (Grömping, 2006).

As seen in table III.6.1, the results show that the influence of the level of activity on investment is higher in economies that are larger and that are more diversified such as Argentina, Brazil and Mexico. Commodity prices are important in economies of medium size and that are specialized in natural resources (Chile, Colombia and Peru). In these countries, natural resources explain a large part of the behaviour of both exports and investment. Natural resource exploitation is also the main determinant of long-term financial flows. For its part, the domestic monetary policy rate and the long-term interest rate explain a small percentage of the goodness of fit of the regression. This finding is explained, in part, by the fact that the pass-through of policy rates to the banking system tends to be weak. It also agrees with the literature on the subject (Claessens and Kose, 2018) that shows the impact of interest rates on the real economy is more complex than is generally thought, and that it depends on companies' balance sheets, including the terms of maturity of assets and liabilities. The real exchange rate is important in the case of Brazil and Chile in reflecting greater flexibility of the exchange-rate regime. In Latin America, variations in the real exchange rate tend to be driven by variations in the nominal exchange rate.

This analysis shows that, in general, in the case of the larger economies, investment is largely driven by economic activity. As a result, these economies can have more space to undertake demand-oriented policies to increase growth. Sustainability of investment-driven growth will depend on the ability to finance imports (investment has a significant import content) and the potential to absorb the

(continued)

a The variables are entered as panel data on a quarterly basis. The number of observations varies by country: for Argentina, the data correspond to the period 2005–2017; for Brazil, 2004–2017; for Chile, 2004–2017; for Colombia, 2006–2017; for Mexico, 1994–2017; and for Peru, 2004–2017.

Box III.6 (*continued*)

Table III.6.1
Latin America (selected countries): results of the estimation of the relative importance of investment determinants, 1995–2017

Country	Goodness of Fit R^2	Rate of variation in index of economic activity (IA)	Commodity price index (IPCM)	External interest rate (TLP)	Emerging Market Bond Index (EMBI)	Monetary policy rate (TPM)	Rate of variation in the real exchange rate (TCR)
		Per cent contribution to the Goodness of Fit measure					
Argentina	90.7	67.9	2.2	2.7	21.2	6.0	...
Brazil	90.5	67.2	11.8	2.7	6.5	11.7	24.7
Chile	58.0	34.7	39.7	4.6	4.3	16.8	44.7
Colombia	55.4	12.8	67.7	4.7	10.2	4.6	4.7
Mexico	77.8	71.0	10.7	10.9	6.0	1.3	1.8
Peru	87.1	49.0	31.6	12.6	3.3	3.5	13.4
Average	76.6	50.4	27.3	6.4	8.6	7.3	17.9

Source: ECLAC, on the basis of Grömping (2006).

consequent capital and production capacity expansion. In this sense, articulating capacity utilization, given the interlinkages between investment, imports, output and capacity, is a significant challenge for economic policy. Medium-sized economies depend to a greater extent on external variables, such as commodity prices, and are thus vulnerable to the fluctuations of commodity cycles. This highlights the need to introduce countercyclical buffer stock mechanisms to confront commodity price volatility, and, in the long run, to diversify their productive matrix. In most countries, the monetary policy rate is not largely significant, which points to the need to better understand how it is transmitted to the financial and real sectors of the economies of the region.

Author: Esteban Perez (UN/ECLAC).

The economic downturn in 2018 has been particularly severe in Argentina. After experiencing a currency crisis in the second quarter, the country has fallen into recession. The macroeconomic adjustment plan agreed upon by the Government and the IMF as part of a Stand-By Arrangement includes severe fiscal and monetary tightening. While these measures aim at restoring market confidence and stabilizing the economy, they come with a high cost. Annual GDP is projected to contract in both 2018 and 2019, before a modest recovery gets underway. Brazil's recovery from its longest-ever recession hit a speed bump in the first half of 2018 amid a truckers' strike and external headwinds, including a stronger dollar and widening risk premiums. With consumer confidence improving and the labour market strengthening, economic activity is projected to gain traction in 2019–2020. However, given pressing needs for fiscal adjustment and an expected tightening of monetary policy, the pace of the recovery will likely remain subdued. At the same time, persistent structural bottlenecks, such as a low savings rate and widespread skill deficits in the workforce, will constrain growth in the medium run.

Venezuela's socioeconomic downward spiral continues

The Bolivarian Republic of Venezuela is in its fifth year of recession. While the true extent of the crisis is difficult to gauge, the economy is estimated to have contracted by more than 40 per cent since 2013. The collapse in economic activity has been accompanied by rapid increases in unemployment and underemployment, shortages of food and medical supplies, and rising violence. The socioeconomic downward spiral has led to mass migration of Venezuelans to other Latin American countries, creating challenges for local infrastructure and administrative capacities. With oil production continuing to decline and inflation soaring, an end to the country's economic collapse is not in sight.

Prospects remain favourable in several South American commodity exporters

The prospects for Bolivia (Plurinational State of), Chile, Colombia, Paraguay and Peru, by contrast, are largely favourable. In 2018, improved terms of trade, along with stronger consumer and business confidence, boosted household consumption and investment. While lower commodity prices, in particular for oil, copper and zinc, could weigh on economic growth, solid macroeconomic fundamentals and robust private sector demand will support activity in 2019–2020.

Mexico and Central America benefit from the strong United States economy....

Mexico and Central America will likely continue to see steady but modest economic growth in the outlook period. After expanding by an estimated 2.4 per cent in 2018, the economy is projected to grow by 2.5 per cent in 2019 and 2.3 per cent in 2020. The subregion continues to benefit from the strong performance of the United States economy, which is not only the main trading partner for most countries, but also the main origin of remittances. The latest data show persistently strong increases in remittance flows to Mexico and Central America, providing support to private consumption, the main driver of growth. However, political uncertainty and structural impediments, such as weak productive capacities, poor infrastructure, a low-skilled work force and high degrees of violence, weigh on economic activity in many countries.

...but the growth outlook remains subdued for many economies

The subregion's modest average growth continues to mask large differences between individual countries. On the one hand, the outlook remains positive in the Dominican Republic and Panama, two of Latin America's fastest-growing economies in the past decade. In both countries, growth is supported by strong investment, especially in infrastructure, and government consumption. On the other hand, growth prospects are subdued in many other economies, most notably in Cuba, El Salvador, Haiti, Mexico and Nicaragua. In Mexico, the newly signed United States-Mexico-Canada Agreement (USMCA) removed some uncertainty over the outlook for trade. A strong domestic labour market—at about 3.5 per cent, the unemployment rate remains near a low for the decade—improved consumer confidence, and a buoyant United States economy continued to support demand. However, relatively tight monetary and fiscal policy, along with institutional weaknesses, will weigh on growth in 2019–2020. Among other economies, Nicaragua has seen a severe deterioration in the economic outlook. Political instability and violent unrest have negatively affected tourism, construction and foreign direct investment. Consequently, economic activity and employment in the formal sector have declined. While further downside risks for growth exist, a mild recovery is projected for the latter part of the forecast period, provided that macroeconomic and financial stability can be preserved.

The economic situation in the Caribbean has improved, but growth remains modest

In the Caribbean, a moderate economic recovery materialized in 2018 as Suriname and Trinidad and Tobago returned to positive growth, benefitting from higher oil prices. Economic growth in Suriname is also supported by increased gold production, whereas Trinidad and Tobago has managed to expand natural gas production. Aggregate GDP in the subregion is projected to expand by 2.0 per cent in both 2019 and 2020, following estimated growth of 1.9 per cent in 2018. This constitutes a significant improvement over the poor performance of recent years. However, the subregion continues to face severe structural obstacles to development, such as high burdens of debt, significant infrastructure deficits and high rates of unemployment, particularly among youth. High exposure to climate risks poses a constant threat to economic prospects for the countries in the subregion.

Accommodative monetary policy continues to support activity

In many of the region's economies, particularly in South America, accommodative monetary policy continues to support activity. Average inflation (excluding the Bolivarian Republic of Venezuela) picked up slightly in 2018. However, in most countries inflation remained within the target range of central banks, due to limited demand pressures and well-anchored inflation expectations. The main exceptions are Argentina and the Bolivarian Republic of Venezuela. In the latter, shortages of consumer goods (partly due to widespread government price controls), the monetization of large fiscal deficits, and a rapid depreciation of the currency in the parallel market have resulted in hyperinflation. Without wide-ranging structural reforms to rebuild public finances, stabilize the currency and resolve the debt situation, the inflationary spiral will continue in 2019. In Argentina, inflation and inflation expectations have risen strongly during 2018, mostly because of a markedly weaker peso. In October, year-on-year inflation reached 45.5 per cent. The central bank has responded by adopting an extremely tight monetary policy stance. The benchmark rate is maintained at a record high of 60 per cent. At the same time, the inflation-targeting regime has been temporarily replaced with a monetary base target, which caps growth of money at 0 per cent per month. These measures are expected to gradually bring down inflation over the forecast period, creating room for the central bank to ease monetary policy.

Some monetary tightening is likely in 2019

Price pressures started to build in the second half of 2018 in parts of the region, caused by higher energy prices and weaker currencies. Several central banks (for example in Brazil, Chile, Colombia, the Dominican Republic and Peru) are likely to raise interest rates in 2019. With United States interest rates projected to further increase, Latin America and the Caribbean is likely to be subjected to capital outflow pressures. A significant challenge for many monetary authorities across the region is to preserve domestic financial stability through this period of tightening global financial conditions, while providing support for the ongoing economic recovery.

Fiscal adjustment remains a priority for many countries

Across the region, fiscal space is constrained. Many Governments will face significant fiscal adjustment pressures during the outlook period. In 2017, all of the region's economies except Jamaica recorded fiscal deficits (figure III.27). Despite some improvements in 2018, primary fiscal deficits often exceeded debt-stabilizing levels. Persistent fiscal deficits over the past few years have led to a notable increase in government debt. The region's weighted average government-to-GDP ratio rose from 48.5 per cent in 2013 to 60 per cent in 2017. Government debt-to-GDP ratios and debt services costs are high in several countries, especially in South America (Argentina, Brazil, Uruguay) and the Caribbean (Barbados, Jamaica). Rising global interest rates, a strong dollar and capital flow volatility add to pressures for fiscal consolidation. When implementing adjustment measures, most Governments will continue to pursue a gradual approach in order to minimize the negative impact on economic activity and on social conditions for the most vulnerable segments of the population.

In Argentina, fiscal policy will remain strongly contractionary in 2019–2020. The Government's deep fiscal adjustment programme includes both large spending cuts and tax increases and aims to eliminate the primary deficit by 2019. Barbados is also undertaking a stringent fiscal adjustment programme, allied with a $290 million lending arrangement under the IMF Extended Fund Facility, targeting a primary surplus of 6 per cent of GDP in 2019/20. In Brazil, a combination of moderate primary deficits and high interest expenditures has resulted in large overall fiscal deficits, averaging almost 9 per cent of GDP in 2015–2018. As a result, general government gross debt increased from 60 per cent of GDP in 2013 to an estimated 88 per cent of GDP in 2018. Brazil's new Government therefore faces strong pressures to consolidate public finances, including a comprehensive reform of the pension system.

Figure III.27
Fiscal balances and government debt in Latin America and the Caribbean, 2017

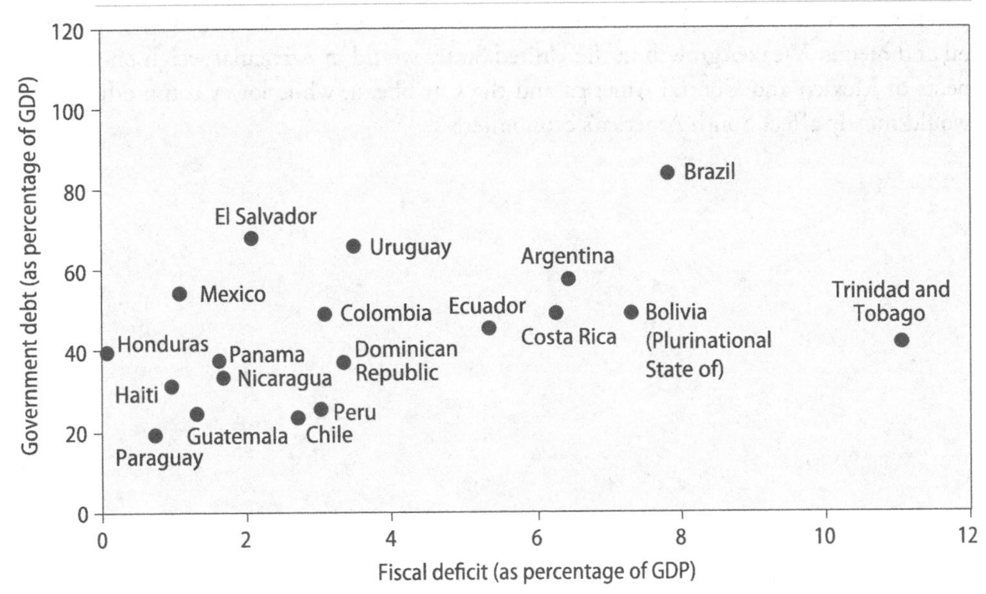

Source: IMF World Economic Outlook October 2018 database.
Note: "Fiscal balance" refers to general government net lending/borrowing. "Government debt" refers to general government gross debt.

Figure III.28
Selected Latin American exchange rates against the US dollar

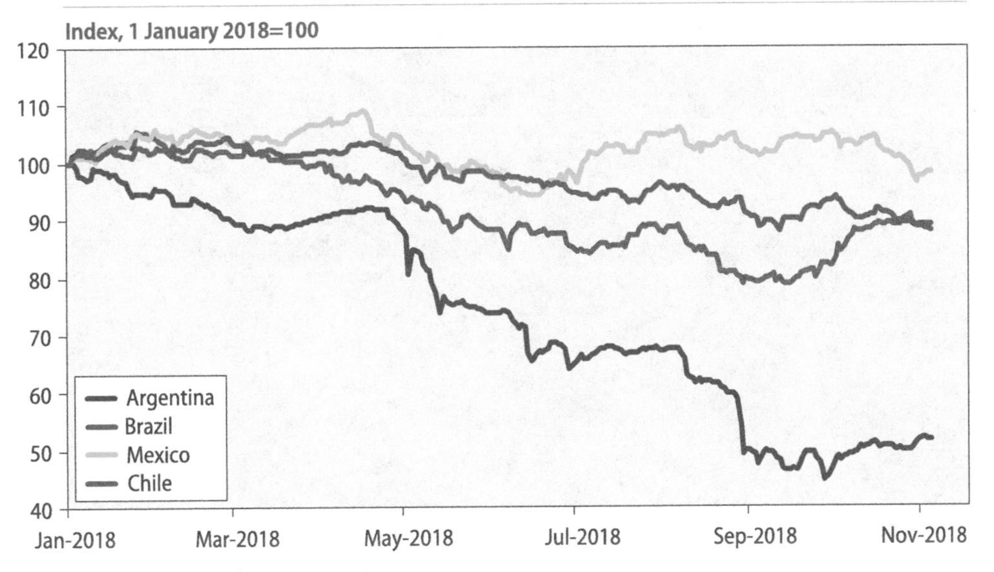

Source: UN/DESA.
Note: A declining value indicates a depreciation of the currency against the US dollar.

Higher United States interest rates and a stronger dollar pose a risk to the outlook

With limited space for countercyclical monetary and fiscal policy, the risks to the Latin America and the Caribbean outlook are tilted to the downside. Over the past year, countries with weaker macroeconomic fundamentals and higher political uncertainties have already been negatively affected by the combination of rising United States interest rates and a stronger dollar. While significant net capital outflows led to a weakening of many local currencies (figure III. 28), the impact on the real economy was concentrated in only a few countries, most notably Argentina. A sharp tightening of global financial conditions during the forecast period could trigger further capital outflows from the region (in particular South America), potentially affecting investment prospects and thus undermining the projected recovery in economic activity. Additional risks are associated with a potential slowdown of the United States economy and a renewed downturn in the prices of oil and metals. Weaker growth in the United States would in particular weigh on the prospects of Mexico and Central America and the Caribbean, while lower commodity prices would mostly affect South America's economies.

Statistical annex

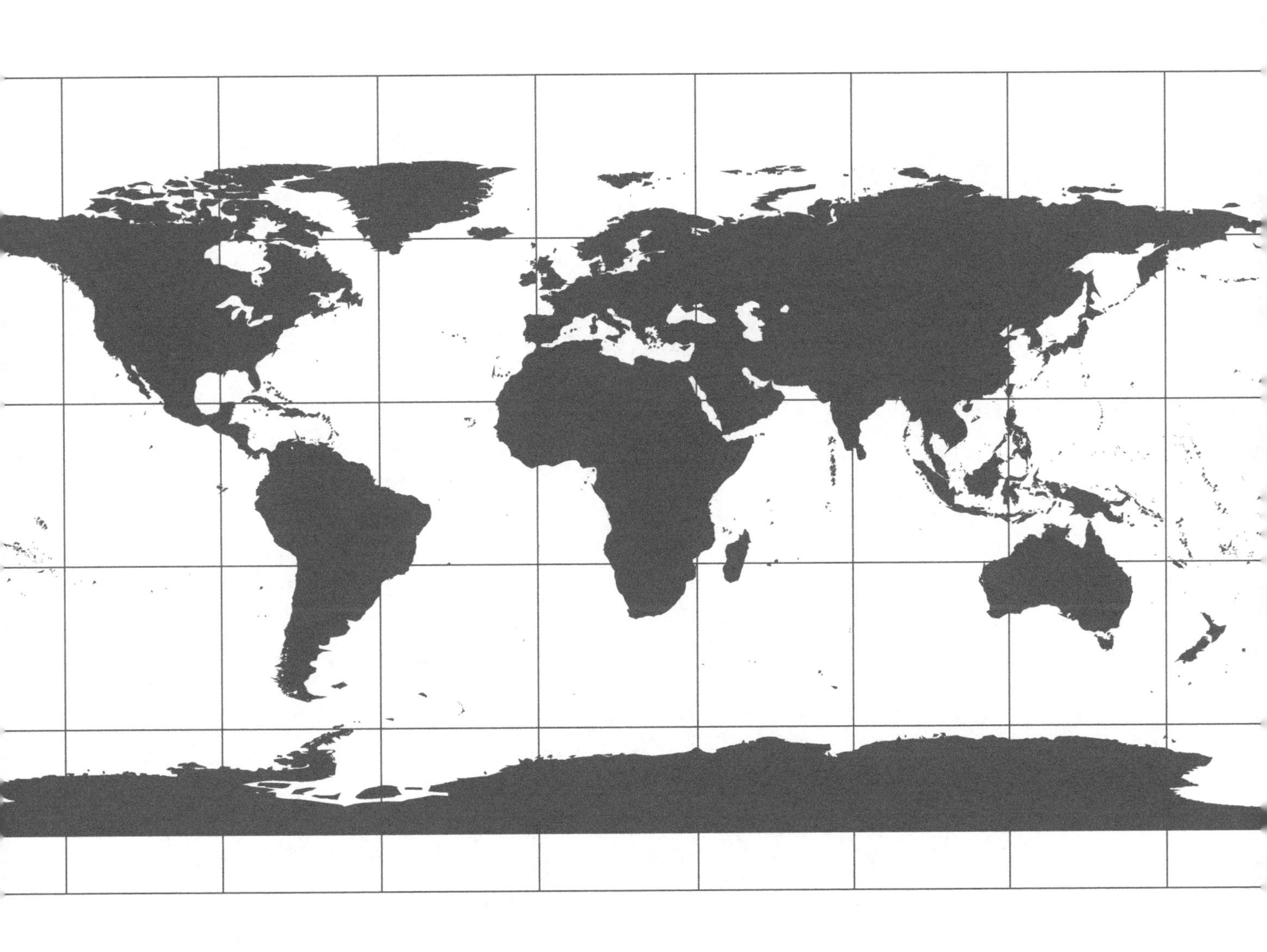

Country classifications

Data sources, country classifications and aggregation methodology

The statistical annex contains a set of data that the *World Economic Situation and Prospects (WESP)* employs to delineate trends in various dimensions of the world economy.

Data sources

The annex was prepared by the Economic Analysis and Policy Division (EAPD) of the Department of Economic and Social Affairs of the United Nations Secretariat (UN/DESA). It is based on information obtained from the Statistics Division and the Population Division of UN/DESA, as well as from the five United Nations regional commissions, the United Nations Conference on Trade and Development (UNCTAD), the United Nations World Tourism Organization (UNWTO), the International Monetary Fund (IMF), the World Bank, the Organization for Economic Cooperation and Development (OECD), and national and private sources. Estimates for the most recent years were made by EAPD in consultation with the regional commissions, UNCTAD, UNWTO and participants in Project LINK, an international collaborative research group for econometric modelling coordinated jointly by EAPD and the University of Toronto. Forecasts for 2019 and 2020 are primarily based on the World Economic Forecasting Model of EAPD, with support from Project LINK.

Data presented in *WESP* may differ from those published by other organizations for a series of reasons, including differences in timing, sample composition and aggregation methods. Historical data may differ from those in previous editions of *WESP* because of updating and changes in the availability of data for individual countries.

Country classifications

For analytical purposes, *WESP* classifies all countries of the world into one of three broad categories: developed economies, economies in transition and developing economies. The composition of these groupings, specified in tables A, B and C, is intended to reflect basic economic country conditions. Several countries (in particular the economies in transition) have characteristics that could place them in more than one category; however, for purposes of analysis, the groupings have been made mutually exclusive. Within each broad category, some subgroups are defined based either on geographical location or on ad hoc criteria, such as the subgroup of "major developed economies", which is based on the membership of the Group of Seven. Geographical regions for developing economies are as follows: Africa, East Asia, South Asia, Western Asia, and Latin America and the Caribbean.[1]

1 Names and composition of geographical areas follow those specified in the statistical paper entitled "Standard country or area codes for statistical use" (ST/ESA/STAT/SER.M/49/Rev). Available from https://unstats.un.org/unsd/publication/SeriesM/Series_M49_Rev4(1999)_en.pdf.

In parts of the analysis, a distinction is made between fuel exporters and fuel importers from among the economies in transition and the developing countries. An economy is classified as a fuel exporter if the share of fuel exports in its total merchandise exports is greater than 20 per cent and the level of fuel exports is at least 20 per cent higher than that of the country's fuel imports (table D). This criterion is drawn from the share of fuel exports in the total value of world merchandise trade. Fuels include coal, oil and natural gas.

For other parts of the analysis, countries have been classified by their level of development as measured by per capita gross national income (GNI). Accordingly, countries have been grouped as high-income, upper-middle-income, lower-middle-income and low-income (table E). To maintain compatibility with similar classifications used elsewhere, the threshold levels of GNI per capita are those established by the World Bank. Countries with less than $995 GNI per capita are classified as low-income countries, those with between $996 and $3,895 as lower-middle-income countries, those with between $3,896 and $12,055 as upper-middle-income countries, and those with incomes of more than $12, 056 as high-income countries. GNI per capita in dollar terms is estimated using the World Bank Atlas method,[2] and the classification in table E is based on data for 2017.

The list of the least developed countries (LDCs) is decided upon by the United Nations Economic and Social Council and, ultimately, by the General Assembly, on the basis of recommendations made by the Committee for Development Policy. The basic criteria for inclusion require that certain thresholds be met with regard to per capita GNI, a human assets index and an economic vulnerability index.[3] As of March 2018, there were 47 LDCs (table F).

WESP also makes reference to the group of heavily indebted poor countries (HIPCs), which are considered by the World Bank and IMF as part of their debt-relief initiative (the Enhanced HIPC Initiative).[4] In October 2017, there were 39 HIPCs (see table G).

Aggregation methodology

Aggregate data are either sums or weighted averages of individual country data. Unless otherwise indicated, multi-year averages of growth rates are expressed as compound annual percentage rates of change. The convention followed is to omit the base year in a multi-year growth rate. For example, the 10-year average growth rate for the decade of the 2000s would be identified as the average annual growth rate for the period from 2001 to 2010.

WESP utilizes exchange-rate conversions of national data in order to aggregate output of individual countries into regional and global totals. The growth of output in each group of countries is calculated from the sum of gross domestic product (GDP) of individual countries measured at 2012 prices and exchange rates. Data for GDP in 2012 in national currencies were converted into dollars (with selected adjustments) and extended forwards and backwards in time using changes in real GDP for each country. This method supplies a reasonable set of aggregate growth rates for a period of about 15 years, centred on 2012.

2 See http://data.worldbank.org/about/country-classifications.

3 *Handbook on the Least Developed Country Category: Inclusion, Graduation and Special Support Measures* (United Nations publication, Sales No. E.07.II.A.9). Available from http://www.un.org/en/development/desa/policy/cdp/cdp_publications/2008cdphandbook.pdf.

4 *International Monetary Fund, Debt Relief Under the Heavily Indebted Poor Countries (HIPC) Initiative.* Available from https://www.imf.org/en/About/Factsheets/Sheets/2016/08/01/16/11/Debt-Relief-Under-the-Heavily-Indebted-Poor-Countries-Initiative.

The exchange-rate-based method differs from the one mainly applied by the IMF for their estimates of world and regional economic growth, which is based on purchasing power parity (PPP) weights. Over the past two decades, the growth of world gross product (WGP) on the basis of the exchange-rate-based approach has been below that based on PPP weights. This is because developing countries, in the aggregate, have seen significantly higher economic growth than the rest of the world in the 1990s and 2000s and the share in WGP of these countries is larger under PPP measurements than under market exchange rates. Table I.1 in chapter I reports world output growth with PPP weights as a comparator.

Table A
Developed economies

	Europe		
North America	**European Union**	**Other Europe**	**Major developed economies (G7)**
Canada	**EU-15**	Iceland	Canada
United States	Austria[a]	Norway	Japan
	Belgium[a]	Switzerland	France
	Denmark		Germany
	Finland[a]		Italy
	France[a]		United Kingdom
	Germany[a]		United States
	Greece[a]		
	Ireland[a]		
	Italy[a]		
	Luxembourg[a]		
	Netherlands[a]		
	Portugal[a]		
	Spain[a]		
	Sweden		
	United Kingdom[b]		
Developed Asia and Pacific	**EU-13**[c]		
Australia	Bulgaria		
Japan	Croatia		
New Zealand	Cyprus[a]		
	Czech Republic		
	Estonia[a]		
	Hungary		
	Latvia[a]		
	Lithuania[a]		
	Malta[a]		
	Poland		
	Romania		
	Slovakia[a]		
	Slovenia[a]		

a Member of Euro area.
b At the time of publishing, the United Kingdom was a member of the EU and is therefore is included in all EU aggregations. The country is scheduled to withdraw from the EU at the end of March 2019.
c Used in reference to the 13 countries that joined the EU since 2004.

Table B
Economies in transition

South-Eastern Europe	Commonwealth of Independent States and Georgia[a]	
Albania	Armenia	Republic of Moldova
Bosnia and Herzegovina	Azerbaijan	Russian Federation
Montenegro	Belarus	Tajikistan
Serbia	Georgia[a]	Turkmenistan
The former Yugoslav Republic of Macedonia	Kazakhstan	Ukraine[b]
	Kyrgyzstan	Uzbekistan

a Georgia officially left the Commonwealth of Independent States on 18 August 2009. However, its performance is discussed in the context of this group of countries for reasons of geographic proximity and similarities in economic structure.
b Starting in 2010, data for the Ukraine excludes the temporarily occupied territory of the Autonomous Republic of Crimea and Sevastopol.

Table C
Developing economies by region[a]

Africa		Asia	Latin America and the Caribbean
North Africa	**Southern Africa**	**East Asia[b]**	**Caribbean**
Algeria	Angola	Brunei Darussalam	Bahamas
Egypt	Botswana	Cambodia	Barbados
Libya	Eswatini	China	Belize
Mauritania	Lesotho	Democratic People's Republic of Korea[c]	Guyana
Morocco	Malawi	Fiji	Jamaica
Sudan	Mauritius	Hong Kong SAR[d]	Suriname
Tunisia	Mozambique	Indonesia	Trinidad and Tobago
Central Africa	Namibia	Kiribati	**Mexico and Central America**
Cameroon	South Africa	Lao People's Democratic Republic	Costa Rica
Central African Republic	Zambia	Malaysia	Cuba
Chad	Zimbabwe	Mongolia	Dominican Republic
Congo	**West Africa**	Myanmar	El Salvador
Equatorial Guinea	Benin	Papua New Guinea	Guatemala
Gabon	Burkina Faso	Philippines	Haiti
Sao Tome and Prinicipe	Cabo Verde	Republic of Korea	Honduras
East Africa	Côte d'Ivoire	Samoa	Mexico
Burundi	Gambia (Islamic Republic of the)	Singapore	Nicaragua
Comoros	Ghana	Solomon Islands	Panama
Democratic Republic of the Congo	Guinea	Taiwan Province of China	**South America**
Djibouti	Guinea-Bissau	Thailand	Argentina
Eritrea	Liberia	Timor-Leste	Bolivia (Plurinational State of)
Ethiopia	Mali	Vanuatu	Brazil
Kenya	Niger	Viet Nam	Chile
Madagascar	Nigeria	**South Asia**	Colombia
Rwanda	Senegal	Afghanistan	Ecuador
Somalia	Sierra Leone	Bangladesh	Paraguay
South Sudan[c]	Togo	Bhutan	Peru
Uganda		India	Uruguay
United Republic of Tanzania		Iran (Islamic Republic of)	Venezuela (Bolivarian Republic of)
		Maldives	
		Nepal	
		Pakistan	
		Sri Lanka	
		Western Asia	
		Bahrain	
		Iraq	
		Israel	
		Jordan	
		Kuwait	
		Lebanon	
		Oman	
		Qatar	
		Saudi Arabia	
		State of Palestine[c]	
		Syrian Arab Republic	
		Turkey	
		United Arab Emirates	
		Yemen	

a Economies systematically monitored by the Global Economic Monitoring Branch of EAPD.

b Throughout the report the term 'East Asia' is used in reference to this set of developing countries, and excludes Japan.

c The country coverage in WESP 2019 was expanded to include South Sudan, State of Palestine and Democratic People's Republic of Korea.

d Special Administrative Region of China.

Table D
Fuel-exporting countries

Developed countries	Economies in transition	Developing countries			
		Latin America and the Caribbean	Africa	East Asia	South Asia
Australia	Azerbaijan	Bolivia (Plurinational State of)	Algeria	Brunei Darussalam	Iran (Islamic Republic of)
Norway	Kazakhstan	Colombia	Angola	Democratic People's Republic of Korea	**Western Asia**
	Russian Federation	Ecuador	Cameroon	Indonesia	Bahrain
	Turkmenistan	Trinidad and Tobago	Chad	Mongolia	Iraq
		Venezuela (Bolivarian Republic of)	Congo	Myanmar	Kuwait
			Equatorial Guinea	Papua New Guinea	Oman
			Gabon		Qatar
			Libya		Saudi Arabia
			Nigeria		United Arab Emirates
			Sudan		

Table E
Economies by per capita GNI in June 2018[a]

High-income	
Argentina[c]	Latvia
Australia	Lithuania
Austria	Luxembourg
Bahamas	Malta
Bahrain	Netherlands
Barbados	New Zealand
Belgium	Norway
Brunei Darussalam	Oman
Canada	Panama[c]
Chile	Poland
Croatia[c]	Portugal
Cyprus	Qatar
Czech Republic	Republic of Korea
Denmark	Saudi Arabia
Estonia	Singapore
Finland	Slovak Republic
France	Slovenia
Germany	Spain
Greece	Sweden
Hong Kong SAR[d]	Switzerland
Hungary	Taiwan Province of China
Iceland	Trinidad and Tobago
Ireland	United Arab Emirates
Israel	United Kingdom
Italy	United States
Japan	Uruguay
Kuwait	

Upper-middle-income	
Albania	Kazakhstan
Algeria	Lebanon
Armenia[c]	Libya
Azerbaijan	Malaysia
Belarus	Maldives
Belize	Mauritius
Bosnia and Herzegovina	Mexico
Botswana	Montenegro
Brazil	Namibia
Bulgaria	Paraguay
China	Peru
Colombia	Romania
Costa Rica	Russian Federation
Cuba	Samoa
Dominican Republic	Serbia
Ecuador	South Africa
Equatorial Guinea	Suriname
Fiji	Thailand
Gabon	The former Yugoslav Republic of Macedonia
Guatemala[c]	Turkey
Guyana	Turkmenistan
Iran (Islamic Republic of)	Venezuela (Bolivarian Republic of)
Iraq	
Jamaica	
Jordan[c]	

Lower-middle-income	
Angola	Lesotho
Bangladesh	Mauritania
Bhutan	Mongolia
Bolivia (Plurinational State of)	Morocco
Cabo Verde	Myanmar
Cambodia	Nicaragua
Cameroon	Nigeria
Congo	Pakistan
Côte d'Ivoire	Papua New Guinea
Djibouti	Philippines
Egypt	Republic of Moldova
El Salvador	São Tomé and Principe
Eswatini	Solomon Islands
Georgia	Sri Lanka
Ghana	State of Palestine
Honduras	Sudan
India	Timor-Leste
Indonesia	Tunisia
Kenya	Ukraine
Kiribati	Uzbekistan
Kyrgyzstan	Vanuatu
Lao People's Democratic Republic	Viet Nam
	Zambia

Low-income			
Afghanistan	Democratic Republic of the Congo	Malawi	Syrian Arab Republic[b]
Benin	Eritrea	Mali	Tajikistan[b]
Burkina Faso	Ethiopia	Mozambique	Togo
Burundi	Gambia	Nepal	Uganda
Central African Republic	Guinea	Niger	United Republic of Tanzania
Chad	Guinea-Bissau	Rwanda	Yemen[b]
Comoros	Haiti	Senegal	Zimbabwe
Democratic People's Republic of Korea	Liberia	Sierra Leone	
	Madagascar	Somalia	
		South Sudan	

a Economies systematically monitored for the World Economic Situation and Prospects report and included in the United Nations' global economic forecast.

b Indicates the country has been shifted downward by one category from previous year's classification.

c Indicates the country has been shifted upward by one category from previous year's classification.

d Special Administrative Region of China.

Table F
Least developed countries *(as of March 2018)*

Africa		East Asia	South Asia	Western Asia	Latin America and the Caribbean
Angola	Malawi	Cambodia	Afghanistan	Yemen	Haiti
Benin	Mali	Kiribati	Bangladesh		
Burkina Faso	Mauritania	Lao People's Democratic Republic	Bhutan		
Burundi	Mozambique	Myanmar	Nepal		
Central African Republic	Niger	Solomon Islands			
Chad	Rwanda	Timor Leste			
Comoros	Sao Tome and Principe	Tuvalu[a]			
Democratic Republic of the Congo	Senegal	Vanuatu			
Djibouti	Sierra Leone				
Eritrea	Somalia				
Ethiopia	South Sudan				
Gambia	Sudan				
Guinea	Togo				
Guinea-Bissau	Uganda				
Lesotho	United Republic of Tanzania				
Liberia	Zambia				
Madagascar					

a Not included in the WESP discussion because of insufficient data.

Table G
Heavily indebted poor countries *(as of October 2017)*

Post-completion point HIPCs[a]		Pre-decision point HIPCs[b]
Afghanistan	Haiti	Eritrea
Benin	Honduras	Somalia
Bolivia	Liberia	Sudan
Burkina Faso	Madagascar	
Burundi	Malawi	
Cameroon	Mali	
Central African Republic	Mauritania	
Chad	Mozambique	
Comoros	Nicaragua	
Congo	Niger	
Côte D'Ivoire	Rwanda	
Democratic Republic of the Congo	Sao Tomé and Principe	
Ethiopia	Senegal	
Gambia	Sierra Leone	
Ghana	Togo	
Guinea	Uganda	
Guinea-Bissau	United Republic of Tanzania	
Guyana	Zambia	

a Countries that have qualified for irrevocable debt relief under the HIPC Initiative.

b Countries that are potentially eligible and may wish to avail themselves of the HIPC Initiative or the Multilateral Debt Relief Initiative (MDRI).

Table H
Small island developing States

United Nations members		Non-UN members/Associate members of the Regional Commissions
Antigua and Barbuda	Marshall Islands	American Samoa
Bahamas	Mauritius	Anguilla
Bahrain	Nauru	Aruba
Barbados	Palau	Bermuda
Belize	Papua New Guinea	British Virgin Islands
Cabo Verde	Saint Kitts and Nevis	Cayman Islands
Comoros	Saint Lucia	Commonwealth of Northern Marianas
Cuba	Saint Vincent and the Grenadines	Cook Islands
Dominica	Samoa	Curaçao
Dominican Republic	São Tomé and Príncipe	French Polynesia
Federated States of Micronesia	Seychelles	Guadeloupe
Fiji	Singapore	Guam
Grenada	Solomon Islands	Martinique
Guinea-Bissau	Suriname	Montserrat
Guyana	Timor-Leste	New Caledonia
Haiti	Tonga	Niue
Jamaica	Trinidad and Tobago	Puerto Rico
Kiribati	Tuvalu	Sint Maarten
Maldives	Vanuatu	Turks and Caicos Islands
		U.S. Virgin Islands

Table I
Landlocked developing countries

Landlocked developing countries		
Afghanistan	Kazakhstan	Republic of Moldova
Armenia	Kyrgystan	Rwanda
Azerbaijan	Lao People's Democratic Republic	South Sudan
Bhutan	Lesotho	Tajikistan
Bolivia (Plurinational State of)	Malawi	The former Yugoslav Republic of Macedonia
Botswana	Mali	Turkmenistan
Burkina Faso	Mongolia	Uganda
Burundi	Nepal	Uzbekistan
Central African Republic	Niger	Zambia
Chad	Paraguay	Zimbabwe
Eswatini		
Ethiopia		

Table J
International Organization for Standardization of Country Codes

ISO Code	Country
AFG	Afghanistan
AGO	Angola
ALB	Albania
AND	Andorra
ARE	United Arab Emirates
ARG	Argentina
ARM	Armenia
ATG	Antigua and Barbuda
AUS	Australia
AUT	Austria
AZE	Azerbaijan
BDI	Burundi
BEL	Belgium
BEN	Benin
BFA	Burkina Faso
BGD	Bangladesh
BGR	Bulgaria
BHR	Bahrain
BHS	Bahamas
BIH	Bosnia and Herzegovina
BLR	Belarus
BLZ	Belize
BOL	Bolivia (Plurinational State of)
BRA	Brazil
BRB	Barbados
BRN	Brunei Darussalam
BTN	Bhutan
BWA	Botswana
CAF	Central African Republic
CAN	Canada
CHE	Switzerland
CHL	Chile
CHN	China
CIV	Côte D'Ivoire
CMR	Cameroon
COD	Democratic Republic of the Congo
COG	Congo
COL	Colombia
COM	Comoros
CPV	Cabo Verde
CRI	Costa Rica
CUB	Cuba
CYP	Cyprus
CZE	Czech Republic
DEU	Germany
DJI	Djibouti
DMA	Dominica
DNK	Denmark
DOM	Dominican Republic
DZA	Algeria
ECU	Ecuador
EGY	Egypt
ERI	Eritrea
ESP	Spain
EST	Estonia
ETH	Ethiopia
FIN	Finland
FJI	Fiji
FRA	France
FSM	Micronesia (Federated States of)
GAB	Gabon
GBR	United Kingdom of Great Britain and Northern Ireland
GEO	Georgia
GHA	Ghana
GIN	Guinea
GMB	Gambia
GNB	Guinea Bissau
GNQ	Equatorial Guinea
GRC	Greece
GRD	Grenada
GTM	Guatemala
GUY	Guyana
HND	Honduras
HRV	Croatia
HTI	Haiti
HUN	Hungary
IDN	Indonesia
IND	India
IRL	Ireland
IRN	Iran (Islamic Republic of)
IRQ	Iraq
ISL	Iceland
ISR	Israel
ITA	Italy
JAM	Jamaica
JOR	Jordan
JPN	Japan
KAZ	Kazakhstan
KEN	Kenya
KGZ	Kyrgyzstan
KHM	Cambodia
KIR	Kiribati
KNA	Saint Kitts and Nevis
KOR	Republic of Korea
KWT	Kuwait
LAO	Lao People's Democratic Republic
LBN	Lebanon
LBR	Liberia
LBY	Libya
LCA	Saint Lucia
LIE	Liechtenstein
LKA	Sri Lanka
LSO	Lesotho
LTU	Lithuania
LUX	Luxembourg
LVA	Latvia
MAR	Morocco
MCO	Monaco
MDA	Republic of Moldova
MDG	Madagascar
MDV	Maldives
MEX	Mexico
MHL	Marshall Islands
MKD	The former Yugoslav Republic of Macedonia
MLI	Mali
MLT	Malta
MMR	Myanmar
MNE	Montenegro
MNG	Mongolia
MOZ	Mozambique
MRT	Mauritania
MUS	Mauritius
MWI	Malawi
MYS	Malaysia
NAM	Namibia
NER	Niger
NGA	Nigeria
NIC	Nicaragua
NLD	Netherlands
NOR	Norway
NPL	Nepal
NRU	Nauru
NZL	New Zealand
OMN	Oman
PAK	Pakistan
PAN	Panama
PER	Peru
PHL	Philippines
PLW	Palau
PNG	Papua New Guinea
POL	Poland
PRK	Democratic People's Republic of Korea
PRT	Portugal
PRY	Paraguay
PSE	State of Palestine
QAT	Qatar
ROU	Romania
RUS	Russian Federation
RWA	Rwanda
SAU	Saudi Arabia
SDN	Sudan
SEN	Senegal
SGP	Singapore
SLB	Solomon Islands
SLE	Sierra Leone
SLV	El Salvador
SMR	San Marino
SOM	Somalia
SRB	Serbia
SSD	South Sudan
STP	Sao Tome and Principe
SUR	Suriname
SVK	Slovakia
SVN	Slovenia
SWE	Sweden
SWZ	Eswatini
SYC	Seychelles
SYR	Syrian Arab Republic
TCD	Chad
TGO	Togo
THA	Thailand
TJK	Tajikistan
TKM	Turkmenistan
TLS	Timor-Leste
TON	Tonga
TTO	Trinidad and Tobago
TUN	Tunisia
TUR	Turkey
TUV	Tuvalu
TZA	United Republic of Tanzania
UGA	Uganda
UKR	Ukraine
URY	Uruguay
USA	United States of America
UZB	Uzbekistan
VCT	Saint Vincent and the Grenadines
VEN	Venezuela (Bolivarian Republic of)
VNM	Viet Nam
VUT	Vanuatu
WSM	Samoa
YEM	Yemen
ZAF	South Africa
ZMB	Zambia
ZWE	Zimbabwe

Annex tables

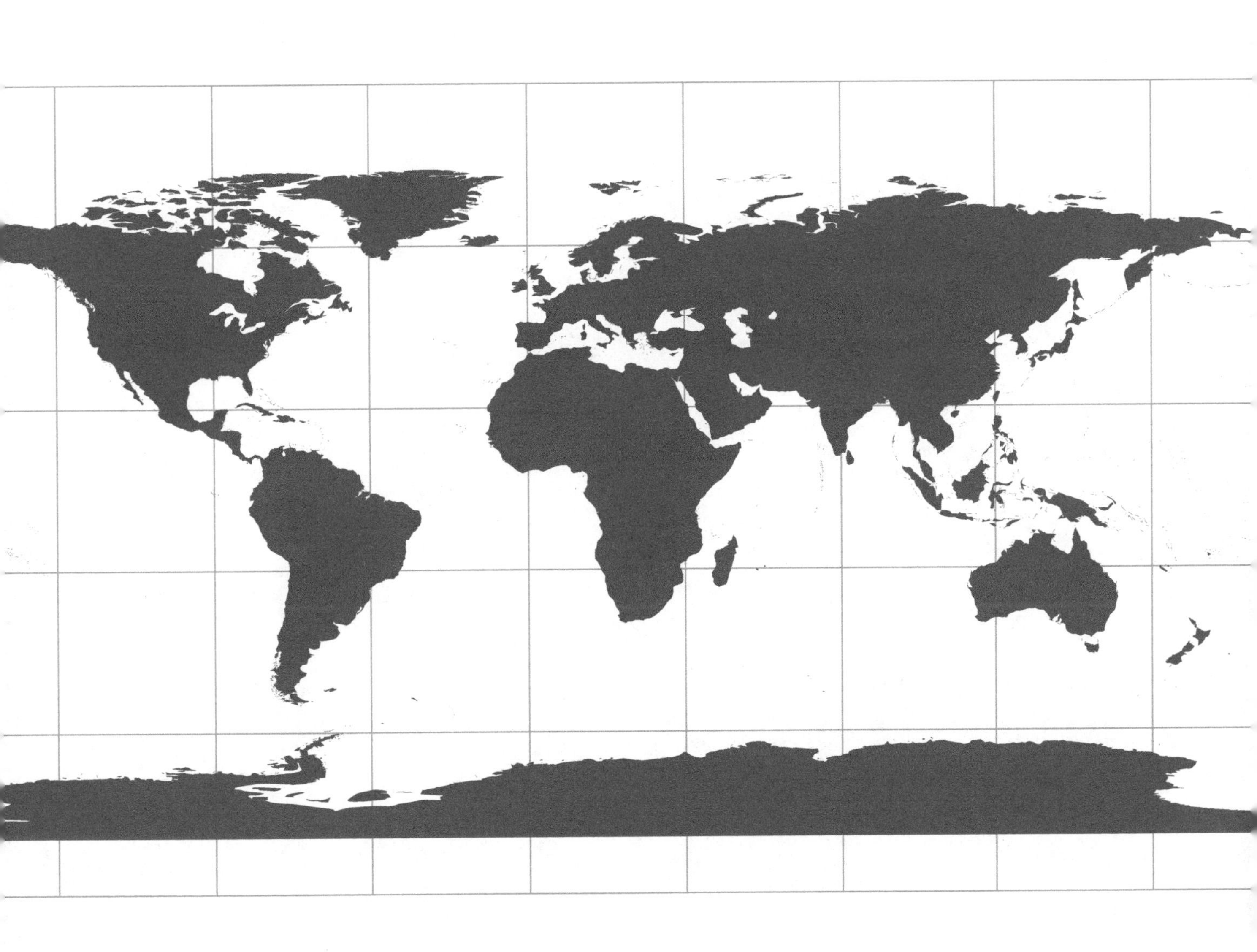

Table A.1
Developed economies: rates of growth of real GDP, 2010–2020

Annual percentage change

	2010-2017[a]	2010	2011	2012	2013	2014	2015	2016	2017	2018[b]	2019[c]	2020[c]
Developed economies	1.8	2.6	1.5	1.1	1.2	2.0	2.3	1.7	2.2	2.2	2.1	1.9
United States	2.2	2.5	1.6	2.2	1.7	2.6	2.9	1.6	2.2	2.8	2.5	2.0
Canada	2.3	3.1	3.1	1.7	2.5	2.9	1.0	1.4	3.0	2.0	2.0	2.2
Japan	1.5	4.2	-0.1	1.5	2.0	0.4	1.4	1.0	1.7	1.0	1.4	1.2
Australia	2.6	2.4	2.7	3.9	2.2	2.6	2.5	2.6	2.2	3.2	2.7	2.4
New Zealand	2.9	2.0	1.9	2.5	2.2	3.2	4.2	4.1	3.0	2.9	2.7	3.0
European Union	1.5	2.1	1.7	-0.4	0.3	1.8	2.3	2.0	2.4	2.0	2.0	2.0
EU-15	1.4	2.1	1.6	-0.5	0.2	1.7	2.2	1.9	2.2	1.8	1.8	1.8
Austria	1.5	1.8	2.9	0.7	0.0	0.8	1.1	1.5	3.0	2.9	1.9	1.8
Belgium	1.4	2.7	1.8	0.2	0.2	1.3	1.4	1.4	1.7	1.5	1.6	1.6
Denmark	1.5	1.9	1.3	0.2	0.9	1.6	1.6	2.0	2.3	1.6	1.9	1.8
Finland	1.0	3.0	2.6	-1.4	-0.8	-0.6	0.1	2.5	2.8	2.5	2.3	2.3
France	1.3	1.9	2.2	0.3	0.6	1.0	1.1	1.2	2.2	1.7	1.8	1.8
Germany	2.1	4.1	3.7	0.5	0.5	1.9	1.7	2.2	2.2	1.8	1.8	1.8
Greece	-3.0	-5.5	-9.1	-7.3	-3.2	0.7	-0.3	-0.2	1.4	1.8	1.9	1.5
Ireland	6.3	1.8	3.0	0.0	1.6	8.3	25.1	5.0	7.2	3.8	4.4	4.2
Italy	0.1	1.7	0.6	-2.8	-1.7	0.1	1.0	0.9	1.5	1.2	1.2	1.0
Luxembourg	3.1	4.9	2.5	-0.4	3.7	5.8	2.9	3.1	2.3	3.1	3.1	3.1
Netherlands	1.3	1.4	1.7	-1.1	-0.2	1.4	2.0	2.2	2.9	2.6	2.5	2.4
Portugal	0.2	1.9	-1.8	-4.0	-1.1	0.9	1.8	1.6	2.7	1.7	1.3	1.9
Spain	0.7	0.0	-1.0	-2.9	-1.7	1.4	3.4	3.3	3.1	2.7	2.3	2.1
Sweden	2.7	6.0	2.7	-0.3	1.2	2.6	4.5	2.7	2.1	2.7	2.2	2.2
United Kingdom	1.9	1.7	1.5	1.5	2.1	3.1	2.3	1.8	1.7	1.3	1.4	1.7
EU-13	2.6	1.7	3.1	0.6	1.3	2.9	3.8	3.2	4.6	4.2	3.6	3.5
Bulgaria	2.1	1.3	1.9	0.0	0.9	1.3	3.5	3.9	3.8	3.4	3.5	3.5
Croatia	0.5	-1.5	-0.3	-2.3	-0.5	-0.1	2.4	3.5	2.9	2.7	2.8	2.7
Cyprus	0.2	1.3	0.3	-3.1	-5.9	-1.4	2.0	4.8	4.2	3.0	2.0	3.2
Czech Republic	2.2	2.3	1.8	-0.8	-0.5	2.7	5.3	2.5	4.3	2.5	3.1	3.3
Estonia	3.6	2.3	7.6	4.3	1.9	2.9	1.9	3.5	4.9	3.8	3.5	3.0
Hungary	2.1	0.7	1.7	-1.6	2.1	4.2	3.4	2.2	4.0	4.8	3.2	3.0
Latvia	2.5	-3.9	6.4	4.0	2.4	1.9	3.0	2.2	4.5	4.6	3.8	4.0
Lithuania	3.3	1.6	6.0	3.8	3.5	3.5	2.0	2.3	3.9	3.2	3.5	3.5
Malta	5.2	3.5	1.3	2.7	4.7	8.1	9.5	5.2	6.7	2.9	2.9	3.6
Poland	3.3	3.6	5.0	1.6	1.4	3.3	3.8	3.0	4.6	5.0	3.8	3.8
Romania	2.8	-2.8	2.0	1.2	3.5	3.1	3.9	4.8	6.8	4.2	3.8	3.6
Slovakia	3.0	5.0	2.8	1.7	1.5	2.8	3.9	3.3	3.4	4.2	4.0	3.6
Slovenia	1.4	1.2	0.6	-2.7	-1.1	3.0	2.3	3.1	4.9	4.2	3.8	3.2
Other Europe	1.7	1.9	1.4	1.7	1.5	2.2	1.6	1.4	1.5	2.1	2.0	1.9
Iceland	2.7	-3.6	2.0	1.3	4.3	2.2	4.5	7.4	4.0	3.5	3.2	4.0
Norway	1.6	0.7	1.0	2.7	1.0	2.0	2.0	1.2	2.0	1.7	2.0	2.1
Switzerland	1.7	3.0	1.7	1.0	1.9	2.4	1.2	1.4	1.1	2.3	2.0	1.7
Memorandum items												
North America	2.2	2.6	1.8	2.2	1.8	2.6	2.7	1.6	2.3	2.7	2.4	2.0
Developed Asia and Pacific	1.8	3.8	0.5	2.0	2.0	0.9	1.6	1.4	1.9	1.5	1.7	1.5
Europe	1.5	2.1	1.7	-0.2	0.4	1.8	2.3	1.9	2.4	2.0	2.0	2.0
Major developed economies	1.8	2.8	1.5	1.4	1.4	1.9	2.1	1.5	2.1	2.1	2.0	1.8
Euro area	1.3	2.1	1.6	-0.9	-0.2	1.3	2.1	1.9	2.4	2.0	1.9	1.9

Source: UN/DESA, based on data of the United Nations Statistics Division and individual national sources.

Note: Regional aggregates calculated at 2012 prices and exchange rates.

a Average percentage change.

b Partly estimated.

c Baseline scenario forecasts, based in part on Project LINK and UN/DESA World Economic Forecasting Model.

Table A.2
Economies in transition: rates of growth of real GDP, 2010–2020

Annual percentage change

	2010–2017[a]	2010	2011	2012	2013	2014	2015	2016	2017	2018[b]	2019[c]	2020[c]
Economies in transition	2.0	4.5	4.7	3.5	2.4	0.9	-2.2	0.4	2.0	2.1	2.0	2.6
South-Eastern Europe	1.8	1.5	1.7	-0.6	2.4	0.1	2.1	3.1	1.9	3.9	3.7	3.7
Albania	2.7	3.7	2.5	1.4	1.0	1.8	2.2	3.4	3.8	4.2	4.0	3.8
Bosnia and Herzegovina	1.7	0.9	1.0	-0.8	2.4	1.1	3.8	3.3	1.3	2.7	3.0	3.0
Montenegro	2.7	2.7	3.3	-2.7	3.5	1.8	3.4	3.8	4.3	4.8	3.7	4.2
Serbia	1.3	0.6	1.4	-1.0	2.6	-1.8	0.8	2.8	1.9	4.5	4.0	4.0
The former Yugoslav Republic of Macedonia	2.3	3.4	2.3	-0.5	2.9	3.6	3.8	2.9	0.0	2.5	3.0	3.0
Commonwealth of Independent States and Georgia[d]	2.0	4.6	4.8	3.7	2.4	1.0	-2.3	0.3	2.0	2.1	2.0	2.5
Commonwealth of Independent States and Georgia - net fuel exporters	2.0	4.8	4.6	3.8	2.4	1.2	-2.2	0.0	1.8	1.8	1.7	2.3
Azerbaijan	1.6	5.0	0.1	2.2	5.8	2.8	1.0	-3.1	0.1	1.1	1.9	1.9
Kazakhstan	4.6	7.3	8.9	4.8	6.0	4.2	1.2	1.1	4.0	4.0	4.0	4.0
Russian Federation	1.7	4.5	4.3	3.7	1.8	0.7	-2.8	-0.1	1.5	1.5	1.4	2.1
Turkmenistan	8.9	9.2	14.7	11.1	10.2	10.3	6.5	6.2	6.5	6.0	5.0	5.0
Commonwealth of Independent States and Georgia - net fuel importers	2.1	3.3	5.9	2.3	2.2	-1.0	-3.5	2.3	3.6	4.0	3.8	4.0
Armenia	4.2	2.2	4.7	7.2	3.3	3.6	3.2	0.2	7.5	6.0	4.0	3.7
Belarus	1.9	7.7	5.5	1.7	1.0	1.7	-3.8	-2.5	2.4	3.6	3.0	3.0
Georgia[d]	4.8	6.2	7.2	6.4	3.4	4.6	2.9	2.8	5.0	5.0	4.5	4.3
Kyrgyzstan	3.9	-0.5	6.0	-0.1	10.9	4.0	3.9	4.3	4.6	2.1	3.0	3.0
Republic of Moldova	4.4	7.1	6.8	-0.7	9.4	4.8	-0.4	4.5	4.0	4.3	4.5	4.5
Tajikistan	6.3	6.5	2.4	7.5	7.4	6.7	6.0	6.6	6.6	7.0	6.0	5.5
Ukraine[e]	-0.4	0.3	5.5	0.2	0.0	-6.6	-9.8	2.4	2.5	3.2	2.9	3.4
Uzbekistan[f]	7.2	8.5	8.3	8.2	8.0	8.0	7.9	6.0	5.3	5.2	5.7	5.8

Source: UN/DESA, based on data of the United Nations Statistics Division and individual national sources.
Note: Regional aggregates calculated at 2012 prices and exchange rates.
a Average percentage change.
b Partly estimated.
c Baseline scenario forecasts, based in part on Project LINK and the UN/DESA World Economic Forecasting Model.
d Georgia officially left the Commonwealth of Independent States on 18 August 2009. However, its performance is discussed in the context of this group of countries for reasons of geographic proximity and similarities in economic structure.
e Starting in 2010, data for the Ukraine excludes the temporarily occupied territory of the Autonomous Republic of Crimea and Sevastopol.
f Based on 2019 criteria, Uzbekistan is now considered a net fuel importer.

Table A.3
Developing economies: rates of growth of real GDP, 2010–2020

Annual percentage change

	2010–2017[a]	2010	2011	2012	2013	2014	2015	2016	2017	2018[b]	2019[c]	2020[c]
Developing countries[d]	5.1	7.7	6.3	5.1	5.0	4.5	4.1	3.9	4.5	4.4	4.3	4.6
Africa	3.1	5.1	0.7	6.1	1.8	3.5	2.6	1.6	3.4	3.2	3.4	3.7
North Africa	1.6	4.0	-6.7	9.9	-4.1	0.2	2.3	2.9	5.3	3.7	3.4	3.5
Algeria	3.1	3.6	2.9	3.4	2.8	3.8	3.7	3.3	1.6	2.7	2.2	2.8
Egypt[e]	3.4	5.1	1.8	2.2	2.2	2.9	4.4	4.3	4.2	5.8	5.2	4.7
Libya	-19.9	4.3	-61.3	124.7	-52.1	-50.1	-45.5	-16.1	70.8	11.0	1.5	4.0
Mauritania	4.2	4.8	4.7	5.8	6.1	5.6	1.0	2.4	3.5	3.2	5.1	6.9
Morocco	3.9	4.0	6.3	2.3	4.9	4.0	4.5	1.1	4.1	3.5	3.8	3.9
Sudan[e]	2.6	8.8	-0.3	-2.2	2.2	3.2	3.0	3.5	3.2	-2.0	-1.1	4.3
Tunisia	1.7	3.0	-1.9	3.9	2.3	2.4	0.9	1.1	1.9	2.4	3.4	3.6
East Africa	6.0	6.9	6.7	0.9	8.0	7.8	6.6	5.5	6.1	6.2	6.4	6.5
Burundi	3.1	5.1	4.0	4.4	4.9	4.2	-0.4	2.8	0.0	0.1	0.8	2.2
Comoros	4.9	4.8	5.9	6.3	8.9	3.9	2.0	4.1	3.4	3.7	3.8	5.0
Democratic Republic of the Congo	6.5	7.1	6.9	7.1	8.5	9.5	6.9	2.4	3.7	4.2	4.4	4.5
Djibouti	6.1	3.5	4.5	4.8	5.0	8.9	9.7	8.7	4.1	6.8	6.7	4.8
Eritrea	4.3	2.2	8.7	7.0	4.6	2.9	2.6	1.9	5.0	4.1	4.4	5.8
Ethiopia	10.3	12.9	10.8	9.6	10.4	10.3	9.0	9.3	10.3	7.6	7.5	7.7
Kenya	5.8	8.4	6.1	4.6	5.9	5.4	5.8	5.6	4.8	5.9	6.0	6.0
Madagascar	2.5	0.6	1.8	2.5	1.4	2.7	3.1	4.2	4.1	4.9	5.4	5.2
Rwanda	7.1	7.3	7.8	8.8	4.7	7.6	8.9	6.0	6.1	7.0	7.2	7.1
Somalia	2.5	2.6	2.6	2.6	2.6	2.6	2.6	2.6	1.8	3.3	3.9	3.6
South Sudan	-2.4	-1.8	1.9	-51.5	30.2	22.2	5.1	0.3	1.3	7.4	8.2	8.5
Uganda	5.0	8.2	5.9	3.2	4.7	4.5	5.7	2.6	5.0	6.0	6.0	6.8
United Republic of Tanzania	6.8	6.4	7.9	5.1	7.3	7.0	7.0	7.0	7.1	6.8	6.9	6.6
Central Africa	2.3	4.0	4.8	7.3	-0.5	4.7	-1.1	-0.5	-0.2	2.2	2.5	3.8
Cameroon	4.7	3.4	4.1	4.5	5.4	5.9	5.7	4.6	3.5	4.1	4.6	4.4
Central African Republic	-2.9	3.6	2.0	2.9	-36.7	1.0	4.8	4.5	4.0	4.2	4.0	3.5
Chad	3.2	13.4	6.3	12.5	-5.9	3.4	4.4	-3.4	-3.1	5.2	2.8	4.3
Congo	1.2	15.0	1.2	9.6	-2.5	9.7	-13.2	-2.8	-4.6	1.9	2.1	3.3
Equatorial Guinea	-2.5	-8.9	6.5	8.3	-4.1	0.4	-9.1	-8.6	-3.2	-3.8	-2.7	1.7
Gabon	4.5	7.1	7.1	5.3	5.6	4.3	3.9	2.1	1.1	1.9	2.7	4.1
Sao Tome and Principe	4.7	6.7	4.4	3.1	4.8	6.5	3.9	4.2	3.9	5.0	5.4	5.0
West Africa	4.4	7.3	5.0	5.2	5.8	6.1	3.2	0.2	2.4	3.2	3.4	3.8
Benin	4.8	2.1	3.0	4.6	6.9	6.5	5.0	5.0	5.6	6.0	6.3	4.9
Burkina Faso	6.0	8.4	6.6	6.5	5.8	4.3	3.9	5.9	6.3	7.0	6.2	6.4
Cabo Verde	2.1	1.5	4.0	1.1	0.8	0.6	1.0	3.8	4.0	3.8	4.1	3.5
Côte D'Ivoire	6.3	2.0	-4.2	10.1	9.3	8.8	8.8	8.3	8.1	7.9	7.8	7.6
Gambia (Islamic Republic of the)	2.8	6.5	-4.3	5.9	4.8	-0.9	5.9	0.4	4.6	4.0	4.3	4.1
Ghana	7.3	7.9	14.0	9.3	7.3	4.0	3.8	3.7	8.5	7.5	7.4	6.5
Guinea	5.6	4.8	5.6	5.9	3.9	3.7	3.8	10.5	6.7	6.4	6.2	5.8
Guinea Bissau	3.9	4.6	8.1	-1.7	3.3	0.2	6.1	5.8	5.5	6.2	5.2	4.9
Liberia	5.9	7.3	8.2	11.3	4.6	5.2	9.3	-0.5	2.5	3.8	4.8	4.8
Mali	8.2	10.9	7.7	11.2	7.0	7.8	7.6	7.9	5.3	5.2	5.3	5.6
Niger	6.1	8.4	2.3	11.8	5.3	7.5	4.3	4.9	4.9	5.2	5.6	5.2

Table A.3
Developing economies: rates of growth of real GDP, 2010–2020 *(continued)*

Annual percentage change

	2010–2017[a]	2010	2011	2012	2013	2014	2015	2016	2017[b]	2018[c]	2019[c]	2020[c]
Nigeria	3.8	7.8	4.9	4.3	5.4	6.3	2.7	-1.6	0.8	1.9	2.1	2.7
Senegal	4.3	4.2	1.8	4.0	3.9	4.1	6.4	2.8	7.2	7.0	6.7	6.5
Sierra Leone	4.6	5.3	6.3	15.2	20.7	4.6	-20.5	6.3	3.8	5.8	6.4	7.4
Togo	5.8	6.1	6.4	6.5	6.1	5.9	5.7	5.6	4.4	4.9	5.5	5.4
Southern Africa	2.7	4.1	3.9	4.2	3.6	2.9	1.5	0.3	1.5	1.2	2.1	2.6
Angola	3.2	4.9	3.5	8.5	5.0	4.8	0.9	-2.6	0.7	1.0	2.4	3.0
Botswana	4.9	8.6	6.0	4.5	11.3	4.1	-1.7	4.3	2.4	4.4	4.0	4.1
Eswatini	2.8	3.8	2.2	4.7	6.4	1.9	0.4	1.4	1.5	1.3	1.0	1.3
Lesotho	4.0	6.1	6.9	6.0	1.8	3.1	2.5	2.4	3.1	2.0	1.5	2.6
Malawi	4.2	5.5	6.2	-0.6	6.3	6.2	3.3	2.7	4.0	3.6	5.1	5.2
Mauritius	3.8	4.4	4.1	3.5	3.4	3.7	3.6	3.8	3.8	3.7	3.9	3.2
Mozambique	6.2	6.7	7.1	7.2	7.1	7.4	6.6	3.8	3.7	3.4	3.4	4.1
Namibia	4.2	6.0	5.1	5.1	5.6	6.4	6.1	0.7	-0.8	1.0	2.6	3.5
South Africa	2.0	3.0	3.3	2.2	2.5	1.7	1.3	0.6	1.3	0.8	1.7	2.1
Zambia	5.5	10.3	5.6	7.6	5.1	4.7	2.9	3.8	4.1	3.1	3.9	3.8
Zimbabwe	6.8	12.6	15.4	14.8	5.5	2.1	1.7	0.6	3.0	1.5	1.0	4.0
Africa - net fuel exporters	2.0	5.9	-3.5	10.3	-1.5	2.6	1.2	-0.5	1.7	2.1	1.7	3.0
Africa - net fuel importers	3.9	4.5	4.1	3.0	4.4	4.1	3.7	3.1	4.6	3.9	4.5	4.2
East and South Asia	6.6	9.2	7.4	6.0	6.1	6.2	5.8	6.1	6.1	5.8	5.5	5.6
East Asia	6.8	9.5	7.7	6.6	6.5	6.2	5.8	5.7	6.1	5.8	5.6	5.5
Brunei Darussalam	0.1	2.6	3.7	0.9	-2.1	-2.5	-0.4	-2.5	1.3	2.4	2.7	3.0
Cambodia	7.0	6.0	7.1	7.3	7.5	7.1	7.0	6.9	7.0	7.1	7.0	6.6
China	7.9	10.6	9.5	7.9	7.8	7.3	6.9	6.7	6.9	6.6	6.3	6.2
Democratic People's Republic of Korea	0.4	-0.5	0.8	1.3	1.1	1.0	-1.1	3.9	-3.5	-1.0	1.5	1.0
Fiji	3.2	3.0	2.7	1.4	4.7	5.6	3.8	0.4	3.8	3.5	3.3	3.4
Hong Kong SAR[f]	3.4	6.8	4.8	1.7	3.1	2.8	2.4	2.2	3.8	3.4	3.1	3.2
Indonesia	5.5	6.2	6.2	6.0	5.6	5.0	4.9	5.0	5.1	5.1	5.1	5.1
Kiribati	2.9	-0.9	1.6	4.6	4.3	-0.6	10.3	1.1	3.1	2.1	2.0	2.3
Lao People's Democratic Republic	7.6	8.1	8.0	7.9	8.0	7.6	7.3	7.0	6.9	6.7	7.0	7.1
Malaysia	5.5	7.4	5.3	5.5	4.7	6.0	5.1	4.2	5.9	4.6	4.4	4.3
Mongolia	8.0	6.4	17.3	12.3	11.6	7.9	2.5	1.4	5.2	6.2	6.1	5.8
Myanmar[e]	7.4	10.2	5.6	7.3	8.4	8.0	7.0	5.9	6.8	6.9	7.2	7.2
Papua New Guinea	5.9	11.2	3.4	4.0	3.6	12.5	8.0	2.4	2.5	0.8	2.7	3.1
Philippines	6.3	7.6	3.7	6.7	7.1	6.1	6.1	6.9	6.7	6.3	6.5	6.4
Republic of Korea	3.4	6.5	3.7	2.3	2.9	3.3	2.8	2.9	3.1	2.6	2.5	2.6
Samoa	2.1	4.3	3.6	-2.3	0.5	1.9	2.9	6.5	-0.4	0.7	2.1	3.0
Singapore	5.3	15.2	6.4	4.1	5.1	3.9	2.2	2.4	3.6	3.2	2.6	2.7
Solomon Islands	4.2	10.6	6.4	2.6	3.0	2.3	2.5	3.5	3.2	3.0	3.1	3.3
Taiwan Province of China	3.4	10.6	3.8	2.1	2.2	4.0	0.8	1.4	2.9	2.7	2.4	2.3
Thailand	3.7	7.5	0.8	7.2	2.7	1.0	3.0	3.3	3.9	4.1	3.8	3.7
Timor-Leste	-1.0	-1.2	11.8	5.0	-11.0	-26.0	20.9	0.8	-0.5	0.5	4.5	4.0
Vanuatu	2.1	1.6	1.2	1.8	2.0	2.3	0.2	3.5	4.2	3.3	3.1	3.4
Viet Nam	6.1	6.4	6.2	5.2	5.4	6.0	6.7	6.2	6.8	6.9	6.7	6.5

Table A.3
Developing economies: rates of growth of real GDP, 2010–2020 *(continued)*

Annual percentage change

	2010–2017[a]	2010	2011	2012	2013	2014	2015	2016	2017[b]	2018[c]	2019[c]	2020[c]
South Asia	5.9	7.7	6.1	3.3	4.3	6.2	5.8	8.0	6.1	5.6	5.4	5.9
Afghanistan[e]	4.5	3.2	8.7	10.9	6.5	3.1	-1.8	3.6	2.5	2.5	2.8	2.5
Bangladesh[e]	6.4	5.6	6.5	6.5	6.0	6.1	6.6	7.1	7.3	7.3	7.4	7.2
Bhutan	6.6	11.7	7.9	5.1	2.1	5.7	6.6	8.0	6.0	6.0	6.4	6.1
India[e]	7.3	10.3	6.6	5.5	6.4	7.4	8.2	7.1	6.7	7.4	7.6	7.4
Iran (Islamic Republic of)[e]	2.6	5.7	2.7	-7.5	-0.1	4.7	-1.1	13.4	4.3	-1.0	-2.4	0.1
Maldives	5.5	7.3	8.6	2.5	7.3	7.3	2.2	6.2	3.2	5.5	6.3	6.1
Nepal[e]	4.3	4.8	3.4	4.8	4.1	6.0	3.3	0.4	7.5	6.3	5.4	5.1
Pakistan[e]	4.1	1.6	2.7	3.5	4.4	4.7	4.7	5.5	5.7	5.4	4.1	3.6
Sri Lanka	5.8	8.0	8.4	9.1	3.4	5.0	5.0	4.5	3.3	3.9	4.1	4.8
East and South Asia - net fuel exporters	4.4	5.7	5.0	1.6	2.9	4.7	3.3	6.6	5.3	3.2	2.4	3.5
East and South Asia - net fuel importers	6.9	9.6	7.7	6.5	6.5	6.4	6.1	6.1	6.2	6.0	5.8	5.8
Western Asia	4.7	5.7	8.7	4.6	5.9	3.3	4.0	3.1	2.5	3.0	2.4	3.4
Western Asia - net fuel exporters	4.4	4.5	9.1	6.1	5.8	3.0	3.9	3.3	-0.1	2.6	2.5	3.9
Bahrain	3.7	4.3	2.0	3.7	5.4	4.4	2.9	3.5	3.8	3.1	2.1	3.1
Iraq	8.4	5.5	10.2	12.6	26.0	0.2	3.8	9.6	1.0	2.4	2.3	6.2
Kuwait	1.9	-2.4	9.6	6.6	1.1	0.5	0.6	2.9	-3.5	3.6	3.2	4.4
Oman	3.7	2.0	2.6	9.1	5.3	1.2	4.7	5.4	-0.3	2.9	2.1	3.5
Qatar	6.1	16.7	13.0	4.7	4.4	4.0	3.6	2.1	1.6	3.3	3.0	4.7
Saudi Arabia	3.9	5.0	10.0	5.4	2.7	3.7	4.1	1.7	-0.9	2.1	2.1	3.1
United Arab Emirates	3.9	1.6	6.9	4.5	5.1	4.4	5.1	3.0	0.8	2.8	3.1	3.4
Western Asia - net fuel exporters	5.1	7.2	8.2	2.6	5.9	3.8	4.1	2.9	6.0	3.4	2.2	2.9
Israel	3.8	5.5	5.2	2.2	4.2	3.5	2.5	4.0	3.4	3.5	3.2	3.7
Jordan	2.5	2.3	2.6	2.7	2.8	3.1	2.4	2.0	2.0	2.1	2.3	4.1
Lebanon	2.3	8.0	0.9	2.8	2.6	1.9	0.4	1.6	0.6	0.9	1.7	2.4
State of Palestine	5.0	8.1	12.4	6.3	2.2	-0.2	3.4	4.7	3.1	-0.8	1.3	1.8
Syrian Arab Republic	-9.2	3.4	4.6	-26.3	-26.3	-14.7	-6.1	-4.0	1.9	10.1	11.3	8.5
Turkey	6.8	8.5	11.1	4.8	8.5	5.2	6.1	3.2	7.4	3.5	1.7	2.5
Yemen	-10.2	3.3	-15.1	2.2	3.6	-10.6	-30.3	-14.8	-13.8	-2.5	1.9	6.3
Latin America and the Caribbean	2.1	6.1	4.5	2.8	2.9	1.1	-0.1	-1.3	1.0	1.0	1.7	2.3
South America	1.7	6.6	4.8	2.5	3.3	0.4	-1.5	-2.9	0.5	0.4	1.4	2.3
Argentina	2.3	10.1	6.0	-1.0	2.4	-2.5	2.7	-1.8	2.9	-2.8	-1.8	1.2
Bolivia (Plurinational State of)	5.0	4.1	5.2	5.1	6.8	5.5	4.9	4.3	4.2	4.3	4.4	4.0
Brazil	1.3	7.5	4.0	1.9	3.0	0.5	-3.5	-3.5	1.0	1.4	2.1	2.5
Chile	3.5	5.8	6.1	5.3	4.0	1.9	2.3	1.3	1.5	3.9	3.3	3.2
Colombia	3.8	4.0	6.6	4.0	4.9	4.4	3.0	2.0	1.8	2.7	3.3	3.1
Ecuador	3.3	3.5	7.9	5.6	4.9	4.0	0.1	-1.6	2.4	1.0	0.9	1.2
Paraguay	5.8	13.1	4.3	-1.2	14.0	4.7	3.1	4.3	5.2	4.5	4.7	4.3
Peru	4.8	8.3	6.3	6.1	5.9	2.4	3.3	4.0	2.5	3.9	3.8	3.6
Uruguay	3.6	7.8	5.2	3.5	4.6	3.2	0.4	1.7	2.7	1.9	1.5	2.4
Venezuela (Bolivarian Republic of)	-4.1	-1.5	4.2	5.6	1.3	-3.9	-5.7	-16.5	-14.0	-15.0	-8.0	-2.0

Table A.3
Developing economies: rates of growth of real GDP, 2010–2020 *(continued)*

Annual percentage change

	2010–2017[a]	2010	2011	2012	2013	2014	2015	2016	2017[b]	2018[c]	2019[c]	2020[c]
Mexico and Central America	3.3	4.9	3.8	3.8	1.9	3.1	3.7	3.1	2.4	2.4	2.5	2.3
Costa Rica	3.9	5.0	4.3	4.8	2.3	3.5	3.6	4.2	3.3	3.2	3.1	3.3
Cuba	2.3	2.4	2.8	3.0	2.7	1.0	4.4	0.5	1.8	1.1	1.3	1.5
Dominican Republic	5.6	8.3	3.1	2.7	4.9	7.6	7.0	6.6	4.6	5.6	5.3	5.5
El Salvador	2.5	2.1	3.8	2.8	2.4	2.0	2.4	2.6	2.3	2.4	2.4	2.2
Guatemala	3.5	2.9	4.2	3.0	3.7	4.2	4.1	3.1	2.8	2.9	3.0	3.2
Haiti[e]	1.7	-5.5	5.5	2.9	4.2	2.8	1.2	1.5	1.2	1.8	2.0	2.1
Honduras	3.7	3.7	3.8	4.1	2.8	3.1	3.8	3.8	4.8	3.6	3.7	3.4
Mexico	3.1	5.1	3.7	3.6	1.4	2.8	3.3	2.9	2.0	2.2	2.3	2.0
Nicaragua	5.2	4.4	6.3	6.5	4.9	4.8	4.8	4.7	4.9	-3.1	-0.3	2.7
Panama	7.1	5.8	11.3	9.8	6.9	5.1	7.5	5.0	5.3	4.8	5.3	4.7
Caribbean	0.5	1.8	1.1	1.4	1.4	-0.2	-0.1	-0.7	-0.4	1.9	2.0	2.0
Bahamas	0.3	1.5	0.6	3.1	-0.6	-1.2	-3.1	0.2	1.8	2.5	2.2	2.2
Barbados	0.6	0.3	0.8	0.3	-0.1	0.1	0.9	1.6	0.9	0.0	0.8	1.1
Belize	2.2	3.3	2.2	3.7	0.7	4.0	3.8	-0.5	0.5	2.6	2.0	2.7
Guyana	4.0	4.1	5.2	5.3	5.0	3.9	3.1	3.4	2.2	3.0	3.7	4.3
Jamaica	0.5	-1.5	1.7	-0.6	0.5	0.7	0.9	1.4	1.0	1.7	1.9	2.0
Suriname	1.0	5.2	5.8	2.7	2.9	0.3	-2.6	-5.1	-0.7	1.7	2.8	2.2
Trinidad and Tobago	0.1	3.3	-0.3	1.3	2.3	-1.0	0.2	-2.3	-2.6	1.9	1.7	1.6
Latin America and the Caribbean - net fuel exporters	0.7	1.5	5.4	4.8	3.4	0.8	-0.8	-5.5	-3.5	-2.8	0.1	1.6
Latin America and the Caribbean - net fuel importers	2.3	7.0	4.4	2.4	2.8	1.1	0.0	-0.6	1.8	1.5	2.0	2.4
Memorandum items:												
Least Developed Countries	4.8	6.4	4.7	4.7	5.6	5.3	3.7	3.6	4.6	5.0	5.0	5.7
Africa (excluding Libya)	3.7	5.2	4.1	3.7	4.2	4.6	3.1	1.7	3.1	3.1	3.4	3.7
North Africa (excluding Libya)	3.4	3.9	2.8	2.4	2.8	3.6	3.8	3.2	4.4	3.5	3.5	3.5
East Asia (excluding China)	4.5	7.7	4.5	4.2	4.0	4.1	3.6	3.7	4.2	4.0	3.9	3.9
South Asia (excluding India)	3.7	4.5	4.1	-0.7	1.2	4.4	2.5	8.0	5.9	2.4	0.7	2.6
Western Asia (excluding Israel and Turkey)	3.8	4.5	8.2	4.8	4.9	2.5	3.2	3.0	-0.2	2.6	2.6	3.9
Arab States[g]	3.2	4.3	3.5	6.3	2.3	1.9	2.9	2.9	1.3	2.9	2.8	3.8
Landlocked developing economies	5.2	7.3	7.0	4.3	7.0	5.6	3.4	3.0	4.5	4.5	4.7	4.7
Small island developing economies	4.2	9.3	4.6	3.4	4.1	3.5	3.2	2.4	3.0	3.0	2.8	2.9

Source: UN/DESA, based on data of the United Nations Statistics Division and individual national sources.
Note: Regional aggregates calculated at 2012 prices and exchange rates.
a Average percentage change.
b Partly estimated.
c Baseline scenario forecasts, based in part on Project LINK and the UN/DESA World Economic Forecasting Model.
d Covering countries that account for 98 per cent of the population of all developing countries.
e Fiscal year basis.
f Special Administrative Region of China.
g Currently includes data for Algeria, Bahrain, Comoros, Djibouti, Egypt, Iraq, Jordan, Kuwait, Lebanon, Libya, Mauritania, Morocco, Oman, Qatar, Saudi Arabia, Somalia, Sudan, Syrian Arab Republic, Tunisia, United Arab Emirates, and Yemen.

Table A.4
Developed economies: consumer price inflation, 2010–2020

Annual percentage change[a]

	2010	2011	2012	2013	2014	2015	2016	2017	2018[b]	2019[c]	2020[c]
Developed economies	1.5	2.5	1.9	1.3	1.4	0.3	0.7	1.7	2.0	2.2	2.1
United States	1.6	3.2	2.1	1.5	1.6	0.1	1.3	2.1	2.5	2.5	2.4
Canada	1.8	2.9	1.5	0.9	1.9	1.1	1.4	1.6	2.3	2.2	2.1
Japan	-0.7	-0.3	-0.1	0.3	2.8	0.8	-0.1	0.5	1.2	1.4	1.5
Australia	2.9	3.3	1.8	2.4	2.5	1.5	1.3	1.9	2.1	2.2	2.2
New Zealand	2.3	4.0	1.1	1.1	1.2	0.3	0.6	1.9	1.8	2.1	2.1
European Union	1.9	3.0	2.6	1.5	0.6	0.0	0.3	1.7	1.9	2.1	2.1
EU-15	1.9	2.9	2.5	1.5	0.6	0.1	0.4	1.7	1.9	2.1	2.1
Austria	1.7	3.6	2.6	2.1	1.5	0.8	1.0	2.2	2.0	2.4	2.4
Belgium	2.3	3.4	2.6	1.2	0.5	0.6	1.8	2.2	1.9	2.2	2.2
Denmark	2.2	2.7	2.4	0.5	0.4	0.2	0.0	1.1	1.0	1.6	1.8
Finland	1.7	3.3	3.2	2.2	1.2	-0.2	0.4	0.8	1.3	1.9	2.2
France	1.7	2.3	2.2	1.0	0.6	0.1	0.3	1.2	2.2	2.3	2.0
Germany	1.2	2.5	2.1	1.6	0.8	0.1	0.4	1.7	1.9	1.9	1.9
Greece	4.7	3.1	1.0	-0.9	-1.4	-1.1	0.0	1.1	0.7	2.0	2.2
Ireland	-1.6	1.2	1.8	0.5	0.3	0.0	-0.2	0.3	0.7	1.1	1.9
Italy	1.6	2.9	3.3	1.3	0.2	0.1	-0.1	1.4	1.3	1.9	1.9
Luxembourg	2.8	3.7	2.9	1.7	0.7	0.1	0.0	2.1	1.5	2.6	3.3
Netherlands	0.9	2.5	2.8	2.6	0.3	0.2	0.1	1.3	1.5	2.0	2.1
Portugal	1.4	3.6	2.8	0.4	-0.2	0.5	0.6	1.6	1.3	2.0	2.0
Spain	2.1	3.0	2.4	1.5	-0.2	-0.6	-0.3	2.0	1.4	1.8	1.8
Sweden	1.9	1.4	0.9	0.4	0.2	0.7	1.1	1.9	2.2	2.6	2.5
United Kingdom	3.2	4.5	2.9	2.5	1.5	0.0	0.7	2.7	2.6	2.6	2.4
EU-13	2.7	3.8	3.7	1.5	0.2	-0.4	-0.2	1.8	2.4	2.3	2.3
Bulgaria	2.4	4.2	3.0	0.9	-1.4	-0.1	-0.8	2.1	2.9	2.5	2.6
Croatia	1.0	2.3	3.4	2.2	-0.2	-0.5	-1.1	1.1	1.6	1.8	1.8
Cyprus	2.4	3.3	2.4	-0.4	-1.4	-2.1	-1.7	0.5	0.6	1.5	1.8
Czech Republic	1.2	2.2	3.6	1.3	0.5	0.2	0.7	2.4	2.3	2.3	2.0
Estonia	2.7	5.1	4.2	3.2	0.5	0.1	0.8	3.7	3.3	3.0	2.9
Hungary	4.7	3.9	5.7	1.7	0.0	0.1	0.5	2.4	2.9	2.9	2.7
Latvia	-1.2	4.2	2.3	0.0	0.7	0.2	0.1	2.9	2.4	2.5	2.3
Lithuania	1.2	4.1	3.2	1.2	0.2	-0.7	0.7	3.7	2.6	2.3	1.9
Malta	1.5	2.7	2.4	1.4	0.3	1.1	0.6	1.4	1.9	2.4	2.3
Poland	2.7	3.9	3.6	0.8	0.1	-0.7	-0.2	1.6	1.5	1.9	1.9
Romania	6.1	5.8	3.3	4.0	1.1	-0.6	-1.5	1.3	4.5	3.5	3.5
Slovakia	0.7	4.1	3.7	1.5	-0.1	-0.3	-0.5	1.4	2.7	2.2	2.2
Slovenia	2.1	2.1	2.8	1.9	0.4	-0.8	-0.2	1.6	2.3	2.1	2.0
Other European countries	1.4	0.6	-0.2	1.0	0.8	0.4	1.4	1.1	1.7	1.9	2.1
Iceland	7.5	4.2	6.0	4.1	1.0	0.3	0.8	-1.6	1.7	3.1	3.6
Norway	2.3	1.3	0.3	2.0	1.9	2.0	3.9	1.8	3.0	2.6	2.5
Switzerland	0.6	0.1	-0.7	0.1	0.0	-0.8	-0.5	0.6	0.8	1.3	1.7
Memorandum items:											
North America	1.7	3.1	2.0	1.4	1.7	0.2	1.3	2.1	2.5	2.5	2.4
Developed Asia and Pacific	0.1	0.5	0.3	0.8	2.7	0.9	0.2	0.8	1.4	1.6	1.7
Europe	1.9	2.8	2.4	1.5	0.6	0.1	0.4	1.7	1.9	2.1	2.1
Major developed economies	1.3	2.5	1.8	1.3	1.6	0.3	0.7	1.7	2.1	2.2	2.1
Euro area	1.6	2.7	2.5	1.4	0.5	0.0	0.2	1.5	1.7	2.0	2.0

Sources: UN/DESA, based on OECD *Main Economic Indicators*; Eurostat; and individual national sources.

a Data for country groups are weighted averages, where weights for each year are based on 2012 GDP in United States dollars.

b Partly estimated.

c Baseline scenario forecasts, based in part on Project LINK and the UN/DESA World Economic Forecasting Model.

Table A.5
Economies in transition: consumer price inflation, 2010–2020

Annual percentage change[a]

	2010	2011	2012	2013	2014	2015	2016	2017	2018[b]	2019[c]	2020[c]
Economies in transition	7.1	9.6	6.1	6.4	7.8	15.6	7.8	5.1	4.0	4.9	4.3
South-Eastern Europe	4.1	7.3	4.9	4.4	1.0	0.8	0.5	2.3	2.0	2.3	2.3
Albania	3.6	3.5	2.0	1.9	1.6	1.9	1.3	2.0	2.3	2.4	2.3
Bosnia and Herzegovina	2.1	3.7	2.1	-0.1	-0.9	-1.0	-1.1	1.2	1.5	1.8	1.8
Montenegro	0.7	3.5	4.1	2.2	-0.7	1.5	-0.3	2.4	3.0	2.5	2.5
Serbia	6.1	11.1	7.3	7.7	2.1	1.4	1.1	3.1	2.0	2.5	2.5
The former Yugoslav Republic of Macedonia	1.5	3.9	3.3	2.8	-0.3	-0.3	-0.2	1.3	1.5	2.1	2.1
Commonwealth of Independent States and Georgia[d]	7.2	9.6	6.1	6.4	8.0	16.1	8.0	5.1	4.0	4.9	4.4
Commonwealth of Independent States and Georgia - net fuel exporters	**6.8**	**8.5**	**5.0**	**6.5**	**7.5**	**14.2**	**7.6**	**4.3**	**3.2**	**4.5**	**4.0**
Azerbaijan	5.7	7.9	1.1	2.4	1.4	4.0	12.4	12.9	2.5	3.5	3.0
Kazakhstan	7.4	8.5	5.2	5.9	6.8	6.7	14.4	7.4	6.7	6.0	5.4
Russian Federation	6.8	8.4	5.1	6.8	7.8	15.5	7.0	3.7	2.9	4.4	4.0
Turkmenistan	2.3	12.9	8.3	1.2	0.7	-5.2	-4.8	5.6	6.0	4.8	4.0
Commonwealth of Independent States and Georgia - net fuel exporters	**10.3**	**18.2**	**14.2**	**6.0**	**12.1**	**29.8**	**11.1**	**11.5**	**10.1**	**8.1**	**7.1**
Armenia	8.2	7.7	2.6	5.8	3.0	3.7	-1.4	1.0	2.8	3.4	2.9
Belarus	7.7	53.2	59.2	18.3	18.1	13.5	11.8	6.0	4.9	4.9	4.5
Georgia[d]	7.1	8.5	-0.9	-0.5	3.1	4.0	2.1	6.0	2.9	3.0	3.0
Kyrgyzstan	8.0	16.6	2.8	6.6	7.5	6.5	0.4	3.2	2.4	3.0	3.0
Republic of Moldova	7.5	7.7	4.5	4.6	5.1	9.7	6.4	6.6	3.5	3.6	3.5
Tajikistan	6.4	12.4	5.8	5.0	6.1	5.7	6.0	8.0	6.0	5.0	5.0
Ukraine[e]	9.4	8.0	0.6	-0.2	12.1	48.7	13.9	14.4	12.2	10.3	8.8
Uzbekistan[f]	19.2	16.5	14.8	14.0	11.9	9.1	8.9	14.4	15.9	9.0	8.0

Sources: UN/DESA, based on data of the United Nations Statistics Division and individual national sources.

Note: Regional aggregates calculated at 2012 prices and exchange rates.

a Average percentage change.

b Partly estimated.

c Baseline scenario forecasts, based in part on Project LINK and the UN/DESA World Economic Forecasting Model.

d Georgia officially left the Commonwealth of Independent States on 18 August 2009. However, its performance is discussed in the context of this group of countries for reasons of geographic proximity and similarities in economic structure.

e Starting in 2010, data for the Ukraine excludes the temporarily occupied territory of the Autonomous Republic of Crimea and Sevastopol.

f Based on 2019 criteria, Uzbekistan is now considered a net fuel importer.

Table A.6
Developing economies: consumer price inflation, 2010–2020

Annual percentage change[a]

	2010	2011	2012	2013	2014	2015	2016	2017	2018[b]	2019[c]	2020[c]
Developing countries by region[d]	**5.3**	**6.6**	**5.4**	**5.7**	**5.0**	**4.3**	**5.2**	**4.4**	**5.2**	**5.1**	**4.4**
Africa	**7.7**	**9.1**	**9.1**	**6.9**	**6.8**	**7.2**	**13.3**	**14.4**	**11.1**	**8.5**	**7.2**
North Africa	**6.8**	**8.4**	**8.6**	**7.7**	**7.7**	**7.8**	**11.6**	**18.4**	**12.8**	**7.8**	**6.0**
Algeria	3.9	4.5	8.9	3.3	2.9	4.8	6.4	5.6	3.9	2.9	2.2
Egypt	11.3	10.1	7.1	9.4	10.1	10.4	13.8	29.5	14.2	10.7	8.9
Libya	2.8	15.5	6.1	2.6	2.4	9.0	26.7	28.4	12.0	11.0	10.0
Mauritania	6.3	5.7	4.9	4.1	3.5	3.3	1.5	2.3	3.4	5.4	6.5
Morocco	1.0	0.9	1.3	1.9	0.4	1.6	1.6	0.8	1.4	1.1	1.4
Sudan	13.2	18.1	35.6	36.5	36.9	16.9	17.6	32.6	64.1	19.4	9.2
Tunisia	4.4	3.5	5.1	5.8	4.9	4.9	3.7	5.3	7.3	3.9	2.7
East Africa	**5.7**	**18.7**	**15.3**	**5.5**	**5.3**	**7.8**	**20.5**	**18.0**	**11.3**	**6.9**	**6.0**
Burundi	6.5	9.6	18.2	7.9	4.4	5.5	5.6	16.1	6.8	10.5	13.2
Comoros	3.4	1.8	6.3	-4.3	0.6	-8.1	7.6	2.2	0.5	1.0	1.2
Democratic Republic of the Congo	7.1	15.3	9.7	0.8	1.2	0.7	2.9	13.2	11.0	7.1	4.6
Djibouti	4.0	5.1	3.7	2.7	1.3	-0.8	2.7	0.6	1.6	1.5	1.2
Eritrea	15.2	25.3	20.7	7.3	15.2	1.0	21.9	7.5	6.0	4.5	3.7
Ethiopia	8.1	33.3	24.1	8.1	7.4	10.1	7.3	9.8	11.5	10.0	9.7
Kenya	4.0	14.0	9.4	5.7	6.9	6.6	6.3	8.0	5.1	4.6	4.3
Madagascar	9.2	9.5	5.7	5.8	6.1	7.4	6.7	8.3	7.2	6.5	5.8
Rwanda	-0.2	3.1	10.3	5.9	2.4	2.5	7.2	8.3	2.9	4.5	4.8
Somalia	-15.3	-3.0	-2.0	-3.2	-4.2	-5.5	-3.6	2.2	0.8	1.3	1.5
South Sudan	1.2	47.3	45.1	0.0	1.7	52.8	351.3	239.1	109.3	22.6	10.9
Uganda	4.0	16.2	12.7	4.9	3.1	5.6	5.7	5.2	3.9	4.7	5.2
United Republic of Tanzania	6.2	12.7	16.0	7.9	6.1	5.6	5.2	5.3	4.6	4.9	4.6
Central Africa	**2.2**	**1.8**	**5.1**	**2.4**	**3.1**	**3.2**	**17.3**	**1.9**	**2.6**	**2.7**	**2.5**
Cameroon	1.3	2.9	2.7	2.1	1.9	2.7	0.9	0.6	1.6	1.9	1.8
Central African Republic	1.5	1.3	5.8	1.5	25.3	37.1	5.6	21.7	11.0	7.9	5.3
Chad	-2.1	-3.7	14.0	0.1	1.7	3.7	-0.5	-1.7	1.4	2.3	2.4
Congo	0.4	0.8	6.1	6.0	0.1	4.5	95.2	4.0	3.3	2.6	2.0
Equatorial Guinea	7.8	4.8	3.7	2.9	4.3	1.7	1.4	0.7	3.4	3.7	3.8
Gabon	1.5	1.3	2.7	0.5	4.7	-0.3	2.1	3.9	2.7	2.5	2.3
Sao Tome and Principe	13.3	14.3	10.6	8.1	7.0	5.2	5.4	5.7	5.7	3.8	2.3
West Africa	**11.6**	**9.7**	**10.4**	**7.6**	**7.3**	**8.3**	**13.3**	**13.8**	**13.4**	**12.1**	**10.2**
Benin	2.3	2.7	6.7	0.9	-1.0	0.3	-0.8	0.1	2.2	2.2	1.5
Burkina Faso	-0.8	2.8	3.8	0.5	-0.3	1.0	-0.2	0.4	1.9	2.2	1.9
Cabo Verde	2.1	4.5	2.5	1.5	-0.2	0.1	-1.4	0.8	1.3	2.1	1.9
Côte D'Ivoire	1.2	4.9	1.3	2.6	0.4	1.3	0.7	0.7	2.1	3.1	3.3
Gambia (Islamic Republic of the)	5.0	4.8	4.3	5.7	5.9	6.8	7.2	8.6	4.1	4.0	4.0
Ghana	10.7	8.7	7.1	11.7	15.5	17.1	17.5	12.4	8.3	12.2	12.0
Guinea	15.5	21.4	15.2	11.9	9.7	8.2	8.2	8.9	9.2	7.4	7.1
Guinea Bissau	2.5	5.0	2.1	1.2	-1.5	1.4	1.6	1.4	1.8	2.4	2.4
Liberia	7.3	8.5	6.8	7.6	9.9	7.7	8.8	12.4	11.2	6.5	3.9
Mali	1.1	3.0	5.3	-0.6	0.9	1.5	-1.8	1.8	2.5	2.7	2.5
Niger	0.8	2.9	0.5	2.3	-0.9	1.0	0.2	2.4	4.1	3.5	2.6
Nigeria	13.7	10.8	12.2	8.5	8.1	9.0	15.7	16.5	16.2	14.1	11.6
Senegal	1.2	3.4	1.4	0.7	-1.1	0.1	0.8	1.3	1.7	2.3	2.1
Sierra Leone	7.2	6.8	6.6	5.5	4.6	6.7	10.9	18.2	11.7	9.1	7.8

Table A.6
Developing economies: consumer price inflation, 2010–2020 (*continued*)

Annual percentage change[a]

	2010	2011	2012	2013	2014	2015	2016	2017	2018[b]	2019[c]	2020[c]
Togo	0.0	3.6	2.6	1.8	0.2	1.8	0.9	-0.8	1.3	1.6	1.6
Southern Africa	**6.6**	**7.0**	**6.8**	**6.5**	**6.2**	**5.8**	**12.3**	**10.8**	**8.1**	**7.3**	**6.9**
Angola	14.5	13.5	10.3	8.8	7.3	10.3	32.4	31.7	20.8	14.7	13.0
Botswana	6.9	8.5	7.5	5.9	4.4	3.1	2.8	3.3	3.6	4.2	4.5
Eswatini	4.5	6.1	8.9	5.6	5.7	5.0	7.8	6.2	5.7	5.5	5.0
Lesotho	3.6	5.0	6.1	5.0	5.3	3.2	6.6	5.3	5.0	4.4	3.9
Malawi	7.4	7.6	21.3	27.3	23.8	21.9	21.7	11.5	9.7	6.8	5.8
Mauritius	2.9	6.5	3.9	3.5	3.2	1.3	1.0	3.7	3.8	3.8	3.7
Mozambique	12.4	11.2	2.6	4.3	2.6	3.6	17.4	15.1	5.5	6.5	6.7
Namibia	4.9	5.0	6.7	5.6	5.3	3.4	6.7	6.1	4.3	4.4	4.3
South Africa	4.1	5.0	5.7	5.8	6.1	4.5	6.6	5.2	4.8	5.5	5.4
Zambia	8.5	6.4	6.6	7.0	7.8	10.1	17.9	6.6	8.3	7.1	6.8
Zimbabwe	3.0	3.5	3.7	1.6	-0.2	-2.4	-1.6	0.9	2.1	2.6	3.0
Africa - net fuel exporters	**9.7**	**9.9**	**11.3**	**7.9**	**7.4**	**8.1**	**17.2**	**16.8**	**15.2**	**10.8**	**8.8**
Africa - net fuel importers	**6.0**	**8.4**	**7.3**	**6.2**	**6.3**	**6.4**	**10.2**	**12.6**	**7.9**	**6.6**	**5.9**
East and South Asia	**4.7**	**6.4**	**4.6**	**5.2**	**3.4**	**2.6**	**2.6**	**2.3**	**3.5**	**4.1**	**3.6**
East Asia	**3.2**	**5.3**	**2.8**	**2.8**	**2.3**	**1.6**	**1.9**	**1.8**	**2.2**	**2.5**	**2.5**
Brunei Darussalam	0.4	0.1	0.1	0.4	-0.2	-0.4	-0.7	-0.2	0.2	0.6	0.9
Cambodia	4.0	5.5	2.9	2.9	3.9	1.2	3.0	2.9	2.7	3.1	3.0
China	3.2	5.6	2.6	2.6	1.9	1.4	2.0	1.6	2.1	2.5	2.6
Democratic People's Republic of Korea	-15.6	6.8	4.0	1.6	3.7	3.1	-0.6	-2.0	-1.0	2.0	2.0
Fiji	3.7	7.3	3.4	2.9	0.5	1.4	3.9	3.4	3.2	3.1	3.0
Hong Kong SAR[e]	2.3	5.3	4.1	4.3	4.4	3.0	2.4	1.5	1.9	2.5	2.7
Indonesia	5.1	5.4	4.3	6.4	6.4	6.4	3.5	3.8	3.3	3.7	3.5
Kiribati	-3.9	1.5	-3.0	-1.5	2.1	0.6	0.7	2.1	2.9	2.4	2.3
Lao People's Democratic Republic	6.0	7.6	4.3	6.4	4.1	1.3	1.6	0.8	2.2	2.5	2.8
Malaysia	1.7	3.2	1.7	2.1	3.1	2.1	2.1	3.9	1.3	2.2	2.3
Mongolia	10.1	8.4	14.3	10.5	12.2	6.6	1.1	4.1	6.8	7.8	6.5
Myanmar	7.7	5.0	1.5	5.5	5.0	9.5	7.0	4.6	6.6	6.0	5.8
Papua New Guinea	6.0	4.4	4.5	5.0	5.2	6.0	6.7	5.9	5.2	4.7	5.3
Philippines	3.8	4.7	3.0	2.6	3.6	0.7	1.3	2.9	5.5	4.0	3.2
Republic of Korea	2.9	4.0	2.2	1.3	1.3	0.7	1.0	1.9	1.6	1.8	2.0
Samoa	0.8	5.2	2.0	0.6	-0.4	0.7	1.3	1.6	3.3	2.7	2.8
Singapore	2.8	5.2	4.6	2.4	1.0	-0.5	-0.5	0.6	0.5	1.1	1.3
Solomon Islands	1.1	7.3	5.9	5.4	5.2	-0.6	0.5	0.5	2.7	2.9	3.0
Taiwan Province of China	1.1	1.4	1.6	1.0	1.3	-0.6	1.0	1.1	1.7	1.6	1.6
Thailand	3.2	3.8	3.0	2.2	1.9	-0.9	0.2	0.7	1.2	1.5	1.6
Timor-Leste	6.8	13.5	11.8	11.1	0.7	0.6	-1.3	0.6	2.3	2.8	2.2
Vanuatu	2.8	1.1	1.1	1.5	0.8	2.5	0.8	2.6	3.1	2.8	3.0
Viet Nam	8.9	18.7	9.1	6.6	4.7	0.9	3.2	3.5	3.7	4.2	4.0
South Asia	**11.3**	**11.6**	**12.7**	**16.2**	**8.6**	**7.1**	**5.6**	**4.6**	**9.6**	**11.4**	**8.7**
Afghanistan	0.9	10.2	7.2	7.7	4.6	-0.7	4.4	5.0	3.7	5.2	5.4
Bangladesh	8.1	11.4	6.2	7.5	7.0	6.2	5.5	5.7	5.7	6.1	6.1
Bhutan	7.0	8.8	10.9	7.0	8.3	4.5	4.3	3.9	4.3	5.0	4.7
India	12.0	8.9	9.3	10.9	6.4	5.9	4.9	2.5	4.5	5.1	4.9

Table A.6
Developing economies: consumer price inflation, 2010–2020 *(continued)*

Annual percentage change[a]

	2010	2011	2012	2013	2014	2015	2016	2017	2018[b]	2019[c]	2020[c]
Iran (Islamic Republic of)	10.1	20.6	26.5	39.3	17.2	13.7	8.6	10.5	28.8	34.9	22.8
Maldives	6.1	11.3	10.9	3.8	2.1	1.0	0.5	2.7	1.6	2.5	3.0
Nepal	9.3	9.2	9.5	9.0	8.4	7.9	8.8	3.2	4.3	5.3	5.1
Pakistan	13.9	11.9	9.7	7.7	7.2	2.5	3.8	4.1	4.8	7.3	6.1
Sri Lanka	6.2	6.7	7.5	6.9	3.2	3.8	4.0	7.7	5.0	4.7	5.1
East and South Asia - net fuel exporters	**6.8**	**10.8**	**12.2**	**18.1**	**10.2**	**9.0**	**5.4**	**6.2**	**12.5**	**15.0**	**10.6**
East and South Asia - net fuel importers	**4.5**	**5.9**	**3.7**	**3.7**	**2.7**	**1.9**	**2.2**	**1.9**	**2.5**	**2.8**	**2.9**
Western Asia	**4.8**	**4.9**	**5.0**	**5.2**	**4.3**	**4.1**	**4.0**	**3.9**	**6.3**	**4.5**	**4.7**
Net fuel exporters	**3.1**	**4.1**	**2.7**	**2.6**	**2.4**	**2.1**	**2.0**	**0.3**	**2.2**	**1.9**	**2.2**
Bahrain	2.0	-0.4	2.8	3.3	2.6	1.9	2.7	1.4	2.8	3.1	3.0
Iraq	2.9	5.8	6.1	1.9	2.2	1.4	0.5	0.2	0.4	1.1	1.6
Kuwait	4.5	4.8	3.3	2.7	3.1	3.7	3.5	1.5	0.5	2.1	3.4
Oman	3.2	4.0	2.9	1.0	1.0	0.1	1.1	1.6	1.1	1.3	1.5
Qatar	-2.4	2.0	1.8	3.2	3.4	1.8	2.7	0.4	0.5	2.9	4.4
Saudi Arabia	5.3	5.8	2.9	3.5	2.2	1.3	2.0	-0.9	2.9	1.8	2.0
United Arab Emirates	0.9	0.9	0.7	1.1	2.3	4.1	1.6	2.0	3.7	1.7	1.2
Yemen	11.2	19.5	9.9	11.0	8.1	23.9	11.9	12.4	13.7	13.4	12.3
Net fuel importers	**7.0**	**6.0**	**8.2**	**8.7**	**6.8**	**6.7**	**6.9**	**8.8**	**11.8**	**8.1**	**8.1**
Israel	2.7	3.5	1.7	1.6	0.5	-0.6	-0.5	0.2	0.9	1.6	1.7
Jordan	4.8	4.2	4.5	4.8	2.9	-0.9	-0.8	3.3	4.5	2.3	1.5
Lebanon	4.0	5.0	6.6	4.8	1.9	-3.7	-0.8	4.4	4.3	1.4	0.8
State of Palestine	3.7	2.9	2.8	1.7	1.7	1.4	-0.2	0.2	0.1	1.0	1.7
Syrian Arab Republic	4.4	4.8	36.7	82.9	10.3	32.7	45.7	20.7	4.3	13.6	16.8
Turkey	8.6	6.5	9.0	7.5	8.9	7.7	7.7	11.1	16.1	10.2	10.0
Latin America and the Caribbean[d]	**6.1**	**6.9**	**6.4**	**6.8**	**8.8**	**7.9**	**9.8**	**6.1**	**6.7**	**6.7**	**5.3**
South America[d]	**6.8**	**7.9**	**7.2**	**7.9**	**10.8**	**10.0**	**12.5**	**6.4**	**7.6**	**7.8**	**5.9**
Argentina	22.1	19.9	21.0	24.5	41.7	23.6	41.0	24.3	33.0	32.0	19.5
Bolivia (Plurinational State of)	2.5	9.9	4.5	5.7	5.8	4.1	3.6	2.8	2.3	3.0	3.4
Brazil	5.0	6.6	5.4	6.2	6.3	9.0	8.7	3.4	3.7	4.1	4.0
Chile	1.4	3.3	3.0	1.9	4.4	4.3	3.8	2.2	2.4	2.9	2.7
Colombia	2.3	3.4	3.2	2.0	2.9	5.0	7.5	4.3	3.2	3.1	3.0
Ecuador	3.6	4.5	5.1	2.7	3.6	4.0	1.7	0.4	0.0	1.3	1.7
Paraguay	4.7	8.3	3.7	2.7	5.0	3.1	4.1	3.6	4.1	4.0	4.2
Peru	1.5	3.4	3.7	2.8	3.2	3.6	3.6	2.8	1.2	2.0	2.4
Uruguay	6.7	8.1	8.1	8.6	8.9	8.7	9.6	6.2	7.6	7.5	6.7
Venezuela (Bolivarian Republic of)	28.2	26.1	21.1	40.6	62.2	121.7	254.9	250.0	...	...	...
Mexico and Central America	**4.1**	**4.3**	**4.2**	**3.7**	**3.8**	**2.5**	**2.9**	**5.5**	**4.6**	**4.1**	**3.8**
Costa Rica	5.7	4.9	4.5	5.2	4.5	0.8	0.0	1.6	2.3	2.9	2.8
Cuba	0.5	11.1	5.6	0.2	1.4	1.8	6.9	5.2	6.4	5.3	4.4
Dominican Republic	6.3	8.7	3.6	4.7	3.1	0.8	1.6	3.3	3.9	3.8	3.8
El Salvador	0.9	5.1	1.7	0.8	1.1	-0.7	0.6	1.0	1.2	1.4	1.5
Guatemala	3.9	6.2	3.8	4.3	3.4	2.4	4.4	4.4	4.3	4.0	3.8
Haiti	5.7	8.4	6.3	5.9	4.6	9.0	13.8	14.7	13.4	12.6	11.5

Table A.6
Developing economies: consumer price inflation, 2010–2020 *(continued)*

Annual percentage change[a]

	2010	2011	2012	2013	2014	2015	2016	2017	2018[b]	2019[c]	2020[c]
Honduras	4.7	6.8	5.2	5.2	6.1	3.2	2.7	3.9	4.3	4.0	3.9
Mexico	4.2	3.4	4.1	3.8	4.0	2.7	2.8	6.0	4.8	4.2	3.8
Nicaragua	5.5	8.1	7.2	7.1	6.0	4.0	3.5	3.9	4.9	4.5	4.5
Panama	3.5	5.9	5.7	4.0	2.6	0.1	0.7	0.9	0.8	1.3	1.6
Caribbean	**8.3**	**6.5**	**6.4**	**4.7**	**4.8**	**3.4**	**6.1**	**4.1**	**2.7**	**3.2**	**3.6**
Bahamas	1.3	3.2	2.0	0.7	1.5	1.9	-0.3	1.5	2.0	2.3	2.4
Barbados	5.8	9.4	4.5	1.8	1.8	-1.1	1.3	4.7	2.6	2.4	2.3
Belize	0.9	1.6	1.3	0.5	1.2	-0.9	0.7	1.2	0.3	1.3	2.0
Guyana	2.1	5.0	2.4	1.9	0.9	-1.0	0.8	1.9	1.4	1.9	2.4
Jamaica	12.6	7.5	6.9	9.3	8.3	3.7	2.3	4.4	4.2	4.0	4.0
Suriname	6.9	17.7	5.0	1.9	3.4	6.9	55.5	22.0	8.3	7.5	6.5
Trinidad and Tobago	10.5	5.1	9.3	5.2	5.7	4.7	3.1	1.9	1.3	2.6	3.6
Latin America and the Caribbean - net fuel exporters	**2.9**	**4.0**	**3.9**	**2.5**	**3.3**	**4.7**	**6.1**	**3.4**	**2.5**	**2.7**	**2.8**
Latin America and the Caribbean - net fuel importers	**6.4**	**7.2**	**6.6**	**7.2**	**9.4**	**8.2**	**10.2**	**6.4**	**7.2**	**7.1**	**5.6**
Memorandum items:											
Least developed countries	**8.2**	**12.6**	**11.1**	**8.6**	**7.8**	**8.4**	**15.2**	**14.8**	**13.8**	**8.6**	**7.2**
East Asia (excluding China)	**3.4**	**4.7**	**3.2**	**3.1**	**3.1**	**1.9**	**1.7**	**2.3**	**2.2**	**2.5**	**2.5**
South Asia (excluding India)	**10.2**	**16.2**	**18.3**	**25.1**	**12.4**	**9.3**	**6.8**	**8.1**	**18.1**	**22.1**	**15.2**
Western Asia (excluding Israel and Turkey)	**3.3**	**4.4**	**3.7**	**4.7**	**2.7**	**3.0**	**3.0**	**1.2**	**2.5**	**2.3**	**2.6**
Arab States[f]	**4.3**	**5.5**	**5.1**	**5.6**	**4.2**	**4.4**	**5.6**	**6.2**	**5.5**	**3.9**	**3.6**
Landlocked developing economies	**6.6**	**10.9**	**8.2**	**5.8**	**5.6**	**5.9**	**12.7**	**10.1**	**7.4**	**5.7**	**5.2**
Small island developing States	**3.7**	**6.4**	**4.8**	**2.9**	**2.0**	**0.9**	**2.1**	**2.4**	**2.4**	**2.6**	**2.7**

Sources: UN/DESA, based on data of the United Nations Statistics Division and individual national sources.
Note: Regional aggregates calculated at 2012 prices and exchange rates.

a Average percentage change.
b Partly estimated.
c Baseline scenario forecasts, based in part on Project LINK and the UN/DESA World Economic Forecasting Model.
d Regional aggregates exclude Venezuela (Bolivarian Republic of), due to the potential distortionary impacts of very high inflation in a single country.
e Special Administrative Region of China.
f Currently includes data for Algeria, Bahrain, Comoros, Djibouti, Egypt, Iraq, Jordan, Kuwait, Lebanon, Libya, Mauritania, Morocco, Oman, Qatar, Saudi Arabia, Somalia, Sudan, Syrian Arab Republic, Tunisia, United Arab Emirates and Yemen..

Table A.7
Developed economies: unemployment rates,[a,b] 2010–2020

Percentage of labour force

	2010	2011	2012	2013	2014	2015	2016	2017	2018[c]	2019[d]	2020[d]
Developed economies	8.7	8.5	8.6	8.5	7.8	7.1	6.5	5.8	5.4	5.1	5.0
United States	9.6	9.0	8.1	7.4	6.2	5.3	4.9	4.4	3.9	3.5	3.6
Canada	8.1	7.5	7.3	7.1	6.9	6.9	7.0	6.3	5.9	5.9	6.0
Japan	5.1	4.6	4.4	4.0	3.6	3.4	3.1	2.8	2.7	2.6	2.6
Australia	5.2	5.1	5.2	5.7	6.1	6.1	5.7	5.6	5.5	5.5	5.6
New Zealand	6.2	6.0	6.4	5.8	5.4	5.4	5.1	4.7	4.7	4.7	4.7
European Union	9.5	9.6	10.4	10.8	10.2	9.4	8.5	7.6	7.0	6.7	6.5
EU-15	9.4	9.6	10.5	11.0	10.5	9.8	9.0	8.2	7.6	7.3	7.2
Austria	4.8	4.6	4.9	5.3	5.6	5.7	6.0	5.5	5.0	5.0	5.0
Belgium	8.3	7.1	7.5	8.4	8.5	8.5	7.8	7.1	6.8	6.8	6.8
Denmark	7.5	7.6	7.5	7.0	6.6	6.2	6.2	5.7	5.8	5.8	5.8
Finland	8.4	7.8	7.7	8.2	8.7	9.4	8.8	8.6	8.6	8.5	8.5
France	8.9	8.8	9.4	9.9	10.3	10.4	10.1	9.4	9.1	9.1	9.1
Germany	7.0	5.8	5.4	5.2	5.0	4.6	4.1	3.7	3.4	3.5	3.5
Greece	12.7	17.9	24.4	27.5	26.5	24.9	23.5	21.5	20.1	19.3	18.8
Ireland	14.5	15.4	15.5	13.7	11.9	9.9	8.4	6.7	5.6	5.0	5.0
Italy	8.4	8.4	10.7	12.1	12.7	11.9	11.7	11.2	10.4	9.7	9.7
Luxembourg	4.4	4.9	5.1	5.8	5.9	6.7	6.3	5.5	5.6	5.5	5.4
Netherlands	4.5	5.0	5.8	7.2	7.4	6.9	6.0	4.8	4.3	4.0	3.9
Portugal	10.8	12.7	15.5	16.2	13.9	12.4	11.1	8.9	7.9	7.7	7.5
Spain	19.9	21.4	24.8	26.1	24.4	22.1	19.6	17.2	15.6	14.1	13.1
Sweden	8.6	7.8	8.0	8.1	8.0	7.4	7.0	6.7	6.6	6.5	6.5
United Kingdom	7.8	8.0	7.9	7.5	6.1	5.3	4.8	4.3	4.1	4.2	4.1
EU-13	9.8	9.9	10.0	10.1	9.0	7.9	6.6	5.4	4.6	4.3	4.0
Bulgaria	10.3	11.3	12.3	13.0	11.4	9.2	7.6	6.2	5.6	5.2	4.8
Croatia	11.8	13.7	15.8	17.4	17.2	16.1	13.4	11.1	10.0	9.4	8.9
Cyprus	6.3	7.9	11.9	15.9	16.1	15.0	13.0	11.1	11.2	11.0	10.8
Czech Republic	7.3	6.7	7.0	7.0	6.1	5.0	4.0	2.9	2.4	2.1	1.9
Estonia	16.7	12.3	10.0	8.6	7.4	6.2	6.8	5.8	5.9	5.7	5.4
Hungary	11.2	11.0	11.0	10.2	7.7	6.8	5.1	4.2	3.8	3.5	3.4
Latvia	19.5	16.2	15.1	11.9	10.8	9.9	9.6	8.7	7.5	7.0	6.8
Lithuania	17.8	15.4	13.4	11.8	10.7	9.1	7.9	7.1	6.7	6.4	6.2
Malta	6.9	6.4	6.2	6.1	5.7	5.4	4.7	4.0	4.1	4.2	4.0
Poland	9.6	9.6	10.1	10.3	9.0	7.5	6.2	4.9	4.0	3.5	3.2
Romania	7.0	7.2	6.8	7.1	6.8	6.8	5.9	4.9	4.5	4.4	4.2
Slovakia	14.4	13.6	14.0	14.2	13.2	11.5	9.7	8.1	6.5	5.9	5.7
Slovenia	7.2	8.2	8.8	10.1	9.7	9.0	8.0	6.6	5.4	4.6	4.2
Other Europe	4.4	4.1	4.0	4.3	4.4	4.6	4.8	4.5	4.5	4.4	4.4
Iceland	7.5	7.0	6.0	5.4	4.9	4.0	3.0	2.7	3.1	3.2	3.1
Norway	3.5	3.2	3.1	3.4	3.5	4.3	4.7	4.2	4.3	4.3	4.3
Switzerland	4.8	4.4	4.5	4.7	4.8	4.8	4.9	4.8	4.7	4.5	4.6
Memorandum items:											
North America	9.5	8.8	8.0	7.3	6.2	5.5	5.1	4.6	4.1	3.8	3.9
Developed Asia and Pacific	5.2	4.7	4.5	4.3	4.0	3.9	3.6	3.3	3.2	3.1	3.1
Europe	9.4	9.5	10.2	10.6	10.0	9.2	8.4	7.5	6.9	6.6	6.5
Major developed economies	8.1	7.6	7.3	7.1	6.4	5.8	5.4	5.0	4.6	4.4	4.4
Euro area	10.1	10.1	11.3	11.9	11.6	10.8	10.0	9.1	8.4	8.0	7.8

Sources: UN/DESA, based on data of the United Nations Statistics Division and individual national sources; OECD; Eurostat.

a Unemployment data are standardized by the OECD and Eurostat for comparability among countries and over time, in conformity with the definitions of the International Labour Organization (see OECD, *Standardized Unemployment Rates: Sources and Methods* (Paris, 1985)).

b Data for country groups are weighted averages, where labour force is used for weights.

c Partly estimated.

d Baseline scenario forecasts, based in part on Project LINK and the UN/DESA World Economic Forecasting Model.

Table A.8

Economies in transition and developing economies: unemployment rates,[a] 2010–2018

Percentage of labour force

	2010	2011	2012	2013	2014	2015	2016	2017	2018[b]
South-Eastern Europe[c]									
Albania	14.0	14.0	13.4	15.9	17.5	17.1	15.2	13.7	12.8
Bosnia and Herzegovina	27.2	27.6	28.0	27.5	27.5	27.7	25.4	20.5	19.6
Montenegro	19.7	19.7	19.7	19.5	18.0	17.6	17.7	16.0	15.4
Serbia	19.2	23.0	23.9	22.1	19.2	17.7	15.3	13.5	12.9
The former Yugoslav Republic of Macedonia	32.0	31.4	31.0	29.0	28.0	26.1	23.8	22.4	21.0
Commonwealth of Independent States and Georgia[c, d]									
Armenia	19.0	18.4	17.3	16.2	17.6	18.5	18.0	17.8	17.6
Azerbaijan	5.6	5.4	5.2	5.0	4.9	5.0	5.0	5.0	4.9
Belarus	0.7	0.6	0.5	0.5	0.5	1.0	0.8	0.5	0.5
Georgia[d]	16.3	15.1	15.0	14.6	12.4	12.0	11.8	11.8	11.7
Kazakhstan	5.8	5.4	5.3	5.2	5.0	5.0	5.0	4.9	4.9
Kyrgyzstan	8.6	8.5	8.4	8.3	8.0	7.6	7.2	6.9	6.9
Republic of Moldova	7.4	6.8	5.6	5.2	4.0	5.0	4.2	4.1	4.0
Russian Federation	7.5	6.5	5.5	5.5	5.2	5.6	5.5	5.2	4.9
Tajikistan	2.1	2.3	2.4	2.3	2.4	2.3	2.3	2.3	2.3
Turkmenistan[f]	4.0	3.7	3.7	3.6	3.6	3.6	3.5	3.4	3.3
Ukraine[e]	8.2	8.0	7.6	7.3	9.3	9.1	9.4	9.5	9.3
Uzbekistan	5.4	5.0	4.9	4.9	5.1	5.2	5.2	5.2	5.1
Africa[f]									
Algeria	10.0	10.0	11.0	9.8	10.2	11.2	10.2	12.0	12.3
Botswana	17.9	17.6	17.5	17.7	17.3	17.0	17.1	17.4	17.6
Egypt	8.8	11.8	12.6	13.2	13.1	13.1	12.4	11.8	11.7
Mauritius	7.7	7.5	7.5	7.3	7.5	7.4	6.8	6.8	6.7
Morocco	9.1	8.9	9.0	9.2	9.7	9.5	9.3	9.3	9.3
South Africa	24.9	24.8	24.9	24.7	25.1	25.4	26.7	27.5	29.1
Tunisia	13.0	18.3	17.6	15.9	15.1	15.2	15.5	15.4	15.3
Latin America and the Caribbean[g]									
Argentina	7.7	7.2	7.2	7.1	7.3	6.5	8.5	8.4	9.5
Barbados	10.8	11.2	11.6	11.6	12.3	11.3	9.7	10.0	10.1
Bolivia (Plurinational State of)	4.3	3.8	3.2	4.0	3.5	4.4	4.9	4.6	4.5
Brazil[f]	6.7	6.0	5.5	5.4	4.8	6.8	11.6	12.8	12.5
Chile	8.2	7.1	6.4	5.9	6.4	6.2	6.5	6.7	6.7
Colombia	11.8	10.9	10.4	9.7	9.2	9.0	9.3	9.4	9.7
Costa Rica	7.1	7.7	10.0	9.2	9.6	9.7	9.6	9.0	9.0
Dominican Republic	5.7	6.7	7.2	7.9	7.2	7.9	7.9	6.1	6.0
Ecuador	6.1	5.0	4.2	4.0	4.3	4.7	5.9	5.0	5.5
El Salvador	6.8	6.6	6.2	5.6	6.7	6.5	6.9	6.8	6.9
Guatemala	4.8	3.1	4.0	3.8	4.0	3.2	3.4	3.2	3.2
Honduras	6.4	6.8	5.6	6.0	7.5	8.8	9.0	8.2	8.2
Jamaica	12.4	12.6	9.3	10.3	9.5	9.8	9.0	7.7	7.6
Mexico[h]	5.3	5.2	4.9	4.9	4.8	4.3	3.9	3.4	3.3
Nicaragua	10.5	8.1	8.7	7.7	8.5	7.7	6.3	5.2	6.1

Table A.8
Economies in transition and developing economies: unemployment rates,[a] 2010–2018 (*continued*)

Percentage of labour force

	2010	2011	2012	2013	2014	2015	2016	2017	2018[b]
Latin America and the Caribbean (*continued*)									
Panama	5.8	3.6	3.6	3.7	4.1	4.5	5.2	5.5	5.4
Paraguay	7.4	6.9	7.9	7.7	7.8	6.5	7.7	8.3	8.1
Peru	5.3	5.1	4.7	4.8	4.5	4.4	5.2	5.0	5.0
Trinidad and Tobago	5.9	5.1	5.0	3.7	3.3	3.5	4.0	4.9	5.1
Uruguay	7.5	6.6	6.7	6.7	6.9	7.8	8.2	8.3	8.3
Venezuela (Bolivarian Republic of)	8.7	8.3	8.1	7.8	7.2	7.0	7.3	...	...
Developing Asia[f]									
China	4.1	4.1	4.1	4.1	4.1	3.8	3.9	3.9	3.9
Hong Kong SAR[i]	4.3	3.4	3.3	3.4	3.3	3.3	3.4	3.1	2.8
India	2.4	2.6	2.7	2.7	2.6	2.6	2.5	2.6	2.5
Indonesia	7.3	6.7	6.2	6.0	5.8	6.0	5.7	5.6	5.5
Iran, Islamic Republic of	13.5	12.5	12.6	10.4	10.6	11.1	12.4	12.1	12.1
Israel	6.6	5.6	6.9	6.2	5.9	5.2	4.8	4.2	4.2
Jordan	12.5	12.9	12.2	12.6	11.9	13.1	15.3	15.4	15.4
Korea, Republic of[h]	3.7	3.4	3.2	3.1	3.5	3.6	3.7	3.7	3.7
Malaysia	3.3	3.1	3.0	3.1	2.9	3.1	3.4	3.4	3.4
Pakistan	0.7	0.8	1.8	3.0	1.8	3.6	4.2	4.4	4.5
Philippines	3.6	3.6	3.5	3.5	3.6	3.0	2.7	2.6	2.5
Saudi Arabia	5.6	5.8	5.5	5.6	5.7	5.6	5.7	5.9	5.9
Singapore	4.1	3.9	3.7	3.9	3.7	3.8	4.1	4.3	4.2
Sri Lanka	4.9	4.1	3.9	4.4	4.4	4.7	4.4	4.2	4.2
Taiwan Province of China	5.2	4.4	4.2	4.2	4.0	3.8	3.9	3.8	3.6
Thailand	0.6	0.7	0.6	0.5	0.6	0.6	0.7	0.6	0.4
Turkey[h]	10.7	8.8	8.2	8.7	9.9	10.2	10.8	10.8	10.8
Viet Nam	1.1	1.0	1.0	1.3	1.3	1.9	1.9	1.9	1.8

Sources: UN/DESA, based on data of the United Nations Statistics Division and individual national sources; Economic Commission for Europe, Economic Comission for Latin America and Caribbean; ILO KILM 9th edition; OECD.

a As a percentage of labour force. Reflects national definitions and coverage. Not comparable across economies.

b Partly estimated.

c Sourced from UNECE Statistical Database.

d Georgia officially left the Commonwealth of Independent States on 18 August 2009. However, its performance is discussed in the context of this group of countries for reasons of geographic proximity and similarities in economic structure.

e Starting in 2010, data for the Ukraine excludes the temporarily occupied territory of the Autonomous Republic of Crimea and Sevastopol.

f Sourced from ILO KILM 9th edition.

g Sourced from CEPALSTAT Database, ECLAC.

h Sourced from OECD Short-Term Labour Market Statistics.

i Special Administrative Region of China.

Table A.9

Selected economies: real effective exchange rates, broad measurement,[a, b] 2009–2018

	2009	2010	2011	2012	2013	2014	2015	2016	2017	2018[c]
Developed economies										
Australia	87.5	100.0	106.9	108.5	102.9	98.2	89.6	90.3	93.3	89.5
Bulgaria	103.6	100.0	101.7	100.2	100.8	99.8	96.7	96.8	98.1	101.5
Canada	91.6	100.0	101.6	100.9	97.2	91.4	83.2	81.5	82.8	82.8
Croatia	103.1	100.0	97.3	95.2	96.3	95.5	92.2	92.6	93.5	95.4
Czech Republic	99.7	100.0	101.7	97.7	95.9	90.6	88.0	90.3	94.1	98.8
Denmark	104.4	100.0	99.2	96.5	97.3	98.2	94.7	96.0	96.4	97.9
Euro area	108.9	100.0	99.3	94.4	97.7	98.2	89.8	91.5	92.5	96.8
Hungary	99.3	100.0	99.6	96.8	95.9	92.0	88.0	88.7	90.4	90.2
Japan	99.4	100.0	101.3	100.0	79.7	75.1	70.3	79.7	75.7	75.1
New Zealand	92.1	100.0	103.9	106.5	109.5	113.0	104.7	105.4	107.1	102.8
Norway	96.2	100.0	100.3	99.6	97.9	93.4	85.2	85.6	86.5	86.9
Poland	95.0	100.0	98.2	95.2	96.1	96.6	92.1	88.4	91.4	93.2
Romania	98.9	100.0	102.5	96.3	100.9	101.7	98.0	96.3	95.0	97.7
Sweden	94.4	100.0	105.8	105.1	106.3	100.9	93.9	94.5	93.5	89.9
Switzerland	96.2	100.0	109.5	105.1	103.4	104.5	111.2	108.9	106.5	103.9
United Kingdom	99.5	100.0	100.5	104.5	103.1	110.3	115.5	103.5	98.1	100.3
United States	104.5	100.0	95.0	97.2	97.5	99.7	110.5	114.5	113.7	114.8
Economies in transition										
Russian Federation	91.5	100.0	103.7	104.9	106.7	96.2	77.8	76.5	88.7	82.3
Ukraine[d]	97.3	100.0	100.3	102.9	99.7	78.3	73.7	72.6	76.0	70.6
Developing economies										
Algeria	100.0	100.0	99.2	103.9	101.5	102.8	97.8	96.1	98.0	92.7
Argentina	103.1	100.0	95.2	98.2	90.1	73.9	86.4	70.9	74.3	65.5
Brazil	87.5	100.0	104.6	94.4	90.0	88.9	74.0	78.3	84.6	80.7
Chile	94.3	100.0	100.8	102.8	101.6	92.0	90.2	91.5	94.5	99.7
China	100.7	100.0	102.5	108.7	115.6	118.3	129.8	124.4	120.6	124.5
Colombia	87.6	100.0	98.5	103.9	100.1	95.3	77.8	74.9	76.5	95.1
Hong Kong SAR[e]	104.1	100.0	95.9	99.4	103.1	107.4	118.1	121.5	120.9	118.4
India	89.6	100.0	100.1	93.8	89.4	90.8	97.8	98.8	103.1	99.0
Indonesia	88.5	100.0	100.0	96.3	93.0	87.1	88.9	92.6	94.0	88.2
Iran, Islamic Republic of	97.0	100.0	109.3	122.4	121.6	91.4	103.3	105.9	106.6	67.1
Israel	95.5	100.0	100.8	95.9	102.2	103.3	103.0	104.5	109.3	107.3
Korea, Republic of	92.4	100.0	99.9	99.5	103.9	109.9	111.0	109.2	112.6	114.1
Malaysia	95.0	100.0	99.8	99.6	99.7	99.3	91.6	87.8	86.3	90.1
Mexico	92.8	100.0	99.4	96.4	101.9	101.0	90.9	79.1	80.9	82.7
Morocco	104.1	100.0	97.8	95.9	97.7	97.8	98.1	100.0	99.6	98.5
Nigeria	91.9	100.0	100.4	111.7	119.1	127.6	126.7	116.3	105.5	97.7
Pakistan	95.0	100.0	102.9	104.5	102.4	110.0	120.2	122.9	124.9	121.6

Table A.9
Selected economies: real effective exchange rates, broad measurement,[a, b] 2009–2018 *(continued)*

	2009	2010	2011	2012	2013	2014	2015	2016	2017	2018[c]
Developing economies *(continued)*										
Peru	96.9	100.0	98.2	105.7	104.8	102.8	101.9	99.9	101.3	113.6
Philippines	96.5	100.0	100.4	105.6	109.0	108.5	115.1	110.9	105.8	102.2
Saudi Arabia	99.0	100.0	97.4	100.3	102.9	105.0	114.9	117.8	114.7	113.3
Singapore	96.7	100.0	105.4	110.4	112.5	112.3	110.6	109.7	108.3	107.7
South Africa	86.8	100.0	98.1	92.2	82.0	77.1	75.5	70.1	79.6	81.5
Taiwan Province of China	99.5	100.0	100.2	100.3	101.0	100.2	102.3	102.0	107.4	106.5
Thailand	94.8	100.0	99.1	99.5	104.9	101.9	104.0	100.2	103.5	106.7
Turkey	90.8	100.0	88.4	91.6	90.4	85.4	84.0	82.4	73.4	62.9
United Arab Emirates	104.7	100.0	93.5	95.2	95.4	96.9	108.4	111.1	110.6	110.6
Uruguay	89.3	100.0	102.0	105.2	112.2	110.3	114.4	119.3	127.7	101.3
Venezuela, Bolivarian Republic of	161.2	100.0	117.5	141.9	137.0	208.3	480.9	852.4	1983.0	318.8

Source: Bank for International Settlements, IMF International Financial Statistics..

a Year 2010=100.

b CPI-based indices. The real effective exchange rate gauges the effect on international price competitiveness of the country's manufactures owing to currency changes and inflation differentials. A rise in the index implies a fall in competitiveness and vice versa.

c Average for the first ten months.

d Starting in 2010, data for the Ukraine excludes the temporarily occupied territory of the Autonomous Republic of Crimea and Sevastopol.

e Special Administrative Region of China.

Table A.10
Indices of prices of primary commodities, 2009–2018

Index: Year 2015=100[a]

	Non-fuel commodities								
	Food	Tropical beverages	Vegetable oilseeds and oils	Agricultural raw materials	Minerals and metals	Combined index	Manufactured export prices	Real prices of non-fuel commodities[a]	Crude petroleum[b]
2009	101	92	107	104	101	113	101	112	123.4
2010	111	110	114	144	136	141	102	138	156.5
2011	134	144	133	178	164	181	113	161	217.1
2012	127	112	145	143	153	176	110	160	221.2
2013	119	90	139	130	138	170	112	152	213.9
2014	118	111	134	115	121	157	111	141	194.6
2015	100	100	100	100	100	100	100	100	100.0
2016	104	97	103	99	105	90	99	91	82.4
2017	102	94	100	105	118	106	104	102	105.9
2018	98	87	104	104	121	124	109	114	143.8
2015									
I	110	103	107	104	107	106	101	105	101.6
II	102	101	102	104	105	111	101	110	121.0
III	94	98	97	98	96	97	101	96	97.6
IV	94	97	94	94	92	86	99	87	80.2
2016									
I	95	91	96	92	96	77	98	78	60.9
II	104	94	111	99	102	90	100	90	85.6
III	109	101	111	101	110	94	100	94	86.7
IV	108	101	111	105	112	100	99	101	96.0
2017									
I	108	99	112	114	118	107	100	107	105.0
II	104	93	103	103	113	102	102	99	97.9
III	100	93	102	102	119	103	106	97	101.0
IV	97	90	108	102	120	113	108	105	119.9
2018									
I	102	90	108	106	125	121	109	111	130.8
II	100	90	107	104	122	126	109	116	145.5
III	92	80	97	102	114	126	...	...	149.8

Source: UNCTAD, *Monthly Commodity Price Bulletin*; United Nations, *Monthly Bulletin of Statistics*; and data from the Organization of the Petroleum Exporting Countries (OPEC) website, available from http://www.opec.org.

a Indices rebased to 2015=100 in 2019.

b Combined index of non-fuel commodity prices in dollars, deflated by manufactured export price index.

c The new OPEC reference basket, introduced on 1 January 2017, is a weighted average of 13 crudes.

Table A.11
World oil supply and demand, 2010–2019

	2010	2011	2012	2013	2014	2015	2016	2017	2018[a]	2019[b]
World oil supply[c, d] *(millions of barrels per day)*	85.6	86.9	89.0	89.3	91.7	94.3	94.7	95.5	97.5	98.5
Developed economies	15.9	16.1	17.0	18.1	20.1	21.4	21.0	22.0	24.0	25.4
Economies in transition	13.7	13.7	13.7	13.9	14.0	14.1	14.3	14.4	14.7	15.0
Developing economies	53.8	55.0	56.2	55.1	55.3	56.6	57.1	56.8	56.5	55.7
OPEC	34.7	35.8	37.5	37.7	37.7	39.1	39.6	39.5	39.5	39.2
Non-OPEC	19.1	19.2	18.7	17.4	17.6	17.6	17.5	17.2	16.9	16.5
Processing gains[e]	2.1	2.1	2.1	2.2	2.2	2.2	2.3	2.3	2.3	2.4
Global biofuels[f]	1.8	1.9	1.9	2.0	2.2	2.3	2.4	2.4	2.6	2.8
World total demand[g]	88.5	89.5	90.7	92.0	93.2	95.0	96.1	97.9	99.2	100.5
Oil prices *(dollars per barrel)*										
OPEC basket[h]	77.4	107.5	109.5	105.9	96.3	49.5	40.8	52.4	71.2	...
Brent oil	79.6	110.9	112.0	108.9	98.9	52.3	43.7	54.2	73.1	71.9

Source: UN/DESA, International Energy Agency; U.S. Energy Information Administration; and OPEC.
a Partly estimated.
b Baseline scenario forecasts.
c Including global biofuels, crude oil, condensates, natural gas liquids (NGLs), oil from non-conventional sources and other sources of supply.
d Totals may not add up because of rounding.
e Net volume gains and losses in the refining process (excluding net gain/loss in the economies in transition and China) and marine transportation losses.
f Global biofuels comprise all world biofuel production including fuel ethanol from Brazil and the United States.
g Including deliveries from refineries/primary stocks and marine bunkers, and refinery fuel and non-conventional oils.
h The new OPEC reference basket, introduced on 1 January 2017, is a weighted average of 13 crudes.

Table A.12

World trade:[a] changes in value and volume of exports and imports, by major country group, 2010–2020

Annual percentage change

	2010	2011	2012	2013	2014	2015	2016	2017	2018[b]	2019[c]	2020[c]
Dollar value of exports											
World	19.3	18.7	1.6	2.7	1.9	-10.9	-1.6	10.2	7.8	5.3	7.1
Developed economies	**14.1**	**15.4**	**-1.5**	**3.3**	**3.1**	**-9.6**	**0.2**	**8.2**	**7.5**	**4.4**	**6.7**
North America	17.4	14.3	3.6	3.0	3.8	-6.2	-2.3	6.2	7.2	5.1	6.2
Europe	10.8	16.4	-3.0	5.0	3.1	-10.4	0.6	8.6	7.6	4.2	6.8
Developed Asia and Pacific	31.0	11.6	-2.3	-6.6	1.8	-11.8	3.3	10.4	7.0	3.8	6.9
Economies in transition	**27.6**	**30.3**	**3.2**	**-0.4**	**-5.7**	**-28.6**	**-11.6**	**21.7**	**17.8**	**7.7**	**7.4**
South-Eastern Europe	14.1	21.3	-6.2	15.5	4.0	-10.4	9.4	15.3	11.3	4.6	6.9
Commonwealth of Independent States and Georgia[d]	28.2	30.6	3.6	-0.9	-6.1	-29.3	-12.7	22.1	18.2	7.9	7.5
Developing economies	**26.6**	**22.2**	**5.5**	**2.3**	**1.1**	**-11.1**	**-3.3**	**12.2**	**7.5**	**6.2**	**7.6**
Latin America and the Caribbean	31.3	17.9	1.9	-0.1	-2.2	-10.4	2.2	19.3	4.9	3.3	4.8
Africa	26.7	15.5	7.9	-10.2	-4.1	-26.6	-7.9	15.1	18.7	7.6	8.2
East Asia	27.2	20.7	5.0	5.1	4.1	-6.1	-3.8	10.2	5.4	6.0	8.1
South Asia	25.9	24.1	0.8	3.7	-4.1	-11.6	1.4	13.9	9.1	9.5	7.1
Western Asia	20.0	35.7	11.2	0.7	-2.5	-23.6	-6.5	12.5	14.6	8.0	7.9
Dollar value of imports											
World	18.7	18.9	1.3	2.7	2.2	-7.8	-1.6	9.0	3.2	6.4	7.7
Developed economies	**14.5**	**16.2**	**-1.9**	**1.6**	**2.9**	**-9.9**	**-0.5**	**8.0**	**6.5**	**6.6**	**7.8**
North America	19.7	13.6	3.0	0.1	3.4	-4.3	-2.0	7.0	8.2	6.2	7.5
Europe	11.1	16.2	-5.1	3.6	2.9	-11.2	0.8	8.3	5.4	6.9	8.2
Developed Asia and Pacific	24.0	22.9	5.3	-5.4	1.5	-16.8	-4.5	9.4	8.9	5.9	6.1
Economies in transition	**22.3**	**26.9**	**8.5**	**3.3**	**-9.1**	**-28.2**	**-4.8**	**19.3**	**7.6**	**6.4**	**7.6**
South-Eastern Europe	2.3	20.0	-6.6	4.8	4.1	-14.1	5.4	14.1	8.4	9.8	10.8
Commonwealth of Independent States and Georgia[d]	24.2	27.4	9.6	3.2	-9.9	-29.2	-5.8	19.8	7.5	6.1	7.2
Developing economies	**25.6**	**22.4**	**5.4**	**4.2**	**2.4**	**-3.3**	**-2.8**	**9.7**	**-1.2**	**6.1**	**7.4**
Latin America and the Caribbean	27.6	20.0	5.7	4.9	2.9	35.4	-1.9	3.1	-33.9	5.5	6.8
Africa	11.1	15.4	3.4	5.3	1.5	-15.5	-7.2	8.3	9.8	5.9	7.5
East Asia	31.5	24.3	4.9	4.9	2.9	-10.2	-2.3	12.6	6.9	6.1	7.8
South Asia	21.7	24.8	6.3	-3.3	-3.7	-9.8	-0.4	16.4	11.2	10.6	10.5
Western Asia	13.7	19.9	7.6	5.2	4.0	-7.6	-5.4	5.5	3.2	3.6	3.7
Volume of exports											
World	11.8	6.9	3.3	3.4	4.0	3.0	2.6	5.1	3.9	3.8	3.9
Developed economies	**11.4**	**5.6**	**2.3**	**2.8**	**4.5**	**4.7**	**2.5**	**4.5**	**3.5**	**3.8**	**3.6**
North America	10.8	6.4	3.3	3.3	4.6	1.2	0.1	2.6	4.1	2.8	3.2
Europe	10.4	6.3	2.1	2.8	3.9	6.0	3.2	4.9	3.2	4.1	3.6
Developed Asia and Pacific	18.8	-0.1	1.3	2.0	8.4	3.9	3.0	5.7	4.3	3.6	4.4
Economies in transition	**6.4**	**2.6**	**1.2**	**2.7**	**-0.5**	**1.7**	**2.5**	**5.3**	**3.9**	**3.6**	**3.7**
South-Eastern Europe	15.9	7.1	0.7	12.9	6.2	8.0	11.0	9.6	4.6	4.3	4.2
Commonwealth of Independent States and Georgia[d]	6.1	2.5	1.2	2.4	-0.7	1.4	2.1	5.1	3.9	3.6	3.7

Table A.12
World trade[a]: Changes in value and volume of exports and imports, by major country group, 2010–2020 *(continued)*

Annual percentage change

	2010	2011	2012	2013	2014	2015	2016	2017	2018[b]	2019[c]	2020[c]
Developing economies	**12.9**	**9.0**	**4.8**	**4.0**	**3.8**	**0.9**	**2.8**	**5.8**	**4.3**	**3.8**	**4.2**
Latin America and the Caribbean	9.8	6.5	2.8	1.3	1.3	4.6	1.7	3.3	3.2	3.2	3.3
Africa	10.1	-1.5	7.2	-5.3	0.1	1.4	5.4	6.0	4.1	4.3	4.4
East Asia	16.6	9.7	4.6	6.7	5.8	0.9	1.9	7.2	4.8	3.8	4.5
South Asia	10.6	10.6	0.1	3.6	3.2	-2.4	9.2	6.2	2.5	3.5	3.9
Western Asia	5.8	14.0	8.1	2.2	1.0	-0.6	3.0	2.8	4.3	3.8	4.2
Volume of imports											
World	12.9	7.5	2.8	3.2	3.6	2.5	2.4	5.4	3.8	3.7	3.9
Developed economies	**10.8**	**5.1**	**1.0**	**2.0**	**4.5**	**5.6**	**2.9**	**4.2**	**3.8**	**3.9**	**3.7**
North America	12.9	5.5	2.5	1.2	4.1	4.6	1.4	4.4	4.7	3.4	4.0
Europe	9.6	4.5	-0.4	2.3	4.4	6.9	4.2	4.0	3.3	4.4	3.8
Developed Asia and Pacific	12.2	7.1	5.3	2.1	6.0	1.1	-1.0	4.6	4.4	2.3	2.4
Economies in transition	**16.5**	**15.9**	**9.0**	**2.5**	**-6.4**	**-17.0**	**0.0**	**12.1**	**6.9**	**4.1**	**3.4**
South-Eastern Europe	3.5	6.1	1.0	2.4	6.9	5.2	9.8	8.8	6.7	6.7	6.0
Commonwealth of Independent States and Georgia[d]	17.6	16.6	9.6	2.5	-7.2	-18.6	-0.9	12.4	6.9	3.8	3.1
Developing economies	**16.1**	**10.4**	**4.9**	**4.9**	**3.2**	**-0.1**	**1.9**	**6.9**	**3.6**	**3.3**	**4.1**
Latin America and the Caribbean	20.2	10.5	4.6	2.8	0.0	-2.0	-2.7	5.4	3.3	2.3	3.4
Africa	7.2	2.7	5.9	5.5	0.9	0.8	2.2	5.5	3.2	2.9	3.5
East Asia	19.9	11.4	4.8	7.0	5.0	1.3	3.4	7.6	3.6	3.3	4.5
South Asia	8.3	11.9	2.9	-5.9	-1.8	-5.6	2.4	11.3	8.5	8.6	7.9
Western Asia	8.0	10.2	7.0	6.0	3.5	-1.5	-0.6	2.7	0.5	1.2	0.5

Source: UN/DESA.

a Includes goods and non-factor services.

b Partly estimated.

c Baseline forecast, based in part on Project LINK.

d Georgia officially left the Commonwealth of Independent States on 18 August 2009. However, its performance is discussed in the context of this group of countries for reasons of geographic proximity and similarities in economic structure.

Table A.13

Balance of payments on current accounts, by country or country group, summary table, 2009–2017

Billions of dollars

	2009	2010	2011	2012	2013	2014	2015	2016	2017
Developed economies	-265.3	-194.5	-223.6	-168.7	0.2	-4.7	25.9	70.8	179.4
Japan	145.3	221.0	129.8	59.7	45.9	36.8	136.4	194.9	196.1
United States	-372.5	-431.3	-445.7	-426.8	-348.8	-365.2	-407.8	-432.9	-449.1
Europe[a]	51.6	123.0	193.1	338.4	419.7	418.0	416.0	403.7	522.7
EU-15	13.5	40.8	126.0	236.4	287.8	308.4	308.9	315.8	424.7
EU-13	-42.0	-50.2	-49.0	-29.9	-0.8	-4.0	1.9	9.2	8.6
Economies in transition[b]	35.7	63.0	98.9	59.1	12.3	51.6	48.8	-3.1	18.4
South-Eastern Europe	-7.5	-5.9	-8.4	-8.3	-5.6	-6.1	-4.3	-3.9	-5.1
Commonwealth of Independent States[c]	44.3	70.1	109.2	69.3	18.9	59.4	54.7	2.6	24.8
Developing economies[d]	415.5	435.6	525.7	529.1	390.6	391.3	186.8	200.0	274.5
Net fuel exporters	57.5	194.7	462.3	428.6	360.8	210.6	-178.0	-123.4	4.4
Net fuel importers	358.0	240.9	63.4	100.6	29.8	180.7	364.8	323.4	270.1
Latin America and the Caribbean	-32.2	-95.5	-111.3	-136.8	-163.1	-184.6	-173.4	-94.8	-81.7
Net fuel exporters	1.5	-0.2	-10.6	3.6	2.4	10.8	36.8	17.1	6.5
Net fuel importers	-33.7	-95.3	-100.8	-140.4	-165.5	-195.4	-210.2	-111.9	-88.2
Africa	-41.4	-10.7	-8.9	-45.1	-60.5	-90.8	-144.0	-114.3	-86.4
Net fuel exporters	-6.5	24.9	38.5	30.4	16.4	-20.6	-81.2	-63.2	-36.8
Net fuel importers	-34.9	-35.6	-47.4	-75.5	-76.9	-70.2	-62.8	-51.1	-49.6
Western Asia	37.0	99.5	273.7	338.9	278.7	197.8	-76.5	-89.1	-7.9
Net fuel exporters	50.7	147.5	352.8	401.3	350.5	243.9	-44.7	-51.2	47.2
Net fuel importers	-13.7	-48.0	-79.0	-62.4	-71.9	-46.1	-31.7	-37.9	-55.2
East and South Asia	412.1	393.5	291.9	279.0	300.2	440.9	558.7	479.7	381.3
Net fuel exporters	16.6	26.4	68.6	13.9	8.9	0.6	-14.2	6.7	-0.4
Net fuel importers	395.5	367.1	223.3	265.1	291.3	440.3	572.9	473.0	381.7
World residual[e]	185.9	304.0	401.1	419.5	403.1	438.2	261.5	267.7	472.4

Source: International Monetary Fund (IMF), *World Economic Outlook* database, October 2018.

Note: IMF-WEO has adopted the sixth edition of the Balance of Payments Manual (BPM6).

a Europe consists of the EU-15, the EU-13 and Iceland, Norway and Switzerland (Table A).

b Includes Georgia.

c Excludes Georgia, which left the Commonwealth of Independent States on 18 August 2009.

d Libya has been excluded in the calculation due to unavailability of data.

e Statistical discrepancy.

Table A.14
Balance of payments on current accounts, by country or country group, 2009–2017

Billions of dollars

	2009	2010	2011	2012	2013	2014	2015	2016	2017
Developed economies									
Trade balance	-401.1	-483.8	-665.2	-618.2	-487.8	-533.8	-432.6	-364.5	-426.6
Services, net	285.2	318.4	412.7	425.8	507.0	570.9	517.4	507.8	605.8
Primary income	192.3	321.3	391.2	376.0	356.0	343.8	288.7	284.5	357.5
Secondary income	-341.7	-350.3	-362.2	-351.6	-375.1	-385.4	-347.5	-356.9	-357.1
Current-account balance	-265.3	-194.5	-223.6	-168.7	0.2	-4.7	25.9	70.8	179.4
Japan									
Trade balance	57.8	108.5	-4.5	-53.9	-90.0	-99.9	-7.4	51.4	44.5
Services, net	-34.9	-30.3	-35.0	-47.8	-35.7	-28.8	-16.0	-10.6	-6.5
Primary income	134.6	155.1	183.1	175.6	181.6	184.6	176.2	173.9	177.0
Secondary income	-12.3	-12.4	-13.8	-14.2	-10.0	-19.0	-16.3	-19.8	-18.9
Current-account balance	145.3	221.0	129.8	59.7	45.9	36.8	136.4	194.9	196.1
United States									
Trade balance	-509.7	-648.7	-741.0	-741.1	-700.5	-749.9	-761.9	-751.1	-807.5
Services, net	125.9	153.4	191.3	203.7	239.4	260.3	263.3	249.0	255.2
Primary income	115.2	168.2	211.1	207.5	206.0	218.4	203.6	193.0	221.7
Secondary income	-103.9	-104.3	-107.0	-96.9	-93.6	-94.0	-112.8	-123.9	-118.6
Current-account balance	-372.5	-431.3	-445.7	-426.8	-348.8	-365.2	-407.8	-432.9	-449.1
Europe[a]									
Trade balance	60.9	52.6	55.0	198.4	302.4	308.2	375.8	362.9	345.9
Services, net	209.4	221.1	288.6	307.3	342.7	372.0	296.2	288.2	375.8
Primary income	3.3	77.7	84.7	67.0	39.9	4.3	-41.8	-37.8	16.8
Secondary income	-222.0	-228.4	-235.1	-233.7	-265.5	-266.3	-214.2	-209.5	-215.8
Current-account balance	51.6	123.0	193.1	338.4	419.7	418.0	416.0	403.7	522.7
EU-15									
Trade balance	49.5	16.3	9.9	123.9	202.1	221.0	310.5	311.4	301.6
Services, net	147.1	159.5	220.5	240.4	271.1	295.9	223.2	209.2	284.9
Primary income	30.5	86.0	122.0	95.2	64.3	33.4	-28.0	-12.0	39.7
Secondary income	-213.5	-221.0	-226.4	-222.5	-249.8	-241.8	-196.9	-192.9	-201.5
Current-account balance	13.5	40.8	126.0	236.4	287.8	308.4	308.9	315.8	424.7
EU-13									
Trade balance	-45.7	-47.7	-51.4	-34.8	-14.4	-17.9	-12.5	-8.9	-22.0
Services, net	36.0	36.2	45.1	45.8	53.0	58.5	55.9	66.1	78.2
Primary income	-36.9	-45.7	-49.9	-45.3	-44.5	-47.3	-44.7	-48.4	-51.4
Secondary income	4.5	7.0	7.3	4.5	5.2	2.6	3.2	0.5	3.8
Current-account balance	-42.0	-50.2	-49.0	-29.9	-0.8	-4.0	1.9	9.2	8.6
Economies in transition[b]									
Trade balance	105.8	154.4	221.7	205.9	179.5	203.3	132.4	62.6	96.1
Services, net	-24.5	-31.1	-36.7	-52.7	-61.5	-62.9	-40.7	-24.5	-29.4
Primary income	-58.9	-72.4	-98.5	-103.9	-112.8	-96.4	-53.8	-52.9	-60.4
Secondary income	13.3	12.0	12.4	9.8	7.1	7.6	10.8	11.7	12.1
Current-account balance	35.7	63.0	98.9	59.1	12.3	51.6	48.8	-3.1	18.4

Table A.14
Balance of payments on current accounts, by country or country group, 2009–2017 *(continued)*

Billions of dollars

	2009	2010	2011	2012	2013	2014	2015	2016	2017
Economies in transition[b] *(continued)*									
South-Eastern Europe									
Trade balance	-19.8	-17.6	-20.8	-19.3	-17.2	-18.0	-14.7	-14.2	-16.1
Services, net	2.3	2.5	3.1	2.7	3.2	3.6	3.7	4.3	5.0
Primary income	-0.3	-0.9	-1.1	-1.5	-1.6	-1.7	-1.8	-2.4	-3.2
Secondary income	10.3	10.1	10.4	9.7	10.0	10.0	8.6	8.4	9.3
Current-account balance	-7.5	-5.9	-8.4	-8.3	-5.6	-6.1	-4.3	-3.9	-5.1
Commonwealth of Independent States[c]									
Trade balance	128.0	174.6	246.0	229.4	200.2	225.6	151.1	80.6	116.1
Services, net	-27.1	-34.0	-40.5	-56.5	-66.1	-67.8	-45.9	-30.4	-36.4
Primary income	-58.6	-71.3	-97.0	-102.3	-110.9	-94.5	-51.6	-49.8	-56.4
Secondary income	2.0	0.9	0.7	-1.3	-4.4	-3.9	1.2	2.3	1.5
Current-account balance	44.3	70.1	109.2	69.3	18.9	59.4	54.7	2.6	24.8
Developing economies[d]									
Trade balance	702.1	850.5	1093.9	1103.2	1082.5	1054.8	832.9	798.9	924.2
Services, net	-213.7	-251.1	-304.7	-342.9	-388.3	-492.4	-428.1	-399.6	-445.2
Primary income	-197.9	-288.4	-370.8	-315.0	-371.0	-263.5	-269.4	-260.5	-281.7
Secondary income	125.1	124.5	107.3	83.8	67.2	92.4	51.4	61.2	77.1
Current-account balance	415.5	435.6	525.7	529.1	390.6	391.3	186.8	200.0	274.5
Net fuel exporters									
Trade balance	319.6	517.4	853.9	831.9	780.7	631.0	178.0	181.6	323.6
Services, net	-188.5	-207.1	-239.2	-251.4	-263.1	-281.6	-227.0	-188.2	-196.7
Primary income	-66.6	-95.2	-122.1	-114.3	-111.2	-97.6	-69.7	-56.0	-73.0
Secondary income	-7.0	-20.4	-30.3	-37.6	-45.7	-41.1	-59.3	-60.8	-49.6
Current-account balance	57.5	194.7	462.3	428.6	360.8	210.6	-178.0	-123.4	4.4
Net fuel importers									
Trade balance	382.4	333.1	239.9	271.3	301.8	423.8	654.9	617.3	600.6
Services, net	-25.2	-44.0	-65.5	-91.4	-125.2	-210.8	-201.1	-211.4	-248.5
Primary income	-131.3	-193.1	-248.7	-200.7	-259.8	-165.9	-199.7	-204.5	-208.6
Secondary income	132.1	144.9	137.6	121.4	112.9	133.5	110.7	122.0	126.7
Current-account balance	358.0	240.9	63.4	100.6	29.8	180.7	364.8	323.4	270.1
Latin America and the Caribbean									
Trade balance	50.3	46.0	69.1	41.4	6.8	-13.4	-49.4	8.1	37.0
Services, net	-35.8	-52.7	-71.2	-75.2	-83.1	-80.5	-58.8	-45.9	-49.2
Primary income	-104.9	-151.5	-173.7	-166.6	-151.1	-158.6	-134.9	-133.2	-149.9
Secondary income	58.3	62.6	64.4	63.6	64.3	68.0	69.7	76.2	80.4
Current-account balance	-32.2	-95.5	-111.3	-136.8	-163.1	-184.6	-173.4	-94.8	-81.7
Africa									
Trade balance	-12.5	31.6	60.4	7.2	-4.9	-52.2	-131.6	-111.8	-72.7
Services, net	-42.8	-46.9	-60.6	-55.8	-55.9	-67.4	-45.3	-36.6	-44.0
Primary income	-49.5	-66.3	-85.0	-78.5	-84.2	-71.0	-53.8	-45.4	-59.0

Table A.14
Balance of payments on current accounts, by country or country group, 2009–2017 *(continued)*

Billions of dollars

	2009	2010	2011	2012	2013	2014	2015	2016	2017
Africa *(continued)*									
Secondary income	63.4	70.9	76.3	82.1	84.5	99.7	86.7	79.5	89.3
Current-account balance	-41.4	-10.7	-8.9	-45.1	-60.5	-90.8	-144.0	-114.3	-86.4
Western Asia									
Trade balance	164.4	263.9	459.0	537.9	490.8	421.5	127.6	95.2	167.5
Services, net	-75.3	-90.4	-99.5	-110.0	-116.7	-130.5	-105.4	-89.8	-84.3
Primary income	-11.7	-16.0	-15.5	-8.7	-5.8	1.9	7.2	9.6	8.8
Secondary income	-40.4	-58.0	-70.2	-80.2	-89.7	-95.1	-106.0	-104.1	-100.0
Current-account balance	37.0	99.5	273.7	338.9	278.7	197.8	-76.5	-89.1	-7.9
East Asia									
Trade balance	481.5	478.6	437.3	486.5	556.7	680.8	880.9	786.5	775.5
Services, net	-50.0	-50.5	-64.7	-93.5	-124.4	-207.2	-213.7	-221.4	-259.9
Primary income	-31.9	-54.9	-97.2	-62.2	-131.0	-37.5	-88.3	-92.3	-81.3
Secondary income	43.8	48.7	36.4	17.8	7.6	19.3	0.6	9.1	6.8
Current-account balance	443.3	421.9	311.9	348.6	309.0	455.3	579.5	481.9	441.0
South Asia									
Trade balance	-127.1	-130.5	-161.5	-212.8	-159.7	-173.3	-172.9	-142.6	-209.8
Services, net	23.2	32.1	53.8	53.3	62.2	67.8	63.3	60.4	66.5
Primary income	-14.4	-23.2	-20.9	-27.0	-30.2	-30.7	-32.7	-35.1	-38.7
Secondary income	87.2	93.1	108.6	116.9	118.8	121.8	121.4	115.0	122.4
Current-account balance	-31.2	-28.4	-20.0	-69.6	-8.8	-14.4	-20.8	-2.2	-59.7
World residual[e]									
Trade balance	406.8	521.1	650.3	690.9	774.3	724.3	532.8	497.0	593.8
Services, net	47.0	36.2	71.4	30.3	57.3	15.6	48.6	83.7	131.1
Primary income	-64.5	-39.5	-78.1	-43.0	-127.8	-16.1	-34.5	-28.9	15.5
Secondary income	-203.3	-213.7	-242.4	-258.0	-300.8	-285.5	-285.2	-283.9	-267.9
Current-account balance	185.9	304.0	401.1	419.5	403.1	438.2	261.5	267.7	472.4

Source: International Monetary Fund (IMF), *World Economic Outlook* database, October 2018.
Note: IMF-WEO has adopted the sixth edition of the Balance of Payments Manual (BPM6).
a Europe consists of the EU-15, the EU-13 and Iceland, Norway and Switzerland (Table A).
b Includes Georgia.
c Excludes Georgia, which left the Commonwealth of Independent States on 18 August 2009.
d Libya has been excluded in the calculation due to unavailability of data.
e Statistical discrepancy.

Table A.15
Net ODA from major sources, by type, 1996–2017

Donor group or country	Growth rate of ODA (2015 prices and exchange rates)					ODA as a percentage of GNI	Total ODA (millions of dollars)	Percentage distribution of ODA by type, 2017			
								Bilateral	Multilateral		
	1996–2006	2006–2014	2015	2016	2017	2017	2017	Total	Total (United Nations & Other)	United Nations	Other
Total DAC countries	5.1	1.5	6.1	10.6	-0.5	0.31	146646	71.5	28.5	4.9	23.6
Total EU	4.8	1.2	12.5	14.4	-1.1	0.49	82718	64.8	35.2	5.2	30.0
Austria	9.9	-4.8	25.3	22.6	-26.1	0.30	1251	48.0	52.0	2.0	50.0
Belgium	6.6	0.4	-7.9	19.3	-8.2	0.45	2204	57.9	42.1	7.5	34.6
Denmark	0.5	1.1	1.5	-7.5	-2.3	0.72	2401	69.7	30.3	10.7	19.6
Finland	6.2	5.7	-7.6	-18.2	-3.3	0.41	1054	49.3	50.7	11.6	39.1
France[a]	2.2	-1.8	0.7	6.4	14.9	0.43	11363	57.5	42.5	6.9	35.5
Germany	2.9	3.7	27.0	36.5	-3.6	0.66	24681	78.8	21.2	2.0	19.2
Greece	7.4	-8.0	16.6	56.4	-16.6	0.16	314	27.0	73.0	4.3	68.7
Ireland	14.2	-2.8	-1.9	12.0	-2.4	0.30	808	57.3	42.7	9.9	32.8
Italy	1.7	-1.0	18.4	26.5	10.2	0.29	5734	50.4	49.6	4.3	45.3
Luxembourg	11.2	1.4	1.2	9.5	4.3	1.00	424	71.7	28.3	10.2	18.1
Netherlands	3.1	-1.5	21.9	-13.5	-2.9	0.60	4955	71.3	28.7	10.0	18.7
Portugal	3.0	-0.8	-16.1	10.2	6.9	0.18	378	29.6	70.4	3.3	67.1
Spain	8.5	-9.8	-11.5	202.5	-44.3	0.19	2415	33.7	66.3	3.4	63.0
Sweden	6.6	3.0	36.9	-31.0	9.9	1.01	5512	68.3	31.7	12.2	19.5
United Kingdom	10.6	5.0	3.3	8.0	2.1	0.70	17940	62.4	37.6	4.3	33.2
Australia	4.3	4.2	-3.7	-6.4	-15.8	0.23	2957	80.0	20.0	4.6	15.4
Canada	3.2	-0.5	17.6	-5.3	4.7	0.26	4305	72.6	27.4	5.3	22.1
Japan	3.3	-2.5	8.7	1.5	13.9	0.23	11475	70.4	29.6	4.1	25.5
New Zealand	6.4	2.9	3.7	-0.4	-6.7	0.23	436	81.9	18.1	10.3	7.8
Norway	3.3	3.4	10.8	7.9	-10.0	0.99	4123	75.8	24.2	10.2	14.0
Switzerland	4.4	5.1	6.0	4.5	-13.9	0.46	3097	73.9	26.1	7.7	18.4
United States	7.3	2.6	-7.4	9.7	0.6	0.18	35261	85.9	14.1	3.4	10.7

Source: UN/DESA, based on OECD/DAC online database, available from http://www.oecd-ilibrary.org/statistics.

a Excluding flows from France to the Overseas Departments, namely Guadeloupe, French Guiana, Martinique and Réunion.

Table A.16
Total net ODA flows from OECD/DAC, by type, 2008–2017

	Net disbursements at current prices and exchange rates (billions of dollars)									
	2008	2009	2010	2011	2012	2013	2014	2015	2016	2017
Official Development Assistance	122.9	120.7	128.5	135.1	127.0	134.8	137.5	131.6	144.9	146.6
Bilateral official development assistance	87.1	84.0	90.6	94.8	88.5	93.5	94.8	94.2	103.1	104.9
in the form of:										
Technical cooperation	17.3	17.6	18.6	18.0	18.2	16.9	17.3	14.9	15.7	...
Humanitarian aid	8.8	8.6	9.3	9.7	8.5	10.5	13.1	13.4	14.4	...
Debt forgiveness	11.1	2.0	4.2	6.3	3.3	6.1	1.4	0.3	2.1	...
Bilateral loans	-1.1	2.5	3.8	1.9	2.6	1.4	5.3	6.0	5.8	...
Contributions to multilateral institutions[a]	35.8	36.7	37.8	40.3	38.6	41.4	42.7	37.3	41.8	41.7
of which are:										
UN agencies	5.9	6.2	6.5	6.5	6.6	6.9	6.8	6.1	5.9	7.2
EU institutions	13.6	14.3	13.7	13.8	12.0	12.8	13.3	11.9	13.8	14.0
World Bank	8.6	7.6	8.8	10.2	8.6	9.4	9.8	8.6	8.8	8.0
Regional development banks	3.2	3.1	3.2	4.1	3.9	3.9	4.0	3.2	4.6	4.2
Others	3.8	4.8	4.9	4.4	6.4	7.2	7.5	6.7	7.8	...
Memorandum item										
Bilateral ODA to least developed countries	23.5	24.3	28.2	30.7	27.4	30.0	26.4	25.0	24.6	...

Source: UN/DESA, based on OECD/DAC online database, available from http://www.oecd.org/dac/stats/idsonline.

a Grants and capital subscriptions. Does not include concessional lending to multilateral agencies.

Table A.17
Commitments and net flows of financial resources, by selected multilateral institutions, 2008–2017

Billions of dollars

	2008	2009	2010	2011	2012	2013	2014	2015	2016	2017
Resource commitments[a]	135.2	193.7	245.4	163.8	189.8	130.8	185.0	119.9	245.4	256.7
Financial institutions, excluding International Monetary Fund (IMF)	76.1	114.5	119.6	106.8	96.5	98.8	99.2	99.9	106.9	108.0
Regional development banks[b]	36.7	55.1	46.2	46.9	43.0	45.8	41.1	46.9	49.8	54.0
World Bank Group[c]	39.4	59.4	73.4	59.9	53.5	53.0	58.1	53.0	57.0	54.0
International Bank for Reconstruction and Development (IBRD)	13.5	32.9	44.2	26.7	20.6	15.2	18.6	23.5	29.7	22.6
International Development Association (IDA)	11.2	14.0	14.6	16.3	14.8	16.3	22.2	19.0	16.2	19.5
International Financial Corporation (IFC)[d]	14.6	12.4	14.6	16.9	9.2	11.0	10.0	10.5	11.1	11.9
International Fund for Agricultural Development (IFAD)	0.6	0.7	0.8	1.0	1.0	0.8	0.7	1.3	0.8	1.3
International Monetary Fund (IMF)	48.7	68.2	114.1	45.7	82.5	19.6	72.7	6.2	123.9	132.9
United Nations operational agencies[e]	10.5	11.0	11.6	11.3	10.8	12.4	13.1	13.7	14.7	15.8
Net flows	43.4	54.6	64.6	78.7	35.1	8.8	-5.1	17.7	32.2	36.3
Financial institutions, excluding IMF	24.5	22.6	27.2	38.0	26.3	22.2	25.0	35.5	33.8	36.6
Regional development banks[b]	21.4	15.7	9.9	10.5	8.6	5.7	11.2	15.4	14.2	13.1
World Bank Group[c]	3.1	6.9	17.2	27.6	17.7	16.5	13.8	20.1	19.6	23.6
International Bank for Reconstruction and Development (IBRD)	-6.2	-2.1	8.3	17.2	8.0	7.8	6.4	9.0	10.0	13.2
International Development Association (IDA)	6.8	7.0	7.0	9.1	7.8	7.0	7.4	9.9	8.8	8.8
International Financial Corporation (IFC)	2.4	2.1	1.9	1.2	1.9	1.6	0.1	1.3	0.8	1.6
International Fund for Agricultural Development (IFAD)	0.2	0.2	0.2	0.3	0.3	0.2	0.2	0.2	0.2	0.3
International Monetary Fund (IMF)	18.9	32.0	37.4	40.7	8.9	-13.4	-30.1	-17.9	-1.5	-0.4

Source: Annual reports of the relevant multilateral institutions, various issues.

a Loans, grants, technical assistance and equity participation, as appropriate; all data are on a calendar-year basis.

b African Development Bank (AfDB), Asian Development Bank (ADB), Caribbean Development Bank (CDB), European Bank for Reconstruction and Development (EBRD), Inter-American Development Bank (IaDB) and the International Fund for Agricultural Development (IFAD).

c Data is for fiscal year.

d Effective 2012, data does not include short-term finance.

e United Nations Development Programme (UNDP), United Nations Population Fund (UNFPA), United Nations Children's Fund (UNICEF), and the World Food Programme (WFP).

Bibliography

A

Adrian, Tobias, Fabio Natalucci and Thomas Piontek (2018). Sounding the alarm on leveraged lending. IMF Blog. 15 November. Available from https://blogs.imf.org/2018/11/15/sounding-the-alarm-on-leveraged-lending/.

Afonso, Helena, and Dawn Holland (2018). Trade policy and the United States labour market. *Journal of Policy Modelling*, vol. 40, pp. 601–613.

Albagli, Elias, Luis Ceballos, Sebastian Claro, and Damian Romero (2018). Channels of US monetary policy spillovers to international bond markets. BIS Working Papers, No 719. Bank for International Settlements. Basel, Switzerland. May.

Alliance for Financial Inclusion (2015). Current State of Practice 2015–National Financial Inclusion Strategies.

Alschner, Wolfgang, J. Seiermann and D. Skougarevskiy (2017). Text-as-data analysis of preferential trade agreements: Mapping the PTA landscape. UNCTAD Research Paper No.5 (UNCTAD/SER.RP/2017/5). Geneva. July.

The American Chamber of Commerce in the People's Republic of China (AmCham China) (2018). Impact of U.S. and Chinese tariffs on American companies in China. Available from https://www.amchamchina.org/uploads/media/default/0001/09/7d5a70bf034247cddac45bdc90e89eb77a580652.pdf.

Antimiani, Alessandro, and Lucian Cernat (2017). Liberalizing global trade in mode 5 services: how much is it worth? Chief Economist Note, DG Trade, Issue 4 (July). European Commission.

Arias, Maria A., and Yi Wen (2015). Trapped: Few developing countries can climb the economic ladder or stay there. Regional Economist. Federal Reserve Bank of St. Louis. October.

Atkinson, Anthony B. (2007). The distribution of earnings in OECD countries. International Labour Review, vol. 146, Issue 1–2 (March–June 2007), pp. 41–60.

Ayyagari, Meghana, Thorsten Beck and Maria Soledad Martinez Peria (2017). Credit growth and macroprudential policies: preliminary evidence on the firm level. BIS Papers, No. 91. Bank for International Settlements. Basel, Switzerland. March.

B

Bank for International Settlements (2018). Statistical release: BIS international banking statistics at end-June 2018. Available from https://www.bis.org/statistics/rppb1810.pdf.

Barattieri, Alessandro, Matteo Cacciatore, and Fabio Ghironi (2018). Protectionism and the Business Cycle, NBER Working Paper No. 24353, February. National Bureau for Economic Research. Cambridge, Massachusetts.

Barrell, Ray, Dilly Karim and Corrado Macchiarelli (2018). Towards an understanding of credit cycles: do all credit booms cause crises? *The European Journal of Finance*. DOI: 10.1080/1351847X.2018.152341.

Barrow, Jennifer (2017). Addressing the challenge of climate change adaptation and resilience building for key international transportation assets: perspectives. Presentation delivered at the UNCTAD Regional Workshop "Climate Change Impacts and Adaptation for Coastal Transport Infrastructure in the Caribbean", held in Bridgetown, Barbados on 5–7 December 2017. Available from https://sidsport-climateadapt.unctad.org/wp-content/uploads/2018/03/JBarrow_CTO_BBWorkshop_p017_en.pdf.

Batten, Sandra, Rhiannon Sowerbutts and Misa Tanaka (2016). Let's talk about the weather: The impact of climate change on central banks. Bank of England Working Paper No. 603. London. May.

Beck, T., A. Demirgüç-Kunt and R. Levine (2007). Finance, inequality and the poor. *Journal of Economic Growth* 12, pp. 27–49.

Berkes, Enrico, Ugo Panizza and Jean-Louis Arcand (2012). Too much finance? IMF Working Papers, No 12/161. Washington, D. C.

Bernard, Andrew B., Bradford J. Jensen, Stephen J. Redding and Peter K. Schott (2018). Global Firms. *Journal of Economic Literature*, vol. 56, No. 2, pp. 565–619.

Bleaney, Michael, and Havard Halland (2014). Natural Resource Exports, Fiscal Policy Volatility and Growth. *Scottish Journal of Political Economy*, vol.61, Issue 5, pp. 502–522.

Bloomberg New Energy Finance (2018). Electric Vehicle Outlook 2018.

Bollen, Johannes, and Hugo Rojas-Romagosa (2018). Trade Wars: Economic impacts of US tariff increases and retaliations, an international perspective. CPB Background Document, July.

Bonnet, Florence (forthcoming). Facts on business informality.

Buch, Claudia M., Matthieu Bussière, Linda Goldberg and Robert Hills (2018). The International Transmission of Monetary Policy. *Federal Reserve Bank of New York Staff Reports*, No. 845. March.

Bueno, Ramón, et al. (2008). The Caribbean and climate change: the costs of inaction. Stockholm Environment Institute—US Center and Global Development and Environment Institute, Tufts University. May.

Burke, Marshall, W. Matthew Davis, and Noah S. Diffenbaugh (2018). Large potential reduction in economic damages under UN mitigation targets. *Nature*, Issue 557, pp. 549–553. 23 May.

C

Ciccone, Antonio, and Marek Jarocinski (2008). Determinants of economic growth: Will data tell? European Central Bank Working Paper, No. 852. January.

Čihák, Martin, Aslı Demirgüç-Kunt, Erik Feyen, and Ross Levine (2012). Benchmarking financial development around the world. World Bank Policy Research Working Paper 6175. Washington, D. C.

Citigroup Global Markets (2011). Global Economic View: Global Growth Generators: Moving beyond 'Emerging Markets' and 'BRIC'. 21 February.

Claessens, Stijn, and M. Ayhan Kose (2018). Frontiers of macrofinancial linkages. BIS papers, No. 95. Bank for International Settlements. Basel, Switzerland.

Collier, Paul (2007). *The Bottom Billion: Why the Poorest Countries are Failing and What Can Be Done About It.* Oxford University Press.

Collier, Paul, and Anke Hoeffler (2004). Greed and grievance in civil war. *Oxford Economic Papers*, No. 56, pp. 563–595.

D

de Zamaróczy, Mario, Vincent Fleuriet and José Gijón (2018). Central African Economic and Monetary Community: a new medium-term approach for international reserve management. International Monetary Fund. African Department Paper Series No. 18/15.

Demirgüç-Kunt, Asli, Leora Klapper, Dorothe Singer, Saniya Ansar, and Jake Hess (2018). The Global Findex Database 2017: Measuring Financial Inclusion and the Fintech Revolution. World Bank, Washington, D. C.

Durlauf, Steven N. (2009). The Rise and Fall of Cross-Country Growth Regressions. *History of Political Economy 41* (annual suppl.), pp. 315-333. Duke University Press.

E

Easterly, William, Roumeen Islam and Joseph Stiglitz (2000). Shaken and stirred: Explaining growth volatility. World Bank Discussion Paper. Washington, D. C.

Edwards, Sebastian (1994). Real and monetary determinants of real exchange rate behaviour: theory and evidence from developing countries. In *Estimating Equilibrium Exchange Rates*, J. Williamson, ed. Institute for International Economics: Washington, D. C.

European Commission (2018a). WTO-EU's proposals on WTO modernisation. WK 8329/2018 INIT. Brussels. 5 July.

European Commission (2018b). A credible enlargement perspective for and enhanced EU engagement with the Western Balkans. Communication to the European Parliament, the Council, the European Economic and Social Committee and the Committee of the Regions. Strasbourg.

European Parliament (2015). Labour market shortages in the European Union, Study conducted by the Policy Department A to the Committee on Employment and Social Affairs, March. Available from http://www.europarl.europa.eu/RegData/etudes/STUD/2015/542202/IPOL_STU%282015%29542202_EN.pdf.

G

Gaspar, Vitor, Laura Jaramillo and Philippe Wingender (2016). Tax capacity and growth: Is there a tipping point? IMF Working Paper 16/234. Washington, D.C.

Goel, Tirupam (2018). The rise of leveraged loans: a risky resurgence? BIS Quarterly Review. September.

Goldberg, Pinelopi K., and Nina Pavcnik (2016). The effects of trade policy. NBER Working Papers, No. 21957. National Bureau of Economic Research. Cambridge, Massachusetts.

Government of the Commonwealth of Dominica (2017). Post-Disaster Needs Assessment Hurricane Maria, September 18, 2017. A report of the Government of the Commonwealth of Dominica. Available from https://reliefweb.int/sites/reliefweb.int/files/resources/dominica-pdna-maria.pdf.

Grömping, Ulrike (2006). Relative importance for linear regression in R: the package relaimpo, *Journal of Statistical Software*, vol. 17, Issue 1.

H

Herring, S. C., N. Christidis, A. Hoell, J. P. Kossin, C. J. Schreck III, and P. A. Stott, eds. (2018). Explaining extreme events of 2016 from a climate perspective. *Bulletin of the American Meteorological Society*, vol. 99, No. 1, January. Special Supplement.

Hsiang, Solomon, et al. (2017). Estimating economic damage from climate change in the United States. *Science*, vol. 356, Issue 6345, pp. 1362–1369. doi:10.1126/science.aal4369.

Huang, Yi, Chen Lin, Sibo Liu and Tang Heiwai (2018). Trade linkages and firm value: Evidence from the 2018 US-China 'Trade War'. August. Available from https://voxeu.org/article/economic-costs-us-china-trade-war

Humphreys, Macartan (2003). Economics and violent conflict. Available from https://www.unicef.org/socialpolicy/files/Economics_and_Violent_Conflict.pdf.

I

Infante, Ricardo (2018). Crecimiento, cambio estructural y formalización. In *Políticas de Formalización en América Latina: Avances y Desafíos*, José Manuel Salazar-Xirinachs and Juan Chacaltana, eds. Organización Internacional del Trabajo, Oficina Regional para América Latina y el Caribe, FORLAC. Perú.

Institute of International Finance (2018). Capital Flows to Emerging Markets Report. October.

Inter-American Development Bank (2016). Social pulse in Latin American and Caribbean 2016: Realities and perspectives. Washington, D. C.

Intergovernmental Forum on Mining, Minerals, Metals and Sustainable Development (2018). Case study Botswana: Downstream linkages. Available from https://www.iisd.org/sites/default/files/publications/case-study-botswana-downstream-linkages.pdf

Intergovernmental Panel on Climate Change (IPCC) (2013). Summary for Policymakers. In *Climate Change 2013: The Physical Science Basis. Contribution of Working Group I to the Fifth Assessment Report of the Intergovernmental Panel on Climate Change.* Stocker, T.F., D. Qin, G.-K. Plattner, M. Tignor, S.K. Allen, J. Boschung, A. Nauels, Y. Xia, V. Bex and P.M. Midgley (eds.). Cambridge University Press, Cambridge, United Kingdom and New York, NY, USA.

Intergovernmental Panel on Climate Change (IPCC) (2014a). *Climate Change 2014: Impacts, Adaptation, and Vulnerability. Part A: Global and Sectoral Aspects.* Contribution of Working Group II to the Fifth Assessment Report of the Intergovernmental Panel on Climate Change, C.B. Field, et al., eds. Cambridge, United Kingdom: Cambridge University Press. Available from https://www.ipcc.ch/report/ar5/wg2/.

Intergovernmental Panel on Climate Change (IPCC) (2014b). *Climate Change 2014: Synthesis Report.* Contribution of Working Groups I, II and III to the Fifth Assessment Report of the Intergovernmental Panel on Climate Change, Rajendra K. Pachauri and Leo Meyer, eds. Geneva. Available from https://www.ipcc.ch/report/ar5/syr/.

Intergovernmental Panel on Climate Change (IPCC) (2018). *Global Warming of 1.5°C.* An IPCC Special Report on the impacts of global warming of 1.5°C above pre-industrial levels and related global greenhouse gas emission pathways, in the context of strengthening the global response to the threat of climate change, sustainable development, and efforts to eradicate poverty. V. Masson-Delmotte, P. Zhai, H. O. Pörtner, D. Roberts, J. Skea, P.R. Shukla, A. Pirani, W. Moufouma-Okia, C. Péan, R. Pidcock, S. Connors, J. B. R. Matthews, Y. Chen, X. Zhou, M. I. Gomis, E. Lonnoy, T. Maycock, M. Tignor, T. Waterfield (eds.). Chapter 3: Impacts of 1.5°C global warming on natural and human systems. Available from http://ipcc.ch/report/sr15/.

Internal Displacement Monitoring Centre (2018). Global Report on Internal Displacement. May.

International Air Transport Association (2017). Assessment of Hurricane Irma and Maria's impacts on aviation. IATA Economics, November. Available from https://www.iata.org/publications/economic-briefings/Impact-of-Hurricanes-Irma-and-Maria.pdf.

International Energy Agency (IEA) (2018). CO_2 Emissions from Fuel Combustion 2018: Overview. Paris.

International Labour Organization (ILO) (2015). Recommendation No. 204 concerning the Transition from the Informal to the Formal Economy. Text of the Recommendation adopted by the Conference at its 104th Session in Geneva, on 12 June. Available from https://www.ilo.org/ilc/ILCSessions/104/texts-adopted/WCMS_377774/lang--en/index.htm.

International Labour Organization (ILO) (2018). *Women and Men in the Informal Economy: A Statistical Picture*, Third edition. Geneva. Available from https://www.ilo.org/wcmsp5/groups/public/---dgreports/---dcomm/documents/publication/wcms_626831.pdf.

International Monetary Fund (IMF) (2016). Nigeria. IMF Country Report No. 16/101. April.

International Monetary Fund (IMF) (2017). Annual report on exchange arrangements and exchange restrictions. October. Washington, D. C.

International Monetary Fund (IMF) (2018a). Global Financial Stability Report. October.

International Monetary Fund (IMF) (2018b). Macroeconomic developments and prospects in low-income developing countries 2018. IMF Policy Paper. March.

International Monetary Fund (IMF) (2018c). Nigeria. IMF Country Report No. 18/63. March.

International Monetary Fund (IMF) (2018d). Central African Economic and Monetary Community (CEMAC). Staff report on the common policies in support of member countries reform programs. IMF Country Report No. 18/210. July.

International Monetary Fund (IMF), World Bank and World Trade Organization (WTO) (2017). Making trade an engine of growth for all: the case for trade and for policies to facilitate adjustment. Available from https://www.imf.org/en/Publications/Policy-Papers/Issues/2017/04/08/making-trade-an-engine-of-growth-for-all.

J

Jessen, Jonas, and Jochen Kluve (2018). Evaluación de impacto (A systematic review of impact evaluations of formalisation policies). In *Políticas de Formalización en América Latina: Avances y Desafíos*, José Manuel Salazar-Xirinachs and Juan Chacaltana, eds. Organización Internacional del Trabajo, Oficina Regional para América Latina y el Caribe, FORLAC. Perú.

Jordà, Òscar, Moritz Schularick and Alan M Taylor (2011). Financial crises, credit booms, and external imbalances: 140 years of lessons. IMF Economic Review, vol. 59, No. 2, p. 340.

K

Koepke, Robin (2016). Determinants of emerging market crises: The role of U.S. monetary policy. IIF Research Note. July. International Institute of Finance. Washington, D. C.

Kumhof, Michael, Romain Rancière and Pablo Winant (2015). Inequality, leverage, and crises. *The American Economic Review*, vol. 105, No. 3 (March), pp. 1217–1245.

L

Levine, Ross (2005). Finance and growth: Theory and evidence. In *Handbook of Economic Growth*, Philippe Aghion and Steven Durlauf, eds., edition 1, vol. 1, chap. 12, pp. 865–934.

Lustig, Nora (2017). Fiscal policy, income redistribution, and poverty reduction in low- and middle-income countries. Center for Global Development Working Paper, No. 448. London and Washington, D. C. January.

M

Mehlum, Halvor, Karl Moene and Ragnar Torvik (2006). Institutions and the resource curse. *The Economic Journal*, vol. 116, Issue 508, pp. 1–20.

Monioudi, Isavela N., et al. (2018). Climate change impacts on critical international transportation assets of Caribbean Small Island Developing States (SIDS): the case of Jamaica and Saint Lucia. *Regional Environmental Change*, vol. 18, Issue 8, pp. 2211–2225 (December). Available form https://rdcu.be/Q1OY.

Mortimore, Michael, and Sebastian Vergara (2004). Targeting winners: Can foreign direct investment policy help developing countries industrialise? *The European Journal of Development Research*, September 2004, vol. 16, Issue 3, pp. 499–530.

MunichRe (2018). Hurricanes cause record losses in 2017: The year in figures. Available from https://www.munichre.com/topics-online/en/2018/01/2017-year-in-figures.

N

Nicita, Alessandro, and Julia Seiermann (2016). G20 policies and export performance of least developed countries. Policy Issues in International Trade and Commodities, Study Series No. 75, UNCTAD/ITCD/TAB/77. Available from https://unctad.org/en/pages/PublicationWebflyer.aspx?publicationid=1684.

O

Organisation for Economic Co-operation and Development (2018). *Development Co-operation Report 2018: Joining Forces to Leave No One Behind*. Paris.

P

Pfeffer, Fabian T., Sheldon Danziger and Robert F. Schoeni (2013). Wealth disparities before and after the great recession. *Annals of the American Academy of Political and Social Science*, vol. 650, Issue 1, pp, 98–122.

R

Rodríguez-Pose, Andrés and Daniel Hardy (2015). Addressing poverty and inequality in the rural economy from a global perspective. Applied Geography, vol. 61, pp. 11–23.

S

Sahay, R., Cihak, M., N'Diaye, P., Barajas, A., Ayala Pena, D., Bi, R. and R. Yousefi. (2015). Rethinking financial deepening: Stability and growth in emerging markets. IMF Staff Discussion Notes, 15(8). Washington, D. C.

Salazar-Xirinachs, José Manuel, and Juan Chacaltana (2018). La informalidad en América Latina y el Caribe: ¿por qué persiste y cómo superarla? In *Políticas de Formalización en América Latina: Avances y Desafíos*, José Manuel Salazar-Xirinachs and Juan Chacaltana, eds. Organización Internacional del Trabajo, Oficina Regional para América Latina y el Caribe, FORLAC. Perú.

Saxena, Sweta (2018). Economic Prospects: East and South Asia. Presentation at LINK Meeting, September 7th, ECLAC, Santiago, Chile.

Saygili, Mesut, Ralf Peters and Christian Knebel (2018). African Continental Free Trade Area: Challenges and opportunities of tariff reductions. UNCTAD Research Paper, No. 15. Geneva. February.

Scott, D. and S. Gössling (2018). Tourism and climate change mitigation: Embracing the Paris Agreement: Pathways to decarbonisation. European Travel Commission.

Scott, D., and S. Verkoeyen (2017). Assessing the climate change risk of a coastal-island destination. In *Global Climate Change and Coastal Tourism*, Jones, A. and M. Phillips, eds. CAB International.

Seiermann, Julia (forthcoming). Only words? How power in trade agreement texts affects international trade flows. UNCTAD Research Paper.

Shim, Ilhyock, and Kwanho Shin (2018). Financial stress in lender countries and capital outflows from emerging market economies. BIS Working Papers, No. 745. Bank for International Settlements, Basel, Switzerland. September.

Stiglitz, Joseph E. (2002). *Globalization and Its Discontents*. W.W Norton and Company, Inc.

T

Taylor, Michael A., et al. (2018). Future Caribbean climates in a world of rising temperatures: The 1.5 vs 2.0 dilemma. *Journal of Climate*, vol. 31, No. 7 (April).

Tobin, J. (1984). On the efficiency of the financial system. *Lloyds Bank Review* 153, pp. 1–15.

Transparency International (2017). Corruption Perceptions Index 2017. Available from https://www.transparency.org/news/feature/corruption_perceptions_index_2017.

U

U.S. Geological Survey (2018). Mineral Commodity Summaries: Cobalt. January.

United Nations (2015). Addis Ababa Action Agenda of the Third International Conference on Financing for Development (Addis Ababa Action Agenda). The final text of the outcome document adopted at the Third Internatinal Conference on Financing for Development (Addis Ababa, Ethiopia, 13–16 July 2015) and endorsed by the General Assembly in its resolution 69/313 of 27 July 2015.

United Nations (2016). *World Economic Situation and Prospects 2016*. Sales No. E.16. II.C.2.

United Nations (2018a). *Financing for Development: Progress and Prospects 2018*. Report of the Inter-agency Task Force on Financing for Development 2018. Sales No. E.18.I.5

United Nations (2018b). *The Sustainable Development Goals Report 2018*. Sales No. E.18.I.6.

United Nations and World Bank (2018). *Pathways for Peace: Inclusive Approaches to Preventing Violent Conflict*. Washington, DC: World Bank.

United Nations Conference on Trade and Development (UNCTAD) (2013). *World Investment Report 2013: Global Value Chains: Investment and Trade for Development*. Sales No. E.13.II.D.5.

United Nations Conference on Trade and Development (UNCTAD) (2014). Small island developing States: Challenges in transport and trade logistics. Note by the UNCTAD secretariat. Available from https://unctad.org/meetings/en/SessionalDocuments/cimem7d8_en.pdf.

United Nations Conference on Trade and Development (UNCTAD) (2016). *State of Commodity Dependence Report*. Sales No. E.17.II.D.9.

United Nations Conference on Trade and Development (UNCTAD) (2017a). *Services and Structural Transformation for Development*. UNCTAD/DITC/TNCD/2017/2. Geneva.

United Nations Conference on Trade and Development (UNCTAD) (2017b). Climate Change Impacts on Coastal Transportation Infrastructure in the Caribbean: Enhancing the Adaptive Capacity of Small Island Developing States (SIDS). Saint Lucia: a case study. UNDA 1415O. Available from https://SIDSport-climateadapt.unctad.org.

United Nations Conference on Trade and Development (UNCTAD) (2017c). Port Industry Survey on Climate Change Impacts and Adaptation. UNCTAD Research Paper No. 18. UNCTAD/SER.RP/2017/18. Available from https://unctad.org/en/pages/PublicationWebflyer.aspx?publicationid=1964.

United Nations Conference on Trade and Development (UNCTAD) (2017d). *Least Developed Countries Report*. Geneva.

United Nations Conference on Trade and Development (UNCTAD) (2017e). *Commodities and Development Report 2017: Commodity Markets, Economic Growth and Development*. Sales No. E.17.II.D.1. Geneva.

United Nations Conference on Trade and Development (UNCTAD) (2017f). *Trade and Development Report 2017: Beyond austerity: Towards a global new deal.* Sales No. E.17.II.D.5.

United Nations Conference on Trade and Development (UNCTAD) (2018a). *Trade and Development Report 2018: Power, Platforms and The Free Trade Delusion.* Sales No. E.18.II.D.7

United Nations Conference on Trade and Development (UNCTAD) (2018b). Investment Trends Monitor. Issue 30. October.

United Nations Conference on Trade and Development (UNCTAD) (2018c). *World Investment Report 2018: Investment and Industrial Policies.* Sales No. E.18. II.D4.

United Nations Conference on Trade and Development (UNCTAD) (2018d). The African Continental Free Trade Area: The Day After the Kigali Summit. UNCTAD Policy Brief, No. 67. May.

United Nations Conference on Trade and Development (UNCTAD) and Food and Agriculture Organization of the United Nations (FAO) (2017). *Commodities and Development Report 2017.*

United Nations Development Programme (2017). Income inequality trends in sub-Saharan Africa: Divergence, determinants and consequences.

United Nations Economic and Social Commission for Asia and the Pacific (ESCAP) (forthcoming). *China's economic transformation: Impacts on Asia and the Pacific.* Bangkok.

United Nations Economic and Social Commission for Asia and the Pacific (ESCAP) (2018). *Inequality in Asia and the Pacific in the ear of the 2030 Agenda for Sustainable Development.* Bangkok.

United Nations Economic and Social Commission for Western Asia (ESCWA) (2018). *Survey of Economic and Social Developments in the Arab Region 2017-2018.* Beirut.

United Nations Economic Commission for Africa (ECA) (2010). Assessing Regional Integration in Africa IV: Enhancing Intra-African Trade. Addis Ababa.

United Nations Economic Commission for Africa (ECA) (2017). *Economic Report on Africa 2017: Urbanization and industrialization for Africa's transformation.* Addis Ababa.

United Nations Economic Commission for Africa (ECA) (2018). African Continental Free Trade Area: Towards the finalization of modalities on goods – Toolkit. ATPC, Addis Ababa.

United Nations Economic Commission for Latin America and the Caribbean (ECLAC) (2011). An assessment of the economic impact of climate change on the transportation sector in Barbados. Sub-regional Headquarters for the Caribbean. October. Available from https://repositorio.cepal.org/bitstream/handle/11362/38610/1/LCCARL309_en.pdf.

United Nations Economic Commission for Latin America and the Caribbean (ECLAC) (2018a). *Foreign Direct Investment in Latin America and the Caribbean 2018.*

United Nations Economic Commission for Latin America and the Caribbean (ECLAC) (2018b). Irma and Maria by Numbers, *FOCUS*, Magazine of the Caribbean Development and Cooperation Committee, Issue 1, January–March.

United Nations Economic Commission for Latin America and the Caribbean (ECLAC) (2018c). *The inefficiency of inequality*. Santiago.

United Nations Economic Commission for Latin America and the Caribbean (ECLAC) (2018d). *Economic Survey of Latin America and the Caribbean*. Santiago.

United Nations International Strategy for Disaster Reduction (UNISDR) and Centre for Research on the Epidemiology of Disasters (CRED) (2018). Economic Losses, Poverty and Disasters 1998-2017.

United Nations World Tourism Organization (UNWTO) (1983). *Risks of Saturation of Tourist Carrying Capacity Overload in Holiday Destinations*.

United Nations World Tourism Organization (UNWTO), Centre of Expertise Leisure, Tourism & Hospitality; NHTV Breda University of Applied Sciences; and NHL Stenden University of Applied Sciences (2018). *'Overtourism'? – Understanding and Managing Urban Tourism Growth beyond Perceptions*.

United States Trade Representative (2018). Joint Statement on Trilateral Meeting of the Trade Ministers of the United States, Japan, and the European Union. 25 September.

V

Van der Ploeg, Frederick, and Steven Poelhekke (2009). Volatility and the natural resource curse. *Oxford Economic Papers*, vol. 61, Issue 4 (1 October), pp. 727–760.

Venables, Anthony J. (2016). Using natural resources for development: Why has it proven so difficult? *The Journal of Economic Perspectives*, vol. 30, No. 1 (Winter), pp. 161–183.

Vergara, Sebastian (2018). The role of productive and technological capabilities on export dynamics in developing countries. MPRA Paper 88937. University Library of Munich, Germany.

W

World Bank (2013). EU11 Regular Economic Report, Issue #27, June. Available from https://openknowledge.worldbank.org/handle/10986/16527.

World Bank (2016). *Poverty and Shared Prosperity 2016: Taking on Inequality*.

World Bank (2018). Nigeria Biannual Economic Update: Connecting to Compete. World Bank Macroeconomic, Trade and Investment Global Practice Nigeria Team. April.

World Health Organization (2018). Ebola virus disease – Democratic Republic of the Congo. Disease outbreak news: Update 8 November 2018. Available from: https://www.who.int/csr/don/08-november-2018-ebola-drc/en/.

The World Inequality Lab (2018). *World Inequality Report 2018*. Available from https://wir2018.wid.world/.

World Travel and Tourism Council (2018). Evaluation of job creation in G20 countries. Available from https://www.wttc.org/publications/2018/job-creation-in-g20-countries/.